International Technical

Threadsafe Considerations for CICS

November 2007

SG24-6351-02

Note: Before using this information and the product it supports, read the information in "Notices" on page xi.

Third Edition (November 2007)

This edition applies to Version 1, Release 3, Version 2 of CICS TS, and Version 3 of CICS TS.

© Copyright International Business Machines Corporation 2004, 2006, 2007. All rights reserved.
Note to U.S. Government Users Restricted Rights -- Use, duplication or disclosure restricted by GSA ADP Schedule Contract with IBM Corp.

Contents

Notices xi
Trademarks xii

Preface xiii
The team that wrote this book xiii
Become a published author xvi
Comments welcome. xvi

Summary of changes xvii
November 2007, Third Edition xvii

Part 1. Introducing threadsafe 1

Chapter 1. Introduction. 3
1.1 The concept of CICS Open Transaction Environment 4
   1.1.1 Improved throughput. 4
   1.1.2 Improved performance 5
1.2 CICS data integrity for shared resources 5
   1.2.1 Quasi-reentrant and threadsafe programs 5
   1.2.2 Shared application resources 6
   1.2.3 Shared CICS resources 6
   1.2.4 Threadsafe applications 6
1.3 Benefits of migrating applications to adhere to threadsafe standards. 7
   1.3.1 Improve performance 7
   1.3.2 Reduce the cost of computing. 9
   1.3.3 Exploitation of OTE 9
   1.3.4 Understand the application - a warning. 9

Chapter 2. OTE and threadsafe overview 11
2.1 Overview of quasi-reentrant and threadsafe programs. 12
   2.1.1 Quasi-reentrant programs. 12
   2.1.2 Threadsafe programs 13
   2.1.3 CICSAPI programs 14
   2.1.4 OPENAPI programs 15
2.2 Open transaction environment - a brief history 15
   2.2.1 Before CICS Transaction Server 1.3. 16
   2.2.2 CICS Transaction Server 1.3 17
   2.2.3 CICS Transaction Server 2.2 18
   2.2.4 CICS Transaction Server 2.3 19

2.2.5 CICS Transaction Server 3.1 21
2.2.6 CICS Transaction Server 3.2 23
2.2.7 Open TCB modes in CICS Transaction Server Version 2 24
2.2.8 Open TCB modes in CICS Transaction Server Version 3 25
2.3 Techniques to ensure threadsafe processing 25
2.4 Program definition 26
2.5 Task-related user exit APIs 28
  2.5.1 CICS DB2 task-related user exit 28
  2.5.2 CICS WebSphere MQ task-related user exit 28
  2.5.3 IP sockets task-related user exit 29
2.6 TCB limits 30
  2.6.1 MAXOPENTCBS. 31
2.7 Open TCB performance 33
  2.7.1 DB2. 34
  2.7.2 WMQ. 34
  2.7.3 IP CICS Sockets 34
  2.7.4 Performance considerations 34
2.8 TCB considerations with UNIX System Services 35
  2.8.1 The implications of setting MAXPROCUSER too low 37
2.9 Static and dynamic calls 37
2.10 Threadsafe API commands. 38
2.11 Threadsafe SPI commands. 40
2.12 Threadsafe XPI commands. 41
2.13 Function shipping considerations 41

Chapter 3. Techniques for threadsafety 43
3.1 Threadsafe standards 44
3.2 Serialization techniques 46
  3.2.1 Recommended serialization techniques 46
  3.2.2 Comparison of recommended options 47
  3.2.3 Generalized Compare and Swap routine 48
  3.2.4 Non-recommended techniques 50
3.3 Application design considerations. 51
  3.3.1 Application design considerations for CICS TS 3.2 52

Part 2. Threadsafe implementation 55

Chapter 4. Threadsafe tasks 57
4.1 Threadsafe migration planning 58
  4.1.1 CICS Transaction Server upgrade/migration path 58
  4.1.2 High-level threadsafe migration path 59
4.2 Load module scanner: DFHEISUP 61
  4.2.1 DFHEISUP filter tables 62
  4.2.2 DFHEISUP - summary mode 63

    4.2.3 DFHEISUP - detail mode 65
    4.2.4 DFHEISUP summary 67

Chapter 5. CICS migration tools 69
5.1 CICS VT performance on CICS TS V3.2 70
5.2 CICS Interdependency Analyzer for z/OS (CICS IA) 70
    5.2.1 CICS IA overview 70
    5.2.2 New in CICS IA for z/OS V2.1. 72
    5.2.3 The components of CICS IA 73
    5.2.4 CICS IA architecture 75
    5.2.5 How CICS IA can assist with threadsafety 76
    5.2.6 Identifying non threadsafe applications using CICS IA 78
5.3 Threadsafe application case study 97
    5.3.1 Non-threadsafe output (QR TCB) 98
    5.3.2 Threadsafe output with unchanged program 100
    5.3.3 Threadsafe output with changed program 103
5.4 CICS Performance Analyzer for z/OS (CICS PA) 104
    5.4.1 CICS PA overview. 105
    5.4.2 Reports and extracts. 106
    5.4.3 How CICS PA can assist with threadsafety 107

Chapter 6. Application review 111
6.1 Application code review. 112
    6.1.1 Ensure that the program logic is threadsafe 112
    6.1.2 Example showing the use of shared resources 114
    6.1.3 Ensure only threadsafe CICS commands are used 122
6.2 Change program definitions 125
    6.2.1 RDO definition. 126
    6.2.2 CICS environment variable CICSVAR 126
    6.2.3 CICSVAR values. 127
    6.2.4 How to code ENVAR. 127
    6.2.5 An example file control application 128

Chapter 7. System programmer tasks. 131
7.1 The role of the system programmer 132
7.2 Understanding threadsafe operation. 132
    7.2.1 Threadsafe performance issues 132
    7.2.2 Threadsafe data integrity issues 136
7.3 Analyze the CICS regions. 139
    7.3.1 The DB2 version 140
    7.3.2 The WMQ version 140
    7.3.3 Required CICS, DB2 and WMQ product maintenance 141
    7.3.4 DB2 system parameters 141
    7.3.5 WMQ system parameters 141

7.3.6 CICS system parameters 141
7.4 Providing a threadsafe CICS operating environment 144
    7.4.1 CICS exits 144
    7.4.2 Analyzing your exits 147
    7.4.3 Running DFH0STAT 148
    7.4.4 Which exits need to be reviewed 152
    7.4.5 Identifying exits in the DB2, WMQ, and file control call paths. 153
    7.4.6 Identifying dynamic plan exits in the DB2 call path 154
    7.4.7 Contacting the owner of vendor product exits. 155
7.5 Making your exits threadsafe 155
    7.5.1 Remove non threadsafe commands 156
    7.5.2 Serializing shared resources. 156
    7.5.3 Change your exit program's CONCURRENCY definition to
            THREADSAFE 157
7.6 Non threadsafe data integrity example 159
    7.6.1 Sample non threadsafe code example 160
    7.6.2 Threadsafe code example. 164
    7.6.3 Code changes to make RMIXIT threadsafe 166
7.7 Coordinating and driving individual application conversions 168
    7.7.1 Changing your program definitions 169
7.8 Post-conversion monitoring. 169
7.9 Summary. 170

Chapter 8. Migration pitfalls 173
8.1 Migrating CICS DB2 regions 174
    8.1.1 The potential pitfall 174
    8.1.2 The solution. 178
8.2 Migrating WebSphere MQSeries regions 183
    8.2.1 The API crossing exit (CSQCAPX) 186
8.3 OPENAPI programs and additional TCB switching. 187
8.4 Function shipped commands 188
8.5 COBOL calls 193
    8.5.1 PROGA (Quasirent) calls PROGB (threadsafe) 194
    8.5.2 PROGA (threadsafe) calls PROGB (Quasirent) 196
8.6 The CSACDTA field 198

Chapter 9. Migration scenario 199
9.1 Application overview 201
    9.1.1 Description of the application 201
9.2 Migration plan 201
9.3 Migration part 1 202
    9.3.1 Step 1: Identify exits in scope for part 1 203
    9.3.2 Step 2: Convert in-scope exits to threadsafe 205

      9.3.3 Step 3: Address non threadsafe commands 210
      9.3.4 Step 4: Confirm performance after migration to CICS TS 2.3 211
  9.4 Migration part 2 218
      9.4.1 Step 1: Identify programs in scope for part 2 218
      9.4.2 Step 2: Convert user exits to be threadsafe 221
      9.4.3 Step 3: Convert application programs to be threadsafe 224
      9.4.4 Step 4: Address non threadsafe commands 228
      9.4.5 Step 5: CICS system changes 235
  9.5 Performance measurement. 236
      9.5.1 Reports 237
      9.5.2 Charts 240
      9.5.3 Conclusions. 242
  9.6 Additional considerations for OPENAPI programs 242

Chapter 10. Performance case studies 245
  10.1 CICS DB2 and file control application 246
      10.1.1 Environment 247
      10.1.2 Results 247
  10.2 CICS WMQ and file control application 252
      10.2.1 Environment 252
      10.2.2 Results 253

Part 3. Customer examples and general questions. 257

Chapter 11. Danske Bank threadsafe conversion 259
  11.1 Hardware and software configuration 260
  11.2 Online application infrastructure 261
  11.3 Threadsafe project definition. 262
  11.4 Threadsafe analysis and results 263
      11.4.1 Programs used in threadsafe analysis 264
      11.4.2 Resolution 264
  11.5 The autoinstall process 264
      11.5.1 Data extract process for the CICS CFDT information. 265
      11.5.2 Data information structure in CICS CFDT. 266
      11.5.3 Danske Bank CICS autoinstall program 266
  11.6 Threadsafe results. 266
  11.7 Threadsafe summary and conclusion 269

Chapter 12. CoreBank benchmark: Quasirent versus threadsafe 271
  12.1 Scope of the benchmark 272
  12.2 Benchmark hardware and software resources 272
  12.3 Determining whether the application code is threadsafe. 274
      12.3.1 Analysis. 274
      12.3.2 Resolution 275

12.4 Results 275
    12.4.1 CICS performance records 275
12.5 Conclusions 285

Chapter 13. Diagnosing performance problems 287
13.1 Introduction 288
13.2 Define the problem 288
13.3 Performance hierarchy 290
13.4 Key performance indicators 292
    13.4.1 Indicators from System Management Facilities (SMF) 292
    13.4.2 Indicators from Resource Management Facility (RMF) 292
13.5 Performance data sources 293
    13.5.1 Message IEF374I 294
    13.5.2 SMF records 294
    13.5.3 RMF Workload Activity reports 299
    13.5.4 CICS PA reports 301
    13.5.5 DFH0STAT 302
13.6 Conclusions 306

Chapter 14. Common threadsafe questions 307
14.1 General threadsafe questions 308
14.2 Questions about CICS exits 312
14.3 Performance questions 313
14.4 Load module scanner questions 313

Part 4. Appendixes 315

Appendix A. CICS, DB2, and WMQ maintenance 317
CICS TS 2.3 APARs 317
CICS TS 3.1 APARs 318
CICS TS 3.2 APARs 318
DB2 7.1 APARs 318
DB2 8.1 APARs 319
WMQ 5.3.1 APARs 319
WMQ 6.1 APARs 319
DFHEISUP APARs 320

Appendix B. COBOL call program listings 321
Program listings for COBOL call examples 322
Program PROGA 322
Program PROGB 324

Appendix C. Assembler routines 327
DB2MANY 328

DB2PROG1 332
DB2PROG4 335
DB2PROG8 338
Planexit. 341
EXITENBL 342
XXXEI exit 343
XXXRMI exit. 344
XXXTS exit. 345

Related publications 347
IBM Redbooks 347
Other publications 347
Online resources 348
How to get IBM Redbooks 348
Help from IBM 348

Index 349

Notices

This information was developed for products and services offered in the U.S.A.

IBM may not offer the products, services, or features discussed in this document in other countries. Consult your local IBM representative for information on the products and services currently available in your area. Any reference to an IBM product, program, or service is not intended to state or imply that only that IBM product, program, or service may be used. Any functionally equivalent product, program, or service that does not infringe any IBM intellectual property right may be used instead. However, it is the user's responsibility to evaluate and verify the operation of any non-IBM product, program, or service.

IBM may have patents or pending patent applications covering subject matter described in this document. The furnishing of this document does not give you any license to these patents. You can send license inquiries, in writing, to:
IBM Director of Licensing, IBM Corporation, North Castle Drive Armonk, NY 10504-1785 U.S.A.

The following paragraph does not apply to the United Kingdom or any other country where such provisions are inconsistent with local law: INTERNATIONAL BUSINESS MACHINES CORPORATION PROVIDES THIS PUBLICATION "AS IS" WITHOUT WARRANTY OF ANY KIND, EITHER EXPRESS OR IMPLIED, INCLUDING, BUT NOT LIMITED TO, THE IMPLIED WARRANTIES OF NON-INFRINGEMENT, MERCHANTABILITY OR FITNESS FOR A PARTICULAR PURPOSE. Some states do not allow disclaimer of express or implied warranties in certain transactions, therefore, this statement may not apply to you.

This information could include technical inaccuracies or typographical errors. Changes are periodically made to the information herein; these changes will be incorporated in new editions of the publication. IBM may make improvements and/or changes in the product(s) and/or the program(s) described in this publication at any time without notice.

Any references in this information to non-IBM Web sites are provided for convenience only and do not in any manner serve as an endorsement of those Web sites. The materials at those Web sites are not part of the materials for this IBM product and use of those Web sites is at your own risk.

IBM may use or distribute any of the information you supply in any way it believes appropriate without incurring any obligation to you.

Information concerning non-IBM products was obtained from the suppliers of those products, their published announcements or other publicly available sources. IBM has not tested those products and cannot confirm the accuracy of performance, compatibility or any other claims related to non-IBM products. Questions on the capabilities of non-IBM products should be addressed to the suppliers of those products.

This information contains examples of data and reports used in daily business operations. To illustrate them as completely as possible, the examples include the names of individuals, companies, brands, and products. All of these names are fictitious and any similarity to the names and addresses used by an actual business enterprise is entirely coincidental.

COPYRIGHT LICENSE:
This information contains sample application programs in source language, which illustrates programming techniques on various operating platforms. You may copy, modify, and distribute these sample programs in any form without payment to IBM, for the purposes of developing, using, marketing or distributing application programs conforming to the application programming interface for the operating platform for which the sample programs are written. These examples have not been thoroughly tested under all conditions. IBM, therefore, cannot guarantee or imply reliability, serviceability, or function of these programs. You may copy, modify, and distribute these sample programs in any form without payment to IBM for the purposes of developing, using, marketing, or distributing application programs conforming to IBM's application programming interfaces.

© Copyright IBM Corp. 2004, 2006, 2007. All rights reserved.

Trademarks

The following terms are trademarks of the International Business Machines Corporation in the United States, other countries, or both:

Redbooks (logo) ®
z/Architecture®
z/OS®
zSeries®
CICS/ESA®
CICS®
CICSPlex®
DB2 Connect™
DB2 Universal Database™

DB2®
IBM®
IMS™
Language Environment®
MQSeries®
MVS™
OMEGAMON®
OS/390®
Redbooks®

RACF®
RMF™
S/390®
SAA®
Tivoli®
VTAM®
WebSphere®

The following terms are trademarks of other companies:

Java, JVM, and all Java-based trademarks are trademarks of Sun Microsystems, Inc. in the United States, other countries, or both.

UNIX is a registered trademark of The Open Group in the United States and other countries.

Linux is a trademark of Linus Torvalds in the United States, other countries, or both.

Other company, product, and service names may be trademarks or service marks of others.

Preface

This IBM® Redbooks® document is a comprehensive guide to threadsafe concepts and implementation in the context of CICS®. In addition to providing detailed instructions for implementing threadsafe in your environment, it describes the real world experiences of users migrating applications to be threadsafe, along with our own experiences. It also presents a discussion of the two most critical aspects of threadsafe, system performance and integrity.

Originally, CICS employed a single TCB to process everything (such as application code, task dispatching, terminal control, file control, and so on) executed on what today is known as the *application* or Quasi-reentrant (QR) TCB. Over time, CICS added specialized TCBs to help offload management tasks from the overcrowded QR TCB. VSAM subtasking, the VTAM® High Performance Option, and asynchronous journaling were all implemented on separate TCBs. Of course, the DB2® and MQ Series attachment facilities also employ TCBs apart from the application TCB. Distributing processing among multiple TCBs in a single CICS address space is not new, but customers and ISVs had little control over which TCB CICS is selected to dispatch a given function.

Beginning with CICS Version 2, all of that has changed. Applications can execute on TCBs apart from the QR TCB. This has positive implications for improving system throughput and for implementing new technologies inside of CICS. Use of the MVS™ JVM™ inside CICS and enabling listener tasks written for other platforms to be imported to run under CICS are examples of implementing new technologies.

CICS Transaction Server for z/OS® Version 3 Release 2 provides additional functions and enhancements. This updated book covers the latest features, including local and RLS File Control threadsafe commands, threadsafe CICS journaling commands, threadsafe definition for system autoinstalled global user exits (GLUE), and threadsafe WMQ commands.

The team that wrote this book

This book was produced by a team of specialists from around the world working at the International Technical Support Organization, Poughkeepsie Center.

Chris Rayns is an IT Specialist and Project Leader at the ITSO, Poughkeepsie Center in New York. Chris writes extensively on all areas of CICS, including

CICS Tools, CICS TG, and CICS TS. Before joining the ITSO, he worked in IBM Global Services in the United Kingdom as a CICS IT Specialist.

Edward Addison is a Software Engineer working in Raleigh, NC as the Technical Lead for CICS Level 2 support. Prior to working at CICS Level 2, he was a member of the VSAM Level 2 support group in San Jose, CA. Edward has been with IBM for 18 years, supporting customer VSAM and CICS. He holds a BS degree in Information Systems from the University of Phoenix.

George Bogner is a CICS IT Specialist working in IBM Global Services, Service Delivery Center, South Geoplex. George has worked at IBM for 19 years, specializing in the DB/DC area working with IMS™, DB2, and CICS. He has worked in Raleigh, North Carolina, for the past eight years supporting CICS and its associated products on external outsourcing accounts.

David Carey is a Senior IT Advisory Specialist with the IBM Support Center in Sydney, Australia, where he provides defect and non-defect support for CICS, CICSPlex/SM, the WebSphere® MQ family of products, and z/OS. David has been working in the IT industry for 27 years and has written extensively about CICS and zOS Diagnostic procedures for the ITSO.

Tony Fitzgerald is a Software Support Specialist in the UK. He has worked for IBM as CICS Level 2 Support for five years and has 15 years of experience working with CICS and DB2 as a Systems Programmer and an Applications Programmer. He holds a degree in Computer Science and Management Science from the University of Keele.

Steve Foley is a Senior IT Specialist in the IBM EMEA Service Delivery Organization. He is based in Edinburgh, Scotland, and provides CICS support for a variety of UK-based customers. He has 15 years of CICS experience and holds a degree in Computer Science from Edinburgh University.

Jim Grauel is now retired while at IBM he was a Senior Technical Staff Member. He joined IBM in 1965 as a Hardware Customer Engineer, in St. Louis, Missouri. In 1972 he transferred to Software as a Program Support Representative, supporting OS R21.7 and CICS (Release 2.3). In 1980 he transferred to the CICS Support Center in San Jose, California, and later to Raleigh, North Carolina, in 1984 and has been working as Level 2 Support in the CICS Support Center.

Fabrice Jarassat is a CICS and CICSPlex® IT Specialist with the zSeries® Benchmark Center at the EMEA ATS Product and Solutions Center in Montpellier, France. He joined IBM four years ago. Before joining IBM he worked at Mag-Info, which is part of the French Galeries Lafayette group, responsible for managing the transaction system based on CICS. He holds a degree in computing from Ecole Superieure Informatique Professionnel Paris. His areas of expertise include CICS, CICSPlex, CICS e-business technologies z/OS, and CICS Tools. He is an IBM Certified Solutions Expert in CICS Web Enablement.

Scott McClure is an Advisory Programmer. He has 15 years of experience in CICS level 2 Support. He has worked at IBM for 17 years. His areas of expertise include security, terminal autoinstall, and console support.

Keith Patterson is an IT Specialist in the IBM Global e-Business Solution Center in Dallas, Texas. Before joining IBM in 1999, he spent over 15 years as a CICS Systems Programmer. His areas of expertise include integrating existing CICS applications into new system architectures, CICS performance, and CICS internals. He has presented CICS topics at SHARE and taught CICS and assembly language programming at the collegiate level.

Christen Plum is a senior I/T specialist certified within system products and has a comprehensive experience within the mainframe platform for more then 30 years. He has worked as an MVS and CICS system programmer for 15+ years and as a performance specialist with MVS, CICS, batch and VSAM. His areas of expertise also includes MVS internals programming and Language Environment®. He joined IBM in 1995.

John Tilling is a Senior Software Engineer working in the CICS Strategy and Planning group at the IBM Hursley Laboratory in the United Kingdom. He joined IBM in 1985 having graduated from York University with a degree in Computer Science and Mathematics. He has 22 years of experience developing CICS, working in data access components including file control, local DLI, CICS-DBCTL, and was responsible for restructuring the CICS-DB2 and CICS-WMQ Adaptors to exploit OTE.

Andy Wright is a Senior Software Engineer working in the CICS Change Team at the IBM Hursley Laboratory in the United Kingdom. He holds a BSc in Physics and Computing from Southampton University, and an MSc in Software Engineering from the University of Oxford. He has 19 years of experience with CICS and related CICS products. He is the author of over 70 technical articles and papers on CICS software, and debugging and diagnostic techniques, and presents on CICS topics at conferences in the United States and Europe.

Thanks to the following people for their contributions to this project:

Chris Baker
Dai Middleton
Anne Roberts
Trevor Clarke
John Burgess
IBM Hursley

Bob Haimowitz
Richard Conway
International Technical Support Organization, Poughkeepsie Center

James Loftus
IBM Farnborough, United Kingdom

Become a published author

Join us for a two- to six-week residency program! Help write an IBM Redbook dealing with specific products or solutions, while getting hands-on experience with leading-edge technologies. You'll team with IBM technical professionals, Business Partners and/or customers.

Your efforts will help increase product acceptance and customer satisfaction. As a bonus, you'll develop a network of contacts in IBM development labs, and increase your productivity and marketability.

Find out more about the residency program, browse the residency index, and apply online at:

ibm.com/redbooks/residencies.html

Comments welcome

Your comments are important to us!

We want our books to be as helpful as possible. Send us your comments about this or other IBM Redbooks documents in one of the following ways:

- Use the online **Contact us** review redbook form found at:

    ibm.com/redbooks

- Send your comments in an Internet note to:

    redbook@us.ibm.com

- Mail your comments to:

    IBM Corporation, International Technical Support Organization
    Dept. HYJ Mail Station P099
    2455 South Road
    Poughkeepsie, NY 12601-5400

Summary of changes

This section describes the technical changes made in this edition of the book and in previous editions. This edition may also include minor corrections and editorial changes that are not identified.

Summary of Changes for SG24-6351-02
Threadsafe Considerations for CICS
as created or updated on November 2, 2007.

November 2007, Third Edition

This revision reflects the addition, deletion, or modification of new and changed information described below.

New information
- CICS File Control interface under CICS TS 3.2
- Threadsafe CICS Journalling commands under CICS TS 3.2
- Threadsafe definition for system autoinstalled GLUEs
- WebSphere MQ interface under CICS TS 3.2
- Chapter 10, Performance case studies
- Chapter 11, Danske Bank threadsafe conversion example

Changed information
- Chapter 1 OPENAPI updated
- Chapter 2 Addition of CICS TS 3.2 new functions
- Chapter 3 updated for CICS TS 3.2
- Chapter 5 updated for CICS IA and CICS VT
- Chapter 6 File control application example added
- Chapter 7 Updated for CICS TS 3.2 new functionallity
- Chapter 8 Updated for CICS TS 3.2 new functionallity
- Chapter 14 updated with new questions related to CICS TS 3.,2
- Appendix A updated with CICS TS 3.2 APARS information

Part 1

Introducing threadsafe

In Part 1 we introduce threadsafe concepts and definitions, provide an overview of threadsafe considerations in CICS, and discuss techniques for ensuring that applications will operate as expected in a multi-processing environment.

Introduction

In this chapter we provide some introductory information about the CICS Open Transaction Environment (OTE), including:

► The benefits of CICS OTE:
   – Increased throughput
   – Non-CICS API introduced
   – Improved performance
► CICS data integrity of shared resources
► Benefits of migrating applications to threadsafe

1.1 The concept of CICS Open Transaction Environment

CICS Open Transaction Environment (OTE) is an architecture that was introduced mainly for three purposes:

- To increase throughput via more concurrency
- To improve performance
- To introduce the possibility to use non-CICS APIs

Prior to OTE, all application code runs under the main CICS TCB called the Quasi-reentrant (QR) TCB (except for some specific VSAM execution, and other specialized activity such as FEPI, security calls, and file opens and closes, which used other TCBs). The CICS dispatcher sub-dispatches the use of the QR TCB between the different CICS tasks. Each task voluntarily gives up control when it issues a CICS service, which then can cause a CICS dispatcher wait. Only one CICS task can be active at any one time on the QR TCB.

But the one and only QR TCB could only execute on one CPU, so CICS execution was only using one physical CPU at a time. For that reason the limit of of a specific CICS system's execution capacity was set by the MIPS size of the single CPU of the related MVS system.

SQL calls were done on attached TCBs to prohibit blocking of the QR TCB when a CICS program was waiting for a conclusion of a DB2 request. This feature was called the CICS/DB2 attachment facility.

CICS Transaction Server Version 3 has now expanded OTE usage to not only those applications making DB2 calls, but to any application by means of a new keyword on the program definition.

z/OS Communications Server Version 1 Release 7 has been enhanced to allow the IP CICS Sockets task-related user exit (TRUE) to be enabled as OPENAPI. At the time of writing we now have three TRUEs that can be enabled as OPENAPI: DB2, IP CICS Sockets, and Websphere MQ.

Note: Blocking means the TCB is halted by an MVS wait.

1.1.1 Improved throughput

OTE introduces a new class of TCB, which can be used by applications, called an *open TCB*. An open TCB is characterized by the fact it is assigned to a CICS task for its sole use, and multiple OTE TCBs can run concurrently in CICS. There are several modes of open TCBs used to support various functions, such as

Java™ in CICS, open API programs, and C and C++ programs, which have been compiled with the XPLink option.

There is no sub-dispatching of other CICS tasks on an open TCB.

The OTE introduces a lot of new engines (TCBs) to CICS program execution. Each new TCB can execute on one CPU in parallel (concurrently). This gives the potential of increased throughput for a single CICS system, as long as the necessary CPU power is present.

1.1.2 Improved performance

Each new TCB represents a thread where a CICS program can execute in parallel. When the CICS program continues to execute on the open TCB, it is called a *threadsafe* execution of the program. The result is a reduced number of TCB switches between the open TCB and the QR TCB. This, in turn, results in reduced CPU consumption corresponding to the number of saved TCB switches. The more CICS commands that are made threadsafe the more probability you will remain executing on the open TCB.

1.2 CICS data integrity for shared resources

This section discusses the concept of quasi-reentrant execution and threadsafe execution in relation to access to shared resources.

1.2.1 Quasi-reentrant and threadsafe programs

Programs are said to be quasi-reentrant programs because they take advantage of the behavior of the CICS dispatcher and the QR TCB—in particular there is only ever one CICS task active under the QR TCB. This means that although the same program can be being executed by multiple CICS tasks, only one of those CICS tasks is active at any given point in time. Compare this with a situation in which multiple instances of the same program are each executing under a separate TCB. In this scenario, multiple tasks would be active in the same program at the same time and the program would have to be fully MVS reentrant at the very least. For a program to be threadsafe, it must go beyond being fully reentrant and use appropriate serialization techniques when accessing shared resources.

Quasi-reentrant programs always run under the QR TCB and can access shared resources such as the Common Work Area (CWA) or shared storage obtained via EXEC CICS GETMAIN SHARED safe in the knowledge they are the only CICS user task running at that point in time. This is because running under the QR TCB guarantees serialized access to those shared resources. An example would be a program that updates a counter in the CWA. The program is sure to be alone to update this counter, and when it stops or gets suspended by the CICS dispatcher, it is sure to know that the counter still has the value that was assigned.

1.2.2 Shared application resources

Since multiple tasks can potentially access shared resources simultaneously, when executing under an open TCB, applications that access shared resources (such as the CWA) must bear the responsibility of ensuring the integrity of those resources by implementing an appropriate serialization technique.

1.2.3 Shared CICS resources

CICS assumes responsibility for ensuring integrity of all the resources it manages. Either the CICS code has been amended to run on multiple TCBs safely (for example, the CICS code that handles temporary storage requests) or CICS will ensure that the code runs on the QR TCB.

The use of non-threadsafe CICS commands that must run on the QR TCB can, depending on the application, have a performance penalty. This is because of the need to switch TCBs when a non-threadsafe CICS command is encountered. If there are many non-threadsafe CICS commands in a program that is otherwise threadsafe, the extra switching back to the QR TCB will have a detrimental effect on performance. However, there will be no risk to data integrity.

In our example of a program using a CWA counter, by implementing an appropriate serialization technique this formerly quasi-reentrant program would run in an OTE environment. Therefore, this allows multiple instances of this program to execute at the same time. The counter value in the CWA could be changed by multiple executors at the same time and one instance would always be sure about the counter value when it stops or gets suspended.

1.2.4 Threadsafe applications

For the purposes of this book, we define the term *threadsafe application* as a collection of application programs that employ an agreed-upon form of serialized access to shared application resources. A program written to *threadsafe standards*, then, is a program that implements the agreed-upon serialization techniques. It is important to understand that a single program operating without the agreed-upon serialization technique can destroy the predictability and therefore the integrity of an entire system of otherwise threadsafe programs. Therefore, an application system cannot be considered *threadsafe* until all programs that share a common resource implement that application's threadsafe standards.

> **Note:** An application that does not use any of the shared resources, which will be discussed later, can be said to be threadsafe even if it uses non-threadsafe CICS commands, unless it is self-modifying and therefore not reentrant.

1.3 Benefits of migrating applications to adhere to threadsafe standards

In this section we identify and outline the potential business drivers that lead CICS customers to migrate their applications to a threadsafe environment.

There are three principle drivers, which are covered in the following sections:
- Improving performance
- Reducing cost
- Exploitation of OTE

This section concludes with a warning: There is a risk associated with defining an application as threadsafe, and this risk must be understood and eliminated before migration is attempted.

1.3.1 Improve performance

Customers who should benefit most from migrating to a threadsafe environment are those who experience poor response times for any of the following reasons:
- The CICS QR TCB is CPU constrained.
- Application programs are waiting excessively for the QR TCB.
- The CICS region in general is CPU constrained.

These situations are described in detail in the following sections.

CICS QR TCB is CPU constrained
In this scenario, the CICS QR TCB is consistently reaching system CP SHARE (QR TCB is running at 100% CPU) and has to wait to be dispatched by the operating system. Every task running under the QR TCB is being delayed.

Defining transactions as threadsafe, processing as many tasks as possible on an open TCB will remove this constraint on the QR TCB and reduce the response times of both threadsafe and non-threadsafe transactions.

> **CP SHARE calculation:** CP SHARE is the amount of a CP an LPAR is guaranteed before it is eligible to have the CP removed. For CICS to perform well, the CP SHARE for the LPAR where it is executing must be fairly high (90+% is great; 80% is good; 70% is workable).
>
> `CP SHARE = ((# available physical CP * 100)/(# logical CP in LPAR)) * FAIR SHARE.`

See Chapter 13, "Diagnosing performance problems" on page 287 for more details on performance.

Application tasks are waiting excessively for the QR TCB

In this scenario, the QR TCB is not CPU constrained, but application tasks are contending for their share of QR.

Again, defining transactions as threadsafe and moving as many tasks as possible to an open TCB will reduce contention for the QR TCB, and reduce the response times of both threadsafe and non-threadsafe transactions.

CICS region in general is CPU constrained

In this scenario, the system as a whole is at or approaching 100% busy, and CICS is being constrained along with everything else.

Depending on how an application is designed, defining it as threadsafe can significantly reduce the path length of application tasks. The transactions that will achieve the greatest CPU reduction are likely to be DB2 applications that have the following characteristics:

- A significant number of EXEC SQL calls are invoked per task.
- All programs invoked between the first and last EXEC SQL or WMQ call in each task are defined as threadsafe.
- All exits invoked as part of an EXEC SQL call are defined as threadsafe, and only contain threadsafe EXEC CICS commands.
- All exits invoked between the first and last EXEC SQL or WMQ call in each task are defined as threadsafe.
- All EXEC CICS statements invoked between the first and last EXEC SQL or WMQ call in each task are threadsafe.

Defining transactions with the preceding characteristics as threadsafe will all but eliminate TCB switches for the associated CICS tasks.

1.3.2 Reduce the cost of computing

Reducing the CPU consumption of an application does not always necessarily result in improved response times. An application may be a heavy user of CPU, but if the processor has spare capacity and the application is not CPU constrained, then a reduction in path length may have a negligible impact on response times.

However, for many customers, the financial cost incurred running their applications is related to the amount of CPU consumed. Under these circumstances, the CPU savings gained by migrating appropriate applications to a threadsafe environment can equate to a financial saving. As we show in Chapter 9, "Migration scenario" on page 199, the CPU savings for some applications can be substantial.

1.3.3 Exploitation of OTE

OTE in CICS has been implemented in three stages, over several releases of the CICS Transaction Server:

- ► Stage 1 - OTE function introduced: Delivered in CICS TS 1.3
- ► Stage 2 - TRUEs can exploit OTE: Delivered in CICS TS 2.2
- ► Stage 3 - Full application use of open TCBs: Delivered in CICS TS 3.1

Applications that can be defined as threadsafe in CICS Transaction Server Version 2 will be able to exploit the enhancements provided at CICS Transaction Server Version 3.1 with minimum migration effort. Moreover, it is a recommendation from IBM that all new application programs should be written to threadsafe standards at whatever level of CICS they are developed.

1.3.4 Understand the application - a warning

What do we mean when we say an application is *threadsafe*?

A threadsafe program is defined as a program that does one of the following:

- ► Uses appropriate serialization techniques, such as Compare and Swap or enqueue, when accessing any shared application resources. It must be capable of running concurrently on multiple TCBs, and must not rely on quasi-reentrancy to serialize access to shared resources and storage.
- ► Uses no shared application resources whatsoever.

For an application to meet these conditions and therefore be considered threadsafe, the application must do both of the following:

- Incorporate threadsafe application logic (which means that the native language code in between the EXEC CICS commands must be threadsafe).
- Be defined to CICS as threadsafe.

> **Important rule:** Only once it is understood whether an application is threadsafe, and all access to all shared resources is serialized, should any of its programs be defined as threadsafe. Failure to follow this rule may result in unpredictable results and put the integrity of application data at risk.

2

OTE and threadsafe overview

In this chapter we begin by discussing the different program types in CICS:
- Quasi-reentrant
- Threadsafe
  - CICSAPI
  - OPENAPI

We explain what determines each type, how to define the associated Program definition, and the requirements CICS expects of each.

We also look at the history of open transaction environment (OTE) in CICS.

The OTE is discussed with regard to open TCBs, task-related user exits (TRUEs), and TCB limits.

2.1 Overview of quasi-reentrant and threadsafe programs

Definitions of important terms that are relevant to the open transaction environment are provided in this section.

2.1.1 Quasi-reentrant programs

CICS runs user programs under a CICS-managed task control block (TCB). If a program is defined as quasi-reentrant, using the CONCURENCY attribute of the program resource definition, CICS will always invoke the program under the CICS quasi-reentrant (QR) TCB. The requirements for a quasi-reentrant program, in a multithreading context, are less stringent than if the program were to execute concurrently on multiple TCBs.

CICS requires an application program to be reentrant to guarantee a consistent state. A program is considered reentrant if it is read only and does not modify storage within itself. In practice, an application program may not be truly reentrant; CICS expects *quasi-reentrancy*. This means the application program should be in a consistent state when control is passed to it, both on entry to the program as well as before and after each EXEC CICS command. Such quasi-reentrancy guarantees that each invocation of an application program is unaffected by previous runs or by concurrent multithreading through the program by multiple CICS tasks.

CICS quasi-reentrant user programs (application programs, user-replaceable modules, global user exits, and task-related user exits) are given control by the CICS dispatcher under the QR TCB. When running under this TCB, a program can be sure that no other quasi-reentrant program can run until it relinquishes control during a CICS request. The user task is suspended at this point, leaving the program still *in use*. The same program can then be re-invoked by another task. This means the application program can be in use concurrently by more than one task although only one task at a time can actually be executing.

To ensure that programs cannot interfere with each other's working storage, CICS obtains a separate copy of working storage for each execution of an application program. Therefore, if a user application program is in use by 11 user tasks, there are 11 copies of working storage in the appropriate dynamic storage area (DSA).

Quasi-reentrancy allows programs to access globally shared resources, for example, the CICS common work area (CWA), without the need to protect those resources from concurrent access by other programs. Such resources are effectively locked by the running program until it relinquishes control. Therefore, an application can update a field in the CWA without using Compare and Swap (CS) instructions or locking (enqueuing on) the resource.

> **Important:** The CICS QR TCB provides protection through exclusive control of global resources *only* if all user tasks accessing those resources run under the QR TCB. It does not provide automatic protection from other tasks that execute concurrently under another (*open*) TCB.

Specifying Quasirent on the program definition *COncurrency* attribute is supported for all executable programs.

2.1.2 Threadsafe programs

In the CICS open transaction environment, threadsafe application programs, OPENAPI task-related user exits, global user exit programs, and user-replaceable modules cannot rely on quasi-reentrancy because they can run concurrently on multiple open TCBs. Furthermore, even quasi-reentrant programs are at risk if they access resources that can also be accessed by a user task running concurrently under an open TCB. This means that the techniques used by user programs to access shared resources must take into account the possibility of simultaneous access by other programs. Programs that use appropriate serialization techniques when accessing shared resources are described as threadsafe.

> **Note:** The term *fully reentrant* is sometimes used but this can be misunderstood; therefore, *threadsafe* is the preferred term.

CICS resources

For CICS resources, such as temporary storage queues, transient data queues and VSAM files, CICS processing automatically ensures access in a threadsafe manner. CICS ensures that its resources are accessed in a threadsafe way either because the CICS API code has been made threadsafe or because CICS ensures that the command is executed on the QR TCB, which effectively serializes access to the resource.

Application resources

For application-maintained shared resources, it is the responsibility of the application program to ensure that the resource is accessed in a threadsafe manner. Typical examples of shared storage are the CICS CWA, global user exit global work areas, and storage acquired explicitly by the application program with the shared option. You can check whether your application programs use these types of shared storage by looking for occurrences of the following EXEC CICS commands:

- ADDRESS CWA
- EXTRACT EXIT
- GETMAIN SHARED

Application programs using these commands *may* not be threadsafe because they allow access to global storage areas that could be updated concurrently by several tasks running on different open TCBs. To ensure it is threadsafe, an application program must include the necessary synchronization logic to guard against concurrent update. To help you find occurrences of these commands, CICS provides DFHEIDTH, a sample command table you can use with the load module scanner utility, DFHEISUP. See Figure 4-2 on page 64 for information about the load module scanner.

> **Important:** It is very important that you understand that DFHEIDTH is not testing the scanned programs for non threadsafe CICS commands, but is merely identifying whether the application is using CICS commands that give rise to the *possibility* that the application logic is non threadsafe.

During your investigation process of identifying programs that use shared resources, you should include any program that modifies itself. Such a program is effectively sharing storage and should be considered at risk.

2.1.3 CICSAPI programs

A program that is CICSAPI is restricted to use only the CICS API. By definition this is:

- The command-level application programming interface (API)
- The system programming interface (SPI)
- The resource manager interface (RMI)
- The exit programming interface (XPI) - for global user exits
- The system application architecture (SAA®) common programming interfaces
  - CPI-C and CPI-RR
- LE callable services

A CICSAPI program commences execution on the QR TCB. Calls to an OPENAPI-enabled TRUE cause a switch to an open TCB to execute the TRUE. Whether the program is defined as threadsafe or quasi-reentrant will dictate whether control returns to the application from the TRUE on the open TCB or the QR TCB.

2.1.4 OPENAPI programs

From CICS Transaction Server Version 3 it is now possible for programs to run on an open TCB from the start of the program. This kind of program is an OPENAPI program.

An OPENAPI program is a program that has been written to threadsafe standards and does not rely on a call to a TRUE to move the program to an open TCB. An OPENAPI program is a program that *must* be run on an open TCB.

An OPENAPI program is also not restricted to the CICS API. An OPENAPI program can use both non CICS APIs as well as CICS APIs. However, the CICS Transaction Server Version 3.1 documentation states that using a non CICS API is entirely at the risk of the user. No testing of non CICS APIs has been performed by IBM.

Note: An OPENAPI program must always be threadsafe.

2.2 Open transaction environment - a brief history

This section charts the history of the open transaction environment and outlines the enhancements that have been introduced in each release of CICS Transaction Server for z/OS.

Figure 2-1 shows the key OTE enhancements introduced in recent releases of CICS, and these are discussed in more detail in the following sections.

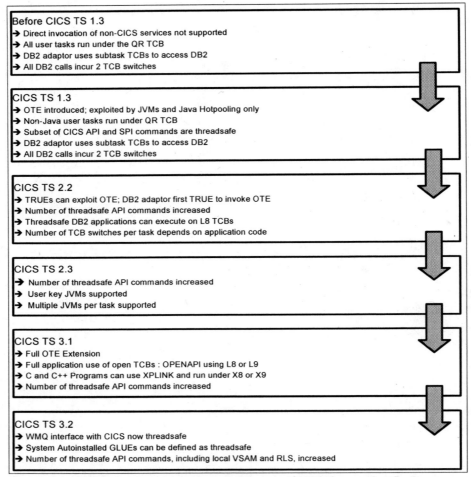

Figure 2-1   OTE enhancements in recent releases of CICS Transaction Server

2.2.1 Before CICS Transaction Server 1.3

Prior to CICS Transaction Server for OS/390® Version 1 Release 3, user applications and user exits operated in a restricted, or closed, environment. Although the applications could use the functionally rich CICS application programming interface (API), direct invocation of other services was not supported. This is because CICS ran all user transactions under a single z/OS TCB, known as the CICS quasi-reentrant (QR) TCB. Direct invocation of other services outside the scope of the CICS-permitted interfaces could interfere with the use by CICS of the QR TCB. In particular, requests resulting in the suspension (*blocking*) of the QR TCB, which happens when an MVS wait is issued, causes all CICS tasks to wait.

CICS-DB2 interface prior to CICS TS 1.3

The CICS DB2 attachment facility created and managed its own subtask thread TCBs with which to access DB2 resources, therefore ensuring that waits for DB2 resources would not block the QR TCB.

CICS used the QR TCB for the CICS DB2 task-related user exit and for the application program's code. The subtask thread TCBs were used for requests to DB2, and switching between the subtask TCB and the QR TCB took place for every DB2 request.

This would continue to be the case in CICS Transaction Server 1.3 (see the following section).

Figure 8-1 on page 175 shows the TCB switches involved in a typical DB2 transaction running under CICS TS 1.3.

2.2.2 CICS Transaction Server 1.3

The open transaction environment function was introduced in CICS Transaction Server for OS/390 Version 1 Release 3 to be exploited initially by Java Virtual Machines and Java Hotpooling applications.

OTE is an environment where CICS application code can use non-CICS services (facilities outside the scope of the CICS API) within the CICS address space, without interfering with other transactions. Applications that exploit OTE run on their own open TCB, rather than on the QR TCB. Unlike the QR TCB, CICS does not perform sub dispatching on an open TCB. If the application running on an open TCB invokes a non-CICS service that blocks the TCB, the TCB blocking does not affect other CICS tasks. For example, some services provided by DB2, MVS, UNIX® System Services, or TCP/IP, might result in TCB blocking.

CICS-DB2 interface under CICS TS 1.3

Although OTE became available in CICS TS 1.3, it was not yet enabled for task-related user exits, and therefore not yet exploited by the CICS DB2 attachment facility. As under previous CICS releases, subtask thread TCBs were used to access DB2 resources to ensure that waits for DB2 resources would not block the QR TCB.

CICS continued to use the QR TCB for the CICS DB2 task-related user exit and for application program code. Subtask thread TCBs are used for requests to

DB2, and switching between the subtask TCB and the QR TCB took place for every DB2 request.

Figure 2-2 shows the TCB switches involved in typical DB2 transactions running under CICS TS 1.3.

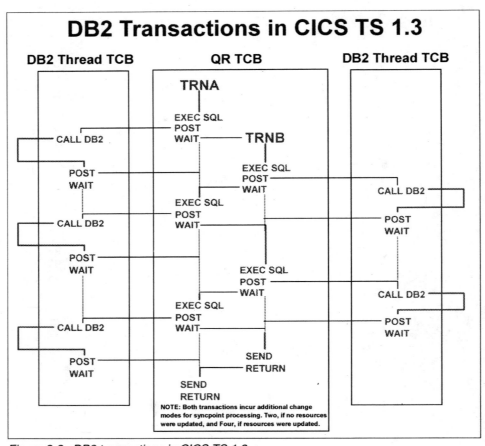

Figure 2-2   DB2 transactions in CICS TS 1.3

2.2.3 CICS Transaction Server 2.2

Enhancements introduced in CICS Transaction Server for z/OS Version 2 Release 2 made it possible for task-related user exits (TRUEs) to exploit the open transaction environment. The CICS DB2 adaptor supplied with this release was the first TRUE to utilize OTE.

> **Note:** The CICS DB2 task-related user exit was converted to exploit this feature and operate as an open API TRUE when CICS is connected to DB2 Version 6 or later, therefore using L8 TCBs for DB2 request processing.

Applications that involve a TRUE enabled using the OPENAPI option on the ENABLE PROGRAM command can exploit OTE to provide performance benefits. Task-related user exits like this are known as OPENAPI TRUEs. An OPENAPI TRUE is given control under an open TCB in L8 mode (known as an L8 TCB) and can use non-CICS APIs without having to create, manage, and switch between subtask TCBs.

CICS DB2 interface under CICS TS 2.2

From CICS TS 2.2, the CICS DB2 attachment facility no longer creates subtask thread TCBs to access DB2 resources, unless connected to DB2 V5 or earlier. Instead, by exploiting OTE, L8 TCBs are used to process EXEC SQL statements. If an application is *not* defined as threadsafe (the default), each task will return to the QR TCB on completion of the EXEC SQL statement.

Existing or new CICS DB2 applications written in any language that accesses DB2 Version 6 or later now have the opportunity to gain the performance benefits provided by OTE. These performance benefits can be gained because open TCBs, unlike the QR TCB or subtask thread TCBs, may be used for both non-CICS API requests (including requests to DB2) and application code. Because application code can be run on the open TCB, the number of TCB switches is significantly reduced.

With OTE, the same L8 TCB can be used by the CICS DB2 task-related user exit.

Figure 2-3 on page 20 shows the TCB switches involved in typical DB2 transactions running under CICS TS 2.2. Threadsafe and non threadsafe tasks are both shown.

2.2.4 CICS Transaction Server 2.3

CICS Transaction Server for z/OS Version 2 Release 3 does not introduce any fundamental changes to the open transaction environment. However, this release does make it easier to maximize the performance improvements that can be achieved by defining appropriate applications as threadsafe.

Issuing non threadsafe EXEC CICS commands will cause a threadsafe program running on an L8 TCB to switch back to the QR TCB, and CICS TS 2.3 helps to prevent this by increasing the number of threadsafe EXEC CICS commands to include, among others, ASKTIME and FORMATTIME.

CICS DB2 interface under CICS TS 2.3

The CICS DB2 attachment facility in CICS Transaction Server 2.3 operates exactly as it does in Version 2.2. Refer to "CICS DB2 interface under CICS TS 2.2" on page 19 for details. The EXEC CICS commands made threadsafe in CICS Transaction Server Version 2.3 will make it easier for some applications to reap the full performance benefits associated with being defined as threadsafe.

Figure 2-3 shows the TCB switches involved in typical DB2 transactions running under CICS TS 2.3. Threadsafe and non threadsafe tasks are both shown.

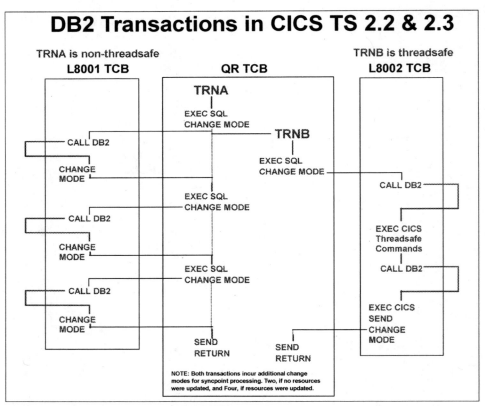

Figure 2-3   DB2 transactions in CICS TS 2.2 and 2.3

2.2.5 CICS Transaction Server 3.1

In CICS TS 3.1, programs can now be defined with API(OPENAPI) and so run almost independently of the QR TCB. Any program defined this way will run on an L8 or L9 open TCB depending on its EXECKEY value. Any program that can be defined as COncurrency(Threadsafe) can now also be defined as API(OPENAPI) and exploit the benefits of running on an open TCB regardless of whether it accesses DB2. For this reason we recommend that *all* programs should be written to threadsafe standards.

Prior to CICS TS 3.1, the OPENAPI option was only available to task-related user exits (TRUEs).

The effect of using the new OPENAPI definition can be seen in Figure 2-4.

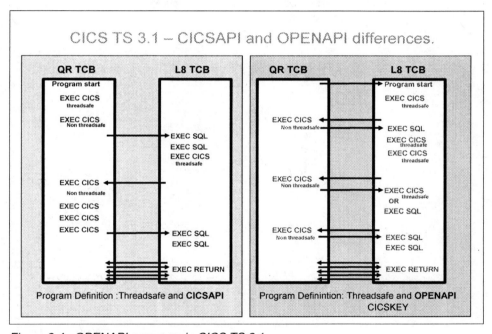

Figure 2-4 OPENAPI programs in CICS TS 3.1

In the example on the left we have a program defined as API(CICSAPI). In this example the behavior is the same as in CICS TS V2, whereby CICS will switch to an L8 TCB when a DB2 command is encountered and will remain there until a non threadsafe CICS command causes a switchback to the QR TCB. The switch to the L8 TCB in this case is made because the CICS DB2 task-related user exit is enabled in OPENAPI mode.

The example on the right of Figure 2-4 on page 21 shows the behavior when an application program is defined using the API(OPENAPI). Using OPENAPI for this program is telling CICS that this program *must* run on an open TCB. CICS immediately moves the task to an L8 or L9 TCB at the start of the program. Only if a non threadsafe CICS command is encountered does CICS move the task to the QR TCB and then *only* for the duration of the CICS command.

> **Note:** A program defined as API(OPENAPI) is not required to have *any* DB2 or WMQ commands.

If our CICS program is now defined as API(OPENAPI) and with EXECKey(UserKey), then CICS will switch to an L9 TCB for execution rather than an L8 TCB. However, CICS will switch the task to an L8 TCB for every DB2 command because OPENAPI TRUEs *must* run in CICS key on an L8 TCB. This is demonstrated in Figure 2-5.

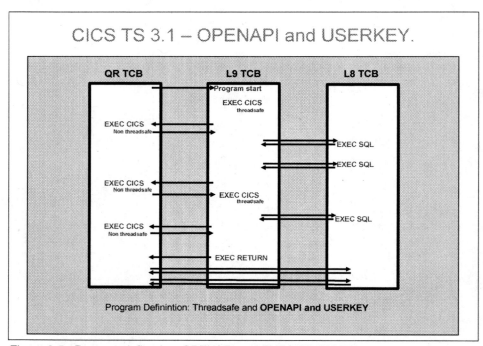

Figure 2-5   Program defined as OPENAPI and EXECKEY(USER)

OPENAPI and CICSAPI candidates

The combination of OPENAPI and EXECKEY attributes at CICS Transaction Server Version 3.1 could therefore lead to extra TCB switching, which would be undesirable. It is important that applications are analyzed correctly before using the OPENAPI attribute, as there are some rules that define what is a good candidate for the OPENAPI attribute (and, by implication, what is a bad candidate). A summary of what are considered good candidates for OPENAPI and CICSAPI can be seen in "OPENAPI good and bad candidates" on page 53.

This is also discussed further in 8.3, "OPENAPI programs and additional TCB switching" on page 187.

XPLINK

Another enhancement to OTE in CICS TS 3.1 is the facility to allow C and C++ programs compiled with the XPLINK option to run under an X8 or X9 open TCB depending on its EXECKey definition.

XPLink is Extra Performance Linkage. It was introduced at OS/390 2.10 to provide a high performance subroutine call and return mechanism for C and C++ programs. XPLink is enabled by using the XPLINK compiler option when compiling C and C++ programs.

A C or C++ program compiled with the XPLINK option will execute on an X8 or an X9 TCB depending on the EXECKEY attribute of the program definition.

TCB switching will still occur when:

- Using non threadsafe CICS commands
- Making SQL calls
- LINKing to a different program
- Using the CICS C++ foundation classes (Currently only non XPLINK versions are available.)

XPLINK programs can be considered a special case of OPENAPI programs. They execute on X8/X9 because XPLINK utilizes batch LE rather than CICS LE. There will be a separate LE enclave for each X8/X9 TCB. However, the storage is still allocated from CICS storage. DFHAPXPO can be used to change the batch LE runtime options.

> **Note:** The same considerations for OPENAPI programs apply to XPLINK programs.

2.2.6 CICS Transaction Server 3.2

Enhancements introduced in CICS Transaction Server for z/OS Version 3 Release 2 include local and RLS file control threadsafe commands, threadsafe CICS journalling commands, threadsafe definition for system autoinstalled global user exits (GLUE), and threadsafe WMQ commands.

CICS File Control interface under CICS TS 3.2

In CICS TS 3.2, the commands for accessing local and Record-Level Sharing (RLS) VSAM files are now threadsafe. These changes will result in improved performance for threadsafe applications that contain a mixture of DB2 and File Control. Also, for pure VSAM applications running on an open TCB, there will be a higher throughput due to utilization of concurrent CPUs. The number of TCB switches will be reduced as well.

The commands that are now threadsafe are READ, READ UPDATE, REWRITE, DELETE, UNLOCK, STARTBR, RESETBR, READNEXT, READPREV, and ENDBR. In addition, the SPI command INQUIRE FILE is also threadsafe.

> **Note:** The commands for accessing files using other methods (remote files, Shared Data Tables, Coupling Facility Data Tables, and BDAM files) remain non-threadsafe.

Threadsafe CICS Journalling commands under CICS TS 3.2

The journalling commands that are now threadsafe are WRITE JOURNALNAME, WRITE JOURNALNUM, WAIT JOURNALNAME and WAIT JOURNALNUM. Also, the XPI command WRITE_JOURNAL_DATA is threadsafe.

Threadsafe definition for system autoinstalled GLUEs

CICS TS 3.2 enables system autoinstalled GLUE programs to be defined as threadsafe. GLUE programs required early during CICS initialization are required to be configured to CICS using the ENABLE command. The ENABLE command can now be specified with an override of THREADSAFE.

WebSphere MQ interface under CICS TS 3.2

The components to connect CICS TS 3.2 and WMQ have been integrated into CICS. This allows the components to become threadsafe. These components are CICS-MQ adapter, the CICS-MQ trigger monitor, and the CICS-MQ bridge.

2.2.7 Open TCB modes in CICS Transaction Server Version 2

The following open TCB modes are available from CICS Transaction Server Version 2:

J8	CICS key JVM requirements
J9	USER key JVM requirements (only at CICS TS 2.3)
L8	OPENAPI TRUEs (TRUEs must run in the CICS key)
H8	High performance Java programs

2.2.8 Open TCB modes in CICS Transaction Server Version 3

CICS Transaction Server V3.1 has extended the number of TCB modes available to CICS. The open TCB modes now available for application use are:

J8 CICS key JVM requirements
J9 User key JVM requirements
L8 OPENAPI TRUEs (TRUEs must run in the CICS key.)
CICS key OPENAPI applications
L9 User key OPENAPI applications
X8 CICS key C and C++ applications compiled with XPLINK
X9 User key C and C++ applications compiled with XPLINK

In addition, there is the S8 TCB mode, which is used internally by CICS for SSL.

2.3 Techniques to ensure threadsafe processing

There are many different techniques you can use to ensure threadsafe processing when accessing a shared resource. The following techniques are only a subset of the possibilities. For further information please refer to Chapter 3, "Techniques for threadsafety" on page 43.

- Enqueue on the resource to obtain exclusive control and ensure no other program can access the resource.
    - An EXEC CICS ENQ command within an application program
    - An XPI ENQUEUE function call within a global user exit program
- Perform accesses to shared resources only in a program defined as Quasirent.

    A linked-to program defined as quasi-reentrant runs under the QR TCB and can take advantage of the serialization provided by CICS quasi-reentrancy. Note that even in quasi-reentrant mode, serialization is provided *only* for as long as the program retains control and does not wait. This is not a recommended technique.

- Place all transactions that access the shared resource into a restricted transaction class(TRANCLASS) defined with the number of active tasks specified as MAXACTIVE(1).

    This approach effectively provides a very coarse locking mechanism, but may have a severe impact on performance.

> **Attention:** Although the term threadsafe is defined in the context of individual programs, a user application as a whole can *only* be considered threadsafe if all the application programs that access shared resources obey the rules. A program written to threadsafe standards cannot safely update shared resources if another program accessing the same resources does not obey the threadsafe rules.

2.4 Program definition

In this section we discuss program definitions.

CONCURRENCY attribute

The CONCURRENCY attribute of the program definition is used to define a program as either Quasirent or threadsafe. Quasirent is the default value.

The CONCURRENCY attribute applies to:

- User application programs
- PLT programs
- User-replaceable programs
- Global user exit programs
- Task-related user exit programs

API attribute

The API attribute, which applies only from CICS Transaction Server V3.1, specifies whether the program is to be defined as CICSAPI or OPENAPI.

The API attribute applies to:

- User application programs
- PLT programs
- User-replaceable programs
- Global user exit programs (CICS always forces CICSAPI)
- Task-related user exit programs

A program defined as API(CICSAPI) will commence on the QR TCB and subsequent behavior will be the same as in CICS versions prior to CICS Transaction Server V3.1.

A program that is defined as API(OPENAPI) will commence its execution on an L8 or an L9 TCB depending on the value of its EXECKEY attribute. It switches to the QR TCB for non threadsafe CICS commands and to the L8 TCB (if it started on L9) to execute SQL commands. Defining a program as API(OPENAPI) automatically implies that the program is also threadsafe.

The main benefit of being able to use the OPENAPI attribute at CICS TS 3.1 is that more applications can now be moved off the QR TCB. Non DB2 applications and highly CPU intensive applications can now benefit from running on an open TCB.

Figure 2-6 on page 27 shows an example program definition as viewed by the CEDA transaction.

```
OBJECT CHARACTERISTICS                                   CICS RELEASE = 0640
 CEDA   View PROGram( DB2PROG5 )
  PROGram          : DB2PROG5
  Group            : THDSAFE
  DEscription      :
  Language         :                    CObol | Assembler | Le370 | C | Pli
  RELoad           : No                 No | Yes
  RESident         : No                 No | Yes
  USAge            : Normal             Normal | Transient
  USElpacopy       : No                 No | Yes
  Status           : Enabled            Enabled | Disabled
  RSl              : 00                 0-24 | Public
  CEdf             : Yes                Yes | No
  DAtalocation     : Any                Below | Any
  EXECKey          : User               User | Cics
  COncurrency      : Quasirent          Quasirent | Threadsafe
  Api              : Cicsapi            Cicsapi | Openapi
 REMOTE ATTRIBUTES
  DYnamic          : No                 No | Yes

                                             SYSID=PJA6 APPLID=SCSCPJA6
```

Figure 2-6   Program definition

The CONCURRENCY and API attribute can both be specified using a program autoinstall exit. The IBM-supplied sample program autoinstall exit defaults to QUASIRENT and CICSAPI.

> **Important:** It is important to understand that the program definition keyword CONCURRENCY(THREADSAFE) is telling CICS that the application logic is threadsafe, not whether CICS commands are threadsafe. CICS will ensure threadsafety of its own logic either because CICS logic can execute on an open TCB or it cannot, and so will be switched to the QR TCB before it executes. In either case, the resource is accessed in a threadsafe way.

A threadsafe application can use non threadsafe CICS commands. It will suffer the overhead of TCB switching, but resource integrity is maintained.

If an application containing non threadsafe logic is incorrectly defined to CICS as CONCURRENCY(THREADSAFE), the results are unpredictable.

2.5 Task-related user exit APIs

Task-related user exits (TRUEs) can be enabled with or without the OPENAPI option. Without the OPENAPI option, the TRUE is enabled as CICSAPI.

- ▶ CICSAPI: The TRUE is enabled as either Quasirent or threadsafe without the OPENAPI option. The TRUE is restricted to the CICS-permitted programming interfaces.
- ▶ OPENAPI: The TRUE is also enabled as threadsafe when the OPENAPI option is specified. The program is assumed to be written to threadsafe standards (serially reusable) and is permitted to use non-CICS APIs. CICS will give control to the TRUE under an L8 mode open TCB, which is dedicated for use by the calling CICS task and is separate from the CICS QR TCB.

For additional information about the OPENAPI option, reference the *CICS Customization Guide*, SC34-6227, for CICS Transaction Server Version 2, and *CICS Transaction Server for z/OS V3.1 CICS Customization Guide,* SC34-6429, for CICS Transaction Server Version 3.

2.5.1 CICS DB2 task-related user exit

The CICS DB2 adapter supplied by CICS is the first to supply a task-related user exits that can be enabled with the OPENAPI attribute. This was first supplied at CICS TS 2.2. This enabled DB2 calls to be executed on an open TCB. As we have already seen, this allowed us to create applications that could remain on the open TCB following a DB2 call depending on the CONCURRENCY attribute of the program definition.

2.5.2 CICS WebSphere MQ task-related user exit

The components that are threadsafe in CICS TS V3.2 are the CICS-MQ adapter, the CICS-MQ trigger monitor, and the CICS-MQ bridge. Exploitation of the Open Transaction Environment will benefit threadsafe applications using WMQ. TCB switching can now be avoided, resulting in saving of CPU and an increase in throughput, since WMQ applications can now run multiple open TCBs.

2.5.3 IP sockets task-related user exit

The IP CICS Sockets component of the Communications Server at z/OS Version 1.7 has been enhanced so that the calls to the IP CICS Sockets task-related user exits can now execute using the CICS Open Transaction Environment. So in the same way that a DB2 call will execute on an L8 TCB, an IP socket call can now run on an L8 TCB.

However, for IP CICS Sockets API calls to utilize OTE it is necessary for the IP CICS Socket configuration file be updated to turn this facility on. Unlike DB2, the TRUE for IP CICS Sockets can be enabled as either OPENAPI or CICSAPI. The default action is for IP sockets to continue managing its own sub task TCBs (that is, be enabled as CICSAPI).

The installation and configuration of IP CICS Sockets is described in detail in *z/OS Communications Server IP CICS Sockets Guide Version 1 Release 7* SC31-8807. The following two sections are a a summary to show where the OTE-related parameters need to be defined.

Building the configuration file using macro EZACICD

The IP CICS Sockets configuration file is initially built from a macro called EZACICD. Once created, the file can be incorporated into CICS using RDO and modified using the supplied configuration transactions.

The macro will create configuration records for each CICS region that uses IP sockets and a configuration record for every listener within each CICS region.

The definition of the CICS region is where OTE for IP sockets is enabled, an example of which can be seen in Example 2-1.

Example 2-1 An example of a CICS region definition in an EZACICD macro

```
EZACICD TYPE=CICS,        CICS record definition              X
        APPLID=CICSPRDB,  APPLID of CICS region using OTE     X
        TCPADDR=TCPIP,    Job/Step name for TCP/IP            X
        CACHMIN=15,       Minimum refresh time for cache      X
        CACHMAX=30,       Maximum refresh time for cache      X
        CACHRES=10,       Maximum number of resident resolvers X
        ERRORTD=CSMT,     Transient data queue for error msgs X
        TCBLIM=12,        Open API TCB Limit                  X
        OTE=YES,          Use Open Transaction Environment    X
        TRACE=NO,         Trace CICS Sockets                  X
        SMSGSUP=NO        STARTED Messages Suppressed?
```

The two parameters that are related to OTE are OTE=YES and TCBLIM=12.

OTE

When OTE=YES is specified, the IP CICS Sockets interface enables its TRUE as OPENAPI, and therefore CICS switches all EZASOKET calls and all IP CICS C socket functions from the QR TCB to an L8 TCB.

TCBLIM

This parameter defines that maximum number of OTE TCBs that the IP CICS Socket TRUE can use. It is a subset of the number of TCBs allocated to the pool of TCBs defined by the MAXOPENTCBS SIT parameter in CICS. This is the same pool of TCBs used by the DB2 TRUE if DB2 is also in use.

Once the socket call is complete, CICS will either leave the task on the L8 TCB or return to the QR TCB depending on the CONCURRENCY attribute of the application program definition. So if the program is defined as CONCURRENCY(THREADSAFE), the program will remain on the L8 until task end or a non threadsafe CICS API command is encountered. If the program is defined as CONCURRENCY(QUASIRENT), the task will be moved back to the QR TCB on completion of the IP socket call. This is exactly the same behavior as for the DB2 task-related user exits. Additionally, at CICS TS 3.1 the application program may be defined as API(OPENAPI) if appropriate, which will enable the program to commence execution on an open TCB. For further information see "OPENAPI good and bad candidates" on page 53.

> **Note:** If you intend to use OTE=YES for IP sockets programs *and* to define the IP sockets application program as threadsafe then you *must* ensure that the programs *are* threadsafe before defining them as such.

Customizing the configuration file

Once the configuration file has been created and defined to the CICS region it can be modified using the supplied configuration transaction EZAC. For example, using EZAC it is possible to turn OTE on or off and to modify the TCBLIM attribute. This transaction is described in detail in *z/OS Communications ServerIP CICS Sockets Guide Version 1 Release 7,* SC31-8807.

2.6 TCB limits

As we have described earlier, CICS manages a number of different TCB pools. For example, at CICS TS 3.1 we have pools for JVM TCBs (J8/J9), OPENAPI and TRUE TCBs(L8/L9), SSL TCBs (S8) and XPLINK TCBs (X8/X9). CICS imposes a limit for each of these TCB pools by means of a SIT parameter for each. The SIT parameter for each pool is as follows:

MAXOPENTCBS	Limits the number of TCBs in the pool of L8 and L9 mode open TCBs
MAXSSLTCBS	Limits the number of TCBs in the pool of S8 mode open TCBs
MAXXPTCBS	Limits the number of TCBs in the pool of X8 and X9 mode open TCBs
MAXJVMTCBS	Limits the number of TCBs in the pool of J8 and J9 mode open TCBs

2.6.1 MAXOPENTCBS

The pool of L8/L9 mode TCBs is managed by the CICS dispatcher. The maximum number of TCBs that will be allocated to the pool is defined by the MAXOPENTCBS System Initialization Table (SIT) parameter. There can be any combination of L8/L9 TCBs in use (allocated to running tasks) and free.

MAXOPENTCBS has a default value of 12 at CICS TS 3.1. It is important to understand which functions now utilize the pool of TCBs defined by MAXOPENTCBS so that a sensible value can be assigned to MAXOPENTCBS. In addition to application programs defined with the OPENAPI attribute or programs calling TRUEs enabled with OPENAPI, CICS itself will perform some tasks on an open TCB taken from the pool of MAXOPENTCBS. Usage of L8 and L9 TCBs can be summarized as follows:

► L9 mode TCBs are used for user key OPENAPI application programs.
► L8 mode TCBs are used:
  – For CICS key OPENAPI application programs
  – For OPENAPI task-related user exits (task-related user exits always run in CICS key)
    • The CICS-DB2 Attachment Facility
    • The IP CICS Sockets interface
    • The CICS-MQ Adapter
  – And by CICS itself, because CICS uses OPENAPI CICS key programs that run on L8 TCBs:
    • When accessing doctemplates and HTTP static responses that are stored on the Hierarchical File System (HFS)
    • When processing Web Service requests and parsing XML

Choosing a value for MAXOPENTCBS will therefore need to take into account all of these factors depending, on which are being used.

Task-related user exit imposed limits

There are currently three TRUEs that can be enabled in CICS using the OPENAPI attribute. They are the TRUEs supplied by the CICS DB2 Attachment Facility, the CICS WMQ Attachment Facility, and the IP CICS Sockets interface. Some of these TRUEs have their own parameter that can be set to limit the number of TCBs that can be used by that TRUE. The TCB limit for each of these TRUEs is part of the TCBs allocated to the pool defined by MAXOPENTCBS.

DB2

The DB2 parameter is TCBLIMIT, which is specified in the DB2CONN definition. TCBLIMIT defines the maximum number of TCBs that can be associated with the CICS DB2 attachment.

WMQ

There is no parameter to limit the number of open TCBs used by WMQ. Therefore, the limit for WMQ is the same as the MAXOPENTCBS parameter.

IP CICS Sockets

The parameter for limiting the number of open TCBs that can be associated with the IP CICS Sockets TRUE is the TCBLIM parameter. This is used when the IP CICS Sockets interface is configured with OTE=YES.

Transaction isolation

When transaction isolation (TRANISO) is used, MAXOPENTCBS should be set equal to or higher than the max task value. When a task defined as using TRANISO is initiated and has accessed DB2 in prior executions of the transaction, CICS assigns an L8 TCB with the correct subspace. This will eliminate TCB stealing on the first DB2 access.

Non transaction isolation

If you are not using transaction isolation you can calculate MAXOPENTCBS using the following steps:

1. Find the value specified for TCBLIMIT in your DB2CONN definition. This represents the number of L8 TCBs required for your DB2 workload.

2. Add a value for the expected peak number of concurrent CICS tasks accessing WMQ.

3. Add a value for the expected peak number of tasks using Web services, XML, DOCTEMPLATEs residing on z/OS UNIX.

4. Add a value for the expected peak number of tasks running as OPENAPI applications that are non DB2.

> **Note:** An application that uses sockets, WMQ, and DB2 will use one L8 open TCB for both purposes. If you have a separate sets of applications that use sockets and DB2 then ensure that MAXOPENTCBS is set greater than or equal to the sum of TCBLIMIT and TCBLIM.

How L8/L9 mode TCBs are allocated

The process for allocating an L8/L9 mode TCB is:

1. If the transaction already has an L8 or L9 mode TCB allocated, it is used. At most only one L8 and L9 TCB is allocated to a task.
2. If a free L8/L9 mode TCB exists for the correct subspace, it is allocated and used.

   > **Note:** If TRANISO is not in use, all tasks use the same space.

3. If the number of open TCBs is below the MAXOPENTCBS limit, a new L8/L9 mode TCB is created and associated with the task's subspace.
4. If the number of open TCBs is at the MAXOPENTCBS limit and there are free L8/L9 mode TCBs with the wrong subspace, the dispatcher will destroy the free TCB and create a new TCB for the required subspace. This avoids suspending the task until the number of TCBs is reduced below the pool limit. This action is reflected in the count of *TCB steals* in the CICS dispatcher TCB mode statistics.
5. If the number of open TCBs is at the MAXOPENTCBS limit and there are no TCBs available to steal, the task is suspended, with an OPENPOOL wait, until one becomes free or the MAXOPENTCBS limit is increased.

> **Important:** CICS TS 2.2 APAR PQ75405 changes the allocation algorithm and should be installed. This code is included in the base level of subsequent CICS releases

2.7 Open TCB performance

Currently, the following IBM software makes use of OTE within CICS:

- The CICS-DB2 Attachment Facility
- The CICS-MQ Adapter
- The IP CICS Sockets interface

2.7.1 DB2

The CICS DB2 attachment facility includes a CICS DB2 task-related user exit, DFHD2EX1, which is written to threadsafe standards and enabled as an open API task-related user exit program. The TRUE is automatically enabled with the OPENAPI option on the ENABLE PROGRAM command during startup of the CICS-DB2 Attachment Facility. This enables the TRUE to receive control on an open L8 mode TCB. DB2 calls are made on this same L8 TCB, so it therefore acts as the thread TCB as well. This results in better performance, as there is no need to switch to a subtask TCB.

2.7.2 WMQ

At CICS TS V3.2 and WebSphere MQSeries® for z/OS the CICS WMQ attachment facility includes a task-related user exit, DFHMQTRU, which is written to threadsafe standards and enabled as an open API task-related user exit program. The TRUE is automatically enabled with the OPENAPI option on the ENABLE PROGRAM during startup of the CICS-MQ Adapter. This enables the TRUE to receive control on an open L8 mode TCB.

2.7.3 IP CICS Sockets

The IP CICS Sockets interface includes a task-related user exit, EZACIC01, which is written to threadsafe standards and can be enabled as an open API task-related user exit program. It will be enabled as OPENAPI only if the OTE parameter in the IP CICS Sockets configuration file for that CICS region is set to YES.

2.7.4 Performance considerations

To gain the best possible performance within an OTE environment:

- Ensure that all applications and exits within the TRUE path are written to threadsafe standards and defined to CICS as threadsafe. Common exits to consider are XPCFTCH, XEIIN, XEIOUT, XRMIIN, XRMIOUT, and Dynamic Plan exits.

  For the DB2, the default sample Dynamic Plan exit, DSNCUEXT, is not defined to CICS as threadsafe.

  – CICS Transaction Server Version 2.3 and Version 3.1 both ship an alternative sample Dynamic Plan exit, DFHD2PXT, which is defined to CICS as threadsafe.

  – For CICS Transaction Server Version 2.2, APAR PQ67351 supplies the alternative sample Dynamic Plan exit, DFHD2PXT.

- Minimize or eliminate the use of non threadsafe CICS commands. Reference "Threadsafe API commands" on page 38, "Threadsafe SPI commands" on page 40, and "Threadsafe XPI commands" on page 41.

    If you are unable to eliminate all non threadsafe commands, consider, if possible, re-arranging the commands within your application so they are not interspersed with SQL calls or IP CICS Sockets calls.

- When using transaction isolation (TRANISO), set MAXOPENTCBS equal to or greater than max task (MXT) coded within the CICS System Initialization Table.

Mode switching, in regard to OTE, is the act of switching from the QR TCB to an open TCB or vice versa.

- For non threadsafe exits, a switch occurs from the open TCB to the QR TCB and returns back to the open TCB when the exit program completes.
- For non threadsafe commands issued from a threadsafe program, a switch occurs from the L8 TCB to the QR TCB and remains there until the next SQL or WMQ call, which would cause a switchback from the QR TCB to the L8 TCB.
- For non threadsafe commands issued from an OPENAPI program, a switch occurs from the open TCB to the QR TCB for the duration of the EXEC CICS command. On return to the application, a switchback from the QR TCB to the open TCB occurs.

2.8 TCB considerations with UNIX System Services

When defining the numbers of TCBs that are allowed in a CICS region, you also need to consider the settings in UNIX System Services that control the number of processes that can run within a CICS region.

In UNIX System Services, the MAXPROCUSER parameter specifies the maximum number of processes one UNIX user identifier (UID) can have concurrently active, regardless of how the processes were created. The value can be in the range 3 to 32767. The default is 25. The MAXPROCUSER parameter is specified in SYS1.PARMLIB member BPXPRMxx. The *z/OS MVS Initialization and Tuning Reference,* SA22-7592, gives guidance on the setting of MAXPROCUSER.

MAXPROCUSER is independent of any particular user ID. However, there is an equivalent RACF® setting to limit the number of processes by user ID for a particular user. This is PROCUSERMAX. It sets the maximum number of processes per user ID field of the RACF OMVS SEGMENT of a user ID's profile.

The following TCBs all contribute to the potential number of processes associated with a particular CICS region:

- MAXOPENTCBS - The maximum number of L8 and L9 TCBs that can exist
- MAXJVMTCBS - The maximum number of J8 and J9 TCBs that can exist
- MAXSSLTCBS - The maximum number of S8 TCBs that can exist
- MAXXPTCBS - The maximum number of X8 and X9 TCBs that exist
- The SO TCB - Used to issue the necessary UNIX System Services and CEEPIPI calls for the socket domain
- The SL TCB - Provides a listening environment for sockets domain requests
- The SP TCB - Owns the S8 TCBs and the SSL cache
- TCBs used by the separate *TCP/IP Socket Interface for CICS* component of the z/OS Communications Server (if applicable)

By adding the number of TCBs from the above list, it is possible to obtain the total number of processes that might be associated with a given CICS region. This total represents a possible upper limit for the region.

Where you have CICS systems that share the same user ID, add the totals together to give the maximum number of processes associated with that user ID. This is because MAXPROCUSER is the number of processes for a UID, not for each job.

When you have determined the total possible number of processes associated with each user ID for your CICS regions, use the largest number and add an extra 10% to this figure when calculating the value of MAXPROCUSER.

If you have a particular user ID with a high result for the total number of processes required, due to several CICS systems sharing the same user ID, setting MAXPROCUSER to such a figure might not be appropriate. In this situation, use the PROCUSERMAX parameter on the OMVS segment of the RACF profile for the user ID to set a suitably high value to accommodate the requirements of the user ID.

The setting of the MAXPROCUSER and PROCUSERMAX parameters does not in itself consume extra resources. These are limiting values. CICS does not generate the open TCBs until they are needed, meaning that processes and system resources are not associated with TCBs until required. Note that TCBs specified in the SSLTCBS system initialization parameter are created at CICS system initialization. The setting of the TCPIP system initialization parameter does not affect the use of open TCBs by OTE. Also, if you specify TCPIP=NO and no OTE-managed services are used by CICS, then two of the MAXPROCUSER entries will be used in the initialization of the sockets domain.

2.8.1 The implications of setting MAXPROCUSER too low

If you do not set a large enough value for MAXPROCUSER for the CICS environment, you might get a number of warning and error messages. These are described below.

Message BPXI040I

This is a UNIX System Services warning message that alerts the operator that system resources are being consumed. The message notifies the operator when a threshold of 85% of the MAXPROCUSER value for a given UNIX Process Identifier (PID) has been reached. It is possible for the percentage to exceed 100%. This is because two special UIDs are allowed to create more processes than MAXPROCUSER would normally allow. The superuser (UID=0) can exceed many of the limits set in BPXPRMxx. Also, the default-UID can exceed the MAXPROCUSER setting. This is because many users can make use of the default-UID, and they each have independent processes. If each user were given an individual UID, then each would be subject to MAXPROCUSER independently. The default-UID refers to a RACF user ID without an OMVS segment defined for it; as such, it uses the default OMVS segment. The default-UID should not to be confused with the CICS default user.

Message DFHKE0500

This message is issued by the CICS TS for z/OS Version 3.1 Kernel when MAXPROCUSER has been exceeded for the user ID of the CICS system. This could occur because a number of CICS systems are sharing the same user ID on UNIX System Services and have a requirement to use a number of TCBs that is greater than the value defined in the MAXPROCUSER parameter.

2.9 Static and dynamic calls

If you defined a program with CONCURRENCY(THREADSAFE), all routines that are statically or dynamically called from this program (for example, COBOL routines) must also be coded to threadsafe standards.

When an EXEC CICS LINK command is used to link from one program to another, the program link stack level is incremented. However, a routine that is statically or dynamically called does not involve passing through the CICS command-level interface. Therefore, it does not cause the program link stack level to be incremented.

With COBOL routines, a static call causes a simple branch and link to an address resolved at link-edit time. For a dynamic call a program definition is required to allow Language Environment to load the program. After the load, a simple branch and link is still used. When a routine is called using either method, CICS does not receive control and is therefore unaware of the program execution change. The program that called the routine is still considered to be executing and its program definition is still considered to be the current program definition.

If the program definition for the calling program states CONCURRENCY(THREADSAFE), the called routine must also comply with this specification. Programs with the CONCURRENCY(THREADSAFE) attribute remain on an open TCB when they return from a DB2 call or any threadsafe EXEC CICS command, which is not appropriate for a program that is not threadsafe. For example, consider a situation in which the initial program of a transaction, program A, issues a dynamic call to program B, which is a COBOL routine. Because the CICS command-level interface was not involved, CICS is unaware of the call to program B and considers the current program to be program A. Program B issues a DB2 call. On return from the DB2 call, CICS needs to determine whether the program can remain on the open TCB or whether the program must switch back to the QR TCB to ensure threadsafe processing. To do this, CICS examines the CONCURRENCY attribute of what it considers to be the current program (program A in this example). If program A is defined as CONCURRENCY(THREADSAFE), CICS allows processing to continue on the open TCB. Program B is currently running. Therefore, if processing is to continue safely, program B must be coded to threadsafe standards. For further details refer to 8.5, "COBOL calls" on page 193.

2.10 Threadsafe API commands

If you write and define a CICS program as threadsafe, it can receive control on an open transaction environment (OTE) TCB. To obtain the maximum performance benefit from OTE, write your CICS programs in a threadsafe manner to avoid CICS having to switch TCBs. However, be aware that not all EXEC CICS commands are threadsafe, and issuing any of the non threadsafe commands causes CICS to switch your task back to the QR TCB to ensure serialization. The CICS API commands that are threadsafe are indicated in the command syntax diagrams in the *CICS Application Programming Reference,* SC34-6232, for CICS Transaction Server Version 2, and *CICS Transaction Server for z/OS V3.1 CICS Application Programming Reference,* SC34-6434, for CICS Transaction Server Version 3, with the statement This command is threadsafe.

Figure 2-7 on page 39 shows CICS V1 and V2 threadsafe API commands. Figure 2-8 on page 39 shows CICS TS V3.1 threadsafe API commands. Figure 2-9 on page 40 shows CICS TS V3.2 threadsafe API commands.

CICS TS V1 and V2 Threadsafe API Commands

CICS TS 1.3
- ABEND
- ADDRESS
- ASSIGN
- DELETEQ TS
- ENTER TRACENUM
- FREEMAIN
- GETMAIN
- HANDLE ABEND
- HANDLE AID
- HANDLE CONDITION
- IGNORE CONDITION
- LINK
- LOAD
- MONITOR
- POP HANDLE
- PUSH HANDLE
- READQ TS
- RELEASE
- RETURN
- WRITEQ TS
- XCTL

CICS TS 2.2
- DEQ
- ENQ
- SUSPEND
- WAIT EXTERNAL

CICS TS 2.3
- ASKTIME
- CHANGE TASK
- DOCUMENT CREATE
- DOCUMENT INSERT
- DOCUMENT RETRIEVE
- DOCUMENT SET
- FORMATTIME

Figure 2-7   Threadsafe API commands for CICS 1.3, 2.2, and 2.3

CICS TS 3.1 Threadsafe Commands

New commands that are threadsafe

- CONVERTTIME
- DELETE CONTAINER (CHANNEL)
- GET CONTAINER (CHANNEL)
- INVOKE WEBSERVICE
- MOVE CONTAINER (CHANNEL)
- PUT CONTAINER (CHANNEL)
- SOAPFAULT ADD
- SOAPFAULT CREATE
- SOAPFAULT DELETE
- WEB CONVERSE
- WEB CLOSE
- WEB OPEN
- WEB PARSE URL
- WEB RECEIVE (Client)
- WEB SEND (Client)

Existing commands that are now threadsafe

- WEB ENDBROWSE FORMFIELD
- WEB ENDBROWSE HTTPHEADER
- WEB EXTRACT
- WEB READ FORMFIELD
- WEB READ HTTPHEADER
- WEB READNEXT FORMFIELD
- WEB READNEXT HTTPHEADER
- WEB RECEIVE (Server)
- WEB RETRIEVE
- WEB SEND (Server)
- WEB STARTBROWSE FORMFIELD
- WEB STARTBROWSE HTTPHEADER
- WEB WRITE HTTPHEADER

Figure 2-8   CICS TS 3.1 threadsafe commands

CICS TS 3.2 Threadsafe Commands

New commands that are threadsafe

- DOCUMENT DELETE

Existing commands that are now threadsafe

- WAIT JOURNALNAME
- WAIT JOURNALNUM
- WRITE JOURNALNAME
- WRITE JOURNALNUM
- DELETE
- ENDBR
- READ
- READNEXT
- READPREV
- RESETBR
- REWRITE
- STARTBR
- UNLOCK
- WRITE

Figure 2-9   CICS TS 3.2 threadsafe commands

Note: The File Control API commands in figure 2-9 are threadsafe if the file to which they refer to is defined as either local VSAM or RLS. If the file is defined as remote, or is a shared data table, a coupling facility data table, or a BDAM file the commands are not threadsafe.

2.11 Threadsafe SPI commands

The CICS SPI commands that are threadsafe are indicated in the command syntax diagrams in the manual *CICS System Programming Reference*, SC34-6233, with the statement `This command is threadsafe`.

Figure 2-10 shows the threadsafe SPI commands and the respective CICS release in which the command was made threadsafe.

```
CICS TS Version V1, V2 and V3  Threadsafe SPI Commands

CICS TS V1.3                          CICS TS v2.2

 • INQUIRE EXITPROGRAM                 • DISCARD DB2CONN
 • INQUIRE TASK                        • DISCARD DB2ENTRY
                                       • DISCARD DB2TRAN
CICS TS V3.2                           • INQUIRE DB2CONN
                                       • INQUIRE DB2ENTRY
 • INQUIRE ASSOCIATION                 • INQUIRE DB2TRAN
 • INQUIRE ASSOCIATION LIST            • SET DB2CONN
 • INQUIRE IPCONN                      • SET DB2ENTRY
 • INQUIRE LIBRARY                     • SET DB2TRAN
 • SET IPCONN
 • PERFORM JVMPOOL                    CICS TS V2.3
 • SET DOCTAMPLATE
 • INQUIRE FILE                        INQUIRE WORKREQUEST
                                       SETWORKREQUEST
                                       INQUIRE DOCTEMPLATE
                                       DISCARD DOCTEMPLATE
```

Figure 2-10 Threadsafe SPI commands

2.12 Threadsafe XPI commands

All the XPI commands are threadsafe with the *exception* of:

► DFHDUDUX TRANSACTION_DUMP

2.13 Function shipping considerations

Terminal control, including Multi-Region Operation (MRO) and Inter System Communication (ISC), is not threadsafe. Therefore CICS must issue a mode switch to the QR TCB in order to function ship a request to a remote region.

This means that any command that is listed as threadsafe will be treated as such when executed locally, but will incur the overhead of a TCB switch if function shipped. See 8.4, "Function shipped commands" on page 188, for more details.

3

Techniques for threadsafety

This chapter is a discussion of some techniques that can be used when migrating to CICS threadsafe.

The following serialization techniques are covered:

- CICS API enqueue/dequeue
- CICS XPI enqueue/dequeue
- Compare and swap

3.1 Threadsafe standards

IBM recommends that all new CICS application programs be written to threadsafe standards. This purpose of this section is to provide the application and system programmer with guidance on how to ensure that this is achieved. By following the rules listed here, existing and new applications will maximize the benefits to be gained from being defined as threadsafe.

1. Ensure that all programs are written to current CICS standards, as documented in the *CICS Application Programming Guide*, SC34-6231, for CICS Transaction Server V2, and *CICS Transaction Server for z/OS V3.2 CICS Application Programming Guide,* SC34-6433, for CICS Transaction Server V3. In particular, programs should:

    – Be compiled and link-edited as reentrant, and reside in read-only storage (SIT parameter RENTPGM=PROTECT).

    This is not an absolute requirement for threadsafe programming, but if a program is capable of overwriting itself, then the program itself is effectively shared storage, and access to it should be serialized. See 3.2, "Serialization techniques" on page 46, for a discussion of appropriate serialization techniques.

    – Use only published CICS interfaces to external resources.

    Again, this is not an absolute requirement for threadsafe programming, but the use of native MVS calls under CICS will, prior to OTE, most likely cause the QR TCB to enter an MVS WAIT state, thereby stopping the whole of CICS. For this reason they are disallowed. This restriction is removed in CICS Transaction Server Version 3.1 by use of OPENAPI programs because they never execute application code on the QR TCB. However, it should be noted that use of non CICS APIs is at the user's own risk and is not formally supported even in CICS Transaction Server 3.1.

    If existing programs are accessing shared application resources, then access should be serialized before defining the programs as threadsafe. See 3.2, "Serialization techniques" on page 46, for a discussion of appropriate serialization techniques.

2. Use of the CICS common work area (CWA) should be avoided if at all possible (that is, set SIT parameter WRKAREA=0). Shared resources that are accessed via CICS APIs can be used instead (for example, CICS temporary storage). If use of the CWA is unavoidable, and the data in it is updated, ensure that an appropriate serialization technique is used by all programs to access it. See 3.2, "Serialization techniques" on page 46, for a discussion of appropriate serialization techniques.

3. All programs (including PLT programs, user exits, and user-replaceable modules) should not create or access shared storage (that is, as created by

the EXEC CICS GETMAIN SHARED command). Shared resources that are accessed via CICS APIs can be used instead (for example, CICS temporary storage). If use of shared storage is unavoidable, and the data in it is updated, ensure that an appropriate serialization technique is used by all programs to access it. See 3.2, "Serialization techniques" on page 46, for a discussion of appropriate serialization techniques.

4. Try to avoid the use of global work areas (GWAs) in user exits, that is, as created by the GALENGTH option of the EXEC CICS ENABLE PROGRAM command, and referenced via parameter UEPGAA in the exit, or via the EXTRACT EXIT command from other application programs. Depending on the exit point, it may be possible to use shared resources that are accessed via CICS APIs instead. If use of a GWA is necessary, and the data in it is updated, ensure that an appropriate serialization technique is used by all user exits and application programs to access it. For example, an application program could use EXEC CICS ENQ / DEQ and a user exit could use XPI ENQUEUE and DEQUEUE as long as they both use the same resource argument. See 3.2, "Serialization techniques" on page 46, for a discussion of appropriate serialization techniques.

5. All programs, user exits, and URMs should use only threadsafe EXEC CICS commands. Check the command syntax diagrams in the *CICS Application Programming Reference* and the *CICS System Programming Reference* for the statement `This command is threadsafe`. If the use of non threadsafe commands is unavoidable, design the application to minimize the performance impact. See 3.3, "Application design considerations" on page 51, for a discussion of threadsafe application design.

6. Ensure that all programs that have been written or identified as threadsafe are defined to CICS with the CONCURRENCY(THREADSAFE) attribute. If program autoinstall is enabled, remember to amend your autoinstall control program to ensure that the correct CONCURRENCY value is set for each program. Alternatively, use the CICS environment variable CICSVAR. This is discussed in 6.2.2, "CICS environment variable CICSVAR" on page 126.

7. Review the use of function shipping within the application. Function shipped commands will cause threadsafe EXEC CICS commands to become non threadsafe, so pay particular attention to temporary storage requests and to EXEC CICS LINK requests that are converted to distributed program links (DPLs). See 8.4, "Function shipped commands" on page 188, for more details. Note that accessing shared temporary storage in a coupling facility is threadsafe, but accessing remote TS queues in a queue owning region is non threadsafe.

8. Check with IBM for the latest threadsafe-related APARs, and apply any maintenance that is appropriate to your environment.

9. Check with your independent software vendors to ensure that their programs and exits comply with threadsafe standards and are defined as threadsafe. If they are not threadsafe, or issue non threadsafe EXEC CICS commands, understand the implications for your application.

3.2 Serialization techniques

As discussed in Chapter 6, "Application review" on page 111, all access to updatable application shared resources (if they exist) must be serialized before the associated programs can be defined as threadsafe. This section outlines a number of techniques that can be used to achieve this. As we will see, some techniques are preferable to others.

Whatever technique is selected, it is important that a shop standard is established, and all programs that access the same resource use the same serialization technique. No program is threadsafe until *all* programs that access the resource have been changed to include serialization.

The following sections discuss a number of serialization techniques.

3.2.1 Recommended serialization techniques

This section outlines techniques that are recommended by the authors of this book.

CICS API enqueue /dequeue
The EXEC CICS ENQUEUE and DEQUEUE commands are ideally suited for CICS application programs to serialize access to shared resources. Both commands are threadsafe, and so will not incur the performance overhead of switching a task back to the QR TCB.

Refer to the *CICS Application Programming Reference*, SC34-6232 for CICS Transaction Server V2, and *CICS Transaction Server for z/OS V3.1 CICS Application Programming Reference,* SC34-6434, for CICS Transaction Server V3, for full details on coding EXEC CICS ENQUEUE and DEQUEUE commands.

CICS XPI enqueue/dequeue
An enhancement to the exit programming interface (XPI) introduced with CICS Transaction Server 1.3 was the DFHNQEDX macro function call, which provides the same ENQUEUE and DEQUEUE capability provided by the CICS API. The XPI commands are threadsafe, so will not incur the performance overhead of switching a task back to the QR TCB.

The XPI ENQUEUE / DEQUEUE is ideal for use within a user exit to serialize access to a global work area (GWA) or any other shared resource. Refer to the *CICS Customization Guide*, SC34-6227, for CICS Transaction Server V2, and *CICS Transaction Server for z/OS V3 CICS Customization Guide*, SC34-6429, for CICS Transaction Server V3, for full details on coding XPI commands.

Compare and swap

Assembler applications and user exits can use one of the conditional swapping instructions, COMPARE AND SWAP (CS) or COMPARE DOUBLE AND SWAP (CDS), to serialize access to shared resources. Refer to the appropriate Principles of Operation manual for full details on coding these instructions.

3.2.2 Comparison of recommended options

Table 3-1 presents a comparison of the recommended options.

Table 3-1   Comparison of options

Option	Advantages	Disadvantages
Compare and swap assembler instruction on shared data element	► Potentially best performance. ► Easiest non-CICS API implementation. ► New locking mechanism is nondisruptive. It can be installed one program at a time.	► Cannot be used for fields greater than 4 bytes (8 bytes for CDS instruction). ► For fields less than 4 bytes, activity on adjacent bytes could cause additional failed lock attempts. ► Storage access is not threadsafe until all programs have been converted. ► Requires assembly language program or subroutine.

Option	Advantages	Disadvantages
Use test and set/Compare and Swap assembler instruction on separate *lock* byte	▸ New locking mechanism is nondisruptive. It can be installed one program at a time. ▸ *Lock* granularity is single byte or word. ▸ *Lock* may be defined for non-contiguous areas. ▸ If using CS, *Locked* status could be something that indicates which CICS task owns the resource (that is, task number, terminal identifier, and so on).	▸ Application failure while holding a lock will cause other TCBs to spin until lock is manually cleared (the effects of this can be mitigated somewhat by adding a retry counter to the lock loop, but access to the resource will still be denied until the lock is cleared). ▸ Storage access is not threadsafe until all programs have been converted. ▸ Requires assembly language program or subroutine.
Use Compare and Swap assembler instruction after moving the shared data element to a new fullword	▸ No interference from non-related tasks. ▸ Guarantees all accesses to shared resource have been identified. ▸ Viable option if a limited number of programs are involved.	▸ No migration path—all affected programs must be installed at the same time. ▸ Not a viable option if a large number of programs are involved. ▸ Requires assembly language program or subroutine.
CICS ENQ (API or XPI)	▸ *Lock* granularity is single byte. ▸ Application failure will not result in held lock. ▸ No knowledge of assembly language required.	▸ Costs more CPU than non-CICS API techniques. ▸ Always has to perform ENQ/DEQ even when no other tasks are interested in the resource. ▸ Must consider implications of MAXLIFETIME option.

3.2.3 Generalized Compare and Swap routine

The following discussion is predicated on the assumption that most accesses to shared resources are for maintaining flags, counters, or chain pointers. In general where this assumption applies, it may be possible to implement a single subroutine (written in assembly language) that protects the integrity of the shared resources, is generally more efficient than ENQ/DEQ, and insulates the application programmer from the details of implementing Compare and Swap instructions for every shared data element.

Except for the actual operation to be performed (increment, decrement, OR, AND, and so on), most Compare and Swap implementations follow exactly the same pattern. For example, to increment a 4-byte counter, the code will always follow the pattern shown in Example 3-1.

Example 3-1   Compare and Swap implementation example

```
* Increment a 4-byte field
INCREMENT DS    0H
          L     ROLD,SHARED         get shared data
RETRY     LR    RNEW,ROLD           save Shared value
          LA    RNEW,1(,RNEW)       increment value
          CS    ROLD,RNEW,SHARED    store new value
          BNZ   RETRY               serialization failed
          B     RETURN              successful completion
```

Retrying the operation without embedding some form of delay may be disconcerting to some in that it looks as though there is a high potential for a CPU loop. This point is addressed in *z/Architecture Principles of Operation*, SA22-7832, and shown in the following note.

> **Note:** This type of a loop differs from the typical *bitspin* loop. In a bitspin loop, the program continues to loop until the bit changes. In this example, the program continues to loop only if the value does change during each iteration. If a number of CPUs simultaneously attempt to modify a single location by using the sample instruction sequence, one CPU will fall through on the first try, another will loop once, and so on until all CPUs have succeeded.

Implementing a retry counter mitigates this worry. A retry counter also provides a convenient method for tracking potential resource contention at a very granular level—simply log the retry count somewhere such as in a CICS trace or monitor entry for offline analysis. Adding a retry counter in the code yields the results shown in Example 3-2. The symbol RCOUNT is a register other than ROLD or RNEW.

Example 3-2   Retry count example

```
* Increment a 4-byte field
INCREMENT DS    0H
          XR    RCOUNT,RCOUNT       clear retry counter
          L     ROLD,SHARED         get shared data
RETRY     LA    RCOUNT,1(,RCOUNT)   increment retry count
          CL    RCOUNT,MAXTRIES     too many attempts?
          BNL   ERROR               yes, quit trying
          LR    RNEW,ROLD           save original value
          LA    RNEW,1(,RNEW)       increment value
          CS    ROLD,RNEW,SHARED    store new value
```

```
          BNZ   RETRY              serialization failed-retry
          B     RETURN             return to caller
ERROR     DS    0H
     < Too many retry attempts >
```

While there are many ways to implement the retry count, the important point to note is that the logic required to set up the CS instruction is always the same.

Likewise, the *increment value* instruction [LA   RNEW,1(,RNEW)] is the only instruction in either of these patterns that has to change to implement a different operation (decrement, AND, OR, and so on). Placing this code in a subroutine in which SHARED is passed by reference could allow the creation of a generalized routine for manipulating shared memory elements. Such a subroutine should handle the most common updates of shared memory.

3.2.4 Non-recommended techniques

This section outlines some other techniques that can be used to serialize access to resources. These techniques are not recommended by the authors of this book, due to the disadvantages associated with each of them.

LINK to a QUASIRENT program

A linked-to program defined as QUASIRENT runs under the QR TCB, and can therefore take advantage of the serialization provided by CICS quasi-reentrancy. Remember, even in quasi-reentrant mode, serialization is provided only for as long as the program retains control and does not wait.

A valid serialization technique is therefore to move all shared resource access to a single program and define it as quasi-reentrant. All other application programs can then be defined as threadsafe, on the condition that they always link to the quasi-reentrant program to access the shared resource.

Although this technique is valid, in that it will protect the integrity of the shared resource, it will not result in the same performance gain as one of the recommended techniques, such as enqueue/dequeue. Whereas the recommended techniques will allow the program to remain on an open TCB (assuming it is there already), this technique will incur the performance overhead of a TCB switch to QR.

CICS transaction class

User-defined CICS transaction classes (TRANCLASS) allow the systems programmer to limit the number of concurrent tasks for transactions that belong to each class. Creating a transaction class with a MAXACTIVE value of 1 is a very crude method of serializing resource access. All transactions belonging to the class will be single threaded.

This technique has one advantage in that it can be achieved without changing any application code. However, even in a moderately busy system, it is likely to have a severe impact on transaction response times, and runs contrary to the whole objective of implementing threadsafe applications in the first place (that is, improved performance).

MVS enqueue/dequeue

Prior to CICS Transaction Server Version 3, issuing non CICS API calls from a CICS program is not supported in releases of CICS Transaction Server (up to and including Version 2 Release 3) because CICS cannot guarantee that such calls will not be issued from the QR TCB. Even if the application and system programmers design the system so that such a call is issued from an open TCB, there is always the risk that a future program change, such as the insertion of a non threadsafe EXEC CICS command, will cause the call to be issued from QR and block all CICS tasks.

The same applies in CICS Transaction Server Version 3 unless the program is defined as THREADSAFE and OPENAPI, which ensures that the program runs on an open TCB. Even in this situation we recommend using CICS services, as CICS provides better facilities to release enqueues in error situations.

3.3 Application design considerations

An ideal candidate application to define as THREADSAFE and CICSAPI, and therefore exploit OTE, is one that contains threadsafe application code, contains only threadsafe EXEC CICS commands, and uses only threadsafe user exit programs. An application like this moves to an L8 TCB when it makes its first call to an OPENAPI TRUE (such as a SQL request, an IP CICS sockets request or a WMQ request), and then continues to run on the L8 TCB through any number of such requests and application code, requiring no TCB switching.

Even if a number of application programs are not threadsafe, or programs contain non threadsafe EXEC CICS commands, it is still possible to design application transactions to minimize the number of TCB switches and obtain the performance benefits associated with running threadsafe.

As can be seen from Figure 2-3 on page 20, the execution path between the first and the last SQL call is key to the performance of a CICS DB2 task running under OTE. It follows that by placing non threadsafe code and commands either prior to the first SQL call or after the final SQL call, the application will avoid incurring the CPU overhead that placing the same code between SQL calls would incur. The same is true for WMQ as well in CICS Transaction Server Version 3.2.

So, to return to the example of the application with both DB2 and VSAM data, pre CICS Transaction Server Version 3.2, by designing the transactions so the VSAM and DB2 calls are not interspersed, an application of this nature can at least partially exploit OTE.

3.3.1 Application design considerations for CICS TS 3.2

At CICS Transaction Server Version 3.2 we now have further enhancements to OTE. It is now possible to define an application program to commence execution on an open TCB rather than wait for a call to an OPENAPI TRUE(DB2, MQ or IP CICS Sockets) to move the task to an open TCB.

Care needs to be taken, however, with applications that are calling OPENAPI-enabled TRUEs. There may be a temptation to define an application that is currently defined as threadsafe, as OPENAPI, so that it commences execution on the open TCB rather than wait for the call to an OPENAPI TRUE. The danger here is that if an application program is defined as OPENAPI and it is also defined as EXECKEY(USER), then the task will begin on an L9 TCB. Then when a call to an OPENAPI TRUE is encountered a switch to an L8 TCB will occur because OPENAPI-enabled TRUEs always run in the CICS key. This situation can lead to TCB switching across three TCBs (QR, L8, and L9). If there are non threadsafe CICS API commands in the program as well, then the performance impact could be very undesirable. This situation can be seen in Figure 2-5 on page 22. The preceding situation is dependant on storage protection being active within the CICS region.

File control

File control for local VSAM and VSAM RLS access is now available via threadsafe API and SPI commands. These include:

- READ
- REWRITE
- WRITE
- DELETE
- UNLOCK
- STARTBR, READNEXT, READPREV, RESETBR, ENDBR
- SPI - INQUIRE FILE

BDAM, SDT, CFDTs and remote files have no threadsafe API.

File control functions that are not threadsafe will still run on the QR TCB. These include:

- Open/Close
- Enable/Disable
- Quiesce functions
- INQ DSNAME
- SET SPI functions

File control exits must be made to be threadsafe, otherwise there will be a switch to the QR TCB when the exit is called and then a switch back when the exit processing completes. Products that have previously located the FCT (File Control Table) via control block interrogation need to be changed because this will no longer be safe to do.

The official interface for access to information in the FCT is via the INQUIRE FILE SPI. No interface to return the addresses of FCT entries, DSNBs, or any other File Control control block will be available.

OPENAPI good and bad candidates

The previous example shows that not all threadsafe application programs are necessarily good candidates to be defined as OPENAPI. If we assume that the program being defined is written to threadsafe standards then we need to decide whether the program is to be defined as CICSAPI or OPENAPI.

There are some guidelines for this, which can be summarized in Figure 3-1 on page 54.

Bad candidates for OPENAPI are user key DB2, IP CICS Sockets, and WMQ programs. This is because the application will start on an L9 TCB and will have to switch to an L8 TCB and back again for each call to an OPENAPI TRUE. Likewise for non threadsafe CICS commands we will switch to QR and back again.

The best candidates for OPENAPI are DB2, IP CICS Sockets, or WMQ programs that have only threadsafe CICS API commands and are defined as EXECKEY(CICS). Also, CPU-intensive programs (that is, those programs that do a lot of processing without giving up control to CICS) are good candidates for OPENAPI, as they can perform the intensive processing without affecting other tasks that might be waiting to execute on the QR TCB.

> **Note:** If storage protection is not active (STGPROT=NO), then the user key is the same as the CICS key and both types of programs run on L8 TCBs if defined as OPENAPI.

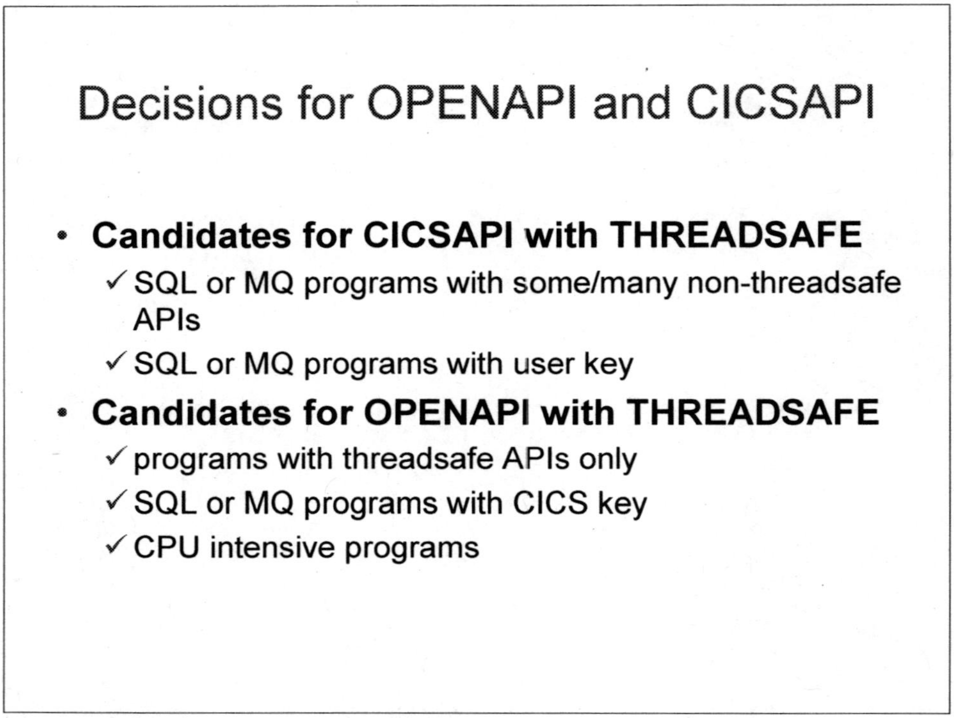

Decisions for OPENAPI and CICSAPI

- **Candidates for CICSAPI with THREADSAFE**
    - ✓ SQL or MQ programs with some/many non-threadsafe APIs
    - ✓ SQL or MQ programs with user key
- **Candidates for OPENAPI with THREADSAFE**
    - ✓ programs with threadsafe APIs only
    - ✓ SQL or MQ programs with CICS key
    - ✓ CPU intensive programs

Figure 3-1   Decisions for OPENAPI and CICSAPI

Part 2

Threadsafe implementation

In Part 2 we discuss the implementation tasks and system programmer tasks and provide a review of application code and a migration scenario.

Threadsafe tasks

This chapter identifies the tasks that are necessary to make a CICS DB2 application threadsafe, thereby allowing it to continue to run on an L8 TCB, following a DB2 command being issued.

While this chapter identifies the tasks needed to make a DB2 application threadsafe, the same principles apply for an application calling one of the other OPENAPI TRUEs, namely Websphere MQSeries or IP Sockets for CICS.

Additionally, this chapter describes how to use a number of tools to identify those programs that contain commands that will cause an application to switch unnecessarily to the QR TCB or wrongly use shared resources. The tools discussed are:

► CICS load module scanner (DFHEISUP)
► CICS Interdependency Analyzer
► CICS Performance Analyzer

4.1 Threadsafe migration planning

Making your application threadsafe is more complex than just defining your application programs as threadsafe and then sitting back to reap the performance benefits. The truth is that without some careful planning and a staged implementation, you could cause a performance degradation to your system or more seriously jeopardize your application's data integrity.

In this section we discuss the high-level plan to safely get you converted from your existing non threadsafe environment to a fully functional threadsafe one.

4.1.1 CICS Transaction Server upgrade/migration path

To achieve your threadsafe goals you need to be running CICS Transaction Server Version 2 or later and DB2 Version 6 or later. Since the OTE enhancements to the CICS-DB2 Attachment Facility are only exploited from DB2 Version 6 or later, you need to be running the correct release of DB2 to realize the benefits of threadsafe technology.

If you upgrade to CICS Transaction Server Version 2 or later, and change program definitions to CONCURRENCY(THREADSAFE) without performing a review of your exits, you will do more harm than good. This brings up the question: In which order should you upgrade your CICS and DB2 products, or does it matter? The answer is that it depends.

There are a couple of ways in which you can approach your threadsafe implementation, as shown in Table 4-1 and Table 4-2, although the method in Table 4-2 on page 59 is recommended.

Table 4-1   Convert to CICS TS V2 or higher first

Task	Description
1	Migrate to CICS TS V2 or later and DB2 V7 or later.
2	Perform a threadsafe analysis of *all* exits defined to CICS.
3	Make any adjustments or conversions to your exits.
4	Use CEDA to define your exit programs as threadsafe.
5	Analyze and convert your applications to be threadsafe.

Table 4-2 Review your exits first

Task	Description
1	Perform a threadsafe analysis of all exits defined to CICS.
2	Make any adjustments or conversions to your exits.
3	Use CEDA to define your exit programs as threadsafe.
4	Migrate to CICS TS V2 or later and DB2 V6 or later.
5	Retest your exits.
6	Analyze and convert your applications to be threadsafe.

We highly recommend that you follow method 2 listed in Table 4-2. The reason for this is the way CICS Transaction Server Version 2 or Version 3 handles exits in the threadsafe environment. Once you are running on the new L8 TCBs, each call to a non threadsafe defined exit in the DB2 path will force a return to the QR TCB to run the exit, and then afterwards return to the L8 TCB, therefore incurring extra TCB switches. See Figure 8-2 on page 176 for more information.

4.1.2 High-level threadsafe migration path

We recommend migration path 2 since the system exits themselves can increase the number of TCB switches you incur when they are defined as non threadsafe. If you are already running a CICS Transaction Server Version 2 or Version 3 system and have not converted your exits, you still may be in good shape since not all exits are directly in the DB2 path.

As mentioned in the previous section, the CICS system exits are a critical point of analysis in ensuring that you receive the benefits of threadsafe applications. A simple way of looking at this is to say that *all exits* must be converted and defined as threadsafe as part of your migration to CICS Transaction Server Version 2 or Version 3.

As well as any exits that you may have written, it is vitally important that you contact vendors of any OEM products you may have installed. They should be able to advise as to whether their exits are already threadsafe or of any maintenance you need to apply to make them threadsafe. Additionally, there may be information about problems known to IBM that can be found by searching the CICS Support Web pages, and that can be found by clicking the support link on the CICS home page:

http://www.ibm.com/cics

A review of the output produced by DFH0STAT will list all your exits and also whether they have already been defined as threadsafe, which may be the case if you have installed a vendor package that installed the exits as threadsafe. An example of DFH0STAT can be found in 7.4.3, "Running DFH0STAT" on page 148.

Table 4-3 outlines a safe migration path that can be followed no matter what release of CICS or DB2 you are currently running.

Table 4-3   High-level threadsafe migration plan

Task	Description
1	Migrate to DB2 V7 or later.
2	Install pre-req CICS PTFs.
3	Install pre-req DB2 PTFs.
4	Review FORCEQR SIT parameter.
5	Address your exits: ► Identify all your exits. ► Contact vendors if necessary about their exits. ► Review each exit for non threadsafe commands. ► Review each exit for use of shared resources. ► Make any coding adjustments and test. ► Define them as threadsafe.
6	Review system parameters and make adjustments: ► MAXOPENTCBS ► TCBLIMIT ► THREADLIMIT ► MXT
7	Upgrade to CICS TS V2 or V3.
8	Retest exits in a threadsafe environment.
9	Create a threadsafe application review plan.
10	Review and identify your candidate applications.
11	Make necessary program changes to conform to threadsafe standards.
12	Define applications that have passed your review or have been converted to threadsafe practices as THREADSAFE to CICS.

We break each of the preceding steps down into further detail in the next two chapters, but first we discuss the use of some tools you can use to analyze your applications.

We are going to treat system exits and application code both as simple applications for our analysis. You review all your code for two basic non threadsafe practices:

1. EXEC CICS commands that generate TCB switches to the QR TCB
2. EXEC CICS commands that reference shared resources:
   - ADDRESS CWA
   - EXTRACT EXIT
   - GETMAIN SHARED

You can use the CICS-supplied load module scanner (DFHEISUP) to scan your code for occurrences of non threadsafe commands that would generate a switchback to the QR TCB and to help you find occurrences of the three CICS commands listed above. In addition, the CICS Interdependency Analyzer (discussed later) includes a similar function.

4.2 Load module scanner: DFHEISUP

The utility DFHEISUP is provided by CICS to allow you to search load modules for specific CICS API and SPI commands. It locates all the EXEC CICS commands in your load modules, and then applies the filter to report on those commands that you have specified.

It returns one of two types of report:

▶ A summary report, giving a list of modules containing the commands specified by your filter, and the number of these commands in each module. This can be used as input to the detailed report to get more information about those modules.

▶ A detailed report shows, for each module, the specific commands it contains, and the offset of the command. Also included is EDF information, if available.

CICS provides an example job DFHEILMS in SDFHINST, which can be edited and used to execute the load module scanner. Its use is documented in the *CICS Operations and Utilities Guide,* SC34-6229, for CICS Transaction Server Version 2, and *CICS Transaction Server for z/OS V3 CICS Operations and Utilities Guide,* SC34-6431, for CICS Transaction Server Version 3.

> **Important:** CICS Transaction Server Version 2.2 users should apply PQ78531 before you run DFHEISUP. This APAR fixes storage problems that occur when running DFHEISUP against very large load libraries or very large load library concatenations. The APAR fix is present at the base code level in later releases of CICS.

4.2.1 DFHEISUP filter tables

Two sample filter tables are provided for use in detemining whether an application is threadsafe:

- DFHEIDTH
- DFHEIDNT

These CICS-supplied filter tables can be found in the SDFHSAMP library on your system.

DFHEIDTH

The first of these, DFHEIDTH, contains a list of the three commands that are *threadsafe inhibitor*, (that is, those commands that *may* cause the program not to be threadsafe because they allow access to shared storage).

The three commands that are listed in DFHEIDTH as being threadsafe inhibitors are:

- EXTRACT EXIT GASET
- GETMAIN SHARED
- ADDRESS CWA

All of these commands return addresses of data areas that can be shared between programs. This means that multiple updates of the data areas pointed at by those addresses may occur by concurrently running tasks.

If your installation has an application standard that allows use of assembler data tables (see "Assembler data tables" on page 122) as a form of shared storage, then you should consider amending DFHEIDTH to add the **LOAD** * command to find which applications load and use this form of shared storage. By default, the LOAD command is not included as part of DFHEIDTH because it would find *too* many legitimate uses of EXEC CICS LOAD (for example, loading a read-only program into a read-only DSA).

If any of these commands are identified as being used in any one application program, then a more detailed analysis of the whole application *must* be performed. This is to identify how and when the addresses returned by these commands are used to access the underlying data. It is possible the address returned by one of these commands can be passed to another program that does none of the above commands itself, but will still modify the data at the address passed to it. Only when you have identified how the address is used can you decide how to serialize access to the data.

DFHEIDNT

The second filter table contains a list of all those commands that *will* cause a TCB switchback to the QR TCB. Note that this table is provided by APAR PQ82603 for both CICS Transaction Server Version 2.2 and Version 2.3. The tables are provided at the base code level in CICS Transaction Server Version 3.

Use of these commands will not prevent you from defining the program as threadsafe. They could, however, prevent your application from achieving the performance benefits of allowing programs to stay on an open TCB following a DB2 call.

4.2.2 DFHEISUP - summary mode

Running the load module scanner run in summary mode produces two groups of information. Both groups will be written to SYSPRINT DD:

- A summary of the whole load library detailing how many modules were scanned, how many modules are in the library, how many were not scanned, and how many of the requested commands were found in the whole library.

```
LOAD LIBRARY STATISTICS
=======================
Total modules in library                               =    41
Total modules Scanned                                  =    41
Total CICS modules/tables not scanned                  =     0
Total modules possibly containing requested commands   =    19
```

Figure 4-1   Load library statistics

▶ A list of members in the library that contain any of the commands that have been specified in the filter table. The list will specify how many commands are in the load module and in what language the program was originally written. See Figure 4-2.

```
SUMMARY LISTING OF CICSRS3.U.LOAD
========================================
Module Name                   Commands Found  Language
'CICSRS3.U.LOAD(DB2MANY)'                  2  Assembler
'CICSRS3.U.LOAD(DB2ONCE)'                  3  Assembler
'CICSRS3.U.LOAD(DB2PGMA)'                  1  Assembler
'CICSRS3.U.LOAD(DB2PGMB)'                  1  Assembler
'CICSRS3.U.LOAD(DB2PGMO)'                  1  Assembler
'CICSRS3.U.LOAD(DB2PROGA)'                 2  Assembler
'CICSRS3.U.LOAD(DB2PROG1)'                 2  Assembler
'CICSRS3.U.LOAD(DB2PROG2)'                 2  Assembler
'CICSRS3.U.LOAD(DB2PROG3)'                 2  Assembler
'CICSRS3.U.LOAD(DB2PROG4)'                 2  Assembler
'CICSRS3.U.LOAD(DB2PROG5)'                 2  Assembler
'CICSRS3.U.LOAD(DB2PROG6)'                 2  Assembler
'CICSRS3.U.LOAD(DB2PROG7)'                 2  Assembler
'CICSRS3.U.LOAD(DB2PROG8)'                 2  Assembler
'CICSRS3.U.LOAD(DB2PROG9)'                 2  Assembler
'CICSRS3.U.LOAD(DB2SAMPL)'                 1  Assembler
'CICSRS3.U.LOAD(FUNCSHIP)'                 1  Assembler
'CICSRS3.U.LOAD(INITXIT)'                  1  Assembler
'CICSRS3.U.LOAD(INITXIT2)'                 1  Assembler
```

Figure 4-2   Module listing from summary report

This list of modules can also be optionally written to a file that is allocated to the DFHDTL DD statement by specifying the DETAILMODS parameter along with the SUMMARY parm on the EXEC statement of the jobstep. Example 4-1 demonstrates this.

Example 4-1   DFHEILMS summary run

```
//DFHSCNR  JOB (accounting information),CLASS=A,MSGCLASS=A
//DFHSCAN  EXEC PGM=DFHEISUP,PARM=('SUMMARY, DETAILMODS'),REGION=512M
//STEPLIB  DD DSN=&HLQ.SDFHLOAD,DISP=SHR
//SYSPRINT DD SYSOUT=*
//SYSERR   DD SYSOUT=*
//* Filter table
//DFHFLTR  DD DSN=&HLQ.FILTER,DISP=SHR
//* Module list for input to detail run
```

```
//DFHDTL   DD DSN=&HLQ.MODLIST,DISP=(NEW,CATLG,DELETE),
//            DCB=(RECFM=FB,LRECL=80,BLKSIZE=8000),SPACE=(CYL,(1,1))
//DFHIN    DD DSN=&HLQ.SDFHLOAD,DISP=SHR
```

This file can then be fed into the detail run via the DFHLIST DD statement. Again the report is written out to the SYSPRINT DD statement.

4.2.3 DFHEISUP - detail mode

The load module scanner, when run in detail mode, writes a report to the SYSPRINT DD statement showing exactly which commands are in each of the load modules scanned. An example of the JCL to run the detail report is shown in Example 4-2.

Example 4-2   DFHEILMS detail run

```
//DFHSCNR  JOB (accounting information),CLASS=A,MSGCLASS=A
//DFHSCAN  EXEC PGM=DFHEISUP,PARM=('DETAIL'),REGION=512M
//STEPLIB  DD DSN=&HLQ.SDFHLOAD,DISP=SHR
//SYSPRINT DD SYSOUT=*
//SYSERR   DD SYSOUT=*
//* Filter table
//DFHFLTR  DD DSN=&HLQ.FILTER,DISP=SHR
//* Module list for input to detail run
//DFHIN    DD DSN=&HLQ.SDFHLOAD,DISP=SHR
//* Module list from the summary run - DO NOT SPECIFY ALL with this
//DFHLIST  DD DSN=&HLQ.MODLIST,DISP=SHR
```

The detail run will scan only those modules listed in the input file pointed to by DD DFHLIST unless you add ALL to the parm statement.

An example of the output from a detail run is shown in Figure 4-3. Most of the entries have been edited from the example to save space.

```
CICS LOAD MODULE SCANNER UTILITY
SCAN PERFORMED ON Thu May  6 16:18:04 2004 USING TABLE RSTABLE2.3

DETAILED LISTING OF DD:DFHLIST
======================================

Module Name        'CICSRS3.U.LOAD(DB2MANY)'
Module Language    Assembler
Offset/EDF         Command
-----------------  -------------------------------------------
00001962/no-edf    START TRANSID FROM LENGTH INTERVAL
00001971/no-edf    SEND TEXT FROM LENGTH FREEKB TERMINAL

Module Name        'CICSRS3.U.LOAD(DB2ONCE)'
Module Language    Assembler
Offset/EDF         Command
-----------------  -------------------------------------------
00001961/no-edf    INQUIRE CLASSCACHE PROFILE
00001974/no-edf    INQUIRE JVM PROFILE
00002000/no-edf    ASKTIME ABSTIME

Module Name        'CICSRS3.U.LOAD(DB2PGMA)'
Module Language    Assembler
Offset/EDF         Command
-----------------  -------------------------------------------
00000840/no-edf    START TRANSID INTERVAL

Module Name        'CICSRS3.U.LOAD(INITXIT2)'
Module Language    Assembler
Offset/EDF         Command
-----------------  -------------------------------------------
00000716/no-edf    EXTRACT EXIT PROGRAM GASET GALENGTH

Total possible commands located = 32

LOAD LIBRARY STATISTICS
=======================
Total modules in library                                 =    19
Total modules Scanned                                    =    19
Total CICS modules/tables not scanned                    =     0
Total modules possibly containing requested commands     =    19
```

Figure 4-3 Detail report from DFHEISUP

4.2.4 DFHEISUP summary

For CICS Transaction Server Version 2.2 ensure that APAR PQ78531 is applied if you intend to scan very large libraries of load modules in a single run (the APAR fix is present at the base code level in higher releases). This will prevent possible storage problems when running against load libraries with 80 or more load modules. DFHEISUP is still a CPU intensive program and will obviously take longer to run against larger load libraries or load library concatenations.

The summary run is specified by PARM=SUMMARY on the PARM statement. Specifying PARM='SUMMARY,DETAILMODS' will direct a copy of the load module list to the file pointed to by DFHDTL as well as writing this information to SYSPRINT. This file can then be used as input to the detail run.

The detail run is specified by PARM=DETAIL on the PARM statement. If you supply, as input to the detail run, the module list generated by the summary run, do not specify PARM='DETAIL,ALL', as this will override the list of modules in this file and scan the whole library again. If ALL is omitted only those modules listed in the DFHLIST DD will be scanned.

5

CICS migration tools

This chapter focuses on the CICS tools that can assist you in migrating your applications to be threadsafe. The following topics are covered:

- A note about CICS VSAM Transparency for z/OS (CICS/VT)
- CICS Interdependency Analyzer for z/OS (CICS IA)
- A threadsafe application case study
- CICS Performance Analyzer for z/OS (CICS PA)

5.1 CICS VT performance on CICS TS V3.2

CICS VSAM Transparency (CICS VT) enables the migration of data from VSAM files to DB2 tables and ensures continued access to this data without modification to existing CICS and batch application programs. CICS VT supports CICS TS V3.2 without any modification.

The threadsafe File Control API in CICS TS V3.2 provides significant performance benefits for CICS VT.

CICS VT uses File Control GLUE programs to intercept File Control API calls and processes these requests as SQL calls to DB2. Although these GLUE programs have always been threadsafe, non-threadsafe CICS File Control APIs in releases of CICS TS prior to CICS TS V3.2 had resulted in a switch back to the QR TCB for every File Control API call.

Basic tests were completed in a laboratory controlled environment using sample CICS applications and comparing CICS VT running in CICS TS V3.1 and CICS TS V3.2 regions. The same workload showed overall CPU improvement ranging from 3.5% to 15.4% when running on CICS TS V3.2. The number of TCB switches dropped from 74 down to 8. Most importantly, up to 80% of the CPU usage shifted from the QR TCB to an L8 TCB. This allowed the QR TCB to process other work that could not run on an OPEN TCB, thus allowing for greater throughput.

5.2 CICS Interdependency Analyzer for z/OS (CICS IA)

This section covers the CICS IA tool, including its purpose, components, architecture, and detailed steps for configuring and using it.

5.2.1 CICS IA overview

The CICS Interdependency Analyzer for z/OS (CICS IA) is a runtime and batch system for use with CICS Transaction Server for z/OS (CICS TS). It is used for the following two purposes:

- To identify CICS application resources and their interdependencies

  This function enables you to understand the makeup of your application set, such as:
  - Which transactions use which programs
  - Which programs use which resources (files, maps, queues, and so on)
  - Which resources are no longer used
  - What applications does a CICS region contain

- To analyze transaction affinities

    Affinities require particular groups of transactions to be run either in the same CICS region or in a particular region.

    Affinities information is useful in a dynamic routing environment, since you need to know of any restrictions that *prevent* particular transactions from being routed to particular application-owning regions (AORs) or that *require* particular transactions to be routed to particular AORs.

CICS IA captures either affinity or interdependency information while CICS is running and stores it in VSAM files. Subsequently the VSAM files are used to load the DB2 database tables. Sample SQL queries are provided to analyze the DB2 tables, or the users can use the online query interface. Detailed batch reports can be produced from the VSAM files, if desired.

Many large organizations have been using CICS since the early 1970s and their systems have grown and evolved with the business. During this time, many techniques for implementing applications have been used as a result of new functions, changing corporate standards, technical requirements, and business pressures.

Frequently, this growth has not been as structured as it might have been, with the result that many applications and services share common resources, and changes in one area typically affect many other areas. This can reach such a level that the system can no longer develop in a controlled manner without a full understanding of these interrelationships. CICS IA can help you achieve this understanding.

For example, if you need to change the content or structure of a file, you need to know which programs use this file, because they will need to be changed also. CICS IA can tell you this, as well as the transactions that drive the programs. CICS IA records the interdependencies between resources (such as files, programs, and transactions) by monitoring programming commands that operate on resources.

The application that issues such a command has a dependency on the resource named in the command. For example, if an application program issues the command EXEC CICS WRITE FILE(myfile), it has a dependency on the file called myfile. It might have similar dependencies on transient data queues, temporary storage queues, transactions, other programs, and so on.

The commands that are monitored are typically CICS application programming interface (API) and system programming interface (SPI) commands that operate on CICS resources. However, you can also instruct CICS IA to monitor some types of non-CICS commands that operate on non-CICS resources, for example:

- WMQ calls
- DLI calls to IMS Database resources
- DB2 calls
- Dynamic COBOL calls to other programs

Potentially, the inclusion of any non-CICS resources gives you a fuller picture of the resources used by a transaction.

The *collector* component of CICS IA collects the dependencies or affinities that apply to a single CICS region — that is, a single application-owning region (AOR) or a single, combined routing region/AOR. It can be run against production CICS regions, and is also useful in a test environment, to monitor possible dependencies introduced by new or changed application suites or packages.

From the interactive interface of CICS IA you can control collectors running on multiple regions.

> **Note:** To ensure that you monitor as many potential dependencies or affinities as possible, use CICS IA with all parts of your workload, including rarely used transactions and abnormal situations. It is possible to store the collected information from several CICS regions into the same database. You can then review the collected dependencies and affinities using CICS IA's query interface, or produce your own SQL queries based on samples provided.

5.2.2 New in CICS IA for z/OS V2.1

The following features and capabilities are introduced in CICS Interdependency Analyzer for z/OS V2.1:

- An Eclipse-based client interface and improved query management facilities
  - This interface makes it easy for you to access the collected data and use it in the day-to-day analysis.
  - The client is based on the XML API, so automated processes can query the database as well.
- Timer-based collector control

  This control allows the user to start the collector for a given time of day to enable targeted data collection. For example, you can set the tool to schedule collection in different regions throughout the data collection process.

It helps you to:
- Work around high volume time periods.
- Target collection for when an application is active.

▶ Enhanced single point of control capabilities
- You can turn data collection for multiple CICS regions on and off with a single CINT command to speed selection.
- You can select default options for all your CICS regions with a single setting or you can specify collection options to be region specific.

▶ A selective program and transaction Exclude list eliminates extraneous data and reduces overhead during data capture

▶ Provision of CSD data set name and group-list information

▶ Automation of tracking of runtime impact on application change by providing program version information, enabling removal of old data by version and comparison of data by program version

▶ Improved installation and customization, as well as other enhancements

5.2.3 The components of CICS IA

The CICS IA architecture is described later in this chapter. This section describes the components that make up CICS IA.

The design of CICS IA centers around the concept of examining the EXEC CICS commands used by applications and systems programmers. Each command and its parameters indicates the resources that will be used by the program. An analysis of these calls provides a view of resource interdependencies.

The scanner component

It is possible to write a program to examine the program load modules and report on the EXEC CICS commands and their parameters. The *scanner* component of CICS IA is just such a program. It produces a report that tells, for each program, the commands issued, the programming language used, and the resources involved. The scanner also indicates whether the command is a possible affinity, a possible dependency, or both.

The collector component

The problem with only using the scanner is that it does not show the execution-time path through the code and which commands are, in fact, executed. An approach is needed that intercepts the commands as they are executed and captures the name of the program and its context (for example, which program called it, which transaction initiated it, and so on). The *collector* component is that part of CICS IA that does this capture function and stores the data in an MVS data space.

The collector function can be activated across multiple CICS regions from a single point of control, and the data can be collected across these regions and written to a VSAM file shared between these regions using a file owning region (FOR) or using RLS. The collector can collect either dependency or affinity information; it cannot collect both at once. At specified intervals or on operator command the data space is written to VSAM files.

Once the data is collected, CICS IA provides a set of utilities to enable this data to be loaded into a DB2 database. Having the data in DB2 provides many opportunities for detailed analysis using standard SQL queries or using the online CICS BMS interface that CICS IA provides. This analysis can help you to:

- Use CICS resources more efficiently.
- Balance application workload for continuous availability.
- Improve the speed and reduce the cost of application maintenance.
- Minimize the impact of routine application maintenance for the end user.
- Plan reuse of existing applications as e-business applications and build new applications more efficiently.

The reporter component

The *reporter* component is a set of batch programs that can produce reports from these files. A summary report can be run or, if desired, a detailed report can be run.

The query component

The VSAM files are loaded into a DB2 database. Once the data is available in the DB2 database, the *query* component can be used to view resource interdependencies. This component comprises a set of CICS transactions (COBOL/BMS).

CICS IA also provides sample SQL queries for use with SPUFI or other DB2 query tools from IBM or other ISVs.

The CICS IA client

CICS IA V2.1 provides an Eclipse-based client to query the DB2 database.

5.2.4 CICS IA architecture

The components of CICS IA described in the previous section are shown in Figure 5-1. Detailed discussion about how to use the components is in subsequent sections.

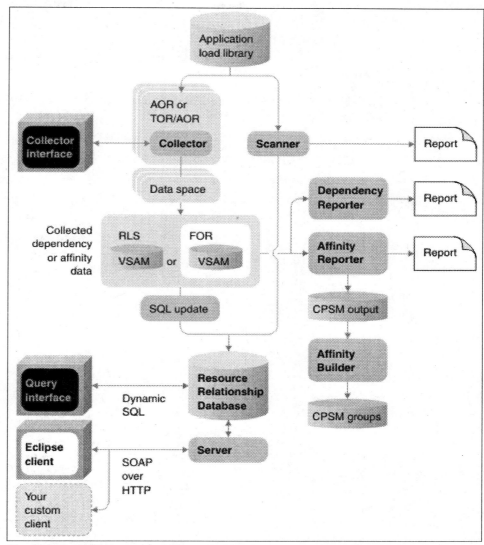

Figure 5-1   CICS IA component architecture

5.2.5 How CICS IA can assist with threadsafety

In a similar way to DFHEISUP and use of filter table DFHEIDTH, CICS IA can detect use of CICS commands that are *threadsafe inhibitors*—those commands that *may* cause the program not to be threadsafe in that they allow access to shared storage.

While CICS IA has an offline scanner that performs a similar role to DFHEISUP, the advantage CICS IA brings is the runtime collector component. This reports on applications executed, rather than applications residing in load libraries, some of which may be obsolete.

CICS IA collects resource information that can be stored in a DB2 table and then queried using SQL. For example:

▶ Show us all programs that execute an ADDRESS CWA command:

    SELECT PROGRAM OBJECT FROM CIU3_CICS_DATA WHERE FUNCTION='ADDRESS';

▶ Show us all transactions and programs that use shared resources:

    SELECT TRANSID, PROGRAM, FUNCTION, OBJECT FROM CIU3_CICS_DATA
    WHERE FUNCTION IN ('LOAD ','EXTRACT ','GETMAIN ','ADDRESS ');

Figure 5-2 shows an example of the results from such a query.

```
TRANSID   PROGRAM   FUNCTION   OBJECT
--------+---------+---------+---------+--
VA90      EQZ1RCV   LOAD       EQZTSCT
VA90      EQZ1REL   LOAD       EQZTSCT
VA90      EQZ1SET   LOAD       EQZTSCT
V220      EQZ1IDEN  LOAD       EQZTSCT
V220      EQZ1IPGV  LOAD       EQZTSCT
V220      EQZ1MONS  LOAD       EQZTSCT
V220      EQZ1RCV   LOAD       EQZTSCT
V220      EQZ1REL   LOAD       EQZTSCT
V895      CAMA895C  LOAD       CAMTACTH
V895      CAMA895C  LOAD       CAMTAPTH
V895      CAMA895C  LOAD       CAMTAXTH
V200      EQZ1SWCH  LOAD       EQZTSCT
V800      CAMA800C  LOAD       EZPSCCIL
V800      EZPACTLC  GETMAIN    ADDR
V800      EZPACTLC  LOAD       CAMLICIL
V800      EZPACTLC  LOAD       CAMLMTSL
V800      EZPACTLC  LOAD       CAMNL01L
V800      EZPACTLC  LOAD       EZPLD01L
V800      EZPACTLC  LOAD       EZPNL01L
V800      EZPACTLC  LOAD       EZPSLNGL
TST4      EMSTEST4  ADDRESS    CWA
```

Figure 5-2   CICS IA output: Looking for threadsafe inhibitors

CICS programmers converting programs to be threadsafe can use CICS IA reports during testing to determine which TCB modes their programs use. These reports can help them to identify programs that have CICS API calls that are not threadsafe and cause TCB mode switching. An example is shown in Figure 5-3.

```
Tran  Program  Offset   Command         Resource
                Sysid    Usage  First Run        Last Run              Term  TCBmode
TS01  TS010001 00000366 READQ TSQUEUE   TS1A+TE+
                ----     33     2004-12-21 17.43.59 2004-12-21 17.44.14  Y     QR

               000004D0 READQ TSQUEUE   TS1M+TE+
                ----     33     2004-12-21 17.43.59 2004-12-21 17.44.14  Y     QR

               000007C4 WRITEQ TSQUEUE  TS1A+TE+
                ----     320    2004-12-21 17.43.59 2004-12-21 17.44.15  Y     QR

               0000088C WRITEQ TSQUEUE  TS1M+TE+
                ----     320    2004-12-21 17.43.59 2004-12-21 17.44.15  Y     QR
```

Figure 5-3   CICS IA output: Reporting the TCB mode

In this section we take the two application programs that we identified as non-threadsafe and make them threadsafe. We use the ENQ/DEQ method to serialize any use of shared storage.

In this section we demonstrate the following:

► Making a sample application threadsafe
► Identifying non-threadsafe programs using IA
► Displaying TCB modes using IA
► Showing what can go wrong if you do not take threadsafe seriously

Prior to enabling any application program to be defined as threadsafe, a review of the application code must be performed. This cannot be emphasized strongly enough. It is necessary for two reasons:

► To maintain application data integrity

   Prior to CICS Transaction Server 2.2 user applications and exits ran on the QR TCB, which is a restricted or closed environment. CICS provided the serialization needed to ensure that application data integrity was never compromised. In this environment programs could be sure that no more than one quasi-reentrant program could run at the same time. For applications that have DB2 calls (or calls to other TRUEs that have been enabled as OPENAPI), it is possible for two or more programs to be running concurrently on different open TCBs and the QR TCB. Therefore it becomes very important that shared resources used by an application are serialized to prevent any application integrity problems due to more than one program accessing the same resource at the same time.

- To ensure that once CICS moves an application over to an open TCB it remains there for as long as possible after the DB2 call has been completed

    CICS will switch the application program back to the QR TCB in order to execute CICS API or SPI commands that are non threadsafe. CICS must do this to maintain the integrity of such things as the CSA and other control blocks used by the commands.

In order to demonstrate the potential problems with defining an application as threadsafe we wrote a simple file update application. The following sections describe this application and the various tests we performed.

We also recommend that CICS PA be used to compare performance before and after converting a program to threadsafe. For more information about the use of CICS PA see 5.4, "CICS Performance Analyzer for z/OS (CICS PA)" on page 104.

5.2.6 Identifying non threadsafe applications using CICS IA

This section describes the steps required to identify applications that are non threadsafe. It discusses the following:

- Using the CICS IA Scanners
- Using the CICS IA Collector
- Identifying non-threadsafe programs

Using the CICS IA Scanners

In CICS IA V2R1 you have two load module scanners:

- The original load module scanner that reports on possible affinities and dependencies in a program. It also reports the program language. It produces a batch report and populates two DB2 tables:
    - CIU4_SCAN_SUMMARY
    - CIU4_SCAN_DETAIL
- A new CSECT scanner that reports on linkage and compiler attributes of all CSECTs within a program. It produces a batch report and populates two DB2 tables:
    - CIU4_CSECT_INFO
    - CIU4_PROGRAM_INFO

Running the load module scanner

To run the load module scanner we must first edit and run the customized job CIUJCLTS to produce a summary report.

The job appears in Example 5-1. The values that require editing in this job are:

scan   The load library to be scanned. We scan REDBK23.APPL.LOADLIB.

ciudet   The output data set to be used as input to the detailed job CIUJCLTD. We use REDBK23.APPL.DETMODS.

Example 5-1   CIUJCLTS: IA summary scanner JCL

```
//CIUJCLTS JOB USER=EYJ,NOTIFY=EYJ,
//         CLASS=A,MSGCLASS=Y,REGION=0M
//****************************************************************
//*                                                               *
//* JCL NAME = CIUJCLTS                                           *
//*                                                               *
//* DESCRIPTIVE NAME = IBM CICS INTERDEPENDENCIES UTILITY          *
//*                    RUN SCANNER IN SUMMARY MODE WITH DB2 OUTPUT *
//*                                                               *
//* CHANGES TO BE MADE                                            *
//*                                                               *
//*   1) CHANGE THE JOB CARD TO SUIT YOUR SYSTEM CONVENTIONS      *
//*   2) CHANGE THE FOLLOWING PARAMETERS:-                        *
//*   DB2P                                                        *
//*   THE DB2 ID                                                  *
//*   CIU                                                         *
//*   DATASET HLQ FOR CIU PRODUCT                                 *
//*   DSN710                                                      *
//*   DATASET HLQ FOR DB2 SDSNLOAD and RUNLIB.LOAD                *
//*   _scan_                                                      *
//*   CICS LOAD DATASET TO BE SCANNED                             *
//*   _ciudet_                                                    *
//*   Output dataset created by SCANNER SUMMARY JOB               *
//*   3) EDIT THE MEMBER CIUDB2BT IN                              *
//*      REDBK23.MIG23T31.SCIUCLIS                                *
//*      AND CHANGE THE FOLLOWING:-                               *
//*   CIU                                                         *
//*   DATASET HLQ FOR CIU PRODUCT                                 *
//*                                                               *
//****************************************************************
//* FUNCTION =                                                    *
//*    Sample JCL to run the Load Module Scanner component of the *
//*    Interdependencies Utility (SUMMARY mode, DB2 output).      *
//****************************************************************
//SCAN     EXEC PGM=IKJEFT1B,DYNAMNBR=20,
```

```
//                   PARM=('%CIUDB2BT','SYS(DB2P)','PROG(CIULMS)',
//                   'PLAN(CIUBTCH4)','PARM(''$SUMMARY,DETAILMODS,TABLE'')')
//STEPLIB  DD DSN=CIU.SCIULOAD,DISP=SHR
//         DD DSN=CIU.SCIULODE,DISP=SHR
//         DD DSN=DSN710.SDSNLOAD,DISP=SHR
//SYSPROC  DD DSN=REDBK23.MIG23T31.SCIUCLIS,DISP=SHR
//INPUT    DD DSN=REDBK23.APPL.LOADLIB,DISP=SHR
//SYSPRINT DD SYSOUT=*
//SYSUDUMP DD SYSOUT=*
//SYSTSIN  DD DUMMY
//SYSTSPRT DD SYSOUT=*
//SYSABOUT DD SYSOUT=*
//SYSOUT   DD SYSOUT=*
//INTMOD   DD DSN=REDBK23.APPL.DETMODS,DISP=(NEW,CATLG,DELETE),
//            DCB=(RECFM=FB,LRECL=80,BLKSIZE=8000),SPACE=(CYL,(1,1))
//DETAIL   DD DUMMY
//
```

The output from this job can be seen in Example 5-2.

Example 5-2 IA scanner summary output

```
CICS INTERDEPENDENCY ANALYZER    Version 2.1.0
LOAD MODULE SCANNER  -   SUMMARY LISTING OF REDBK23.APPL.LOADLIB

Module      Module      Module       Language    Possible statements......
Name        Length      Language     Version     Affinities    Dependencies
--------    --------    ----------   --------    ----------    ------------
CCVSREMP    00003E28    ASSEMBLER                    70             72
CDCB001#    00001F38    COBOL        Non LE           0              2
CDCB0010    00002090    COBOL        Non LE           0              2
CDCB0020    000020D0    COBOL        Non LE           0              5
CDCB0510    00002090    COBOL        Non LE           0              2
CDCB0710    00002090    COBOL        Non LE           0              2
CICB0010    000020B8    COBOL        Non LE           0              7
CICB0020    00001EB0    COBOL        Non LE           0              8
CICB0030    00001EB0    COBOL        Non LE           0              8
CICB0050    00001A90    COBOL        Non LE           0              5
COBOLVS1    00001318    COBOL        Non LE           1              2
COBOLVS2    00001318    COBOL        Non LE           1              2
CSCB0010    00001358    COBOL        Non LE           0              1
CSCB0030    00004BC0    COBOL        Non LE           0              2
CSCB0200    00001250    COBOL        Non LE           0              1
REDBK1      00001630    C/370        LE               4              6
REDBK1A     00001630    C/370        LE               4              6
REDBK1B     00001630    C/370        LE               4              6
REDBK1C     00001630    C/370        LE               4              6
REDBK1D     00001630    C/370        LE               4              6
```

```
REDBK1E      00001630    C/370      LE         4           6
REDBK2       000026D8    PL/I       LE         6           6
REDBK3       00001720    C/370      LE         0           4
REDBK4       00001738    COBOL      Non LE     0           1
REDBK5       00001780    C/370      LE         2           6
CICS INTERDEPENDENCY ANALYZER    Version 2.1.0
LOAD MODULE SCANNER -  SUMMARY LISTING OF REDBK23.APPL.LOADLIB

                       LOAD LIBRARY STATISTICS
==========================================================================
Total modules in library                             =         25
Total modules scanned                                =         25
Total CICS modules/tables (not scanned)              =          0
Total modules in error (not scanned)                 =          0
Total modules containing possible MVS POSTs          =          0
Total modules containing possible Dependency commands =         25
Total modules containing possible Affinity commands  =         11
  Total ASSEMBLER modules                            =          1
  Total C/370 modules                                =          8
  Total COBOL modules                                =         15
  Total COBOL II modules                             =          0
  Total PL/I modules                                 =          1
```

To run the detailed report for the load module scanner we must edit and run the customized job CIUJCLTD. The job appears in Example 5-3. The values that require editing in this job are:

scan   The load library to be scanned. We scan REDBK23.APPL.LOADLIB.

ciudet   The input data set created by the summary job. We use REDBK23.APPL.DETMODS.

Example 5-3   CIUJCLTS - IA detailed scanner

```
//CIUJCLTD JOB USER=EYJ,NOTIFY=EYJ,
//         CLASS=A,MSGCLASS=Y,REGION=0M
//**********************************************************************
//* JCL NAME = CIUJCLTD                                                 *
//*                                                                    *
//* DESCRIPTIVE NAME = IBM CICS INTERDEPENDENCIES UTILITY               *
//*                    RUN SCANNER IN DETAIL MODE WITH DB2 OUTPUT       *
//*                                                                    *
//* CHANGES TO BE MADE                                                  *
//*                                                                    *
//*    1) CHANGE THE JOB CARD TO SUIT YOUR SYSTEM CONVENTIONS           *
//*    2) CHANGE THE FOLLOWING PARAMETERS:-                             *
//*    DB2P                                                             *
//*    THE DB2 ID                                                       *
//*    CIU                                                              *
```

```
//*      DATASET HLQ FOR CIU PRODUCT                                  *
//*      DSN710                                                       *
//*      DATASET HLQ FOR DB2 SDSNLOAD and RUNLIB.LOAD                  *
//*      _scan_                                                       *
//*      The load library to be scanned                                *
//*      _ciudet_                                                     *
//*      Input dataset created from a SCANNER SUMMARY JOB              *
//*                                                                   *
//*   3) EDIT THE MEMBER CIUDB2BT IN                                   *
//*         REDBK23.MIG23T31.SCIUCLIS                                  *
//*         AND CHANGE THE FOLLOWING:-                                 *
//*      CIU                                                          *
//*      DATASET HLQ FOR CIU PRODUCT                                  *
//*                                                                   *
//*********************************************************************
//* FUNCTION =                                                        *
//*                                                                   *
//*    Sample JCL to run the Load Module Scanner component of the     *
//*    Interdependencies Utility (DETAIL mode, DB2 output).            *
//*                                                                   *
//SCAN     EXEC PGM=IKJEFT1B,DYNAMNBR=20,
//             PARM=('%CIUDB2BT','SYS(DB2P)','PROG(CIULMS)',
//             'PLAN(CIUBTCH4)','PARM(''$DETAIL,TABLE'')')
//STEPLIB  DD DSN=CIU.SCIULOAD,DISP=SHR
//         DD DSN=CIU.SCIULODE,DISP=SHR
//         DD DSN=DSN710.SDSNLOAD,DISP=SHR
//SYSPROC  DD DSN=REDBK23.MIG23T31.SCIUCLIS,DISP=SHR
//INPUT    DD DSN=REDBK23.APPL.LOADLIB,DISP=SHR
//SYSPRINT DD SYSOUT=*
//SYSUDUMP DD SYSOUT=*
//SYSTSIN  DD DUMMY
//SYSTSPRT DD SYSOUT=*
//SYSABOUT DD SYSOUT=*
//SYSOUT   DD SYSOUT=*
//DETAIL   DD DSN=REDBK23.APPL.DETMODS,DISP=(OLD,DELETE)
//INTMOD   DD DUMMY
//
```

The output from this job is shown in Example 5-4.

Example 5-4   IA Scanner detailed output

```
CICS INTERDEPENDENCY ANALYZER   Version 2.1.0                                 06/27/06    Page    1
LOAD MODULE SCANNER - DETAILED LISTING OF REDBK23.APPL.LOADLIB

Module Name - REDBK1    /  Load Module Length - 00001630  /  Module Entry Point - 00000028
Offset     Storage Content (HEX)                             EDF DEBUG   Possible Command          Depcy   Affinity
--------   ----------------------------------------------    ---------   ---------------------     ------  --------
000008A4   020880002F1F0000000000000000000000000000           00007000    ASSIGN    APPLID           Yes
00000904   020280002F020000000000000000000000000000           00007400    ADDRESS   CWA              Yes     Trans
00000924   0A02E0002F00004100                                 00007800    WRITEQ    TS               Yes     Trans
00000964   0604F0002F28004400                                 00010000    WRITE     FILE             Yes
00000978   0A02E0002F00004100                                 00010600    WRITEQ    TS               Yes     Trans
```

```
0000098C  0A02E0002F00004100              00011000    WRITEQ   TS              Yes      Trans
Total possible Affinity commands    =         4
Total possible Dependency commands  =         6
Total possible MVS POSTs            =         0

CICS INTERDEPENDENCY ANALYZER   Version 2.1.0                          06/27/06    Page    10
LOAD MODULE SCANNER - DETAILED LISTING OF REDBK23.APPL.LOADLIB
                    LOAD LIBRARY STATISTICS
==============================================================
Total modules in DETAIL file                        =         25
Total modules scanned                               =         25
Total CICS modules/tables (not scanned)             =          0
Total modules in error (not scanned)                =          0
Total modules containing possible MVS POSTs         =          0
Total modules containing possible Dependency commands =       25
Total modules containing possible Affinity commands =         11
    Total ASSEMBLER modules                         =          1
    Total C/370 modules                             =          8
    Total COBOL modules                             =         15
    Total COBOL II modules                          =          0
    Total PL/I modules                              =          1
```

Running the CSECT scanner

In order to use the CSECT scanner we must first populate the DB2 table CIU4_TRANSLATORS with a list of translator and compiler names. To do this we must edit and run the customized job CIUTLOAD. To run the CSECT scanner we must edit and run the customized job CIUJCLCS. The job appears in Example 5-5. The value that requires editing in this job is **_scan_**, the load library to be scanned. We scan REDBK23.APPL.LOADLIB.

Example 5-5   CIUJCLCS - IA CSECT Scanner JCL

```
//CIUJCLCS JOB USER=EYJ,NOTIFY=EYJ,
//         CLASS=A,MSGCLASS=Y,REGION=0M
//****************************************************************
//* JCL NAME = CIUJCLCS                                           *
//* DESCRIPTIVE NAME = IBM CICS INTERDEPENDENCIES UTILITY         *
//*                    Sample JCL for running CSECT Scanner with  *
//*                    DB2 output.                                *
//*                                                               *
//* CHANGES TO BE MADE                                            *
//*                                                               *
//*   1) CHANGE THE JOB CARD TO SUIT YOUR SYSTEM CONVENTIONS      *
//*   2) CHANGE THE FOLLOWING PARAMETERS:-                        *
//*   DB2P                                                        *
//*   THE DB2 ID                                                  *
//*   CIU                                                         *
//*   DATASET HLQ FOR CIU PRODUCT                                 *
//*   DSN710                                                      *
//*   DATASET HLQ FOR DB2 SDSNLOAD and RUNLIB.LOAD                *
//*   _scan_                                                      *
//*   CICS LOAD DATASET TO BE SCANNED                             *
//*                                                               *
//*   3) EDIT THE MEMBER CIUDB2BT IN                              *
//*      REDBK23.MIG23T31.SCIUCLIS                                *
```

```
//*          AND CHANGE THE FOLLOWING:-                              *
//*        CIU                                                       *
//*        DATASET HLQ FOR CIU PRODUCT                               *
//*                                                                  *
//*******************************************************************
//SCAN     EXEC PGM=IKJEFT1B,DYNAMNBR=20,
//             PARM=('%CIUDB2BT','SYS(DB2P)','PROG(CIUCSS)',
//             'PLAN(CIUBTCH4)','PARM(''$TABLE'')')
//STEPLIB  DD DSN=CIU.SCIULOAD,DISP=SHR
//         DD DSN=CIU.SCIULODE,DISP=SHR
//         DD DSN=DSN710.SDSNLOAD,DISP=SHR
//SYSPROC  DD DSN=REDBK23.MIG23T31.SCIUCLIS,DISP=SHR
//LOADLIB  DD DSN=REDBK23.APPL.LOADLIB,DISP=SHR
//SYSPRINT DD SYSOUT=*
//SYSUDUMP DD SYSOUT=*
//SYSTSIN  DD DUMMY
//SYSTSPRT DD SYSOUT=*
//SYSABOUT DD SYSOUT=*
//SYSOUT   DD SYSOUT=*
//
```

The output from this job can be seen in Example 5-6.

Example 5-6   IA CSECT scanner output

```
CICS INTERDEPENDENCY ANALYZER Version 2.1.0               06/27/06      Page   1
CSECT SCANNER - LISTING OF: REDBK23.APPL.LOADLIB
REDBK4    00001738  00000020    5695PMB01  01.07  2006163104940    24     24
    DFHECI    1997256 569623400  01.02
    REDBK4    2006163 5740CB103  02.04
    ILBOCOM0  1983194 5734AS100  05.01     1983194 RSI31940368
    ILBOSRV   1983194 5734AS100  05.01     1983194 RSI31940563
    ILBOMSG   1983194 5734AS100  05.01     1983194 RSI31940572
    ILBOBEG   1983194 5734AS100  05.01     1983194 RSI31940346
```

Using the CICS IA Collector

The collector consists of:

- A control transaction, CINT
- An autosave transaction, CINB
- A number of global user exit programs

In this section we describe how to:

- Configure the collector
- Start the collector
- Stop the collector
- Load the collected data into DB2

Configuring the collector

To configure the collector we use transaction CINT. Figure 5-4 shows the initial screen when CINT is entered.

```
CIU000          CICS Interdependency Analyzer for z/OS - V2R1M0        2006/06/09
                          Main Administration Menu                      11:25:23AM

Select one of the following.  Then press Enter.


        1    Operations Menu.
        2    Configure Region Options.
        3    Configure Global Options.




CICS Sysid:  RB23    CICS Applid:  REDBKV23    TermID:  CP51
CIU7000I 5697-J23 (C) Copyright IBM Corp. 2001,2005
F1=Help         F2=             F3=Exit         F4=             F5=             F6=
F7=             F8=             F9=             F10=            F11=            F12=Exit
```

Figure 5-4   CINT: Administration panel

Select option **3** to configure global options. The global options panel is shown in Figure 5-5.

```
CIU300          CICS Interdependency Analyzer for z/OS - V2R1M0       2006/06/09
                           Global Options Menu                         11:26:09AM
Modify the options and press Enter to update, or press PF12 to cancel.
 Control options
    VSAM file sharing  . . . . . . : N  (Yes/No)
    High Level Trace . . . . . . . : N  (Yes/No)

 National Language Option . . . : E   Code: ENU

 Date and Time Formats
    Date . . . . . . 4 1. MMDDYY  2. DDMMYY      Separator . . . . . . . . /
                       3. YYMMDD  4. YYYYMMDD

    Time . . . . . . 1 1. 12 hrs  2. 24 hrs      Separator . . . . . . . . :



 CICS Sysid:  RB23    CICS Applid:  REDBKV23    TermID:  CP51

 F1=Help         F2=              F3=End         F4=             F5=Refresh      F6=
 F7=             F8=              F9=            F10=            F11=            F12=Cancel
```

Figure 5-5   CINT: Global Options Menu

Select option **2** from the initial screen to configure region options. Figure 5-6 shows the region options panel.

```
CIU200           CICS Interdependency Analyzer for z/OS - V2R1M0     2006/06/09
                          Region Configuration Menu                  11:26:35AM
Type action code then press ENTER.                                   More :
1=Add Region      3=Delete Region    5=DB2/IMS/MQ Options    7=Affinity Options
2=Copy Region     4=CICS Options     6=General Options       8=Time/Date Options
           CICS     CICS    New        New
    Act    Applid   Sysid   Applid     Sysid   Status        Collecting
    4      DEFAULTS DFTS    _____    _____
    _      REDBKV23 RB23    _____    _____   STOPPED
    _                       _____    _____
    _                       _____    _____
    _                       _____    _____
    _                       _____    _____
    _                       _____    _____
    _                       _____    _____

CICS Sysid:  RB23    CICS Applid:  REDBKV23    TermID:   CP51

F1=Help       F2=              F3=Exit      F4=           F5= Refresh   F6=
F7=Page Up    F8=Page Down     F9=          F10=          F11=          F12=
```

Figure 5-6   CINT: Region Configuration Menu

Select option **4** to configure the CICS default options. Figure 5-7 on page 88 shows the CICS default options panel.

To collect all dependencies make sure all options are set to **Y** for YES.

```
CIU240         CICS Interdependency Analyzer for z/OS - V2R1M0        2006/06/09
                         CICS Resources Options for                    11:27:07AM
          CICS Sysid    : DFTS     CICS Applid    : DEFAULTS
Modify the options and press Enter to update, or PF12 to Cancel.

Detect command types: Y=Yes, N=No

APIs
  START    . . . . Y   XCTL . . . . . Y   LOAD . . . . . Y   LINK . . . . . Y
  RETURN TRANSID Y     Handle Abend . Y   Task Control . Y   File Control . Y
  BMS  . . . . . Y     TS Queues  . . Y   TD Queues  . . Y   Journals . . . Y
  DTP  . . . . . Y     Counters . . . Y   FEPI . . . . . Y   WEB Services . Y
  Others . . . . Y

SPIs (Create/Inquire/Set/Discard/Perform)
  Programs . . . Y     Files  . . . . Y   Transactions . Y   Temp Storage . Y
  Transient Data Y     DB2  . . . . . Y   DJAR . . . . . Y   BRFacility . . Y
  Corbaserver  . Y     TCPIPService . Y   FEPI . . . . . Y   Journals . . . Y

CICS Sysid: RB23      CICS Applid: REDBKV23      TermID: CP51

F1=              F2=              F3=Exit          F4=              F5=              F6=
F7=              F8=              F9=              F10=             F11=             F12=Cancel
```

Figure 5-7   CINT: CICS Resource Options

Starting the collector

To start the collector enter transaction CINT and choose option **1** on the operations menu. Figure 5-8 shows the Operations panel.

Select **1** to start CICS IA.

```
CIU100         CICS Interdependency Analyzer for z/OS - V2R1M0        2006/06/09
                              Operations Menu                         11:48:14AM
Type action code then press ENTER.                              More :

1= Start 2= Stop 3= Pause 4= Continue 5= Statistics

        CICS      CICS                    Start         Start
  Act   Applid    Sysid  Status           Date          Time        Collecting
   1    REDBKV23  RB23   STOPPED
   _
   _
```

Figure 5-8   CINT: IA start

CICS IA then asks you to confirm the start of the region, as shown in Figure 5-9. Press Enter to confirm.

```
CICS Sysid:  RB23    CICS Applid:  REDBKV23    TermID:  CP51
CIU2120I Press Enter to confirm Start with data restore or PF12 to cancel
F1=Help        F2=           F3=End      F4=           F5=Refresh   F6=
F7=Page Up     F8=Page Down  F9=         F10=          F11=         F12= CANCEL
```

Figure 5-9   CINT: Confirm start

The operations panel will then refresh to show CICS IA running and collecting dependencies, as shown in Figure 5-10.

```
CIU100        CICS Interdependency Analyzer for z/OS - V2R1M0      2006/06/09
                            Operations Menu                         11:50:38AM
Type action code then press ENTER.                                  More :

1= Start 2= Stop 3= Pause 4= Continue 5= Statistics

         CICS       CICS
  Act    Applid     Sysid  Status   Start Date   Start Time   Collecting
   *     REDBKV23   RB23   RUNNING  2006/06/09   11:50:38AM   Dependencies
   -
```

Figure 5-10   CINT: Collecting dependencies

Stopping the collector

To stop the collector enter transaction `CINT` and choose option **1** for the operations menu. Figure 5-11 shows the Operations screen.

Select **2** to stop CICS IA.

```
CIU100        CICS Interdependency Analyzer for z/OS - V2R1M0      2006/06/09
                            Operations Menu                         11:51:57AM
Type action code then press ENTER.                                  More :

1= Start 2= Stop 3= Pause 4= Continue 5= Statistics

         CICS       CICS
  Act    Applid     Sysid  Status   Start Date   Start Time   Collecting
   2     REDBKV23   RB23   RUNNING  2006/06/09   11:50:38AM   Dependencies
   -
```

Figure 5-11   CINT: IA stop

CICS IA asks you to confirm the stop of the region, as shown in Figure 5-12. Press Enter to confirm.

```
CICS Sysid:   RB23    CICS Applid:   REDBKV23    TermID:   CP51
CIU2122I Press Enter to confirm Stop or PF12 to cancel
F1=Help         F2=            F3=End          F4=             F5=Refresh   F6=
F7=Page Up      F8=Page Down   F9=             F10=            F11=         F12= CANCEL
```

Figure 5-12   CINT: Stop confirmation

CICS IA shows the statistics screen for the region once it has stopped. This is shown in Figure 5-13.

```
CIU150          CICS Interdependency Analyzer for z/OS - V2R1M0       2006/06/09
                            Statistics Menu for                       11:52:38AM

          CICS Sysid    : RB23      CICS Applid    : REDBKV23

    CINT state . . . . . . . . : STOPPED      Collecting Dependencies
    Number of pauses . . . . . : 0
    Number of saves. . . . . . : 1
    Records written last save. : 13
    Total records on file. . . : 46

    Date/time of last start. . : 2006/06/09 11:50:38AM
    Date/time of last save . . : 2006/06/09 11:52:37AM
    Date/time of last change . : 2006/06/09 11:51:47AM

    Total time RUNNING . . . . : 0000:01:41   (HHHH:MM:SS)
    Total time PAUSED. . . . . :              (HHHH:MM:SS)

    Table dataspace name . . . :                  % full
 CICS Sysid:  RB23    CICS Applid:   REDBKV23    TermID:   CP51

 F1=Help         F2=             F3=End          F4=          F5=Refresh   F6=
 F7=            F8=             F9=             F10=          F11=         F12=
```

Figure 5-13   CINT: Collection statistics

Loading the collected data into DB2

To load the collected data into DB2 we must edit and run the customized job CIUUPDB1. The DB2 update JCL is shown in Example 5-7 on page 91.

Example 5-7   CIUUPDB1: DB2 update JCL

```
//CIUUPDB1 JOB USER=EYJ,NOTIFY=EYJ,
//         CLASS=A,MSGCLASS=Y,REGION=0M
//********************************************************************
//* JCL NAME = CIUUPDB1                                               *
//*                                                                   *
//* DESCRIPTIVE NAME = IBM CICS INTERDEPENDENCIES UTILITY             *
//*                    UPDATE THE DATABASE WITH CICS DEPENDENCIES.    *
//*                                                                   *
//* CHANGES TO BE MADE                                                *
//* PLEASE CONSULT WITH YOUR DB2 ADMINISTRATOR                        *
//*                                                                   *
//*    1) CHANGE THE JOB CARD TO SUIT YOUR SYSTEM CONVENTIONS         *
//*                                                                   *
//*    2) CHANGE THE FOLLOWING PARAMETERS:-                           *
//*                                                                   *
//*    DB2P                                                           *
//*    THE DB2 ID                                                     *
//*                                                                   *
//*    CIU                                                            *
//*    THE HLQ FOR CIU PRODUCT                                        *
//*                                                                   *
//*    DSN710                                                         *
//*    THE DATASET HLQ FOR DB2 SDSNLOAD                               *
//*                                                                   *
//*    REDBK23.MIG23T31                                               *
//*    THE HLQ FOR THE CIU FILE RESOURCES. THESE SHOULD BE            *
//*    THE SAME AS THOSE DEFINED IN JOBS CIUJCLCA/CIUJCLCC            *
//*                                                                   *
//*    3) EDIT THE SCIUCLIS MEMBER CIUDB2BT IN                        *
//*                                                                   *
//*       REDBK23.MIG23T31.SCIUCLIS                                   *
//*                                                                   *
//*       AND CHANGE THE FOLLOWING:-                                  *
//*                                                                   *
//*    CIU                                                            *
//*    THE HLQ FOR CIU PRODUCT                                        *
//*                                                                   *
//*    4) IF YOU WISH TO UPDATE THE DATABASE WITH THE LAST USED       *
//*       TIME STAMP FOR EACH DB2 ROW THEN CHOOSE PARM(UPD)           *
//********************************************************************
//*-----------------------------------------------------------------
//*       RUN THE BATCH PROGRAM CIUUREG
//*-----------------------------------------------------------------
//STEP000   EXEC PGM=IKJEFT1B,
//             DYNAMNBR=20,
//             PARM=('%CIUDB2BT','SYS(DB2P)','PROG(CIUUREG)',
//             'PLAN(CIUBTCH4)')
```

```jcl
//*----------------------------------------------------------------
//*        IF YOU WISH TO UPDATE THE DATABASE WITH THE LAST USED
//*        TIME STAMP FOR EACH DB2 ROW THEN CHOOSE PARM(UPD)
//*----------------------------------------------------------------
//STEPLIB  DD  DSN=CIU.SCIULOAD,DISP=SHR
//         DD  DSN=CIU.SCIULODE,DISP=SHR
//         DD  DSN=DSN710.SDSNLOAD,DISP=SHR
//SYSPROC  DD  DSN=REDBK23.MIG23T31.SCIUCLIS,DISP=SHR
//SYSUDUMP DD  SYSOUT=*
//SYSTSIN  DD  DUMMY
//SYSTSPRT DD  SYSOUT=*
//SYSABOUT DD  SYSOUT=*
//SYSOUT   DD  SYSOUT=*
//CIUCNTL  DD  DSN=REDBK23.MIG23T31.CIUCNTL,
//             DISP=SHR
//*----------------------------------------------------------------
//*        CONVERT COLLECTED DATA TO QSAM FILE
//*----------------------------------------------------------------
//STEP010  EXEC PGM=IDCAMS
//SYSPRINT DD  SYSOUT=*
//IN       DD  DSN=REDBK23.MIG23T31.CIUINT1,DISP=SHR
//OUT      DD  DSN=&&DATA1,DISP=(,PASS),SPACE=(CYL,(5,5),RLSE),
//             UNIT=SYSDA,DCB=(RECFM=VB,LRECL=131,BLKSIZE=13100)
//SYSIN    DD  *
 REPRO IFILE(IN),OFILE(OUT)
//****************************************************************
//*----------------------------------------------------------------
//*        CONVERT COLLECTED DATA TO QSAM FILE - LONG FILE
//*----------------------------------------------------------------
//STEP015  EXEC PGM=IDCAMS
//SYSPRINT DD  SYSOUT=*
//IN       DD  DSN=REDBK23.MIG23T31.CIUINT5,DISP=SHR
//OUT      DD  DSN=&&DATA0,DISP=(,PASS),SPACE=(CYL,(5,5),RLSE),
//             UNIT=SYSDA,DCB=(RECFM=VB,LRECL=361,BLKSIZE=36100)
//SYSIN    DD  *
 REPRO IFILE(IN),OFILE(OUT)
//*----------------------------------------------------------------
//*        REFORMAT INPUT FILE
//*----------------------------------------------------------------
//STEP020  EXEC PGM=CIUU040
//STEPLIB  DD  DSN=CIU.SCIULOAD,DISP=SHR
//         DD  DSN=CIU.SCIULODE,DISP=SHR
//SYSPRINT DD  SYSOUT=*
//INPUT    DD  DSN=&&DATA1,DISP=(OLD,DELETE)
//INPUT2   DD  DSN=&&DATA0,DISP=(OLD,DELETE)
//OUTPUT   DD  DSN=&&DATA2,DISP=(,PASS),SPACE=(CYL,(5,5),RLSE),
//             UNIT=SYSDA,DCB=(RECFM=FB,LRECL=384,BLKSIZE=38400)
//*----------------------------------------------------------------
//*        SORT THE INPUT FILE
```

```
//*----------------------------------------------------------------
//STEP030   EXEC PGM=SORT,COND=(0,NE,STEP020)
//SORTLIB   DD  DSN=SYS1.SORTLIB,DISP=SHR
//SYSUDUMP  DD  SYSOUT=*
//SYSOUT    DD  SYSOUT=*
//SORTIN    DD  DSN=&&DATA2,DISP=(OLD,DELETE)
//SORTOUT   DD  DSN=&&DATA3,DISP=(,PASS),SPACE=(CYL,(5,5),RLSE),
//              UNIT=SYSDA,DCB=*.SORTIN
//SYSIN     DD  *
 SORT FIELDS=(1,8,A,13,4,A,17,8,A,41,255,A),
 FORMAT=CH
 RECORD TYPE=F,LENGTH=(384)
/*
//*----------------------------------------------------------------
//*        RUN THE BATCH PROGRAM CIUU050
//STEP040   EXEC PGM=IKJEFT1B,COND=(0,NE,STEP020),
//              DYNAMNBR=20,
//              PARM=('%CIUDB2BT','SYS(DB2P)','PROG(CIUU050)',
//              'PLAN(CIUBTCH4)','PARM(NOPARM)') <-- NO TIMESTAMP UPDATE
//*             'PLAN(CIUBTCH4)','PARM(UPD)')   <-- TIMESTAMP UPDATE
//*----------------------------------------------------------------
//*    IF YOU WISH TO UPDATE THE DATABASE WITH THE LAST USED
//*    TIME STAMP FOR EACH DB2 ROW THEN CHOOSE PARM(UPD)
//*----------------------------------------------------------------
//STEPLIB   DD  DSN=CIU.SCIULOAD,DISP=SHR
//          DD  DSN=CIU.SCIULODE,DISP=SHR
//          DD  DSN=DSN710.SDSNLOAD,DISP=SHR
//SYSPROC   DD  DSN=REDBK23.MIG23T31.SCIUCLIS,DISP=SHR
//SYSUDUMP  DD  SYSOUT=*
//SYSTSIN   DD  DUMMY
//SYSTSPRT  DD  SYSOUT=*
//SYSABOUT  DD  SYSOUT=*
//SYSOUT    DD  SYSOUT=*
//CIUINT1   DD  DSN=&&DATA3,DISP=(OLD,DELETE)
//*----------------------------------------------------------------
//*              REFRESH CIU4_CICS_CHAIN                          *
//*----------------------------------------------------------------
//STEP050   EXEC PGM=IKJEFT1B,COND=(0,NE,STEP020),
//              DYNAMNBR=20,
//              PARM=('%CIUDB2BT','SYS(DB2P)','PROG(CIUU100)',
//              'PLAN(CIUBTCH4)')
//STEPLIB   DD  DSN=CIU.SCIULOAD,DISP=SHR
//          DD  DSN=CIU.SCIULODE,DISP=SHR
//          DD  DSN=DSN710.SDSNLOAD,DISP=SHR
//SYSPROC   DD  DSN=REDBK23.MIG23T31.SCIUCLIS,DISP=SHR
//SYSUDUMP  DD  SYSOUT=*
//SYSTSIN   DD  DUMMY
//SYSTSPRT  DD  SYSOUT=*
//SYSABOUT  DD  SYSOUT=*
```

```
//SYSOUT   DD SYSOUT=*
//*-----------------------------------------------------------------
//*                REFRESH CIU4_CICS_CHAINP
//*-----------------------------------------------------------------
//STEP051  EXEC PGM=IKJEFT1B,COND=(0,NE,STEP020),
//             DYNAMNBR=20,
//             PARM=('%CIUDB2BT','SYS(DB2P)','PROG(CIUU200)',
//             'PLAN(CIUBTCH4)')
//STEPLIB  DD DSN=CIU.SCIULOAD,DISP=SHR
//         DD DSN=CIU.SCIULODE,DISP=SHR
//         DD DSN=DSN710.SDSNLOAD,DISP=SHR
//SYSPROC  DD DSN=REDBK23.MIG23T31.SCIUCLIS,DISP=SHR
//SYSUDUMP DD SYSOUT=*
//SYSTSIN  DD DUMMY
//SYSTSPRT DD SYSOUT=*
//SYSABOUT DD SYSOUT=*
//SYSOUT   DD SYSOUT=* //*          REFRESH CIU4_CICS_CHAINP
```

The load job produces output to indicate how many records were extracted from the VSAM file and how many were added/updated in the DB2 table, as shown in Example 5-8.

Example 5-8 CIUUPDB1 - Sample output

```
********************************************
**** CICS records extracted =       8 ****
********************************************
14390710 CIU6003I LAST USE TIMESTAMPS WILL NOT BE UPDATED
14390715 CIU6005I NUMBER OF NEW ROWS ADDED TO CIU4_CICS_DATA = 000000008
14390715 CIU6006I NUMBER OF EXISTING ROWS IN CIU4_CICS_DATA = 000000000
14390715 CIU6007I NUMBER OF ROWS UPDATED IN CIU4_CICS_DATA = 000000000
```

We can now query the database to find which programs are defined as non threadsafe.

Identifying non threadsafe programs

To identify which programs are non threadsafe we can query either the CIU4_SCAN_DETAIL table populated by job CIUJCLTD (load module scanner) or the CIU4_CICS_DATA table populated by data from the collector.

Querying the CIU4_SCAN_DETAIL table

The following query tells us all programs that have possible commands that would cause the program to be non threadsafe (that is, the program executes a LOAD, EXTRACT, GETMAIN, or ADDRESS CWA). The query is restricted to the REDBK23.APPL.LOADLIB data set only. This is shown in Example 5-12 on page 99.

Example 5-9 Threadsafe query using the scan detail table

```
--Show me all possible programs that are not threadsafe in data set
--REDBK23.APPL.LOADLIB using the load module scanner detail
  SELECT PROGRAM , COMMAND , RESOURCE_TYPE
  FROM CIU4_SCAN_DETAIL
  WHERE COMMAND IN ('LOAD    ', 'EXTRACT ', 'GETMAIN ', 'ADDRESS ')
  AND DSNAME='REDBK23.APPL.LOADLIB';
---------+---------+---------+---------+---------+---------+---------+--------+
PROGRAM    COMMAND   RESOURCE_TYPE
---------+---------+---------+---------+---------+---------+---------+--------+
COBOLVS1   ADDRESS   CWA
COBOLVS2   GETMAIN   SHARED
REDBK1     ADDRESS   CWA
REDBK1A    ADDRESS   CWA
REDBK1B    ADDRESS   CWA
REDBK1C    ADDRESS   CWA
REDBK1D    ADDRESS   CWA
REDBK1E    ADDRESS   CWA
REDBK5     ADDRESS   CWA
DSNE610I NUMBER OF ROWS DISPLAYED IS 9
DSNE616I STATEMENT EXECUTION WAS SUCCESSFUL, SQLCODE IS 100
---------+---------+---------+---------+---------+---------+---------+--------+
```

Querying the CIU4_CICS _DATA table

The query in Example 5-10 shows us all resources used in CICS region REDBKV23.

Example 5-10 All resources query for region REDBKV23 using CICS table

```
--Show me all resources in region REDBKV23
--from the collector
  SELECT DISTINCT PROGRAM , FUNCTION,  TYPE , OBJECT
  FROM CIU4_CICS_DATA
  WHERE APPLID='REDBKV23'
  ORDER BY 1;
---------+---------+---------+---------+---------+---------+---------+--------+
PROGRAM    FUNCTION  TYPE     OBJECT
---------+---------+---------+---------+---------+---------+---------+--------+
REDBK1     ADDRESS   CWA      CWA
REDBK1     ASSIGN    APPLID   REDBKV23
REDBK1     WRITE     FILE     REDBOOKF
REDBK1     WRITEQ    TD       CESE
REDBK1     WRITEQ    TSSHR    REDBOOKQ
REDBK2     START     TRANSID  RDBA
REDBK2     START     TRANSID  RDBB
REDBK2     START     TRANSID  RDBC
REDBK2     START     TRANSID  RDBD
REDBK2     START     TRANSID  RDBE
```

```
REDBK2      START       TRANSID     RDB1
REDBK3      ASSIGN      APPLID      REDBKV23
REDBK3      ENDBR       FILE        REDBOOKF
REDBK3      READNEXT    FILE        REDBOOKF
REDBK3      STARTBR     FILE        REDBOOKF
REDBK4      LINK        PROGRAM     REDBK3
REDBK5      ADDRESS     CWA         CWA
REDBK5      ASSIGN      APPLID      REDBKV23
REDBK5      ENDBR       FILE        REDBOOKF
REDBK5      READNEXT    FILE        REDBOOKF
REDBK5      STARTBR     FILE        REDBOOKF
DSNE610I NUMBER OF ROWS DISPLAYED IS 21
DSNE612I DATA FOR COLUMN HEADER OBJECT COLUMN NUMBER 4 WAS TRUNCATED
DSNE616I STATEMENT EXECUTION WAS SUCCESSFUL, SQLCODE IS 100
```

> **Note:** The output from this query only shows programs that have actually been executed while the CICS IA collector was running. For example, program COBOLVS1 in the output in Example 5-9 is not in the output in Example 5-10 because it has not been executed.

The query shown in Example 5-11 will tell us all programs that have possible commands that would cause the program to be non threadsafe (that is, the program executes a LOAD, EXTRACT, GETMAIN, or ADDRESS CWA). The query is restricted to the CICS region that is to be migrated, REDBKV23.

Example 5-11   Threadsafe query using CICS table

```
--Show me all programs that are not threadsafe in region REDBKV23
--from the collector
  SELECT DISTINCT PROGRAM , FUNCTION, OBJECT
  FROM CIU4_CICS_DATA
  WHERE FUNCTION IN ('LOAD    ', 'EXTRACT ', 'GETMAIN ', 'ADDRESS ')
  AND APPLID='REDBKV23'
  ORDER BY 1;
---------+---------+---------+---------+---------+---------+---------+--------+
PROGRAM    FUNCTION   OBJECT
---------+---------+---------+---------+---------+---------+---------+--------+
REDBK1     ADDRESS    CWA
REDBK5     ADDRESS    CWA
DSNE610I NUMBER OF ROWS DISPLAYED IS 2
DSNE612I DATA FOR COLUMN HEADER OBJECT COLUMN NUMBER 3 WAS TRUNCATED
DSNE616I STATEMENT EXECUTION WAS SUCCESSFUL, SQLCODE IS 100
```

Programs REDBK1 and REDBK5 contain EXEC CICS ADDRESS CWA commands and therefore would need careful investigation prior to being defined as threadsafe. If the reference to the CWA is for read-only purposes then these programs could potentially be defined as an OPENAPI program, which allows them to run under their own OTE TCB from the start.

In Example 5-10 on page 95 we can see that program REDBK2 consists of only EXEC CICS STARTs and could be considered to be defined as threadsafe.

5.3 Threadsafe application case study

We used programs REDBK1 and REDBK5, which are both non threadsafe. Both programs issue an EXEC CICS ADDRESS CWA.

The sample application program, REDBK5, initializes the key in the CWA from the last key stored in VSAM file REDBOOKF.

Our sample application program, REDBK1, shown in outline in Figure 5-14, simply addresses the CWA and uses an integer value in the CWA as the next key to use in an EXEC CICS WRITE command. In a non threadsafe environment (that is, with the program running on the QR TCB) we would not expect there to be any duplicate file records (DUPREC) since there is only one instance of this program executing at the time of addressing the CWA, incrementing its value and using the increment value as the key in the subsequent WRITE command.

In order to test this application we started 75 instances of the invoking transaction RDB1.

```
000001 int *CWAptr;                           /* Pointer to CWA                  */
000002 int RidFld;                            /* Rid field for EXEC CICS WRITE   */
000003                                        /* request                         */
000004 struct CWA_INFO {
000005    int  Counter;                       /* Just a number                   */
000006    char Userid[9];                     /* This userid                     */
000007    char Date[9];                       /* The current Date                */
000008    char Time[9];                       /* the current Time                */
000009 };
000010 CWA_INFO  *CWA;
000011 EXEC CICS ADDRESS CWA(CWAptr) RESP(resp);
000012 CWA = (CWA_INFO *)CWAptr;
---> missing code section to loop for a period of time <---
000013 CWA->Counter++;
000014 RidFld = CWA->Counter;
000015 EXEC CICS WRITE FILE(File) RIDFLD(RidFld)
000016      FROM(FileRec) LENGTH(sizeof(FILEINFO)) RESP(resp);
---> missing code section to write any errors to a TS queue <---
000017 EXEC CICS RETURN ;
```

Figure 5-14   Extract of sample application program REDBK1

5.3.1 Non-threadsafe output (QR TCB)

When running in non threadsafe mode (Program REDBK1 being defined as QUASIRENT as shown in Figure 5-15) we had no error messages in our error message TS QUEUE (Figure 5-16). And, the last 10 records written to the file had sequential key values, as shown in Figure 5-17 on page 99.

Example 5-12 on page 99 shows us the EXEC CICS calls issued by program REDBK1 running in QR mode. The SQL output shows us the TCBMODE for each command (in this case QR).

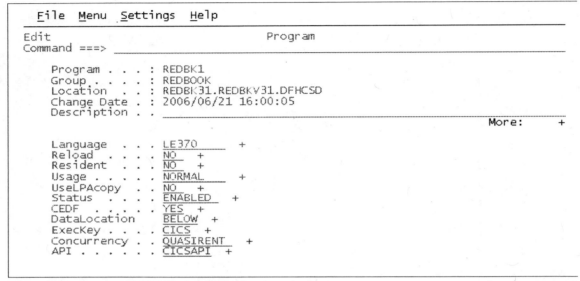

Figure 5-15   Program REDBK1 definition: Non threadsafe

```
CEBR   TSQ REDBOOKQ           SYSID RB31 REC     1 OF      0    COL    1 OF      0
ENTER COMMAND ===>
          **************************   TOP OF QUEUE    **************************
          **************************  BOTTOM OF QUEUE  **************************
```

Figure 5-16   CEBR display of error message queue

```
RDB3 LAST 10 UPDATES TO REDBOOKF

    ITEM 1     KEY=0000006B written by EYJ
    ITEM 2     KEY=0000006A written by EYJ
    ITEM 3     KEY=00000069 written by EYJ
    ITEM 4     KEY=00000068 written by EYJ
    ITEM 5     KEY=00000067 written by EYJ
    ITEM 6     KEY=00000066 written by EYJ
    ITEM 7     KEY=00000065 written by EYJ
    ITEM 8     KEY=00000064 written by EYJ
    ITEM 9     KEY=00000063 written by EYJ
    ITEM 10    KEY=00000062 written by EYJ
```

Figure 5-17   Transaction RDB3 output

Example 5-12   IA report for program REDBK1 in QR mode

```
---------+---------+---------+---------+---------+---------+---------+---------+
-- SHOW ME ALL RESOURCES USED BY PROGRAM REDBK1 IN REGION REDBV31
SELECT DISTINCT PROGRAM, FUNCTION, TYPE, OBJECT, TCBMODE
  FROM CIU4_CICS_DATA
  WHERE PROGRAM='REDBK1' AND APPLID='REDBKV31';
---------+---------+---------+---------+---------+---------+---------+---------+
PROGRAM   FUNCTION  TYPE     OBJECT                TCBMODE
---------+---------+---------+---------+---------+---------+---------+---------+
REDBK1    ASSIGN    APPLID   REDBKV31              QR
REDBK1    ADDRESS   CWA      CWA                   QR
REDBK1    WRITE     FILE     REDBOOKF              QR
DSNE610I NUMBER OF ROWS DISPLAYED IS 3
```

5.3.2 Threadsafe output with unchanged program

The REDBK1 program definition was changed to be THREADSAFE and OPENAPI, as shown in Figure 5-18.

> **Note:** During the testing of this program it was determined that program REDBK1 was not compiled and linked with the RENT option. All programs defined as threadsafe must be reentrant.

```
 File   Menu   Settings   Help
Edit                            Program
Command ===>

     Program . . . : REDBK1
     Group . . . . : REDBOOK
     Location  . . : REDBK31.REDBKV31.DFHCSD
     Change Date . : 2006/06/21 16:00:05
     Description . .
                                                         More:    +

     Language  . . . LE370      +
     Reload  . . . . NO         +
     Resident  . . . NO         +
     Usage . . . . . NORMAL     +
     UseLPAcopy  . . NO         +
     Status  . . . . ENABLED    +
     CEDF  . . . . . YES        +
     DataLocation  . BELOW      +
     ExecKey . . . . CICS       +
     Concurrency . . THREADSAFE +
     API . . . . . . OPENAPI    +
```

Figure 5-18 Program REDBK1 definition: Threadsafe

We again ran 75 instances of transaction RDB1. On this occasion, multiple instances of program REDBK1 were executing concurrently on L8 TCBs, so there was the potential for the same CWA key value to be used more than once. This did in fact happen, as shown in Figure 5-19.

```
CEBR   TSQ REDBOOKQ          SYSID RB31 REC    1 OF    12    COL    1 OF    80
  ENTER COMMAND ===>
**************************   TOP OF QUEUE    *******************************
00001 WRITE Failure resp=14..
00002 DUPREC RID=137..
00003 WRITE Failure resp=14..
00004 DUPREC RID=147..
00005 WRITE Failure resp=14..
00006 DUPREC RID=176..
00007 WRITE Failure resp=14..
00008 DUPREC RID=180..
**************************   BOTTOM OF QUEUE  ******************************
```

Figure 5-19 TS QUEUE logo showing DUPREC errors

```
RDB3 LAST 10 UPDATES TO REDBOOKF

    ITEM 1     KEY=000000B4 written by AYS
    ITEM 2     KEY=000000B2 written by AYS
    ITEM 3     KEY=000000B0 written by AYS
    ITEM 4     KEY=000000AF written by AYS
    ITEM 5     KEY=000000AE written by AYS
    ITEM 6     KEY=000000AC written by AYS
    ITEM 7     KEY=000000AA written by AYS
    ITEM 8     KEY=000000A8 written by AYS
    ITEM 9     KEY=000000A7 written by AYS
    ITEM 10    KEY=000000A6 written by AYS
```

Figure 5-20 RDB3 output showing missing record keys

Example 5-13 shows us the EXEC CICS COMMANDS called when running program REDBK1 as THREADSAFE program, in the OPENAPI and a storage key of CICS. There are three things to note here:

- EXEC CICS WRITEQ to a shared temporary storage queue called REDBOOKQ. As seen previously, this command is only executed during error conditions. CICS IA therefore indicates that an error message has been written to the queue (Figure 5-19 on page 101).
- The program starts on an L8 TCB. This is because it is defined as having a storage key of CICS.
- All EXEC CICS FILE commands are made threadsafe by CICS by switching to the QR TCB. Note that this causes two TCB switches in this case.

> **Note:** There would not be a TCB switch for File Control in CICS TS V3.2 since local VSAM and RLS are now threadsafe.

Example 5-13   IA report for program REDBK1 in threadsafe mode running on the OPENAPI

```
---------+---------+---------+---------+---------+---------+---------+---------+
-- SHOW ME ALL RESOURCES USED BY PROGRAM REDBK1 IN REGION REDBV31
SELECT DISTINCT PROGRAM, FUNCTION, TYPE, OBJECT, TCBMODE
   FROM CIU4_CICS_DATA
   WHERE PROGRAM='REDBK1' AND APPLID='REDBKV31';
---------+---------+---------+---------+---------+---------+---------+---------+
PROGRAM   FUNCTION  TYPE     OBJECT                TCBMODE
---------+---------+---------+---------+---------+---------+---------+---------+
REDBK1    ADDRESS   CWA      CWA                   L8
REDBK1    ASSIGN    APPLID   REDBKV31              L8
REDBK1    WRITE     FILE     REDBOOKF              QR
REDBK1    WRITEQ    TSSHR    REDBOOKQ              L8
DSNE610I NUMBER OF ROWS DISPLAYED IS 4
```

5.3.3 Threadsafe output with changed program

One solution to enable our sample application to run as threadsafe is to put an ENQ and DEQ around the address CWA and its subsequent increment. We did this (see Figure 5-21) and ran the 75 instances of transaction RDB1 again. The results this time were the same as the non threadsafe example (that is, there were no DUPREC errors and there were sequential key values in the file).

```
000001 int *CWAptr;                          /* Pointer to CWA              */
000002 int RidFld;                           /* Rid field for EXEC CICS WRITE */
000003                                       /* request                     */
000004 struct CWA_INFO {
000005   int  Counter;                       /* Just a number               */
000006   char Userid[9];                     /* This userid                 */
000007   char Date[9];                       /* The current Date            */
000008   char Time[9];                       /* the current Time            */
000009 };
000010 CWA_INFO  *CWA;
       EXEC CICS ENQ RESOURCE(EnqName) LENGTH(sizeof(EnqName))
000011 EXEC CICS ADDRESS CWA(CWAptr) RESP(resp);
000012 CWA = (CWA_INFO *)CWAptr;
---> missing code section to loop for a period of time <---
000013 CWA->Counter++;
000014 RidFld = CWA->Counter;
       EXEC CICS DEQ RESOURCE(EnqName) LENGTH(sizeof(EnqName))
000015 EXEC CICS WRITE FILE(File) RIDFLD(RidFld)
000016       FROM(FileRec) LENGTH(sizeof(FILEINFO)) RESP(resp);
---> missing code section to write any errors to a TS queue <---
000017 EXEC CICS RETURN ;
```

Figure 5-21 Extract of sample application program REDBK1 with ENQ DEQ

Example 5-14 shows us the EXEC CICS COMMANDS called when running program REDBK1 with the changes described previously. We can now see that the ADDRESS CWA command is serialized by using the ENQ/DEQ technique.

> **Note:** The ORDER BY TRANSLATE(HEX(OFFSET),'B','F') clause sorts the query by program offset.

Example 5-14 IA report on the modified REDBK1 program

```
---------+---------+---------+---------+---------+---------+---------+---------+
-- SHOW ME ALL RESOURCES USED BY PROGRAM REDBK1 IN REGION REDBV31
SELECT TRANSID, PROGRAM,
       OFFSET,PROGRAM, FUNCTION, TYPE, OBJECT, TCBMODE
  FROM CIU4_CICS_DATA
  WHERE PROGRAM='REDBK1' AND APPLID='REDBKV31' AND TRANSID='RDB1'
  ORDER BY TRANSLATE(HEX(OFFSET),'B','F');
---------+---------+---------+---------+---------+---------+---------+---------+
TRANSID  PROGRAM   OFFSET    PROGRAM   FUNCTION  TYPE      OBJECT    TCBMODE
---------+---------+---------+---------+---------+---------+---------+---------+
RDB1     REDBK1    000001E8  REDBK1    ASSIGN    APPLID    REDBKV31  L8
RDB1     REDBK1    00000288  REDBK1    ENQ       ENQNAME   REDBKENQ  L8
RDB1     REDBK1    000002B0  REDBK1    ADDRESS   CWA       CWA       L8
RDB1     REDBK1    0000074C  REDBK1    DEQ       ENQNAME   REDBKENQ  L8
RDB1     REDBK1    00000956  REDBK1    WRITE     FILE      REDBOOKF  QR
DSNE610I NUMBER OF ROWS DISPLAYED IS 5
```

5.4 CICS Performance Analyzer for z/OS (CICS PA)

This section describes CICS Performance Analyzer for z/OS (CICS PA) and how it can help with threadsafe decisions.

For details of how you can use CICS PA to compare CICS performance before and after application threadsafe conversion, see *Migration Considerations for CICS Using CICS CM, CICS PA, and CICS IA*, SG24-7294.

CICS Performance Analyzer complements IBM Tivoli® OMEGAMON® XE for CICS on z/OS by helping you to respond quickly to online performance issues by drilling down deeply into CICS performance data to identify the cause of the problem. When used in conjunction with OMEGAMON XE for CICS, you can create CICS Performance Analyzer reports that detail your application's use of Adabas, CA-Datacom, SUPRA, and CA-IDMS, as well as reporting on those transactions that have exceeded OMEGAMON XE for CICS resource-limiting thresholds.

Simplified and extended integration with OMEGAMON XE for CICS allows CICS Performance Analyzer to process SMF type 112 records containing third-party database management systems, and OMEGAMON XE for CICS resource-limiting metrics can give you better insight into all of your CICS data resources.

5.4.1 CICS PA overview

CICS PA provides comprehensive performance reporting and analysis for CICS Transaction Server and related subsystems, including DB2, WMQ, IMS (DBCTL), and the z/OS System Logger.

Use the CICS PA Interactive System Productivity Facility (ISPF) dialog to generate your report and extract requests. The CICS PA dialog assists you in building the reports and extracts requests specific to your requirements. This avoids having to understand the complexity of the CICS Monitoring Facility (CMF) data, CICS statistics, CICS server statistics data, DB2 accounting and WMQ accounting data. It has extensive online help facilities and a powerful command language that is used to select, sort, and customize the report formats and data extracts.

CICS PA provides a comprehensive suite of reports and data extracts for use by:

- System programmers, to track overall CICS system performance and evaluate the effects of CICS system tuning efforts
- Applications programmers, to analyze the performance of their applications and the resources they use
- DBAs, to analyze the usage and performance of CICS Resource Managers such as WMQ, and database systems such as DB2 and IMS (DBCTL)
- Managers, to ensure that transactions are meeting their required service levels and measure trends to help plan future requirements and strategies

The Historical Database (HDB) facility provides a flexible and easy way to manage and report historical performance and statistics data for your CICS systems.

The components of CICS PA are shown in Figure 5-22.

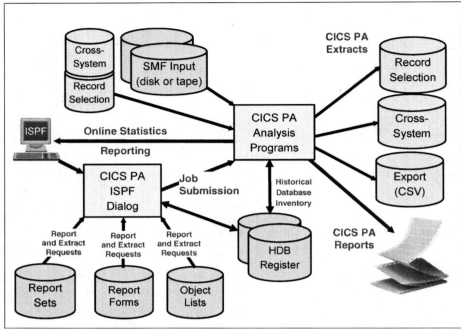

Figure 5-22   CICS PA overview: The big picture

5.4.2 Reports and extracts

Report sets are where you specify, save, and run your report requests. A report set contains a set of report and extract requests to be submitted and run as a single job. You can define any number of report sets, and any number of reports and extracts can be included in a single report set. CICS PA provides a comprehensive set of reports, graphs, and data extracts:

- The performance list, list extended, and summary reports provide detailed analysis of CICS transaction activity and performance.

- The performance wait analysis report provides a detailed analysis of transaction activity by wait time. This report summarizes, by transaction ID, the resources that cause a transaction to be suspended and highlights the CICS system resource bottlenecks that may be causing bad response time.

- The cross-system work report combines the CICS CMF performance class records from connected CICS (via MRO or ISC) systems to produce a consolidated network unit-of-work (UOW) report.

- The DB2 reports combine CICS CMF (SMF 110) performance class records and DB2 accounting (SMF 101) records to produce detail or summary reports of the DB2 usage by your CICS systems. The DB2 list report shows the DB2 activity of each transaction and the DB2 summary report (short or long) summarizes the DB2 activity by transaction and program within an APPLID.

For more information about CICS PA see the IBM Redbooks publication *CICS Performance Analyzer*, SG24-6063.

5.4.3 How CICS PA can assist with threadsafety

CICS PA can be used to help answer the following questions:

- Which TCBs did my transactions use?
  - How many different TCB modes did my transaction use?
- How much dispatch and CPU time did they use?
- How many TCB switches (change modes) were there?
  - What was the change mode delay time?
- Which transactions use GETMAIN SHARED?
  - Who GETMAINed it? How much? And where?
  - Are transactions FREEMAINing shared storage?

CICS PA performance summary, performance list, and performance list extended reports answer these questions. CICS PA provides extensive sample report forms that show CPU and TCB usage, TCB delays, change mode delays, and more, as shown in Figure 5-23.

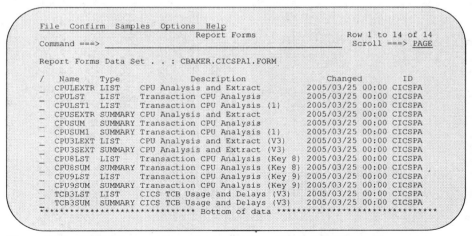

Figure 5-23 CICS PA report forms for transaction CPU and TCB usage

An example of a CICS TCB CPU analysis report is shown in Figure 5-24.

```
V1R4M0                                    CICS Performance Analyzer
                                              Performance Summary

SUMM0001 Printed at 14:58:28  8/15/2005     Data from 10:45:23  2/20/2005 to 11:18:07  2/20/2005            Page    1
Transaction CICS TCB CPU Analysis - Summary

              Avg       Max      Avg      Avg      Avg      Avg      Avg      Avg      Avg      Avg      Avg
Tran  #Tasks Response Response Dispatch User CPU Suspend DispWait QR CPU  MS CPU  RO CPU  KY8 CPU  KY9 CPU
              Time      Time    Time     Time    Time     Time    Time    Time    Time    Time     Time
ABRW       7   .0506    .2705   .0456    .0050   .0050    .0008   .0013   .0037   .0014   .0000    .0000
ADT1       4  1.2787   5.0652  1.2782    .2160   .0005    .0005   .0007   .0005   .0005   .0000    .2147
CALL       4  2.1675   2.2519   .0061    .0014  2.1614    .0003   .0007   .0006   .0006   .0001    .0000
CATA       2   .0241    .0420   .0190    .0033   .0051    .0001   .0019   .0013   .0013   .0000    .0000
CATR       1   .0109    .0109   .0108    .0027   .0001    .0000   .0005   .0022   .0022   .0000    .0000
CBAM       1  4.3257   4.3257   .0106    .0033  4.3152    .0001   .0010   .0023   .0023   .0000    .0000
CEBR       2  7.4248  11.1982   .0498    .0044  7.3749    .0001   .0013   .0031   .0031   .0000    .0000
CECI       2 31.7902  33.4010   .0523    .0078 31.7378    .0003   .0036   .0042   .0042   .0000    .0000
CEDA       4 10.5878  17.3655   .4513    .1893 10.1366    .0013   .1653   .0235   .0047   .0005    .0000
CEJR       3   .0337    .0622   .0209    .0030   .0128    .0121   .0006   .0006   .0006   .0018    .0000
CEMT      12 17.7283 116.4639   .0691    .0093 17.6592    .0038   .0060   .0033   .0016   .0000    .0000
....
CFQR       1 1955.858 1955.858  .0002    .0003 1955.858   .0003   .0003   .0000   .0000   .0000    .0000
CFQS       1 1955.858 1955.851  .0077    .0023 1955.851   .0025   .0005   .0018   .0018   .0000    .0000
CGRP       1   .0944    .0944   .0196    .0025   .0748    .0138   .0007   .0017   .0017   .0000    .0000
CMAC      13   .0628    .7314   .0602    .0054   .0026    .0002   .0010   .0044   .0005   .0000    .0000
CPIR       9   .2211    .6758   .1688    .0030   .0523    .0021   .0011   .0004   .0004   .0016    .0000
....
CXRE       1   .0808    .0808   .0238    .0021   .0570    .0569   .0004   .0018   .0018   .0000    .0000
ENAB       1   .0776    .0776   .0775    .0054   .0001    .0001   .0005   .0048   .0048   .0000    .0000
STAT       5 137.5680 335.4007  .8607   6.5560 136.7072   .0025   .6503   .0057   .0057   .0080    .0000
Total    106 154.0982 1955.858  .2038    .0647 153.8944   .0130   .0513   .0051   .0031   .0002    .0081
```

Figure 5-24 CICS PA transaction CICS TCB CPU analysis: Summary

An example report showing TCB usage and number of change modes is shown in Figure 5-25.

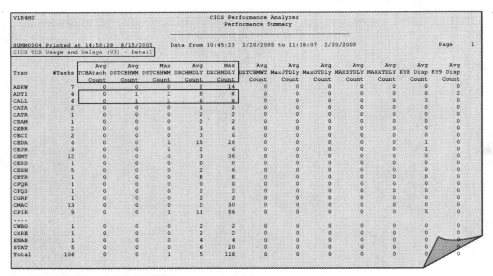

Figure 5-25 CICS PA TCB usage and delays

> **Note:** Prior to CICS Transaction Server Version 3, the field in the CICS SMF 110 record that contained the count of TCB switches (change modes) is called CHMODECT.
>
> In CICS Transaction Server Version 3 the CHMODECT field has been removed and replaced by a composite field called DSCHMDLY. This composite field consists of a time and a count:
>
> ► The time portion represents the elapsed time the user task waited for redispatch after change mode requests. For example, a change mode request from an L8 TCB back to the QR TCB may have to wait for the QR TCB because another task is currently dispatched on the QR TCB.
>
> ► The count portion represents the number of change modes and is equivalent to CHMODECT in previous releases.

An example report on shared storage use is shown in Figure 5-26.

```
V1R4M0                                        CICS Performance Analyzer
                                                    Performance List
LIST0003 Printed at 13:53:01  8/16/2005    Data from 10:45:24  2/20/2005                              Page    1
Transaction Shared Storage Analysis - Detail

Tran Userid       TaskNo Stop         SC24SGet SC24GShr SC24FShr SC31SGet SC31GShr SC31FShr
                         Time
CSSY CBAKER          11 10:45:24.716        0        0        0        0        0        0
CSSY CBAKER          14 10:45:25.133        0        0        0        0        0        0
CSSY CBAKER         III 10:45:32.173        8   208032     2096        1      288        0
CPIR CBAKER          23 10:45:32.183        0        0        0        0        0        0
```

Figure 5-26 CICS PA transaction shared storage analysis

6

Application review

This chapter describes the actions necessary to make a CICS DB2 application threadsafe, therefore allowing it to continue to run on an L8 TCB following a DB2 command being performed.

While this chapter demonstrates a DB2 application, the same principles will apply for an application calling one of the other OPENAPI TRUEs, namely WebSphere MQSeries or IP Sockets for CICS.

This chapter addresses three different areas which must be investigated before defining your application as threadsafe:

- Use of non threadsafe native code
- Use of shared resources
- Use of non threadsafe CICS commands

The chapter concludes with a short example of a COBOL program using File Control commands. This is to demonstrate how, at CICS Transaction Server Version 3.2, file control commands will execute on an open TCB.

6.1 Application code review

Prior to enabling any application as threadsafe, a review of the application code *must* be performed. This is necessary for two reasons:

- First, application data integrity must be maintained. Prior to CICS Transaction Server 2.2 all user applications and exits ran on the QR TCB, which is a restricted or closed environment. CICS provided the serialization needed to ensure that application data integrity was never compromised. In this environment programs could be sure that no more than one quasi-reentrant program could run at the same time. Now, for applications that make calls to TRUEs that have been enabled as OPENAPI or, for application programs that have been defined as OPENAPI, it is possible for two or more programs to be running concurrently on different open TCBs and the QR TCB. Therefore it is now imperative that shared resources used by an application are serialized to prevent any application integrity problems due to more than one program accessing the same resource at the same time.

- The second reason for conducting a review of your application code is to ensure that once CICS moves an application over to an open TCB it remains there for as long as possible. CICS will switch the application program back to the QR TCB in order to execute CICS API or SPI commands that are non threadsafe. CICS must do this to maintain the integrity of such things as the CSA and other control blocks used by these commands.

6.1.1 Ensure that the program logic is threadsafe

There are several things that must be reviewed in order to ensure that the program logic is threadsafe.

Check native code

The native language logic is the application code in between any CICS commands. This code must be also be threadsafe. If you define a program to be threadsafe but the application logic is not threadsafe, then unpredictable results could occur that could compromise your data integrity.

To be threadsafe the first thing that needs to happen is that the program must be reentrant. Language Environment (LE) programs can be guaranteed reentrant by compiling with the RENT option. This means that the compiler for the language concerned will generate fully reentrant (and therefore) threadsafe code. Pre-LE language compilers cannot be guaranteed to be reentrant, and so programs compiled using a pre-LE compiler cannot be made threadsafe.

Assembler programs are probably the most common place where non threadsafe code can be generated. For example, this can be achieved by storing variable data in a DC in a CSECT. In doing this the program is altering itself to store variable data and is therefore creating a shared resource that could be updated by more than one transaction running the same program at the same time.

Test for non reentrant native code

The simplest way to check that the native code in between EXEC CICS commands is reentrant is to link-edit the program with the RENT option. CICS then places any program linked with the RENT option into a read-only DSA (the RDSA for RMODE(24) programs and the ERDSA for RMODE(ANY) programs). By default, the storage for these DSAs is allocated from read-only, key-0, protected storage. This protects any modules loaded into a read-only DSA, from being modified, by all programs except those running in key-0 or in supervisor state. So, as long as CICS is *not* initialized with RENTPGM=NOPROTECT, any attempt by a program to modify itself will result in an ASRA abend. We would suggest that this be done in a pre production environment where the application can be tested thoroughly to identify any possible programs that are not reentrant.

Check for shared resources

The next stage in identifying issues that can make an application non threadsafe is to analyze the use of shared resources by your applications. Shared resources are those storage areas that result from use of the following:

- The CWA
- Shared getmains
- Global work areas for global user exits
- Loaded assembler data tables

Using these resources does not automatically imply that a program is not threadsafe. The application must be analyzed to determine how these areas are subsequently used by the application as a whole. In particular, if the shared area is updated at any point then *all* accesses to the shared area will need to be serialized.

DFHEISUP

CICS provides a utility (DFHEISUP) that can be used to scan load modules in order to identify the CICS commands associated with these shared areas. Its use is described fully in 4.2, "Load module scanner: DFHEISUP" on page 61.

The load module scanner should be used against the application load modules with the supplied filter table DFHEIDTH. This will identify all the programs that contain any of the above commands.

In addition to DFHEISUP, the CICS Interdependency Analyzer (CICS IA) provides the ability to scan for these commands both statically and at runtime. This is discussed in 5.2.5, "How CICS IA can assist with threadsafety" on page 76.

> **Important:** If any of these commands are identified as being used in any one application program then a more detailed analysis of the whole application *must* be performed to identify how and when the addresses returned by these commands are used to access the underlying data.

It is possible that the address returned by one of these commands can be passed to another program that does none of the above commands itself but will still modify the data at the address passed. Hence, just because the scanner utility does not report any of these commands as being present in a particular load module, this does not necessarily mean a module is threadsafe.

If you can determine that the shared resource is *never* updated by any of your application programs (for example, it could have been initialized by a PLT startup program and then only ever read by the rest of the application), then no further action needs to be taken for that shared resource.

How to serialize

Once analysis of your application has determined that the shared data area is updated, you will need to decide how to serialize access to the data using techniques such as:

- Compare and swap
- Enqueue/dequeue
- Accessing the shared storage only from quasi-reentrant programs

6.1.2 Example showing the use of shared resources

The following example application will be used to demonstrate how use of shared resources can compromise data integrity if resources are not serialized.

Starter program CWAPROG

The example application consists of one starter program that initializes some shared storage, in this case the CWA, and then passes on the address of the CWA to five transactions. Each instance of these five transaction uses this address to access and update the data in the shared area. The five transactions are started 25 times each, and each transaction will start the same program: TXNPROG.

CWAPROG is listed in Example 6-1 on page 115.

Example 6-1   CWAPROG

```
        IDENTIFICATION DIVISION.
        PROGRAM-ID. CWAPROG.
        ENVIRONMENT DIVISION.
        DATA DIVISION.
        WORKING-STORAGE SECTION.

        01  ws-queue                    pic x(08)
               value 'OUTPUTQ'.
        01  ws-ptr                      pointer.

        LINKAGE SECTION.
        01  common-work-area.
            03  cwa-counter             pic s9(8) comp.

        PROCEDURE DIVISION.
    *       Delete the output TSQ - don't worry if its not there
            EXEC CICS DELETEQ TS QUEUE(WS-QUEUE) NOHANDLE END-EXEC.

    *       Access our shared storage area - this time the CWA
            EXEC CICS ADDRESS CWA(ADDRESS OF COMMON-WORK-AREA) END-EXEC.

    *       Save address of our shared area so we can pass it on
            set ws-ptr to address of common-work-area.

    *       Initialize the counter in our shared area
            move zero to cwa-counter.

    *
    *       Start our 5 transactions 25 times passing the address of the
    *          CWA (which contains our counter) so that each transaction
    *          can access it
    *
            Perform 25 times
                EXEC CICS START TRANSID('TXN1') FROM(WS-PTR) END-EXEC

                EXEC CICS START TRANSID('TXN2') FROM(WS-PTR) END-EXEC

                EXEC CICS START TRANSID('TXN3') FROM(WS-PTR) END-EXEC

                EXEC CICS START TRANSID('TXN4') FROM(WS-PTR) END-EXEC

                EXEC CICS START TRANSID('TXN5') FROM(WS-PTR) END-EXEC
            End-Perform.

            EXEC CICS RETURN
        END-EXEC.
```

Program TXNPROG

The program executed by each of the transactions, TXNPROG, does the following:

1. Retrieves the address of the shared storage passed to it
2. Makes an EXEC SQL call that causes a switch to an L8 TCB
3. Takes a copy of the counter value in the shared storage and increments it by one
4. Does some processing
5. Writes the new counter value back to the shared storage
6. Writes the result to a temporary storage queue

The program is shown in Example 6-2.

Example 6-2 TXNPROG

```
IDENTIFICATION DIVISION.
PROGRAM-ID. TXNPROG.
ENVIRONMENT DIVISION.
DATA DIVISION.
WORKING-STORAGE SECTION.

 01 ws-enq-queue                     pic x(08) value 'ENQUEUE'.
 01 ws-enqueue-yes-no                pic x(03) value 'NO'.
    88 enqueue-yes                             value 'YES'.

 01 ws-ptr                           pointer.
 01 ws-counter2                      pic s9(8) comp.
 01 ws-count                         pic s9(8) comp.
 01 ws-queue                         pic x(08)
       VALUE 'OUTPUTQ'.
 01 WS-MSG.
    03 WS-TXN                        pic x(05).
    03 filler                        pic x(17)
       value "Counter value :- ".
    03 ws-counter                    pic 9(8).

 01 ws-cwa-ptr                       usage is pointer.
       EXEC SQL
           DECLARE DSN8710.EMP TABLE (
           EMPNO                     CHAR(6),
           FIRSTNME                  CHAR(12),
           MIDINIT                   CHAR(1),
           LASTNAME                  CHAR(15),
           WORKDEPT                  CHAR(3),
```

```
            PHONENO              CHAR(4),
            HIREDATE             DATE,
            JOB                  CHAR(8),
            EDLEVEL              SMALLINT,
            SEX                  CHAR(1),
            BIRTHDATE            DATE,
            SALARY               DECIMAL,
            BONUS                DECIMAL,
            COMM                 DECIMAL )
       END-EXEC.

       EXEC SQL INCLUDE SQLCA END-EXEC.

   LINKAGE SECTION.
   01  SHARED-AREA.
       03  SHARED-COUNTER               PIC S9(8) COMP.

   PROCEDURE DIVISION.
       EXEC CICS READQ TS
           QUEUE(WS-ENQ-QUEUE)
           ITEM(1)
           INTO(WS-ENQUEUE-YES-NO)
           NOHANDLE
       END-EXEC.
       MOVE EIBTRNID TO WS-TXN.

  *    get the address of the shared area which has been passed
       EXEC CICS RETRIEVE INTO(WS-PTR) END-EXEC.

  *    map our linkage section to the address of the shared area
       Set address of shared-area to ws-ptr.
  *
  *    Make DB2 Call which will transfer to the L8
  *
       EXEC SQL
          SELECT count(*)
            INTO :ws-count FROM DSN8710.EMP
                WHERE EMPNO = "000990"
       END-EXEC.

       if enqueue-yes
  *        enqueue before we change the shared storage
           EXEC CICS
               ENQ RESOURCE(shared-area)
           END-EXEC
       end-if.

  *    read the value in shared storage.
       move shared-counter to ws-counter.
```

```
      *     ... and change its value
            Add 1 to ws-counter.

      *     ** Do some important processing **
            move ws-counter to ws-counter2.
            Perform 100000 Times
               add 2 to ws-counter2
               subtract 1 from ws-counter2
            End-Perform.
      *     ***********************************

      *     update the shared storage with our new value
            Move ws-counter to shared-counter.

            if enqueue-yes
      *         remove the enqueue now we have finished updating
      *            the shared storage
                EXEC CICS
                   DEQ RESOURCE(shared-area)
                END-EXEC
            end-if.

      *     output the results ......
            EXEC CICS
               WRITEQ TS MAIN QUEUE(WS-QUEUE) FROM(WS-MSG)
            END-EXEC.

            EXEC CICS RETURN END-EXEC.
```

Results when run as quasi-reentrant

When the program TXNPROG is defined as quasi-reentrant each occurrence of the transaction will be serialized by CICS because only one occurrence of the program can be running at any one time, always on the QR TCB. So, the results will be as expected: each program will process a unique counter, as demonstrated by the output in Figure 6-1.

```
 CEBR   TSQ OUTPUTQ           SYSID PJA6 REC    1 OF    25   COL    1 OF    30
        ENTER COMMAND ===>
              **************************  TOP OF QUEUE
 00001 TXN1 Counter value :- 00000001
 00002 TXN2 Counter value :- 00000002
 00003 TXN1 Counter value :- 00000003
 00004 TXN5 Counter value :- 00000004
 00005 TXN4 Counter value :- 00000005
 00006 TXN3 Counter value :- 00000006
 00007 TXN2 Counter value :- 00000007
 00008 TXN3 Counter value :- 00000008
 00009 TXN4 Counter value :- 00000009
 00010 TXN5 Counter value :- 00000010
 00011 TXN1 Counter value :- 00000011
 00012 TXN2 Counter value :- 00000012
 00013 TXN3 Counter value :- 00000013
 00014 TXN4 Counter value :- 00000014
 00015 TXN5 Counter value :- 00000015
 00016 TXN1 Counter value :- 00000016


 PF1 : HELP             PF2 : SWITCH HEX/CHAR   PF3 : TERMINATE BROWSE
 PF4 : VIEW TOP         PF5 : VIEW BOTTOM       PF6 : REPEAT LAST FIND
 PF7 : SCROLL BACK HALF PF8 : SCROLL FORWARD HALF PF9 : UNDEFINED
 PF10: SCROLL BACK FULL PF11: SCROLL FORWARD FULL PF12: UNDEFINED
```

Figure 6-1 Results when run as quasi-reentrant

Results when defined as threadsafe - without enqueue

If we now take the definition of program TXNPROG and change it to be threadsafe *without* taking any action to ensure the update of the CWA is serialized, the output will look very different. Each instance of TXNPROG will remain on an L8 TCB after completing the EXEC SQL call. The result of this will be that we will have several instances of TXNPROG running concurrently on multiple TCBs. Each instance of the program cannot then rely on the value of the counter in the CWA because access to it is not serialized. So, we end up with a scenario that looks as follows:

- ► TXN1 reads counter (0).
- ► TXN1 increments counter (1).
- ► TXN2 reads counter (0).
- ► TXN1 writes incremented value (1).
- ► TXN2 writes incremented value (1).
- ► TXN3 reads counter (1).
- ► And so on.

The output written to the temporary storage queue will be as shown in Figure 6-2.

```
CEBR  TSQ OUTPUTQ              SYSID PJA6 REC     1 OF    25    COL    1 OF    30
   ENTER COMMAND ===>
           **************************   TOP OF QUEUE   ***************************
 00001 TXN4 Counter value :- 00000001
 00002 TXN1 Counter value :- 00000001
 00003 TXN3 Counter value :- 00000001
 00004 TXN2 Counter value :- 00000002
 00005 TXN5 Counter value :- 00000002
 00006 TXN1 Counter value :- 00000002
 00007 TXN2 Counter value :- 00000003
 00008 TXN3 Counter value :- 00000003
 00009 TXN5 Counter value :- 00000004
 00010 TXN1 Counter value :- 00000004
 00011 TXN4 Counter value :- 00000004
 00012 TXN2 Counter value :- 00000005
 00013 TXN3 Counter value :- 00000005
 00014 TXN4 Counter value :- 00000005
 00015 TXN1 Counter value :- 00000006
 00016 TXN5 Counter value :- 00000006


 PF1 : HELP                PF2 : SWITCH HEX/CHAR    PF3 : TERMINATE BROWSE
 PF4 : VIEW TOP            PF5 : VIEW BOTTOM        PF6 : REPEAT LAST FIND
 PF7 : SCROLL BACK HALF    PF8 : SCROLL FORWARD HALF PF9 : UNDEFINED
 PF10: SCROLL BACK FULL    PF11: SCROLL FORWARD FULL PF12: UNDEFINED
```

Figure 6-2   Results when run as threadsafe without enqueues

In Figure 6-2 we can see that our data has been compromised because each transaction is attempting to concurrently update the counter value.

The solution to this problem is to add an ENQ and DEQ command around the code that reads and then updates the counter value. In our example we have enqueued upon the address of the shared area, which is currently pointed to by linkage section item *shared-area*. Adding the enqueue and dequeue commands will cause the results to return to those seen when the program was defined as quasi-reentrant, as shown in Figure 6-1 on page 119.

The example program uses an IF statement to enclose the enqueue and dequeue commands. This was done so that the ENQUEUE/DEQUEUE can be switched on and off easily without recompiling the program. See Figure 6-3.

```
  if enqueue-yes
* enqueue before we change the shared storage
     EXEC CICS
         ENQ RESOURCE(shared-area)
     END-EXEC
  end-if.
```

Figure 6-3 Enqueue statement

To switch the enqueue on dynamically all that needs to be done is to write the word YES to a temporary storage queue called ENQUEUE.

Example summary

The previous example shows how a program uses the CWA to store a counter value. Under a quasi-reentrant scenario access to this counter value will be serialized by CICS and the counter value returned will always be unique and the next in the series. However, under a threadsafe scenario the serialization must be done by the application. Otherwise, with concurrent tasks running on separate TCBs the counter returned can no longer be relied upon to be unique.

It is important to note that the enqueue and dequeue commands should only enclose the minimum number of program statements that are necessary to ensure that the resource is not updated before this program is ready. In our simple example we could make the enqueue-to-dequeue path shorter by updating the shared resource and dequeuing before we do the *important processing* section of code.

In the example we use the CWA as our shared resource. This could easily be changed to utilize any of the other shared resources listed in "Check for shared resources" on page 113 by replacing the ADDRESS CWA command in Example 6-1 on page 115 with one of these other commands.

Important: If there are several programs (as in our example) that access the shared resource, they must *all* use the *same* serialization technique to serialize access to the shared resource. In our example, if there was another program accessing our CWA area, then it must also ENQUEUE and DEQUEUE on the same resource (in this case the address of the CWA).

Assembler data tables

A technique that has often been used in the past is to load a data-only assembler program containing only DC entries in a CSECT. If the load is done with the HOLD option, the empty assembler program will remain in storage and will therefore become a shared resource that can be updated concurrently from several programs. For example, the following program could be assembled and link edited into a library on the DFHRPL concatenation (Example 6-3).

Example 6-3   Assembler data table

```
TABLE     CSECT
FILLER1   DC     CL16'COUNTER VALUE >>'
COUNTER   DC     F'99'
FILLER2   DC     CL16'<< COUNTER VALUE'
          END
```

It could then be loaded into storage by any program, with an EXEC CICS LOAD command, which could map the data in the table onto a linkage section structure such as in Example 6-4.

Example 6-4   Linkage section

```
LINKAGE SECTION.
01  TABLE-AREA.
    03  filler                pic x(16).
    03  LS-COUNTER            PIC S9(8) COMP.
    03  filler                pic x(16).
```

The address of this area could be passed on and used in the same way the address of the CWA is used in the previous example. This technique would not work if the table is linked with the RENT option and CICS is started with RENTPGM=PROTECT.

6.1.3 Ensure only threadsafe CICS commands are used

Once a program has been switched over to an open TCB it is very important to minimize the number of times CICS switches back to the QR TCB, therefore allowing applications to reap the benefits of running multiple tasks concurrently across different TCBs.

The main inhibitor to staying on an open TCB are those CICS API and SPI commands that are not threadsafe. When a CICS API or SPI command command is executed CICS will execute code that could update any number of CICS control blocks (for example, the CSA). If CICS had not been changed to serialize access to these control blocks and multiple tasks are allowed to run that cause these control blocks to be updated concurrently from several tasks, then the integrity of CICS itself could be compromised and unpredictable results could occur.

To ensure that CICS is not compromised, CICS will automatically switch back to the QR TCB when its is about to execute any API or SPI command that it knows to be non threadsafe. The current list of commands that *are* threadsafe is listed in the appendixes of the *CICS Application Programming Reference*, and the *CICS System Programming Reference*.

> **Note:** If a command is *not* listed in either of these appendixes it is *not* threadsafe and it *will* cause a switch to the QR TCB.

These commands can be identified, again, using the load module scanner, DFHEISUP with filter table DFHEIDNT, or CICS IA.

> **Note:** Using a CICS command that is non threadsafe does not prevent the program from being defined as threadsafe and does not compromise data integrity.
>
> Including these commands will, however, cause CICS to switch back to the QR TCB each time a non threadsafe command is encountered while on an open TCB. Therefore the use of non threadsafe commands has a *performance* penalty, not an *integrity* penalty.

The worst case scenario, in terms of performance, for a DB2 application program would be one where there are many EXEC SQL calls interspersed with non threadsafe EXEC CICS commands, as in Example 6-5.

Example 6-5   Non threadsafe commands causing TCB switches

```
EXEC CICS
EXEC SQL
EXEC CICS <non threadsafe>
EXEC SQL
EXEC CICS <threadsafe>
EXEC CICS <non threadsafe>
EXEC SQL
EXEC CICS <non threadsafe>
EXEC SQL
EXEC CICS <non threadsafe
EXEC SQL

RETURN
```

In this example we would see a TCB switch for each DB2 request and then a switchback to the QR TCB when a non threadsafe EXEC CICS command follows an EXEC SQL call. This clearly would not provide the optimal performance threadsafe applications can deliver due to the number of non threadsafe CICS commands and their distribution throughout the program.

This example could be restructured in such a way that most, or all, of the non threadsafe commands could either be removed or moved to the start of the program before any DB2 request is made. This would remove the excessive number of mode switches and will deliver the performance benefits we are looking for. See Example 6-6.

This kind of simple reorganization is obviously not going to be possible for every program. Once the commands have been identified as being present in the program only then can you assess what, if any, changes can be made.

Example 6-6   Non threadsafe commands moved or deleted

```
EXEC CICS
EXEC CICS <non threadsafe>
EXEC CICS <non threadsafe>
EXEC CICS <non threadsafe>

EXEC SQL
EXEC SQL
EXEC CICS <threadsafe>
EXEC SQL
EXEC SQL

EXEC SQL

RETURN
```

6.2 Change program definitions

Once the applications have been changed or verified to be threadsafe then the final action that is needed to make the application stay on the open TCB is to change the definition of all the programs concerned to define them as threadsafe.

This will be done either by changing the RDO definition of the program, or by modifying your autoinstall exit to install the program as threadsafe, or by using the LE environment variable CICSVAR, which is discussed in 6.2.2, "CICS environment variable CICSVAR" on page 126.

6.2.1 RDO definition

Figure 6-4 shows the RDO definition.

```
 OBJECT CHARACTERISTICS                                 CICS RELEASE = 0640
    CEDA  View PROGram( DB2MANY  )
     PROGram        : DB2MANY
     Group          : THDSAFE
     DEscription    :
     Language       :                  CObol | Assembler | Le370 | C | Pli
     RELoad         : No               No | Yes
     RESident       : No               No | Yes
     USAge          : Normal           Normal | Transient
     USElpacopy     : No               No | Yes
     Status         : Enabled          Enabled | Disabled
     RSl            : 00               0-24 | Public
     CEdf           : Yes              Yes | No
     DAtalocation   : Any              Below | Any
     EXECKey        : User             User | Cics
     COncurrency    : Threadsafe       Quasirent | Threadsafe
     Api            : Cicsapi          Cicsapi | Openapi
    REMOTE ATTRIBUTES
     DYnamic        : No               No | Yes
   + REMOTESystem   :

                                           SYSID=PJA7 APPLID=SCSCPJA7

 PF 1 HELP 2 COM 3 END         6 CRSR 7 SBH 8 SFH 9 MSG 10 SB 11 SF 12 CNCL
```

Figure 6-4   RDO program definition using CEDA

6.2.2 CICS environment variable CICSVAR

Prior to CICS Transaction Server Version 3.1, changing the definitions of programs that were autoinstalled, but had now been made threadsafe, required the introduction of logic into the autoinstall program. This was so it could know which programs were to be auto installed as threadsafe and which were not.

CICS Transaction Server Version 3.1 introduced an environment variable called CICSVAR to allow the CONCURRENCY and API program attributes to be closely associated with the application program by using the ENVAR runtime option. While it may be used in a CEEDOPT CSECT to set an installation default, it is most useful when set in a CEEUOPT CSECT link-edited with an individual program, or set via a #pragma statement in the source of a C or C++ program, or set via a PLIXOPT statement in a PL/I program.

For example, when a program has been coded to threadsafe standards it can be defined as such without having to change a PROGRAM resource definition, or adhere to an installation-defined naming standard to allow a program autoinstall exit to install it with the correct attributes. CICSVAR can be used for the Language Environment conforming assembler, for PLI, for COBOL, and for C and C++ programs (both those compiled with the XPLINK option and those compiled without it) that have been compiled using a Language Environment conforming compiler. CICSVAR cannot be used for assembler programs that are not Language Environment conforming or for Java programs.

> **Note:** Use of CICSVAR overrides the settings on a PROGRAM resource definition installed via standard RDO interfaces or via program autoinstall.

Until a program is executed the first time, an INQUIRE PROGRAM command shows the keyword settings from the program definition. Once the application has been run once, an INQUIRE PROGRAM command shows the settings with any CICSVAR overrides applied.

CICSVAR can take one of three values: QUASIRENT, THREADSAFE, or OPENAPI.

6.2.3 CICSVAR values

The following values for CICSVAR will result in the values shown for CONCURRENCY and API:

CICSVAR=QUASIRENT Results in a program with attributes QUASIRENT and CICSAPI

CICSVAR=THREADSAFE Results in a program with attributes THREADSAFE and CICSAPI

CICSVAR=OPENAPI Results in a program with attributes THREADSAFE and OPENAPI

6.2.4 How to code ENVAR

The following sections show how to code the ENVAR runtime option for different programming environments.

ENVAR CSECT example

Following is an example of ENVAR coded in a CEEUOPT CSECT:

```
CEEUOPT CSECT
CEEUOPT AMODE ANY
CEEUOPT RMODE ANY
        CEEXOPT ENVAR=('CICSVAR=THREADSAFE')
        END
```

This can be assembled and link-edited into a load module and then the CEEUOPT load module link-edited together with any language program supported by Language Environment, as explained above.

ENVAR pragma runopts example

For C and C++ programs, add the following statement at the start of the program source before any other C statements:

```
#pragma runopts(ENVAR(CICSVAR=THREADSAFE))
```

ENVAR PLIXOPT example

For PL/I programs add the following statement after the PL/I MAIN procedure statement:

```
DCL PLIXOPT CHAR(25) VAR STATIC EXTERNAL INIT('ENVAR(CICSVAR=THREADSAFE)');
```

6.2.5 An example file control application

CICS Transaction Server Version 3.2, released in June 2007, expanded the number of API commands that have been made threadsafe to include the file control commands. This would allow applications which currently are not good candidates to be made threadsafe to be converted and enabled as threadsafe.

The following is a simple example of a program that browses through a file. We will demonstrate that a file control API call will now remain on an OPEN TCB, whereas in previous releases of CICS it would have switched back the QR TCB to execute the command.

The program shown in Figure 6-5 browses through the entire FILEA file supplied by CICS.

```
Identification Division.
Program-ID. KSDSPRO1.
Environment Division.
Data Division.
Working-storage Section.

01  ws-file                 pic x(8) value 'FILEA'.

01  ws-record               pic x(80) value low-values.
01  ws-rid                  pic x(06) value low-values.
01  ws-browse-rid           pic x(06) value low-values.

01  ws-resp                 pic s9(8) comp value zero.
01  ws-resp2                pic s9(8) comp value zero.


Procedure Division.

    exec cics
      startbr file(ws-file)
      ridfld(ws-browse-rid)
      resp(ws-resp)
      resp2(ws-resp2)
    end-exec.

    perform until ws-resp not = dfhresp(normal)
       initialize ws-record
       exec cics
         readnext file(ws-file)
             into(ws-record)
             ridfld(ws-rid)
             resp(ws-resp)
             resp2(ws-resp2)
       end-exec
    end-perform.

    exec cics
       endbr file(ws-file)
    end-exec.

    exec cics return end-exec.
```

Figure 6-5 Example File Control Program

This program was defined as OPENAPI. Therefore, as soon as it begins CICS switches the task to an open TCB, where it will remain until the end of the task or until a non threadsafe CICS command is encountered. In this case an L8 TCB (L8005) is used. This can be seen in the trace snippet shown in Figure 6-6. The trace snippet shows trace entries for *one* of the READNEXT commands.

```
00061 L8005 AP 00E1 EIP   ENTRY READNEXT                          0004,266A9900 ..r.,0800060E ....          =000898=
00061 L8005 AP E110 EISR  ENTRY TRACE_ENTRY      266A99F0                                                   =000899=
00061 L8005 AP E160 EXEC  ENTRY READNEXT         'FILEA    ' AT X'266AB040',AT X'266AB048',80 AT X'266AAD18',AT X'266AB
                                                                                                            =000900=
00061 L8005 AP E111 EISR  EXIT  TRACE_ENTRY/OK                                                              =000901=
00061 L8005 AP 04F0 EIFC  ENTRY PROCESS_EXEC_ARGUMENTS 266A99F0,0005C308                                     =000902=
00061 L8005 AP 04E0 FCFR  ENTRY READ_NEXT_INTO   FILEA,266AB048,50,00000000,266AB098,0,FCT_VALUE,KEY,NO,NO   =000903=
00061 L8005 AP 04B0 FCVS  ENTRY READ_NEXT_INTO   FILEA,266AB048,50,00000000,26F393B0,266AB098,26DA2100,0,FCT_VALUE,KEY
                                                                                                            =000904=
00061 L8005 AP 0492 FCVR  EVENT ISSUE_VSAM_RPL_REQUEST GET,SEQ ASY,000000000000                              =000905=
00061 L8005 AP 0493 FCVR  EVENT RETURN_FROM_VSAM  0000,F0F0F0F1F0F0                                          =000906=
00061 L8005 AP 04B1 FCVS  EXIT  READ_NEXT_INTO/OK  50,50,6,00000000,,LENGTH_OK,NO,NO                         =000907=
00061 L8005 AP 04E1 FCFR  EXIT  READ_NEXT_INTO/OK  50,50,6,00000000,,LENGTH_OK,NO,NO                         =000908=
00061 L8005 AP 04E2 FCFR  EXIT  FRAB_FLAB_AND_FRTE                                                           =000909=
00061 L8005 AP 04F1 EIFC  EXIT  PROCESS_EXEC_ARGUMENTS/OK                                                    =000910=
00061 L8005 AP E110 EISR  ENTRY TRACE_EXIT       266A99F0                                                    =000911=
00061 L8005 AP E161 EXEC  EXIT  READNEXT         'FILEA ' AT X'266AB040',' 000100S. D. BORMAN      SURREY, ENGLAND =000912=
00061 L8005 AP E111 EISR  EXIT  TRACE_EXIT/OK                                                                =000913=
00061 L8005 AP 00E1 EIP   EXIT  READNEXT    OK                    00F4,00000000 ....,0000060E ....           =000914=
```

Figure 6-6 File control trace snippets

System programmer tasks

This chapter describes the tasks and steps the CICS System Programmer will normally be responsible for with respect to implementing threadsafe applications.

7.1 The role of the system programmer

Here we discuss the role of the system programmer in making an application threadsafe. In essence, the system programmer does not make an application threadsafe, but prepares the environment and makes it threadsafe so it can efficiently run the customer applications. Additionally, the system programmer may coordinate and guide the conversion of the applications.

To summarize, the system programmer might perform the following actions:

- Analyze the CICS regions
- Provide a threadsafe CICS operating environment
- Coordinate and drive individual application conversions
- Monitor and tune the CICS regions to ensure that they are making efficient use of the open TCBs

7.2 Understanding threadsafe operation

Before we start analyzing and preparing your CICS regions, we go over a few of the concepts to help understand why some of the conversions are necessary.

7.2.1 Threadsafe performance issues

Simply stated, the way to gain the performance benefit of threadsafe applications is to eliminate TCB switches between the QR and open TCBs.

Under CICS Transaction Server Version 2, your program commenced execution on the QR TCB, and when a DB2 call was encountered, your program was swapped over to run on an open TCB. If your program was defined to CICS as CONCURRENCY(THREADSAFE), it would then continue to execute all further instructions on the open TCB until program termination or until a non threadsafe command or exit was encountered.

This behavior is also true, by default, under CICS Transaction Server Version 3. The API attribute of a program definition was introduced in CICS TS Version 3.1 and defaults to a value of CICSAPI. CICSAPI means that the program exploits the traditional CICS programming interfaces. CICSAPI mirrors the behavior of a threadsafe application in CICS TS Version 2. This means that CICS Transaction Server Version 3 CICSAPI applications use open TCBs in the same way as described above for CICS Transaction Server Version 2.

> **Note:** Under CICS Transaction Server Version 3, a threadsafe program may be defined as API(OPENAPI), in which case it will be switched to run under an L8 or L9 TCB *during its initialization*. The open TCB mode that it runs under depends upon the program's EXECKEY parameter. An OPENAPI program will continue to execute its instructions under its L8 or L9 TCB *until program termination*. Any calls to exits or non threadsafe commands requiring TCB switches will be handled by CICS, and upon completion the OPENAPI program will receive control back under its open TCB once more. OPENAPI programs therefore have more extensive threadsafe zones than CICSAPI programs.

Originally, the only TRUE to exploit OTE was the CICS DB2 TRUE. When reviewing the use of L8 TCBs and TCB switching, it was therefore reasonable to discuss this just in terms of CICS DB2 applications. Since then, CICS Transaction Server Version 3.2 has provided an OTE-enabled TRUE for WMQ. In addition, the z/OS Communications Server IP CICS Sockets has also been written to exploit OTE if enabled to do so. As well as these enhancements, CICS Transaction Server Version 3 provides the ability to define applications as OPENAPI programs, to execute under their own L8 or L9 TCBs.

A major enhancement to threadsafe support in CICS Transaction Server Version 3.2 is the change to make the CICS file control API threadsafe for applications. This means that the path for EXEC CICS file control commands should also be reviewed to ensure that this does not result in unwanted TCB switching activity.

The use of open TCBs within CICS has grown. Having said that, the objectives of a system programmer role in terms of preparing CICS for OTE can still be described in terms of calling DB2, since the same basic principles of serialization and data integrity apply, regardless of the reason why open TCBs are being used.

An important objective in reviewing your application or exit programs is to ensure that if a program is executing on an L8 TCB, it stays there until all DB2, WMQ, or IP CICS sockets work has completed. Another objective is to ensure that programs defined as OPENAPI in CICS Transaction Server Version 3 avoid TCB switching if possible. Minimizing TCB switches is a key performance goal for threadsafe implementation.

Let us consider the general case for threadsafe code logic, where a threadsafe CICS application program issues calls to an OTE-enabled TRUE such as DB2 or WMQ. For simplicity, we will assume it is defined as CICSAPI in the CICS Transaction Server Version 3 environment. This can appear as shown in Figure 7-1. Once your program starts to execute on the L8 TCB you are in the threadsafe zone and you need to ensure that you do not get moved off the L8 TCB by executing a non threadsafe command or exit.

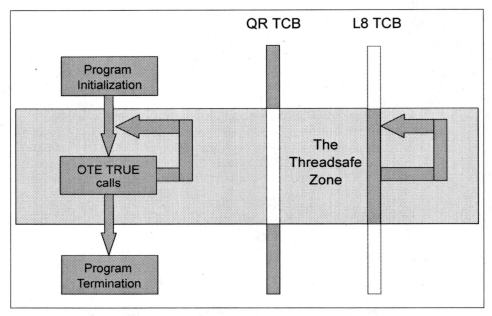

Figure 7-1   CICSAPI program running on an L8 TCB in the threadsafe zone

No matter how your CICSAPI program is coded, it will always start on the QR TCB and finish up on the QR TCB. Therefore, ideally you can place all your non threadsafe EXEC CICS commands at the beginning and end of your application program.

The goal of the system programmer must be to keep the application programs running in the threadsafe zone by not generating TCB switches to the QR TCB in system exits such as GLUEs or URMs, DB2 dynamic plan exits, or the CICS-WMQ API crossing exit CSQCAPX.

Now let us compare this with the case in which an OPENAPI CICS Transaction Server Version 3.2 application program is defined with EXECKEY(USER). (For OPENAPI programs the key of the TCB must match the EXECKEY setting. For an explanation of execution keys in an OPENAPI environment see 9.6, "Additional considerations for OPENAPI programs" on page 242.)

The program issues various threadsafe and non threadsafe EXEC CICS commands, along with a call to WMQ (for example, an MQGET) and an EXEC SQL call to DB2. Note that this combination is not recommended, because it results in additional TCB switching between L9 and L8 TCBs. However, for this very reason it is important to visualize this type of scenario, so we show it graphically in Figure 7-2.

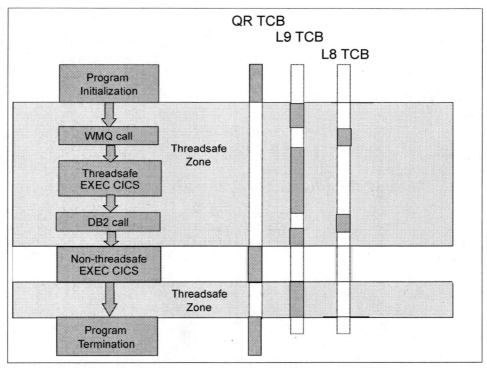

Figure 7-2   OPENAPI user key program running on QR, L9 and L8 TCBs

Here we see that an OPENAPI program enters the threadsafe zone during its program initialization. In fact, an OPENAPI application receives its initial control under an open TCB, so it has to be threadsafe by definition. OPENAPI programs always receive control under their open TCB, both when they start to run and when they receive control back after an EXEC CICS command or a call to a TRUE. The application logic itself has to execute under the open TCB. The key of this open TCB depends upon the program's EXECKEY attribute. As we have chosen to show a user key program, the open TCB selected by CICS is from the pool of L9 TCBs.

In this example, the application runs under this TCB until it issues a call to WMQ. Since WMQ calls run under an L8 TCB in CICS Transaction Server Version 3.2,

CICS switches TCBs for the duration of the request. Upon completion, the application receives control back on its L9 TCB. Here we demonstrate what can happen if the application then issues threadsafe EXEC CICS commands. These have no TCB affinity, and so can be processed under the program's L9 TCB. The application then issues an EXEC SQL call to DB2. As before, the flow of control moves from the L9 to the L8 TCB for the duration of the call to this other OTE-enabled TRUE. Once again, the TCBs are then switched back from L8 to L9 at the end of the call. The application then issues a non threadsafe EXEC CICS command. This must be processed under the QR TCB so CICS switches from the L9 to the QR TCB for the duration of the command. Once again, it switches back to the original L9 TCB when the command completes. The application then terminates, and eventually the L9 TCB returns control to the QR TCB during program termination.

For clarity, this example does not show any additional TCB switches required during any syncpoint processing (for example, at end of task processing if there are no further programs in the task).

7.2.2 Threadsafe data integrity issues

The second type of threadsafe issue you can encounter is data integrity exposures. Once your programs are now enabled to run concurrently on multiple open TCBs you expose your shared resources to update conflicts due to the multiple concurrent program instances running on parallel open TCBs.

> **Note:** Shared resources in this context refers to application shared resources (for example, EXEC CICS GETMAIN SHARED storage), not resources managed by CICS.

In general just removing non threadsafe commands and changing the CICS definition to threadsafe is only half the conversion process. You then must ensure that any shared resource is serialized to prevent data corruption.

To correct this problem you may suggest that application programmers make coding modifications to their programs. Figure 7-3 emphasizes the fact that once you leave the serialized zone and enter the threadsafe zone, you are now in an execution zone where CICS does not provide you with single threaded program execution. All shared resources are now relying on the programmer to code the logic into the program to ensure that multiple instances of the program executing concurrently do not corrupt the shared data. Again, for this example, a CICSAPI program environment with an L8 TCB is shown.

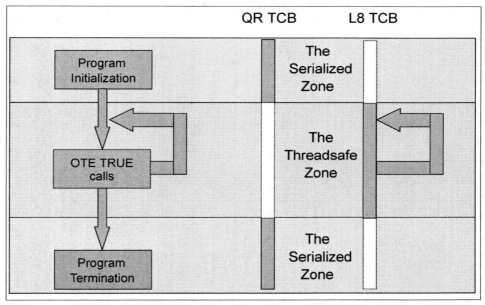

Figure 7-3 Shared data in threadsafe zone must be serialized by your own code logic

Figure 7-4 shows how a non threadsafe program would work. Since all programs execute on the QR TCB, a shared resource is always updated in a serialized fashion forced by the single QR TCB. All secondary instances of your program are waiting for their chance to run on the QR TCB.

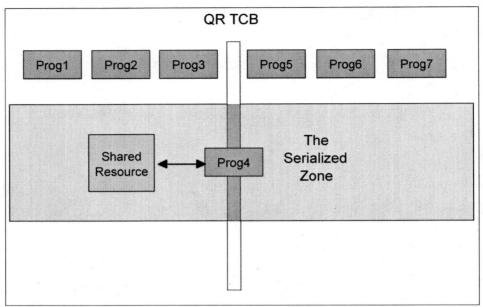

Figure 7-4   Single threaded serialized resource on the QR TCB

Figure 7-5 shows a threadsafe environment where concurrent instances of your CICSAPI program are all running at the same time on their own L8 TCB, all sharing the same common resource.

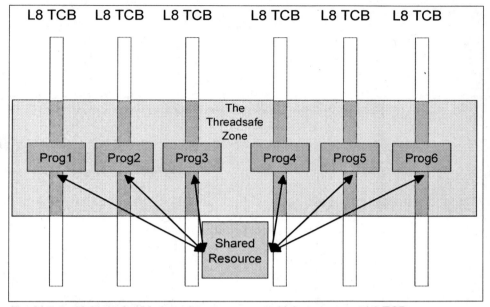

Figure 7-5   Multi-threaded shared resource on multiple concurrent L8 TCBs

The preceding charts help to show how a shared resource can become corrupted due to the nature of threadsafe programs running on open TCBs. Therefore just checking CICS Auxiliary Trace reports and defining a program as threadsafe does not guarantee that a program is threadsafe. Someone needs to review the source code carefully and verify that every shared resource is properly serialized. Such a detailed and thorough analysis is vital, since corruption of shared resources may well not become apparent until some considerable time after it occurs, *if it is noticed at all*. Not all such corruption would result in an abend, for example.

7.3 Analyze the CICS regions

Before converting and running your applications and system exits in threadsafe mode, it is wise to review the status of each individual CICS region to ensure that you have the proper pre-reqs in place. In the next few sections we discuss software and system parameters to be reviewed.

7.3.1 The DB2 version

With CICS Transaction Server Version 2.2, the CICS-DB2 attach code was re-architected to take advantage of the open transaction environment. To enable this change the DB2 product code required an enhancement to facilitate the management of the DB2 side connection control blocks.

From Version 6 onwards, DB2 Universal Database™ utilized the L8 open TCBs provided by the OTE environment. These give the potential for threadsafe applications to see performance improvements over the previous CICS-DB2 attach mechanism, with its pool of subtask TCBs. From this DB2 version onwards, your applications automatically utilize L8 TCBs for their calls to DB2.

> **Note:** For more information about the CICS-DB2 Interface see 2.2, "Open transaction environment - a brief history" on page 15.

7.3.2 The WMQ version

With CICS Transaction Server Version 3.2, the CICS-WMQ attach code was also re-architected to take advantage of the open transaction environment. The CICS-WMQ attach code provided with this release of CICS works with all of the currently supported releases of WMQ (that is, Version 5.3.1 and Version 6).

The CICS Transaction Server Version 3.2 CICS-WMQ attach code utilizes L8 open TCBs. As with the CICS-DB2 attach mechanism, these give the potential for performance improvements over the previous CICS-WMQ attachment mechanism with its proprietary subtask TCBs. From this CICS release onwards, your applications automatically utilize L8 TCBs for their calls to WMQ.

WMQ Version 5.3.1 APAR PK39200 and WMQ Version 6 APAR PK42616 have been shipped to provide support for the new CICS-MQ Adapter in CICS Transaction Server Version 3.2. When WMQ is connected with a CICS Transaction Server Version 3.2 system, the CICS shipped versions of the CICS-WMQ adapter, the CICS-WMQ trigger monitor and the CICS-WMQ bridge must be used. The WMQ APARs ensure that the WMQ shipped versions of the components are immediately terminated if executed when WMQ is connected with a CICS Transaction Server Version 3.2 system. In this circumstance message CSQC330E will be written to the CICS system log and to the CSMT transient data destination.

> **Note:** WMQ will continue to ship its original version of the CICS-WMQ attachment mechanism for use with CICS Transaction Server Version 3.1 and earlier.

7.3.3 Required CICS, DB2 and WMQ product maintenance

Before implementing threadsafe applications you should review and apply the product maintenance listed in Appendix A, "CICS, DB2, and WMQ maintenance" on page 317. Several APARs have been generated to improve performance and system stability. Therefore you should not attempt to run CICS Transaction Server without these APARs.

7.3.4 DB2 system parameters

The CTHREAD parameter, also listed as MAX USERS, is a DB2 subsystem tuning parameter that defines the maximum number of threads that can be concurrently allocated to a DB2 subsystem from any source except for DDF. Since CICS is just one possible front end to DB2, you need to ensure that the value you set for TCBLIMIT is well below the CTHREAD threshold. This parameter is relevant to all currently supported releases of CICS Transaction Server. However, if you have not checked this parameter before, you may want to check with your DB2 support team.

These parameters are set in the DB2 ZPARM.

7.3.5 WMQ system parameters

The CTHREAD parameter is a WMQ subsystem tuning parameter that specifies the total number of threads that can connect to a queue manager. This includes batch, TSO, IMS and CICS.

Prior to CICS Transaction Server Version 3.2, each CICS region took up nine of the threads specified here, plus one thread for each task initiator (CKTI). This is because the original CICS-WMQ attachment mechanism utilized a pool of eight subtask TCBs. In CICS Transaction Server Version 3.2, there is no such hard-coded number of TCBs used for the CICS-WMQ attachment; TCBs are allocated from the OTE pool of L8 TCBs, subject to availability and the limitation set by MAXOPENTCBS. Therefore, to account for the extra threads of work resulting from CICS Transaction Server Version 3.2, the CTHREAD parameter may need to be increased to a higher value.

These parameters are set by the WMQ SET SYSTEM command.

7.3.6 CICS system parameters

To effectively enable threadsafe applications you have to set or tune several CICS system parameters. The parameters described in this section are located in different areas within CICS, and some can be dynamically altered via CEMT commands.

We review each parameter, give you guidelines to start with, indicate where it is defined, and, if possible, show you how to override it.

SIT Parm: MXT

This is not directly a threadsafe-related parameter, but it comes into play when setting your MAXOPENTCBS and TCBLIMIT parameters. If you are running with transaction isolation turned on you should make MAXOPENTCBS greater than or equal to MXT to prevent possible TCB stealing.

Set in the SIT or SYSIN.

Overridden via CEMT SET SYSTEM.

SIT Parm: MAXOPENTCBS

The MAXOPENTCBS parameter sets the maximum number of L8 and L9 TCBs allowed for the CICS region. See 2.6.1, "MAXOPENTCBS" on page 31, for information to assist setting this parameter.

Set in the SIT or SYSIN.

Overridden via CEMT SET DISPATCHER.

> **Note:** MAXOPENTCBS should always be set greater than or equal to TCBLIMIT. Additionally, when running with transaction isolation turned on, MAXOPENTCBS should be set equal to or higher than MXT.

DB2CONN Parm: TCBLIMIT

TCBLIMIT specifies the maximum number of TCBs that can be used to run DB2(R) threads. It is a subset of the MAXOPENTCBS parameter described previously.

Set in the DB2CONN RDO definition.

Overridden via CEMT SET DB2CONN.

> **Note:** Your TCBLIMIT must be greater than or equal to the total of all your THREADLIMIT parameters.

DB2CONN Parm: THREADLIMIT

The DB2CONN THREADLIMIT specifies the maximum number of active DB2 threads for the pool.

Set in the DB2CONN RDO definition.

Overridden via CEMT SET DB2CONN.

DB2ENTRY Parm: THREADLIMIT

The DB2ENTRY THREADLIMIT specifies the maximum number of active DB2 threads for a specific transaction or group of transactions.

Set in the DB2ENTRY RDO definition.

Overridden via CEMT SET DB2ENTRY.

In general you will start at the top of the preceding list, make sure DB2 and WMQ can handle your thread volume, then move up into CICS, set your MXT to the total number of active tasks that can run in your CICS region, and then set your limit for open TCBs via the MAXOPENTCBS parameter.

Furthermore, for DB2, you can then use TCBLIMIT to throttle the number of L8 TCBs used from the MAXOPENTCBS pool. Also ensure that your DB2 Entry and Pool THREADLIMITs total up to a value less than or equal to your TCBLIMIT.

Note that there are also the MAXSSLTCBS, MAXJVMTCBS, and MAXXPTCBS parameters relating to the other types of open TCBs used by OTE. These are not directly relevant when implementing a threadsafe environment in CICS. However, they are important from the overall CICS system programming perspective.

There are two further CICS system parameters that are related to threadsafety:

SIT Parm: FORCEQR

FORCEQR is at first confusing because most people think that it allows you to turn off TCB switching, which is not true, nor is it possible. The FORCEQR parameter is really only used as an emergency stopgap to shift programs back onto the QR TCB to provide resource serialization in the event that you realize that your supposedly threadsafe programs are in fact not threadsafe with respect to data integrity.

FORCEQR overrides all API(CICSAPI),CONCURRENCY(THREADSAFE) program definitions in the CICS region so that they all run as though defined as API(CICSAPI),CONCURRENCY(QUASIRENT).

FORCEQR will not affect the fact that the CICS-DB2 and CICS-WMQ attachment facilities now use L8 TCBs. All DB2 and WMQ calls run on an L8 TCB. FORCEQR will just ensure that you swap back to the QR TCB when returning to the application.

Set in the SIT or SYSIN.

Overridden via CEMT SET SYSTEM.

> **Note:** A change to the FORCEQR parm does not affect programs already running. New tasks that start will use the new FORCEQR setting, but there will be a delay for long-running tasks to pick up the change.
>
> The FORCEQR parameter does not affect API(OPENAPI),CONCURRENCY(THREADSAFE) programs because these *must* run on an open TCB.

SIT Parm: FCQRONLY

FCQRONLY forces CICS Transaction Server Version 3.2 to execute file control requests under the QR TCB, in the same manner as they were in prior releases of CICS. By default, these commands are now threadsafe and so will execute under an open TCB if an application were running under an L8 or L9 TCB at the time a file control command was issued. FCQRONLY also bypasses some of the shared storage locking and concurrency implementations that are required for threadsafe file control support. FCQRONLY defaults to NO. It is provided as a means of deactivating threadsafe file control support for those environments that may choose to do so, perhaps during application testing or validation.

> **Note:** The default for the FCQRONLY parameter will be changed in APAR PK45354. With this APAR the default is now FCQRONLY=YES.

Set in the SIT or SYSIN.

Overridden via CEMT SET SYSTEM.

7.4 Providing a threadsafe CICS operating environment

Now that you have checked each region to make sure that you are running the proper software and have reviewed the system parameters, let us take a look at the major part of the CICS system programmer's conversion process.

7.4.1 CICS exits

Global user exits (GLUEs) are the primary area of concern for the system programmer since a poorly tuned CICS subsystem can experience a performance degradation due to excessive TCB switching caused by non threadsafe exits. To get a better idea of your objective, it can be simplified by saying that all global user exits should be made threadsafe before migrating to CICS Transaction Server Version 2 or later.

With the exploitation of OTE in CICS Transaction Server Version 2.2 and later, the switchover to an L8 TCB happens earlier in the processing of a DB2 request than the switchover to the subtask TCB in pre-CICS Transaction Server Version 2.2 releases. Therefore all your exits now run, or try to run, on L8 TCBs. If you have not converted your GLUEs and defined them as CONCURRENCY(THREADSAFE), then invocation of your exit programs will cause a switchback to the QR TCB for processing and then immediately return back to the L8 TCB to continue processing the DB2 call. This can generate a TCB thrashing effect that results in poor performance.

The same effect is true for exit programs driven during calls to WMQ in CICS Transaction Server Version 3.2.

The design of CICS forces CICSAPI application programs and exit programs to react differently. When an exit program is swapped back to the QR TCB for processing, it always swaps back to the L8 TCB on return. Then if your application program encounters a non threadsafe CICS command, it again swaps back to the QR TCB, but unlike the exits, threadsafe application programs stay on the QR TCB until another call to an OTE-enabled TRUE such as DB2 or WMQ is encountered. (Note that in CICS Transaction Server Version 3, OPENAPI programs are treated in a similar manner to exits in this respect, since they always receive control back under their open TCB, if they happen to invoke non threadsafe commands that require switching to the QR TCB for processing).

Figure 7-6 on page 146 shows the flow of a DB2 call from a threadsafe CICSAPI program, showing how the GLUEs cause processing to bounce between the QR TCB and an L8 TCB.

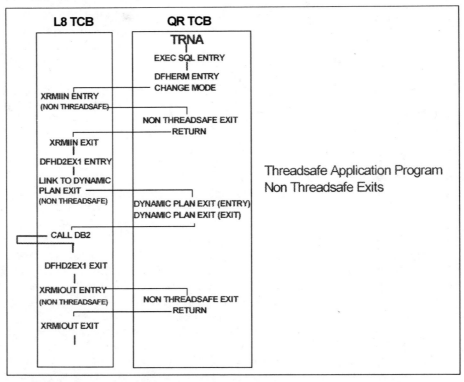

Figure 7-6   Exit flow between the QR and L8 TCBs

The preceding flow shows the application program starting execution on the QR TCB when a DB2 call is encountered and execution is swapped over to an L8 TCB to process the DB2 call. Once on the L8 TCB, the XRMIIN exit is encountered, and due to it being non threadsafe, its processing is swapped back over to the QR TCB. When the XRMIIN exit is complete the process flow is returned to the L8 TCB. CICS will always return back to the TCB where the exit was invoked.

Processing continues on the L8 TCB until the dynamic plan exit is invoked, at which point processing is again swapped back to the QR TCB. On completion of the dynamic plan exit, processing is swapped back onto the L8 TCB to make the actual DB2 call.

Once the DB2 call is complete the XRMIOUT exit is invoked and processing swaps over to the QR TCB to process the exit and then back to the L8 TCB after the exit is complete. At this point all processing would continue on the L8 TCB until either the program terminates, a non threadsafe command is encountered, or a non threadsafe exit is encountered.

Figure 7-6 on page 146 is an example of the switching that might be encountered for exits on the path of a DB2 call. In the case of calls to WMQ in CICS Transaction Server Version 3.2, the same principles apply now that the CICS-MQ Adapter is an OTE-enabled TRUE as well. For WMQ, there is not a dynamic plan exit, but there is the API crossing exit CSQCAPX instead. Note that this is defined as threadsafe in the program definition as supplied in CICS Transaction Server Version 3.2. This means that (by default) the supplied version of CSQCAPX is threadsafe, so if it is active it will not result in a switch back from the L8 to the QR TCB for the link to the CICS-WMQ API crossing exit. Should this exit be changed, take care to ensure that any alterations to its logic are implemented in a threadsafe manner.

Now that we understand that non threadsafe exits are the cause of extra switching in the threadsafe zone, we can start the analysis and conversion process. The preceding discussion has highlighted the fact that the XRMIIN, XRMIOUT, DB2 dynamic plan exit, and CICS-WMQ API crossing exit are key exits to review. Note also that any EXEC CICS command will potentially drive exit programs defined to run at the XEIIN and XEIOUT exit points. Finally, CICS Transaction Server Version 3.2 now provides the EXEC CICS file control commands as threadsafe, so exits invoked from within file control should also be reviewed for potential TCB switching activity. This means analysis of the XFCREQ and XFCREQC exit points.

Additionally, any EXEC CICS calls made in one of the key exit programs may pull in other exits such as XEIIN, XEIOUT, XPCFTCH, or XTSQRIN. Therefore all exits that get invoked during the execution path of a DB2 or WMQ call, or an EXEC CICS file control request, need to be converted to be threadsafe to eliminate a TCB switching.

7.4.2 Analyzing your exits

The first thing you need to do is identify what exits (TRUEs, GLUEs, and dynamic plan exits) are in your system and determine whether they need any modifications to the code or their definition to make them threadsafe. If you are extremely lucky you have no exits and can skip the rest of this section and move on to converting the applications themselves, but those are only a lucky few.

Tools used to identify your exits

The easiest way to get a picture of what exits (TRUEs, GLUEs, and dynamic plan exits) are running in your CICS region is to use the DFH0STAT utility shipped with CICS. Running the STAT transaction generates a report that lists all your TRUE and GLUE exits along with a listing of your DB2 Pool and Entry resources.

You can use the report to identify what exits you have and if they are defined as THREADSAFE or QUASIRENT. The report also helps you identify whether your system exits are using a global work area, which could be a shared resource.

For information on CSQCAPX (the CICS-WMQ API crossing exit), use CEMT or equivalent to review its program definition CONCURRENCY attribute. As mentioned previously, as provided it is defined as threadsafe and written to threadsafe standards. The name of the crossing exit is fixed and cannot be changed. The CKQC display panel will show whether it is active or not.

> **Note:** A shared global work area could be utilized as a non-serialized shared resource and therefore classify your exit program as non threadsafe, in which case you would be required to add serialization techniques to your code. Later we discuss how to serialize shared resources.

7.4.3 Running DFH0STAT

Ensure that the CSD group DFH$STAT has been installed, then run the STAT transaction to get the main menu for DFH0STAT (Figure 7-7).

```
Sample Program - CICS Statistics Print                    07/20/2007 13:10:00

Type in destination fields if required. Press Enter to print

     Jobname. . . : SCSCPJA6
     Applid . . . : SCSCPJA6
     Sysid. . . . : PJA6

     Node . . . . . *           Type in a valid Node. * is default
     Userid . . . . *           Type in a valid Userid. * is default
     Class. . . . . A           Type in a valid Class. A is default

     Abbreviated. . B           Type U or N for abbreviated report. B is default

Current Statistics Settings

     Statistics Recording. : OFF       Collection Interval . . . : 03:00:00
     Last Reset Time . . . : 00:00:00  Elapsed Time Since Reset. : 13:10:00
     Next Collection . . . : 00:00:00  End-of-Day Time . . . . . : 00:00:00


F1=Help F2=Refresh F3=Exit **F4=Report Selection** F5=Print
```

Figure 7-7 Initial CICS STAT/DFH0STAT screen

Using the PF4 key, access the report selection menu (Figure 7-8).

```
Sample Program - CICS Statistics Print Report Selection         07/20/2007 13:10:00

Select the statistics reports required and press 'Enter' to validate

   DB2 Connection . . . . . . . . . . . Y    WebSphere MQ Connection. . . . . . N
   DB2 Entries. . . . . . . . . . . . . Y    Program Autoinstall. . . . . . . . N
                                              Terminal Autoinstall and VTAM. . . N
   JVM Pool and Class Cache . . . . . N      Connections and Modenames. . . . . N
   JVMs . . . . . . . . . . . . . . . N
   JVM Profiles . . . . . . . . . . . N      TCP/IP . . . . . . . . . . . . . . N
   JVM Programs . . . . . . . . . . . N      TCP/IP Services. . . . . . . . . . N
                                              URIMAPs. . . . . . . . . . . . . . N
   CorbaServers and DJARs . . . . . . N      Virtual Hosts. . . . . . . . . . . N
   DJARs and Enterprise Beans . . . . N      PIPELINEs. . . . . . . . . . . . . N
   Requestmodels. . . . . . . . . . . N      WEBSERVICEs. . . . . . . . . . . . N
   EJB System Data Sets . . . . . . . N      Document Templates . . . . . . . . N

   Trace Settings and Levels. . . . . N      Recovery Manager . . . . . . . . . N
   User Exit Programs . . . . . . . . Y      Enqueue Manager. . . . . . . . . . N
   Global User Exits. . . . . . . . . Y      Enqueue Models . . . . . . . . . . N


   F1=Help     F3=Return to Print     F7=Back       F10=Save       F12=Restore
```

Figure 7-8   DFH0STAT report selection menu

Select the **DB2 Connection and Entries** and the **User Exit Pgms/Global User Exits** report with a Y and press Enter, then PF3 to return to the main menu. Press Enter to print your report.

Example 7-1 on page 150 is a sample of the Exit Programs and Global User Exits sections of the DFH0STAT report.

Example 7-1   Output from the DFH0STAT utility showing the exits reports

```
Exit Programs
```

Program Name	Entry Name	Global Area Entry Name	Length	Use Count	No. of Exits	Program Status	API	Concurrency Status	Qual- ifier	Task Area Length	Task Related User Exit Task start	EDF	Shut down	Indoubt	SPI
DFHEDP	DLI		0	0	0	Started	Cics	Quasi Rent		284	No	No	No	No Wait	No
DFHD2EX1	DSNCSQL	DSNCSQL	16	1	0	Started	Open	Thread Safe	D7Q2	222	No	Yes	Yes	Wait	Yes
DFHMQTRU	MQM	MQM	32	1	0	Started	Open	Thread Safe	MQ8G	224	No	No	Yes	Wait	Yes
XXXEI	XXXEI		0	0	2	Started	Cics	Quasi Rent		0	No	No	No	No Wait	No
XXXRMI	XXXRMI		0	0	2	Started	Cics	Quasi Rent		0	No	No	No	No Wait	No
XXXTS	XXXTS	XXXTS	64	1	1	Started	Cics	Quasi Rent		0	No	No	No	No Wait	No

```
Global User Exits
```

Exit Name	Program Name	Entry Name	Global Area Entry Name	Length	Use Count	Number of Exits	Program Status
XTSQRIN	XXXTS	XXXTS	XXXTS	64	1	1	Started
XEIIN	XXXEI	XXXEI		0	0	2	Started
XEIOUT	XXXEI	XXXEI		0	0	2	Started
XRMIIN	XXXRMI	XXXRMI		0	0	2	Started
XRMIOUT	XXXRMI	XXXRMI		0	0	2	Started

The first section of the report, Exit Programs lists the exit programs in the system. The Concurrency Status column shows the concurrency setting for each program.

The other item of interest is the Global Area section of the exit programs or global user exits reports. The Use Count column identifies whether an exit is using a global work area.

In our sample report in Example 7-1, we have exits XTSQRIN, XEIIN, XEIOUT, XRMIIN, and XRMIOUT in use. Of those, exit XTSQRIN has a global work area in use, which could be a shared resource, as identified by the Length and Use Count fields being 64 and 1, respectively.

The User Exit Programs and Global User Exits reports identify your exits. Note, however, that the dynamic plan exit is not defined as a CICS exit. Therefore you need to search the DB2 connection and DB2 entries reports to identify and list all DB2 dynamic plan exits.

The same is true for the CICS-WMQ API crossing exit CSQCAPX. It is not defined as a CICS exit either, and so should be investigated using, for example, CEMT, CKQC, and so forth.

The sample DFH0STAT report in Example 7-2 shows a pool dynamic plan exit called PLANEXIT in use and an entry definition for MIG also using the same dynamic plan exit. Unfortunately, the DFH0STAT report does not indicate whether PLANEXIT is defined as threadsafe or Quasirent. You need to issue a CEMT I PROG to determine its status.

Example 7-2   Output from the DFH0STAT utility showing the DB2 resources

```
DB2 Connection

    DB2 Connection Name. . . . . . . . . . . :  DB2F
    DB2 Sysid. . . . . . . . . . . . . . . . :  D7Q2
    DB2 Release. . . . . . . . . . . . . . . :  7.1.0
    DB2 Connection Status. . . . . . . . . . :  CONNECTED        DB2 Connect™ Date and Time . . . :  05/12/2004  09:47:01.38478
    DB2 Connection Error . . . . . . . . . . :  SQLCODE
    DB2 Standby Mode . . . . . . . . . . . . :  RECONNECT
    DB2 Pool Thread Plan Name. . . . . . . . :
    DB2 Pool Thread Dynamic Plan Exit Name . :  PLANEXIT
    Pool Thread Authtype . . . . . . . . . . :  SIGNID
    Pool Thread Authid . . . . . . . . . . . :
    Command Thread Authtype. . . . . . . . . :  USERID
    Command Thread Authid. . . . . . . . . . :
    Signid for Pool/Entry/Command Threads. . :  CICSTS
    Create Thread Error. . . . . . . . . . . :  N906D            Message TD Queue 1. . . . . . . . . . . :  CDB2
    Protected Thread Purge Cycle . . . . . . :  00.30            Message TD Queue 2. . . . . . . . . . . :
    Deadlock Resolution. . . . . . . . . . . :  ROLLBACK         Message TD Queue 3. . . . . . . . . . . :
    Non-Terminal Intermediate Syncpoint. . . :  RELEASE
    Pool Thread Wait Setting . . . . . . . . :  WAIT             Statistics TD Queue . . . . . . . . . . :  CDB2
    Pool Thread Priority . . . . . . . . . . :  LOW              DB2 Accounting records by . . . . . . . :  NONE
    Current TCB Limit. . . . . . . . . . . .    130
    Current number of TCBs . . . . . . . . .    110
    Peak number of TCBs. . . . . . . . . . .    110
    Current number of free TCBs. . . . . . .    108
    Current number of tasks on TCB Readyq. .      0
    Peak number of tasks on TCB Readyq . . .      0
    Pool Thread Limit. . . . . . . . . . . .      5              Number of Calls using Pool Threads. . . :       0
    Current number of Pool Threads . . . . .      0              Number of Pool Thread Signons . . . . . :       0
    Peak number of Pool Threads. . . . . . .      0              Number of Pool Thread Commits . . . . . :       0
    Number of Pool Thread Waits. . . . . . .      0              Number of Pool Thread Aborts. . . . . . :       0
                                                                 Number of Pool Thread Single Phase. . . :       0
    Current number of Pool Tasks . . . . . .      0              Number of Pool Thread Reuses. . . . . . :       0
    Peak number of Pool Tasks. . . . . . . .      0              Number of Pool Thread Terminates. . . . :       0
    Current Total number of Pool Tasks . . .      0
    Current number of Tasks on Pool Readyq .      0
    Peak number of Tasks on Pool Readyq. . .      0
    Current number of DSNC Command threads .      0              Number of DSNC Command Calls. . . . . . :       0
    Peak number of DSNC Command threads. . .      0              Number of DSNC Command Signons. . . . . :       0
    DSNC Command Thread Limit. . . . . . . .      1              Number of DSNC Command Thread Terminates:       0
                                                                 Number of DSNC Command Thread Overflows :       0

DB2 Entries

    DB2Entry Name. . . . . . . . . . . . . . :  MIG              DB2Entry Status . . . . . . . . . . . . :  ENABLED
    DB2Entry Static Plan Name. . . . . . . . :                   DB2Entry Disabled Action. . . . . . . . :  POOL
    DB2Entry Dynamic Plan Exit Name. . . . . :  PLANEXIT         DB2Entry Deadlock Resolution. . . . . . :  ROLLBACK
    DB2Entry Authtype. . . . . . . . . . . . :  SIGNID           DB2Entry Accounting records by. . . . . :  NONE
    DB2Entry Authid. . . . . . . . . . . . . :
                                                                 Number of Calls using DB2Entry. . . . . :  2,139,282
    DB2Entry Thread Wait Setting . . . . . . :  POOL             Number of DB2Entry Signons. . . . . . . :          0
                                                                 Number of DB2Entry Commits. . . . . . . :          0
    DB2Entry Thread Priority . . . . . . . . :  LOW              Number of DB2Entry Aborts . . . . . . . :          0
    DB2Entry Thread Limit. . . . . . . . . . :    120            Number of DB2Entry Single Phase . . . . :      2,140
    Current number of DB2Entry Threads . . . :      1            Number of DB2Entry Thread Reuses. . . . :      2,140
    Peak number of DB2Entry Threads. . . . . :      2            Number of DB2Entry Thread Terminates. . :          0
                                                                 Number of DB2Entry Thread Waits/Overflows:         0
    DB2Entry Protected Thread Limit. . . . . :    120
    Current number of DB2Entry Protected Threads . . :   1
    Peak number of DB2Entry Protected Threads. . . . :   2
    Current number of DB2Entry Tasks . . . . . . . . :   1
    Peak number of DB2Entry Tasks. . . . . . . . . . :   2
    Current Total number of DB2Entry Tasks . . . . . : 2,141
    Current number of Tasks on DB2Entry Readyq . . . :   0
    Peak number of Tasks on DB2Entry Readyq. . . . . :   0
```

7.4.4 Which exits need to be reviewed

Previously we stated that all system exits must be threadsafe before migrating to CICS Transaction Server Version 2 or later. Actually, the word *all* is a little bit strong. You cannot go wrong if you review all your exits, but the real answer is that exits in the DB2 and WMQ call path must be converted to be threadsafe, along with those exits driven during the processing of threadsafe EXEC CICS commands, in particular those for heavily used API options such as EXEC CICS file control requests.

The DFH0STAT report helps you identify which exits are in your system. However, you may have many and may not be sure which ones need to be converted. A good way to determine which exits are actually in the DB2, WMQ, or EXEC CICS file control command path is to turn on a CICS Auxiliary Trace for a specific DB2, WMQ, or file control application program and review the trace for that one transaction, making notes of all the TCB switching and identifying which exits were involved.

The following CICS Auxiliary Trace shows a typical TCB switch (change mode) from the QR to the L8 TCB to process a DB2 call.

Example 7-3 Sample CICS Auxiliary Trace output for a single TASK

```
04488 QR       AP 00E1 EIP    EXIT  ASKTIME                   OK
04488 QR       AP 2520 ERM    ENTRY ASSEMBLER-APPLICATION-CALL-TO-TRUE(DSNCSQL )
04488 QR       US 0401 USXM   ENTRY INQUIRE_TRANSACTION_USER
04488 QR       US 0402 USXM   EXIT  INQUIRE_TRANSACTION_USER/OK 00000000
04488 QR       RM 0301 RMLN   ENTRY ADD_LINK                  RMI,2302E1E4 , 01010101 ,
04488 QR       RM 0302 RMLN   EXIT  ADD_LINK/OK               0111005A,2302E1E4 , 010101
04488 QR       DS 0002 DSAT   ENTRY CHANGE_MODE         L8    Example 7-4 on page 153
04488 QR       DS 0018 DSDS4  ENTRY ALLOC_OPEN                1,22E4A060
04488 QR       DS 0019 DSDS4  EXIT  ALLOC_OPEN/OK
DSTCB QR       DS 0016 DSDS3  ENTRY PARTITION_EXIT            21D03030
DSTCB QR       DS 0032 DSDS3  EVENT DSDS3_SCAN_HAND_POSTABLES
DSTCB QR       DS 0022 DSDS3  EVENT MVS_WAIT_ENTRY
04488 L8014    DS 0003 DSAT   EXIT  CHANGE_MODE/OK
04488 L8014    AP D500 UEH    EVENT LINK-TO-USER-EXIT-PROGRAM TSTXEII AT EXIT POINT XRMIIN
04488 L8014    DS 0002 DSAT   ENTRY CHANGE_MODE         QR
DSTCB L8014    DS 0016 DSDS3  ENTRY PARTITION_EXIT            23133148
DSTCB L8014    DS 0022 DSDS3  EVENT MVS_WAIT_ENTRY
DSTCB QR       DS 0023 DSDS3  EVENT MVS_WAIT_EXIT
DSTCB QR       DS 0017 DSDS3  EXIT  PARTITION_EXIT/OK
DSTCB QR       DS 0042 DSTCB  EVENT TRACE_DOUBLE_CHAIN_GET
04488 QR       DS 0003 DSAT   EXIT  CHANGE_MODE/OK
04488 QR       AP D501 UEH    EVENT RETURN-FROM-USER-EXIT-PROGRAM TSTXEII WITH RETURN CODE 0
04488 QR       DS 0002 DSAT   ENTRY CHANGE_MODE         L8
DSTCB QR       DS 0032 DSDS3  EVENT DSDS3_SCAN_HAND_POSTABLES
DSTCB QR       DS 0022 DSDS3  EVENT MVS_WAIT_ENTRY
DSTCB QR       DS 0016 DSDS3  ENTRY PARTITION_EXIT            21D03030
DSTCB L8014    DS 0023 DSDS3  EVENT MVS_WAIT_EXIT
DSTCB L8014    DS 0017 DSDS3  EXIT  PARTITION_EXIT/OK
DSTCB L8014    DS 0042 DSTCB  EVENT TRACE_DOUBLE_CHAIN_GET
04488 L8014    DS 0003 DSAT   EXIT  CHANGE_MODE/OK
04488 L8014    AP 3180 D2EX1  ENTRY APPLICATION               REQUEST EXEC SQL SELECT
```

In the preceding example, the program is running on the QR TCB when it performs a DB2 call and then it jumps to an L8 TCB. It then encounters a non threadsafe exit and jumps back to the QR TCB to run it. Upon completion of the exit it returns back to the L8 TCB to process the application's SQL request.

7.4.5 Identifying exits in the DB2, WMQ, and file control call paths

The technique to find exits that are invoked during the DB2, WMQ, or file control call path is to turn on a CICS Auxiliary Trace, then search the output report looking for CHANGE_MODE entry records to the QR TCB followed by RETURN-FROM-USER-EXIT-PROGRAM events and make a note of the exit that was involved.

You may have to make several iterations of your report, for example, turn on your CICS Auxiliary Trace for a short time, run a general report, then look for the CHANGE_MODE records. Then pick one task and re-run the report for that single task only to eliminate extraneous report records and then use the following technique.

The following CICS Auxiliary Trace snippet, an excerpt from the Auxiliary Trace sample in Example 7-3 on page 152, shows a task already running on the L8 TCB linking to exit TSTXEII and then issuing a CHANGE_MODE to the QR TCB.

Shortly after the change mode to the QR TCB you see a few trace records on the QR TCB. One of them is the RETURN-FROM-USER-EXIT-PROGRAM event record showing a return from TSTXEII.

Example 7-4 CICS Auxiliary Trace entries showing the return from an exit

```
04488 L8014 AP D500 UEH    EVENT LINK-TO-USER-EXIT-PROGRAM TSTXEII AT EXIT POINT XRMIIN
04488 L8014 DS 0002 DSAT   ENTRY CHANGE_MODE            QR
DSTCB L8014 DS 0016 DSDS3  ENTRY PARTITION_EXIT         23133148
DSTCB L8014 DS 0022 DSDS3  EVENT MVS_WAIT_ENTRY
DSTCB QR    DS 0023 DSDS3  EVENT MVS_WAIT_EXIT
DSTCB QR    DS 0017 DSDS3  EXIT  PARTITION_EXIT/OK
DSTCB QR    DS 0042 DSTCB  EVENT TRACE_DOUBLE_CHAIN_GET
04488 QR    DS 0003 DSAT   EXIT  CHANGE_MODE/OK
04488 QR    AP D501 UEH    EVENT RETURN-FROM-USER-EXIT-PROGRAM TSTXEII WITH
04488 QR    DS 0002 DSAT   ENTRY CHANGE_MODE            L8
```

These four trace records in this sequence mean that you just invoked a non threadsafe exit, TSTXEII. You can now add TSTXEII to your list of exits you are going to review.

You will need to repeatedly perform the preceding process to identify all your exits in the DB2 or WMQ call paths, and EXEC CICS file control operations.

> **Note:** For CICS Transaction Server Version 2.3, APAR PQ78987 introduced a performance change to eliminate all CHANGE_MODE trace records from DS level 1 traces, and instead write them when DS Level 2 tracing is active.
>
> APAR PQ89845 further refined this for CICS Transaction Server Version 2.3 so the trace entries are written when either DS Level 2 or DS Level 3 trace is active. Both these changes are present at the base code level for CICS Transaction Server Version 3.
>
> If you are not getting any CHANGE_MODE trace records then use CETR to turn on DS Level 2 or Level 3 tracing.

7.4.6 Identifying dynamic plan exits in the DB2 call path

To identify the dynamic plan exits in the DB2 call path, we again use the CICS Auxiliary Trace output.

The following Auxiliary Trace sample, Example 7-5, shows the invocation of a dynamic plan exit called DB2PLAN. Notice that we are already on an L8 TCB, as seen by the second column containing L8000, which is the name of the TCB. Therefore we are in the middle of the DB2 call path.

Example 7-5 Auxiliary Trace showing invocation of a Dynamic Plan exit DB2PLAN

```
00258 L8000 AP 3180 D2EX1 ENTRY APPLICATION            REQUEST EXEC SQL SELECT
00258 L8000 PG 0A01 PGLU  ENTRY LINK_URM               DB2PLAN,22BE7678 , 0000001C,NO,NO
00258 L8000 DD 0301 DDLO  ENTRY LOCATE                 21C27B70,22BE7574,PPT,DB2PLAN
00258 L8000 DD 0302 DDLO  EXIT  LOCATE/OK              D7D7E3C5 , 22DA5B88
00258 L8000 LD 0001 LDLD  ENTRY ACQUIRE_PROGRAM        22C87258
00258 L8000 LD 0002 LDLD  EXIT  ACQUIRE_PROGRAM/OK     A43002D8,243002B0,D8,0,REUSABLE,ESDSA,OLD_COPY
00258 L8000 AP 1940 APLI  ENTRY START_PROGRAM          DB2PLAN,CEDF,FULLAPI,URM,NO,22F89C10,22BE7678
00258 L8000 DS 0002 DSAT  ENTRY CHANGE_MODE            QR
00258 QR    DS 0003 DSAT  EXIT  CHANGE_MODE/OK
00258 QR    SM 0C01 SMMG  ENTRY GETMAIN                190,YES,00,TASK
00258 QR    SM 0C02 SMMG  EXIT  GETMAIN/OK             226E1788
00258 QR    AP 00E1 EIP   ENTRY RETURN 0004,226E1798   .>.q,08000E08 ....
00258 QR    AP E160 EXEC  ENTRY RETURN                 ASM
00258 QR    SM 0301 SMGF  ENTRY FREEMAIN               226E1788,TASK
00258 QR    SM 0302 SMGF  EXIT  FREEMAIN/OK
00258 QR    AP 1941 APLI  EXIT  START_PROGRAM/OK       ....,NO,DB2PLAN
00258 QR    LD 0001 LDLD  ENTRY RELEASE_PROGRAM        22C87258,A43002D8
00258 QR    LD 0002 LDLD  EXIT  RELEASE_PROGRAM/OK     243002B0,D8,ESDSA
00258 QR    DS 0002 DSAT  ENTRY CHANGE_MODE            L8
00258 L8000 DS 0003 DSAT  EXIT  CHANGE_MODE/OK         QR
00258 L8000 PG 0A02 PGLU  EXIT  LINK_URM/OK
00258 L8000 AP 3250 D2D2  ENTRY DB2_API_CALL           230D7030
00258 L8000 AP 3251 D2D2  EXIT  DB2_API_CALL/OK
00258 L8000 AP 3181 D2EX1 EXIT  APPLICATION-REQUEST    SQLCODE 0 RETURNED ON EXEC SQL SELECT
00258 L8000 MN 0201 MNMN  ENTRY ACCUMULATE_RMI_TIME    DSNCSQL
```

As part of invoking the dynamic plan exit, DB2PLAN, CICS detects that the exit is not threadsafe and immediately switches to the QR TCB, and upon return from the dynamic plan exit it switches back to the L8 TCB.

The following three CICS Auxiliary Trace snippets, pulled from the AUX Trace sample in Example 7-5 on page 154, shows a task already running on an L8 TCB that invokes a user replaceable module (URM), in this case our dynamic plan exit DB2PLAN.

Shortly after the LINK_URM record we see CICS starting program DB2PLAN and then detecting that it is not threadsafe, causing a switch to the QR TCB.

Example 7-6   Auxiliary Trace entries showing

```
00258 L8000 PG 0A01 PGLU  ENTRY LINK_URM            DB2PLAN,22BE7678 , 0000001C,NO,NO
00258 L8000 DD 0301 DDLO  ENTRY LOCATE              21C27B70,22BE7574,PPT,DB2PLAN
00258 L8000 DD 0302 DDLO  EXIT  LOCATE/OK           D7D7E3C5 , 22DA5B88
00258 L8000 LD 0001 LDLD  ENTRY ACQUIRE_PROGRAM     22C87258
00258 L8000 LD 0002 LDLD  EXIT  ACQUIRE_PROGRAM/OK  A43002D8,243002B0,D8,0,REUSABLE,ESDSA,OLD_COPY
00258 L8000 AP 1940 APLI  ENTRY START_PROGRAM       DB2PLAN,CEDF,FULLAPI,URM,NO,
00258 L8000 DS 0002 DSAT  ENTRY CHANGE_MODE         QR
```

The sequence of trace records shown in Example 7-6 identifies all your dynamic plan exits in the DB2 call path.

You can now add DB2PLAN to your list of exits you are going to review.

You will need to repeatedly perform this process to identify all your dynamic plan exits in the DB2 call path.

7.4.7 Contacting the owner of vendor product exits

If you have various monitors and debugging products installed, you may see their product exits in the DB2 and WMQ call paths. If so, you need to contact the product vendor directly to have them determine the exit's threadsafe status and make adjustments according to their recommendations.

7.5 Making your exits threadsafe

Now that you have identified what exits are in your system and reviewed their source code for potential code changes it is time to make the code adjustments to make them threadsafe.

The steps required to make your programs threadsafe are:
1. Serialize shared resources.
2. Change your exit programs CONCURRENCY definition to THREADSAFE.

Additionally, we recommend removing non threadsafe EXEC CICS commands if possible. While the existence of such commands in the exit does not make the exit non threadsafe, it will cause additional TCB switching, which should be avoided if at all possible. This is especially important for exits that are invoked on the mainline DB2 and WMQ call paths.

7.5.1 Remove non threadsafe commands

For those exit programs that run at exit points where CICS allows use of the CICS command-level API, review your exit code for use of EXEC CICS commands that would cause a switch to the QR TCB. Consider ways of eliminating use of these commands. Can an XPI command be used instead? For a complete list of threadsafe commands, see these publications:

- Appendix L, "Threadsafe Command List," in the *CICS Application Programming Reference*, SC34-6232, for CICS Transaction Server Version 2, and *CICS Application Programming Reference,* SC34-6434, for CICS Transaction Server Version 3.
- Appendix D, "Threadsafe SPI commands," in the *CICS System Programming Reference*, SC34-6233, for CICS Transaction Server Version 2, and *CICS System Programming Reference,* SC34-6435, for CICS Transaction Server Version 3.
- Appendix G, "Threadsafe XPI commands," in the *CICS Customization Guide*, SC34-6227, for CICS Transaction Server Version 2, and *CICS Customization Guide*, SC34-6429, for CICS Transaction Server Version 3.

If your assembler exit program links other high-level language programs then these need to be reviewed and changed as required.

The DFHEISUP utility can be used to search for non threadsafe commands.

7.5.2 Serializing shared resources

This step is a bit more difficult. It basically involves modifying your program code to add serialization techniques around code that is accessing application-shared resources.

The following EXEC CICS commands can be used to access a shared resource and are the key commands to search for in your code:

- ADDRESS CWA
- EXTRACT EXIT
- GETMAIN SHARED

Techniques that you can use to serialize access to your shared storage are:

- Assembler language Compare and Swap instructions
- EXEC CICS ENQ / DEQ commands
- XPI ENQUEUE / DEQUEUE commands

"Serialize access to GWAs" on page 223 walks through the process of converting an exit and shows use of the Compare and Swap instruction to serialize an application shared resource.

Compare and swap techniques

You may have read about using Compare and Swap as one of the possible serialization techniques. You can find more information about Compare and Swap in the manual *z/Architecture Principles of Operations*, SA22-7832.

There are several instructions you can use, and Compare and Swap is one of many. The following is the recommended list from the manual *z/Architecture Principles of Operations*, SA22-7832:

- Compare and Swap
- Compare and Swap and purge
- Compare double and Swap
- Test and set
- Perform locked operation

Additionally, when using one of the preceding techniques you must also pay attention to what instructions you used to load your data initially. In our example code we are using a COMPARE DOUBLE AND SWAP instruction, which acts on two words of data at once. Therefore when we loaded the initial two words of data, there was a small window of opportunity between each individual word being loaded where they could change. The answer, again from the *Principles of Operations* manual, is to use the LOAD MULTIPLE instruction to load your data. It acts like the COMPARE AND SWAP instruction where the storage is locked during the time the instruction executes.

7.5.3 Change your exit program's CONCURRENCY definition to THREADSAFE

In this section we go through a sample exit, running it in both quasirent and threadsafe modes, and making modifications to the code to remove a data integrity issue created by running it in threadsafe mode

Display the program in question via CEMT and if necessary change its definition via CEDA to be threadsafe.

Example 7-7 CEMT display showing both a Quasirent and threadsafe program

```
I PROG(RMIXIT*)
STATUS:  RESULTS - OVERTYPE TO MODIFY
 Prog(RMIXIT  ) Leng(0000000000)        Pro Ena Pri         Ced
       Res(000) Use(0000000000) Any Uex Ful Thr Cic
 Prog(RMIXIT2 ) Leng(0000000000)        Pro Ena Pri         Ced
       Res(000) Use(0000000000) Any Uex Ful Qua Cic
```

In the preceding display program RMIXIT shows up as Thr, which means it is defined to CICS as CONCURRENCY(THREADSAFE), and program RMIXIT2 shows up as Qua, which means it is defined to CICS as CONCURRENCY(QUAISRENT). Note also that the programs are both defined to CICS as API(CICSAPI).

The CEDA definitions for the preceding programs are listed here (Example 7-8).

Example 7-8 Quasirent program RMIXIT2

```
CEDA ALter PROGram( RMIXIT2  )
 PROGram       : RMIXIT2
 Group         : THDSAFEE
 DEscription  ==>
 Language     ==>                   CObol | Assembler | Le370 | C | Pli
 RELoad       ==> No                No | Yes
 RESident     ==> No                No | Yes
 USAge        ==> Normal            Normal | Transient
 USElpacopy   ==> No                No | Yes
 Status       ==> Enabled           Enabled | Disabled
 RSl           : 00                 0-24 | Public
 CEdf         ==> Yes               Yes | No
 DAtalocation ==> Any               Below | Any
 EXECKey      ==> User              User | Cics
 COncurrency  ==> Quasirent         Quasirent | Threadsafe
 Api          ==> Cicsapi           Cicsapi | Openapi
REMOTE ATTRIBUTES
 DYnamic      ==> No                No | Yes
 REMOTESystem ==>
```

Example 7-9   Threadsafe program RMIXIT

```
CEDA  View PROGram( RMIXIT   )
 PROGram        : RMIXIT
 Group          : THDSAFEE
 DEscription    :
 Language       :                    CObol | Assembler | Le370 | C | Pli
 RELoad         : No                 No | Yes
 RESident       : No                 No | Yes
 USAge          : Normal             Normal | Transient
 USElpacopy     : No                 No | Yes
 Status         : Enabled            Enabled | Disabled
 RSl            : 00                 0-24 | Public
 CEdf           : Yes                Yes | No
 DAtalocation   : Any                Below | Any
 EXECKey        : User               User | Cics
 COncurrency    : Threadsafe         Quasirent | Threadsafe
 Api            : Cicsapi            Cicsapi | Openapi
 REMOTE ATTRIBUTES
 DYnamic        : No                 No | Yes
 REMOTESystem   :
```

7.6 Non threadsafe data integrity example

Since data integrity threadsafe exposures are hard to diagnose and find, we give you a short example of an exit that does not serialize a shared global work area and show you the disastrous effects.

A short simple assembler GLUE exit program will be used that shares a global work area (GWA) that simulates a storage chain. The data structure used by the sample exit program is a two-word header containing the next available address of storage to update and a counter of how many updates are being made.

The program reads in the two-word header, bumps the address value in the first word to the next address, and increments the counter in the second word by one. It then saves the header back into the shared storage area and processes the header chain by using the address value to store a word of information. In this example we are exclusive ORing ones into memory so that you can see the changes.

If the storage is serialized then each program picks up then next sequential chain address stored in the header and builds a sequential list of ones and increments the counter by one. When the program fails to serialize the shared storage, the address value gets re-used and instead of ORing ones into the shared storage it can reverse the effect and turn a word of ones into zeros. Therefore, you would see pockets of zeros interspersed throughout the shared storage area. Additionally, the counter will not be incremented sequentially and will have an invalid total.

7.6.1 Sample non threadsafe code example

Example 7-10 shows a GLUE exit program called RMIXIT, which is not threadsafe, as the shared storage is not serialized.

Example 7-10   Sample GLUE with non threadsafe code

```
RMIXIT   DFHEIENT
RMIXIT   AMODE 31
RMIXIT   RMODE ANY
         LR    R2,R1                DFHUEPAR PLIST PROVIDED BY CALLER
         USING DFHUEPAR,R2          ADDRESS UEPAR PLIST
         L     R4,UEPGAA            GET GWA ADDRESS
         LA    R4,12(R4)            BUMP TO A DOUBLE WORD ADDR
         USING GWA,R4               ADDRESSABILITY
*
         L     R6,0(R4)             LOAD SAVED PGM ADDR
         L     R7,4(R4)             LOAD CTR
         LA    R8,4(R6)             BUMP SAVED PGM ADDR BY 4
         LA    R9,1(R7)             BUMP CTR BY 1
         L     R5,LOOPCTR           DELAY LOOP TO GET SOME OVERLAP
LOOP     EQU   *                      SO THAT WE CAN GENERATE SOME
         BCT   R5,LOOP                TCB CONTENTION
         ST    R8,0(R4)             STORE PGM ADDR AT HEADER ADDR
         ST    R9,4(R4)             STORE THE CTR AT WORD 2 IN HEADER
         L     R7,0(R8)             LOAD DATA AT PGM ADDR
         X     R7,ONES              FLIP THE BITS
         ST    R7,0(R8)             STORE THE DATA AT PGM ADDR
*
         LA    R15,UERCNORM         SET OK RESPONSE
         ST    R15,RETCODE            IN WORKING STORAGE
*
RETURN   EQU   *
         L     R15,RETCODE          FETCH RETURN CODE
         DFHEIRET RCREG=15          RETURN TO CICS
**********************************************************************
         DC    F'0'
ONES     DC    X'11111111'          ONES
LOOPCTR  DC    F'00777777'          TIME DELAY LOOP
**********************************************************************
         LTORG
         END   RMIXIT
```

DFH0STAT report showing RMIXIT defined to the system

Using the DFH0STAT we generated a report to show how the program is defined to the system and to show the global work area we are using.

> **Note:** The DFH0STAT report in Example 7-11 was run under CICS TS 2.3, as opposed to the report in Example 7-1 on page 150. You can see a slight difference in the report formats.

Example 7-11 DFH0STAT report showing XRMIIN and XRMOUT using a global work area

```
User Exit Programs

                    <---- Global Area ---->   No.
   Program    Entry  Entry            Use     of    Program    Program       Exit Program
   Name       Name   Name     Length  Count  Exits  Status     Concurrency   Use Count

   DFHEDP     DLI                 0       0     0   Started    Quasi Rent         0
   DFHD2EX1   DSNCSQL DSNCSQL    16       1     0   Started    Quasi Rent         6
   RMIXIT     RMIXIT  RMIXIT  2,008       1     2   Started    Quasi Rent         0


   Program   Entry         Concurrency                         <------- Task Related User Exit Options -------->
   Name      Name    API   Status       Qualifier  Length   Taskstart  EDF   Shutdown  Indoubt   SPI  Purgeable

   DFHEDP    DLI     Base  Quasi Rent                284       No      No      No      No Wait   No     No
   DFHD2EX1  DSNCSQL Open  Thread Safe  D7Q2         222       No      Yes     Yes     Wait      Yes    Yes
   RMIXIT    RMIXIT  Base  Quasi Rent                  0       No      No      No      No Wait   No     No
   Applid SCSCPJA7  Sysid PJA7  Jobname SCSCPJA7      Date 05/04/2004  Time 09:14:11          CICS 6.3.0


Global User Exits

   Exit     Program  Entry   <------- Global Area ------->  Number    Program   Program
   Name     Name     Name    Entry Name  Length  Use Count  of Exits  Status    Concurrency

   XRMIIN   RMIXIT   RMIXIT  RMIXIT      2,008       1          2     Started   Quasi Rent
   XRMIOUT  RMIXIT   RMIXIT  RMIXIT      2,008       1          2     Started   Quasi Rent
```

The report shows that program RMIXIT is in use at two exit points, XRMIIN and XRMOUT, which means that it will get invoked twice for each DB2 call. Both exits share the same global work area using the first two words as a header to communicate between programs.

QUASIRENT results running on the QR TCB

We initially defined the program as QUASIRENT to show that the program runs successfully on the QR TCB.

Figure 7-9 shows the header format used by RMIXIT. The first word is the next available storage address in the global work area to be updated and the second word represents the number of words updated in the global work area.

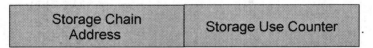

Figure 7-9 Sample header format

While running in QUASIRENT mode on the QR TCB you can see the last address updated was 00412B8. If you look down to the end of the storage area you can see that the word at 00412BC is all zeros, since it has not been used yet. See Example 7-12.

The third word of the storage area is always skipped and left blank, so technically you could say the header is three words. Starting at 004103C program RMIXIT has inserted sequential words of ones all the way up to and including address 00412B8.

The storage use counter has a hex value of A0, which translates to decimal 160. When RMIXIT starts out the header address is initialized to 0041038, so 00412B8 - 0041038 = 000280, which translates to decimal 640, and dividing this by 4 gives you 160 words updated (4 bytes per word).

Example 7-12   Results of running the non threadsafe GLUE defined as QUASIRENT

```
0041030    00000C    000412B8 000000A0 00000000 11111111
0041040    00001C    11111111 11111111 11111111 11111111
0041050    00002C    11111111 11111111 11111111 11111111
0041060    00003C    11111111 11111111 11111111 11111111
0041070    00004C    11111111 11111111 11111111 11111111
0041080    00005C    11111111 11111111 11111111 11111111
0041090    00006C    11111111 11111111 11111111 11111111
00410A0    00007C    11111111 11111111 11111111 11111111
00410B0    00008C    11111111 11111111 11111111 11111111
00410C0    00009C    11111111 11111111 11111111 11111111
00410D0    0000AC    11111111 11111111 11111111 11111111
00410E0    0000BC    11111111 11111111 11111111 11111111
00410F0    0000CC    11111111 11111111 11111111 11111111
0041100    0000DC    11111111 11111111 11111111 11111111
0041110    0000EC    11111111 11111111 11111111 11111111
0041120    00000C    11111111 11111111 11111111 11111111
0041130    00001C    11111111 11111111 11111111 11111111
0041140    00002C    11111111 11111111 11111111 11111111
0041150    00003C    11111111 11111111 11111111 11111111
0041160    00004C    11111111 11111111 11111111 11111111
0041170    00005C    11111111 11111111 11111111 11111111
0041180    00006C    11111111 11111111 11111111 11111111
0041190    00007C    11111111 11111111 11111111 11111111
00411A0    00008C    11111111 11111111 11111111 11111111
00411B0    00009C    11111111 11111111 11111111 11111111
00411C0    0000AC    11111111 11111111 11111111 11111111
00411D0    0000BC    11111111 11111111 11111111 11111111
00411E0    0000CC    11111111 11111111 11111111 11111111
00411F0    0000DC    11111111 11111111 11111111 11111111
0041200    0000EC    11111111 11111111 11111111 11111111
0041210    00000C    11111111 11111111 11111111 11111111
```

```
0041220    00001C    11111111 11111111 11111111 11111111
0041230    00002C    11111111 11111111 11111111 11111111
0041240    00003C    11111111 11111111 11111111 11111111
0041250    00004C    11111111 11111111 11111111 11111111
0041260    00005C    11111111 11111111 11111111 11111111
0041270    00006C    11111111 11111111 11111111 11111111
0041280    00007C    11111111 11111111 11111111 11111111
0041290    00008C    11111111 11111111 11111111 11111111
00412A0    00009C    11111111 11111111 11111111 11111111
00412B0    0000AC    11111111 11111111 11111111 00000000
```

THREADSAFE results of running on an L8 TCB

Running the exact same exit with no modifications but redefining it as THREADSAFE shows that we have exposed an underlying data integrity problem.

The RMIXIT program does not contain any EXEC CICS commands that would move it off the L8 TCB. Therefore once it is defined as THREADSAFE to CICS, it always runs on an L8 TCB. If a programmer performed a quick code review someone could actually think the code is threadsafe and go ahead and allow it to be defined as THREADSAFE, but as you can see, the results would be disastrous.

Example 7-13   Results of running the non threadsafe GLUE defined as THREADSAFE

```
0041030    00000C    00041104 00000033 00000000 11111111
0041040    00001C    11111111 11111111 11111111 11111111
0041050    00002C    11111111 00000000 00000000 00000000
0041060    00003C    11111111 00000000 11111111 00000000
0041070    00004C    11111111 11111111 11111111 11111111
0041080    00005C    00000000 00000000 00000000 00000000
0041090    00006C    11111111 11111111 11111111 11111111
00410A0    00007C    11111111 11111111 11111111 11111111
00410B0    00008C    11111111 11111111 11111111 11111111
00410C0    00009C    11111111 11111111 11111111 11111111
00410D0    0000AC    11111111 11111111 11111111 11111111
00410E0    0000BC    11111111 11111111 11111111 11111111
00410F0    0000CC    11111111 11111111 11111111 11111111
0041100    0000DC    11111111 11111111 00000000 00000000
0041110    0000EC    00000000 00000000 00000000 00000000
```

Interestingly enough, we had to add a loop in the middle of the program to slow it down to generate the contention. Without the loop the program appears to run OK, which means that it could run like this for years, and then all of a sudden corrupt some data.

7.6.2 Threadsafe code example

To make the code threadsafe in regards to data integrity, we have to make a few code changes. We will review the changes necessary in a later section, but for now here is the complete code snippet with the adjustments. In our example we chose to use the Compare and Swap method to serialize the storage. Due to the header being two words long we had to use the compare double and swap instruction.

This method allows you to read the data and update it, and then a single instruction that is serialized across all CPUs in the LPAR does a final compare against storage to verify what you originally read in is still in storage. It then stores the new changed results or fails and makes you retry via a code loop.

Example 7-14   Sample GLUE with threadsafe code

```
RMIXIT   DFHEIENT
RMIXIT   AMODE 31
RMIXIT   RMODE ANY
         LR    R2,R1                DFHUEPAR PLIST PROVIDED BY CALLER
         USING DFHUEPAR,R2          ADDRESS UEPAR PLIST
         L     R4,UEPGAA            GET GWA ADDRESS
         LA    R4,12(R4)            BUMP TO A DOUBLE WORD ADDR
         USING GWA,R4               ADDRESSABILITY
*
         LM    R6,R7,0(R4)          LOAD PGM ADDR AND CTR
AGAIN    EQU   *
         LA    R8,4(R6)             BUMP SAVED PGM ADDR BY 4
         LA    R9,1(R7)             BUMP CTR BY 1
         L     R5,LOOPCTR           DELAY LOOP TO GET SOME OVERLAP
LOOP     EQU   *                    SO THAT WE CAN GENERATE SOME
         BCT   R5,LOOP              TCB CONTENTION
         CDS   R6,R8,0(R4)          SAVE DATA VIA THD SAFE CMD
         BC    7,AGAIN              THD SAFE COMP LOOP
         L     R7,0(R8)             LOAD DATA AT PGM ADDR
         X     R7,ONES              FLIP THE BITS
         ST    R7,0(R8)             STORE THE DATA AT PGM ADDR
*
         LA    R15,UERCNORM         SET OK RESPONSE
         ST    R15,RETCODE            IN WORKING STORAGE
RETURN   EQU   *
         L     R15,RETCODE          FETCH RETURN CODE
         DFHEIRET RCREG=15          RETURN TO CICS
***************************************************************
         DC    F'0'
ONES     DC    X'11111111'          ONES
LOOPCTR  DC    F'00777777'          TIME DELAY LOOP
```

```
***************************************************************
         LTORG
         END   RMIXIT
```

QUASIRENT results running on the QR TCB

Running the fully threadsafe version of our exit in QUASIRENT mode worked perfectly, as we expected. Therefore there is no reason to show the results. So let us move on to the real test.

THREADSAFE results of running on an L8 TCB

We redefined the RMIXIT program as THREADSAFE, disabled it, copied it, and reenabled the GLUE at XRMIIN and XRMIOUT for another test.

Running in THREADSAFE mode on L8 TCBs we are now hitting the single shared global work area from multiple programs running concurrently. The data integrity has been maintained due to the compare double and swap logic we added to the program. We can now run our new RMIXIT in any mode with the knowledge that we are not going to corrupt any data.

Comparing the first two words of data against the previous run in Example 7-12 on page 162 shows that our count is again correct at 0A0 and the next address is again 00412B8.

Example 7-15   Results of running the threadsafe GLUE defined as THREADSAFE

```
0041030    00000C    000412B8 000000A0 00000000 11111111
0041040    00001C    11111111 11111111 11111111 11111111
0041050    00002C    11111111 11111111 11111111 11111111
0041060    00003C    11111111 11111111 11111111 11111111
0041070    00004C    11111111 11111111 11111111 11111111
0041080    00005C    11111111 11111111 11111111 11111111
0041090    00006C    11111111 11111111 11111111 11111111
00410A0    00007C    11111111 11111111 11111111 11111111
00410B0    00008C    11111111 11111111 11111111 11111111
00410C0    00009C    11111111 11111111 11111111 11111111
00410D0    0000AC    11111111 11111111 11111111 11111111
00410E0    0000BC    11111111 11111111 11111111 11111111
00410F0    0000CC    11111111 11111111 11111111 11111111
0041100    0000DC    11111111 11111111 11111111 11111111
0041110    0000EC    11111111 11111111 11111111 11111111
0041120    00000C    11111111 11111111 11111111 11111111
0041130    00001C    11111111 11111111 11111111 11111111
0041140    00002C    11111111 11111111 11111111 11111111
0041150    00003C    11111111 11111111 11111111 11111111
0041160    00004C    11111111 11111111 11111111 11111111
0041170    00005C    11111111 11111111 11111111 11111111
```

```
0041180    00006C    11111111 11111111 11111111 11111111
0041190    00007C    11111111 11111111 11111111 11111111
00411A0    00008C    11111111 11111111 11111111 11111111
00411B0    00009C    11111111 11111111 11111111 11111111
00411C0    0000AC    11111111 11111111 11111111 11111111
00411D0    0000BC    11111111 11111111 11111111 11111111
00411E0    0000CC    11111111 11111111 11111111 11111111
00411F0    0000DC    11111111 11111111 11111111 11111111
0041200    0000EC    11111111 11111111 11111111 11111111
0041210    00000C    11111111 11111111 11111111 11111111
0041220    00001C    11111111 11111111 11111111 11111111
0041230    00002C    11111111 11111111 11111111 11111111
0041240    00003C    11111111 11111111 11111111 11111111
0041250    00004C    11111111 11111111 11111111 11111111
0041260    00005C    11111111 11111111 11111111 11111111
0041270    00006C    11111111 11111111 11111111 11111111
0041280    00007C    11111111 11111111 11111111 11111111
0041290    00008C    11111111 11111111 11111111 11111111
00412A0    00009C    11111111 11111111 11111111 11111111
00412B0    0000AC    11111111 11111111 11111111 00000000
```

7.6.3 Code changes to make RMIXIT threadsafe

First let us go through the code and break it down by function so the new changes make sense (Example 7-16). In our example we chose to use the compare double and swap instruction to serialize our data. We could also have used ENQ/DEQ. In fact, we used both methods. We include the ENQ/DEQ sample later.

Example 7-16 Code broken down into function

```
         (A) Load the two word header

         L    R6,0(R4)           LOAD SAVED PGM ADDR
         L    R7,4(R4)           LOAD CTR

         (B) Update the Header Address value and counter

         LA   R8,4(R6)           BUMP SAVED PGM ADDR BY 4
         LA   R9,1(R7)           BUMP CTR BY 1

         (C) Artificial loop used to simulate real program workload

         L    R5,LOOPCTR         DELAY LOOP TO GET SOME OVERLAP
LOOP     EQU  *                  SO THAT WE CAN GENERATE SOME
         BCT  R5,LOOP            TCB CONTENTION
```

(D) Save the updated header back into the shared storage

```
ST    R8,0(R4)        STORE PGM ADDR AT HEADER ADDR
ST    R9,4(R4)        STORE THE CTR AT WORD 2 IN HEADER
```

(E) Store Ones into the shared storage using the header address value

```
L     R7,0(R8)        LOAD DATA AT PGM ADDR
X     R7,ONES         FLIP THE BITS
ST    R7,0(R8)        STORE THE DATA AT PGM ADDR
```

Sections (A) and (D) need to be modified. Sections (B) and (E) stay the same, and section (C) is an artificial loop added to the code to create real-world processing time delays to generate concurrent TCB contention.

Section (A) loads the header from shared storage via two load instructions. For our case only, the manual *z/Architecture Principles of Operation*, SA22-7832, recommends using a load multiple to load both registers without introducing a window between the two loads where the data could be changed.

Example 7-17   Modifying section (A), loading the header

```
LM    R6,R7,0(R4)        LOAD PGM ADDR AND CTR
```

In section (D) we convert the two store instructions into a single compare double and swap instruction.

Example 7-18   Modifying section (D), saving the updated header

```
AGAIN  EQU   *
       LA    R8,4(R6)        BUMP SAVED PGM ADDR BY 4
       LA    R9,1(R7)        BUMP CTR BY 1
       L     R5,LOOPCTR      DELAY LOOP TO GET SOME OVERLAP
LOOP   EQU   *               SO THAT WE CAN GENERATE SOME
       BCT   R5,LOOP         TCB CONTENTION
       CDS   R6,R8,0(R4)     SAVE DATA VIA THD SAFE CMD
       BC    7,AGAIN         THD SAFE COMP LOOP
```

What the Compare and Swap instruction does is compare what you originally loaded with what is in storage and, based on the result, do one of following two actions:

- If the original data is unchanged it stores your new updates, as in registers 8 and 9, in the storage location.
- If the original data changed, it reloads registers 6 and 7 with the new values from storage.

You then check the return codes from the CDS command and branch accordingly. In our case, for option 1 we drop through the code into unchanged section (E) to store our ones into memory. The address we have is already locked in and is ours, so we can perform this function after the fact.

For option 2 the CDS instruction simulates section (A) for us so we need to go backwards in the code and redo our updates and then retry to store our data again. Notice that this is actually coded as an infinite loop, which could be dangerous. It might have been cleaner to put a loop counter in there and abend the transaction if it cannot serialize the data. However, due to the fact it was difficult getting contention, we felt it was a very low chance we would ever go into an infinite loop.

7.7 Coordinating and driving individual application conversions

Once you have converted all appropriate GLUEs, TRUEs, URMs, and exits, the next step in the conversion process is the application programs themselves. Depending on how each shop is set up, you may have a varying role in helping coordinate the application conversions to threadsafe applications.

Your key role may be to identify what CICS region is ready for the conversion or you may have, in your region-by-region analysis, collected statistics on how many TCB switches are taking place for individual application programs. Armed with performance data on TCB switches you may be the key person to help identify the application conversion selection order.

Obviously applications that perform large amounts of DB2 calls, as opposed to single table lookups, will benefit the most from the conversion. The same principle applies to applications with large volumes of WMQ calls.

By using tools like CICS PA the systems programmer can help identify which applications are the best candidates for conversion first. See 5.4.3, "How CICS PA can assist with threadsafety" on page 107.

Chapter 6, "Application review" on page 111, describes the process of making applications threadsafe.

7.7.1 Changing your program definitions

Once the applications have been changed or verified to be threadsafe, then the final action that is needed to make the application stay on the L8 TCB is to change the definition of all the programs concerned to define them as threadsafe.

```
 OBJECT CHARACTERISTICS                                   CICS RELEASE = 0630
   CEDA   View PROGram( DB2MANY  )
    PROGram        : DB2MANY
    Group          : THDSAFE
    DEscription    :
    Language       :                       CObol | Assembler | Le370 | C | Pli
    RELoad         : No                    No | Yes
    RESident       : No                    No | Yes
    USAge          : Normal                Normal | Transient
    USElpacopy     : No                    No | Yes
    Status         : Enabled               Enabled | Disabled
    RSl            : 00                    0-24 | Public
    CEdf           : Yes                   Yes | No
    DAtalocation   : Any                   Below | Any
    EXECKey        : User                  User | Cics
    COncurrency    : Threadsafe            Quasirent | Threadsafe
    Api            : Cicsapi               Cicsapi | Openapi
 REMOTE ATTRIBUTES
    DYnamic        : No                    No | Yes
  + REMOTESystem   :

                                              SYSID=PJA7 APPLID=SCSCPJA7

 PF 1 HELP 2 COM 3 END          6 CRSR 7 SBH 8 SFH 9 MSG 10 SB 11 SF 12 CNCL
```

Figure 7-10 Changing program definitions

For more information about changing a program's concurrency definition see 7.5.3, "Change your exit program's CONCURRENCY definition to THREADSAFE" on page 157.

7.8 Post-conversion monitoring

The concept of making a program threadsafe can seem simple. However, in reality it can be extremely complex. Identifying which EXEC CICS commands may cause a program to have excessive TCB switching is straightforward. You can look up a list of all the threadsafe commands and search your code and then make the appropriate adjustments.

Making a program threadsafe is much harder because you first have to identify any shared resources. This may be disguised due to the fact that the address of shared storage is obtained from a commarea passed into the program.

There really is no tool or process you can use to monitor for changes in application programs. However, you can periodically monitor your region for TCB switches via tools such as CICS PA. The fact is that a programmer could introduce a non threadsafe EXEC CICS command into a program that has already been converted and therefore introduce extra TCB switches.

To help combat this you may want to alter any existing performance reports you currently run to add change mode counts to your reports then if you can identify any changes in TCB switching.

7.9 Summary

In review, the system programmer is responsible for making the CICS environment threadsafe so that application programs can take advantage of the performance benefits of threadsafe DB2 and WMQ applications.

To make the CICS environment threadsafe the system programmer will need to:

- Review the DB2 version and system parameters.
- Review the WMQ environment and system parameters.
- Review and adjust the CICS system parameters.
- Review and convert any GLUEs in the DB2 and WMQ call paths to threadsafe standards.
- Do the same for those GLUEs on the path of threadsafe EXEC CICS commands, particularly for heavily used API options such as file control.
- Assist application programmers with analyzing their programs by using utilities such as DFH0STAT and DFHEISUP, or tools such as CICS IA and CICS PA.
- Potentially work with the application teams to help prioritize their application threadsafe migrations.
- Convert the actual program definition changes to CONCURRENCY(THREADSAFE).

- The autoinstall program needs to be modified to change the CONCURRENCY value if used, or the environment variable CICSVAR can be used.

Additionally, system programmers may perform periodic reviews of their CICS regions using tools such as CICS PA to monitor the L8 to QR TCB statistics checking to see if applications are really in effect running on the L8 TCBs.

> **Note:** Prior to CICS Transaction Server Version 3, the field in the CICS SMF 110 record that contained the count of TCB switches (change modes) is called CHMODECT.
>
> In CICS Transaction Server Version 3 the CHMODECT field has been removed and replaced by a composite field called DSCHMDLY. This composite field consists of a time and a count.
> - The time portion represents the elapsed time the user task waited for redispatch after change mode requests. For example, a change mode request from an L8 TCB back to the QR TCB may have to wait for the QR TCB because another task is currently dispatched on the QR TCB.
> - The count portion represents the number of change modes and is equivalent to CHMODECT in previous releases.

8

Migration pitfalls

In this chapter we highlight some of the pitfalls you might encounter when migrating a CICS region. In particular we discuss the following:

- The need to examine the use of CICS global user exits for applications that call DB2 or WMQ
- Use of OPENAPI and additional TCB switching
- Function shipping in your CICS systems
- Use of COBOL Call
- The CSACDTA/CSAQRTCA field

8.1 Migrating CICS DB2 regions

When migrating a CICS region to CICS Transaction Server Version 2 or Version 3 you must ensure that your DB2 applications do not suffer any adverse effects because of the change to using open TCBs for calls to DB2. This is independent of whether you are intending to make your application code threadsafe.

8.1.1 The potential pitfall

The CICS DB2 adapter includes the task-related user exit (TRUE) DFHD2EX1. This TRUE is THREADSAFE and automatically enabled with the OPENAPI option on the ENABLE PROGRAM command during the connect process. If your program is defined as THREADSAFE (rather than OPENAPI), when your program makes a DB2 call, CICS switches the task to an OPEN L8 TCB by performing a TCB switch from the QR TCB to the L8 TCB.

If your program is defined as QUASIRENT and you are running exits XRMIIN, XRMIOUT, or a dynamic plan exit enabled as QUASIRENT, there is the potential of experiencing additional TCB switches back to the QR TCB. These switches are easily avoided if these exits are written to threadsafe standards and then enabled as THREADSAFE.

The following two scenarios show the program flow and TCB switches of a program making one DB2 call.

- The first scenario is from a CICS Transaction Server Version 1.3 region.
- The second shows the same application running in a CICS Transaction Server Version 2 or Version 3 region with exits XRMIIN, XRMIOUT, and a dynamic plan exit all enabled as QUASIRENT.

DB2 application in CICS Transaction Server 1.3

Figure 8-1 shows transaction TRANA running in a CICS Transaction Server Version 1.3 environment and making one DB2 call. Notice that the application as well as all exit programs run on the QR TCB, and the actual call to DB2 is made on the thread TCB. The diagram shows that two TCB switches are made around the call to DB2—one to switch to the thread TCB and one to switch back to the QR TCB afterwards.

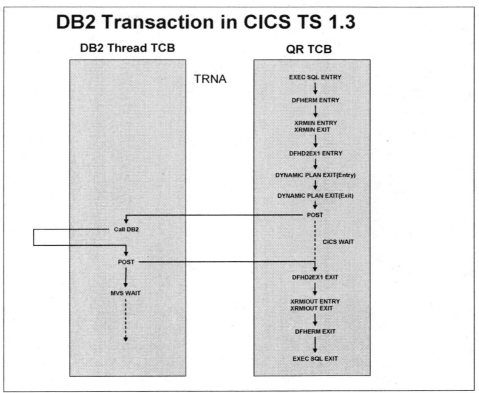

Figure 8-1   TCB switch in CICS TS 1.3

DB2 application in CICS Transaction Server 2 or 3

Figure 8-2 on page 176 shows the same transaction, TRANA, running in a CICS Transaction Server Version 2 or Version 3 environment and making one DB2 call. The transaction was migrated to CICS Transaction Server Version 2 or Version 3 with *no* consideration of threadsafe, which means that the program associated with transaction TRANA is defined as QUASIRENT and all exits are enabled as QUASIRENT. This diagram shows that there is a potential to experience additional TCB switches from the L8 TCB to the QR TCB and back. The non threadsafe exits must run on the QR TCB to ensure that serialization occurs. In this example we see eight TCB switches occur, compared with two switches in the previous example. If the exits were written to threadsafe standards and then enabled as THREADSAFE their associated programs would be allowed to continue running on the L8 TCB and the additional switches would not be necessary. This is shown in the next section.

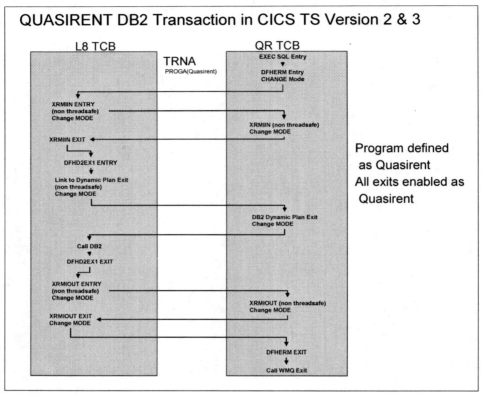

Figure 8-2   TCB switches before exits are enabled as threadsafe on CICS TS Version 2 and Version 3

Example 8-1 is a CICS auxtrace showing the additional TCB switches shown in Figure 8-2 on page 176.

Example 8-1   CICS trace of potential switches with non threadsafe exits

```
00258 QR         AP 2520 ERM    ENTRY ASSEMBLER-APPLICATION-CALL-TO-TRUE(DSNCSQL )                                                     =003356=
00258 QR         US 0401 USXM   ENTRY INQUIRE_TRANSACTION_USER                                                                          =003357=
00258 QR         US 0402 USXM   EXIT  INQUIRE_TRANSACTION_USER/OK 00000000                                                              =003358=
00258 QR         RM 0301 RMLN   ENTRY ADD_LINK              RMI,22F914A4 , 00000000 , 00000008,000949D0 , 00000000 , 00000008,22F       =003359=
00258 QR         RM 0302 RMLN   EXIT  ADD_LINK/OK           01C80006,22F914A4 , 00000000 , 00000008,000949D0 , 00000000 , 00000000      =003360=
00258 QR         DS 0002 DSAT   ENTRY CHANGE_MODE           0000000C                                                                    =003361=
00258 L8000      DS 0003 DSAT   EXIT  CHANGE_MODE/OK                                                                                    =003369=
00258 L8000      AP D500 UEH    EVENT LINK-TO-USER-EXIT-PROGRAM XXXRMI AT EXIT POINT XRMIIN                                             =003370=
00258 L8000      DS 0002 DSAT   ENTRY CHANGE_MODE           QR                                                                          =003371=
00258 QR         DS 0003 DSAT   EXIT  CHANGE_MODE/OK                                                                                    =003377=
00258 QR         SM 0C01 SMMG   ENTRY GETMAIN               198,YES,00,TASK                                                             =003378=
00258 QR         SM 0C02 SMMG   EXIT  GETMAIN/OK            226E1788                                                                    =003379=
00258 QR         SM 0D01 SMMF   ENTRY FREEMAIN              226E1788                                                                    =003380=
00258 QR         SM 0D02 SMMF   EXIT  FREEMAIN/OK           USER storage at 226E1788                                                    =003381=
00258 QR         AP D501 UEH    EVENT RETURN-FROM-USER-EXIT-PROGRAM XXXRMI WITH RETURN CODE 0                                           =003382=
00258 QR         DS 0002 DSAT   ENTRY CHANGE_MODE           L8                                                                          =003383=
00258 L8000      DS 0003 DSAT   EXIT  CHANGE_MODE/OK                                                                                    =003384=
00258 L8000      AP 3180 D2EX1  ENTRY APPLICATION           REQUEST EXEC SQL SELECT                                                     =003385=
00258 L8000      PG 0A01 PGLU   ENTRY LINK_URM              DB2PLAN,22BE7678 , 0000001C,NO,NO                                           =003386=
00258 L8000      DD 0301 DDLO   ENTRY LOCATE                21C27B70,22BE7574,PPT,DB2PLAN                                               =003387=
00258 L8000      DD 0302 DDLO   EXIT  LOCATE/OK             D7D7E3C5 , 22DA5B88                                                         =003388=
00258 L8000      LD 0001 LDLD   ENTRY ACQUIRE_PROGRAM       22C87258                                                                    =003389=
00258 L8000      LD 0002 LDLD   EXIT  ACQUIRE_PROGRAM/OK    A43002D8,243002B0,D8,0,REUSABLE,ESDSA,OLD_COPY                              =003390=
00258 L8000      AP 1940 APLI   ENTRY START_PROGRAM         DB2PLAN,CEDF,FULLAPI,URM,NO,22F89C10,22BE7678 , 0000001C,3                  =003391=
00258 L8000      DS 0002 DSAT   ENTRY CHANGE_MODE           QR                                                                          =003392=
00258 QR         DS 0003 DSAT   EXIT  CHANGE_MODE/OK                                                                                    =003393=
00258 QR         SM 0C01 SMMG   ENTRY GETMAIN               190,YES,00,TASK                                                             =003394=
00258 QR         SM 0C02 SMMG   EXIT  GETMAIN/OK            226E1788                                                                    =003395=
00258 QR         AP 00E1 EIP    ENTRY RETURN                                       0004,226E1798 .>.q,08000E08 ....                    =003396=
00258 QR         AP E160 EXEC   ENTRY RETURN                ASM                                                                         =003397=
00258 QR         SM 0301 SMGF   ENTRY FREEMAIN              226E1788,TASK                                                               =003398=
00258 QR         SM 0302 SMGF   EXIT  FREEMAIN/OK                                                                                       =003399=
00258 QR         AP 1941 APLI   EXIT  START_PROGRAM         ....,NO,DB2PLAN                                                             =003400=
00258 QR         LD 0001 LDLD   ENTRY RELEASE_PROGRAM       22C87258,A43002D8                                                           =003401=
00258 QR         LD 0002 LDLD   EXIT  RELEASE_PROGRAM/OK    243002B0,D8,ESDSA                                                           =003402=
00258 QR         DS 0002 DSAT   ENTRY CHANGE_MODE           L8                                                                          =003403=
00258 L8000      DS 0003 DSAT   EXIT  CHANGE_MODE/OK        QR                                                                          =003404=
00258 L8000      PG 0A02 PGLU   EXIT  LINK_URM/OK                                                                                       =003405=
00258 L8000      AP 3250 D2D2   ENTRY DB2_API_CALL          230D7030                                                                    =003406=
00258 L8000      AP 3251 D2D2   EXIT  DB2_API_CALL/OK                                                                                   =003407=
00258 L8000      AP 3181 D2EX1  EXIT  APPLICATION-REQUEST   SQLCODE 0 RETURNED ON EXEC SQL SELECT                                       =003408=
00258 L8000      MN 0201 MNMN   ENTRY ACCUMULATE_RMI_TIME   DSNCSQL                                                                     =003409=
00258 L8000      MN 0202 MNMN   EXIT  ACCUMULATE_RMI_TIME/OK                                                                            =003410=
00258 L8000      AP D500 UEH    EVENT LINK-TO-USER-EXIT-PROGRAM XXXRMI AT EXIT POINT XRMIOUT                                            =003411=
00258 L8000      DS 0002 DSAT   ENTRY CHANGE_MODE           QR                                                                          =003412=
00258 QR         DS 0003 DSAT   EXIT  CHANGE_MODE/OK                                                                                    =003413=
00258 QR         SM 0C01 SMMG   ENTRY GETMAIN               198,YES,00,TASK                                                             =003414=
00258 QR         SM 0C02 SMMG   EXIT  GETMAIN/OK            226E1788                                                                    =003415=
00258 QR         SM 0D01 SMMF   ENTRY FREEMAIN              226E1788                                                                    =003416=
00258 QR         SM 0D02 SMMF   EXIT  FREEMAIN/OK           USER storage at 226E1788                                                    =003417=
00258 QR         AP D501 UEH    EVENT RETURN-FROM-USER-EXIT-PROGRAM XXXRMI WITH RETURN CODE 0                                           =003418=
00258 QR         DS 0002 DSAT   ENTRY CHANGE_MODE           L8                                                                          =003419=
00258 L8000      DS 0003 DSAT   EXIT  CHANGE_MODE/OK                                                                                    =003420=
00258 L8000      RM 0301 RMLN   ENTRY SET_LINK              01C80006,22F914AC , 0000000C , 00000008,YES,NECESSARY                       =003421=
00258 L8000      RM 0302 RMLN   EXIT  SET_LINK/OK           22F914AC , 0000000C , 00000008,                                             =003422=
00258 L8000      DS 0002 DSAT   ENTRY CHANGE_MODE           00000001                                                                    =003423=
00258 QR         DS 0003 DSAT   EXIT  CHANGE_MODE/OK                                                                                    =003424=
00258 QR         AP 2521 ERM    EXIT  ASSEMBLER-APPLICATION-CALL-TO-TRUE(DSNCSQL )                                                      =003425=
```

8.1.2 The solution

In order to demonstrate how to avoid this pitfall we now examine two additional scenarios:

- The first shows the effect of having only the exits on the DB2 call path written to threadsafe standards and enabled as threadsafe (XRMIIN and XRMIOUT exits and the dynamic plan exit).

- The second shows the true benefit threadsafe has to offer having coded *both* the application program and programs associated with all the exits on the DB2 call path to threadsafe standards and defining them as THREADSAFE.

Enable exits on the DB2 call path to be THREADSAFE

Figure 8-3 on page 179 shows the same transaction, TRNA, running in a CICS Transaction Server Version 2 or Version 3 environment and making one DB2 call. The transaction was migrated to CICS Transaction Server Version 2 or Version 3 *with* threadsafe consideration in mind.

The program associated with transaction TRNA is still defined as Quasirent. However, XRMIIN, XRMIOUT, and the dynamic plan exits have been coded to threadsafe standards and then enabled as THREADSAFE. This diagram shows that the number of TCB switches is back to the original two switches, as seen in the CICS Transaction Server Version 1.3 scenario. However, a TCB switchback to the QR TCB must still take place upon completion of the DB2 call due to TRNA's program not being threadsafe. Therefore, there are two TCB switches for each DB2 call.

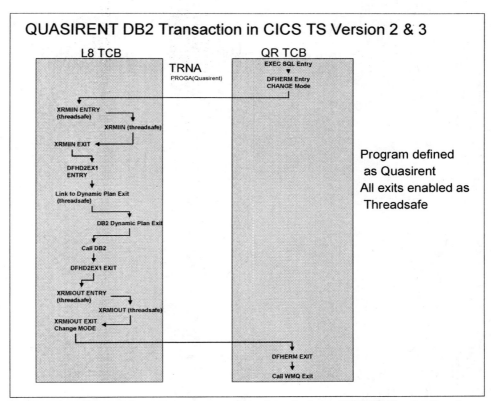

Figure 8-3 TCB switches after exits are made threadsafe on CICS TS Version 2 and Version 3

Example 8-2 on page 180 is a CICS auxiliary trace that demonstrates the TCB switches described by Figure 8-3.

Example 8-2   CICS trace of TCB switches with threadsafe exits

```
00307 QR    AP 2520 ERM    ENTRY ASSEMBLER-APPLICATION-CALL-TO-TRUE(DSNCSQL )                              =000266=
00307 QR    US 0401 USXM   ENTRY INQUIRE_TRANSACTION_USER                                                  =000267=
00307 QR    US 0402 USXM   EXIT  INQUIRE_TRANSACTION_USER/OK 00000000                                      =000268=
00307 QR    RM 0301 RMLN   ENTRY ADD_LINK             RMI,22F914A4 , 00000000 , 00000008,000949D0 , 00000000 , 00000008,22F =000269=
00307 QR    RM 0302 RMLN   EXIT  ADD_LINK/OK          01C80011,22F914A4 , 00000000 , 00000008,000949D0 , 00000000 , 0000000 =000270=
00307 QR    DS 0002 DSAT   ENTRY CHANGE_MODE          0000000C                                             =000271=
00307 L8000 DS 0003 DSAT   EXIT  CHANGE_MODE/OK                                                            =000279=
00307 L8000 AP D500 UEH    EVENT LINK-TO-USER-EXIT-PROGRAM XXXRMI AT EXIT POINT XRMIIN                     =000280=
00307 L8000 SM 0C01 SMMG   ENTRY GETMAIN              198,YES,00,TASK                                      =000281=
00307 L8000 SM 0C02 SMMG   EXIT  GETMAIN/OK           226E1788                                             =000282=
00307 L8000 SM 0D01 SMMF   ENTRY FREEMAIN             226E1788                                             =000283=
00307 L8000 SM 0D02 SMMF   EXIT  FREEMAIN/OK          USER storage at 226E1788                             =000284=
00307 L8000 AP D501 UEH    EVENT RETURN-FROM-USER-EXIT-PROGRAM XXXRMI WITH RETURN CODE 0                   =000285=
00307 L8000 AP 3180 D2EX1  ENTRY APPLICATION          REQUEST EXEC SQL SELECT                              =000286=
00307 L8000 PG 0A01 PGLU   ENTRY LINK_URM             DB2PLAN,22BE7678 , 0000001C,NO,NO                    =000287=
00307 L8000 DD 0301 DDLO   ENTRY LOCATE               21C27B70,22BE7574,PPT,DB2PLAN                        =000288=
00307 L8000 DD 0302 DDLO   EXIT  LOCATE/OK            D7D7E3C5 , 22DA5B30                                  =000289=
00307 L8000 LD 0001 LDLD   ENTRY ACQUIRE_PROGRAM      22C871A0                                             =000290=
00307 L8000 LD 0002 LDLD   EXIT  ACQUIRE_PROGRAM/OK   A43002D8,243002B0,D8,0,REUSABLE,ESDSA,OLD_COPY       =000291=
00307 L8000 AP 1940 APLI   ENTRY START_PROGRAM        DB2PLAN,CEDF,FULLAPI,URM,NO,22F89A94,22BE7678 , 0000001C,3 =000292=
00307 L8000 SM 0C01 SMMG   ENTRY GETMAIN              190,YES,00,TASK                                      =000293=
00307 L8000 SM 0C02 SMMG   EXIT  GETMAIN/OK           226E1788                                             =000294=
00307 L8000 AP 00E1 EIP    ENTRY RETURN                                   0004,226E1798 .>.q,08000E08 ...  =000295=
00307 L8000 AP E160 EXEC   ENTRY RETURN               ASM                                                  =000296=
00307 L8000 SM 0301 SMGF   ENTRY FREEMAIN             226E1788,TASK                                        =000297=
00307 L8000 SM 0302 SMGF   EXIT  FREEMAIN/OK                                                               =000298=
00307 L8000 AP 1941 APLI   EXIT  START_PROGRAM/OK     ....,NO,DB2PLAN                                      =000299=
00307 L8000 LD 0001 LDLD   ENTRY RELEASE_PROGRAM      22C871A0,A43002D8                                    =000300=
00307 L8000 LD 0002 LDLD   EXIT  RELEASE_PROGRAM/OK   243002B0,D8,ESDSA                                    =000301=
00307 L8000 PG 0A02 PGLU   EXIT  LINK_URM/OK                                                               =000302=
00307 L8000 AP 3250 D2D2   ENTRY DB2_API_CALL         230D7030                                             =000303=
00307 L8000 AP 3251 D2D2   EXIT  DB2_API_CALL/OK                                                           =000309=
00307 L8000 AP 3181 D2EX1  EXIT  APPLICATION-REQUEST  SQLCODE 0 RETURNED ON EXEC SQL SELECT                =000310=
00307 L8000 MN 0201 MNMN   ENTRY ACCUMULATE_RMI_TIME  DSNCSQL                                              =000311=
00307 L8000 MN 0202 MNMN   EXIT  ACCUMULATE_RMI_TIME/OK                                                    =000312=
00307 L8000 AP D500 UEH    EVENT LINK-TO-USER-EXIT-PROGRAM XXXRMI AT EXIT POINT XRMIOUT                    =000313=
00307 L8000 SM 0C01 SMMG   ENTRY GETMAIN              198,YES,00,TASK                                      =000314=
00307 L8000 SM 0C02 SMMG   EXIT  GETMAIN/OK           226E1788                                             =000315=
00307 L8000 SM 0D01 SMMF   ENTRY FREEMAIN             226E1788                                             =000316=
00307 L8000 SM 0D02 SMMF   EXIT  FREEMAIN/OK          USER storage at 226E1788                             =000317=
00307 L8000 AP D501 UEH    EVENT RETURN-FROM-USER-EXIT-PROGRAM XXXRMI WITH RETURN CODE 0                   =000318=
00307 L8000 RM 0301 RMLN   ENTRY SET_LINK             01C80011,22F914AC , 0000000C , 00000008,YES,NECESSARY =000319=
00307 L8000 RM 0302 RMLN   EXIT  SET_LINK/OK          22F914AC , 0000000C , 00000008,                      =000320=
00307 L8000 DS 0002 DSAT   ENTRY CHANGE_MODE          00000001                                             =000321=
00307 QR    DS 0003 DSAT   EXIT  CHANGE_MODE/OK                                                            =000322=
00307 QR    AP 2521 ERM    EXIT  ASSEMBLER-APPLICATION-CALL-TO-TRUE(DSNCSQL )                              =000323=
00307 QR    AP 00E1 EIP    ENTRY RETURN                                   0004,226E1458 .>..,08000E08 ...  =000324=
```

Enable both the application program and all exits on the DB2 call path to be THREADSAFE

Figure 8-4 on page 181 shows the same transaction, TRANA, running in a CICS Transaction Server Version 2 or Version 3 environment and making one DB2 call.

The transaction was migrated to CICS Transaction Server Version 2 or Version 3 *with* threadsafe consideration in mind. The program associated with transaction TRANA *and* the programs associated with XRMIIN, XRMIOUT, and the dynamic plan exits are all written to threadsafe standards and defined as THREADSAFE.

This diagram shows a TCB switch from the QR TCB to the L8 TCB for the first DB2 call. Upon completion of the DB2 call the program remains on the L8 TCB. The number of DB2 calls that could be made without another TCB switch is only limited by the design of the application. There would only have to be a TCB switchback to the QR TCB at task termination time, unless non threadsafe EXEC CICS commands were issued. This is where you begin to see what threadsafe can offer with regard to potential savings in both CPU and response time.

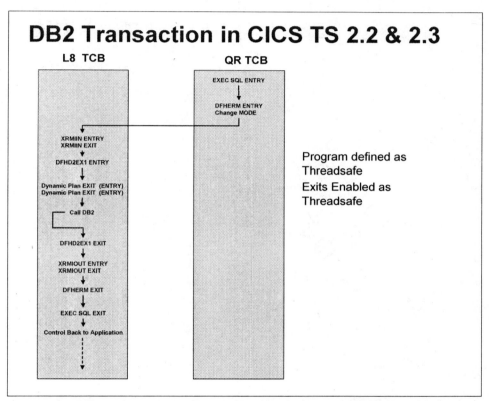

Figure 8-4   TCB switches with programs and exits running as threadsafe on CICS TS Version 2 or Version 3

Example 8-3 on page 182 is an example CICS trace showing the TCB switches described by Figure 8-4 after XRMIIN, XRMIOUT, the dynamic plan exit *and* the application program associated with transaction TRNA were written to threadsafe standards and then defined or enabled as THREADSAFE.

To be consistent, the diagram in Figure 8-4 only shows one DB2 call. However, the associated trace in Example 8-3 continues on to reflect a second DB2 call. You can see that the second DB2 call runs on the L8 TCB and no TCB switch was made.

Example 8-3   CICS trace of TCB switches with threadsafe program and exits

```
00772 QR         AP 2520 ERM    ENTRY ASSEMBLER-APPLICATION-CALL-TO-TRUE(DSNCSQL )                                                        =000242=
00772 QR         US 0401 USXM   ENTRY INQUIRE_TRANSACTION_USER                                                                            =000243=
00772 QR         US 0402 USXM   EXIT  INQUIRE_TRANSACTION_USER/OK 00000000                                                                =000244=
00772 QR         RM 0301 RMLN   ENTRY ADD_LINK              RMI,24C57CE4 , 00000000 , 00000008,000949D0 , 00000000 , 00000008,24C         =000245=
00772 QR         RM 0302 RMLN   EXIT  ADD_LINK/OK           0154000C,24C57CE4 , 00000000 , 00000008,000949D0 , 00000000 , 0000000         =000246=
00772 QR         DS 0002 DSAT   ENTRY CHANGE_MODE           0000000C                                                                      =000247=
00772 L8001 DS 0003 DSAT        EXIT  CHANGE_MODE/OK                                                                                      =000255=
00772 L8001 AP D500 UEH         EVENT LINK-TO-USER-EXIT-PROGRAM XXXRMI AT EXIT POINT XRMIIN                                               =000256=
00772 L8001 SM 0C01 SMMG        ENTRY GETMAIN               198,YES,00,TASK                                                               =000257=
00772 L8001 SM 0C02 SMMG        EXIT  GETMAIN/OK            226E1788                                                                      =000258=
00772 L8001 SM 0D01 SMMF        ENTRY FREEMAIN              226E1788                                                                      =000259=
00772 L8001 SM 0D02 SMMF        EXIT  FREEMAIN/OK           USER storage at 226E1788                                                      =000260=
00772 L8001 AP D501 UEH         EVENT RETURN-FROM-USER-EXIT-PROGRAM XXXRMI WITH RETURN CODE 0                                             =000261=
00772 L8001 AP 3180 D2EX1       ENTRY APPLICATION           REQUEST EXEC SQL SELECT                                                       =000262=
00772 L8001 PG 0A01 PGLU        ENTRY LINK_URM              DB2PLAN,22C1E678 , 0000001C,NO,NO                                             =000263=
00772 L8001 DD 0301 DDLO        ENTRY LOCATE                21C27B70,22C1E574,PPT,DB2PLAN                                                 =000264=
00772 L8001 DD 0302 DDLO        EXIT  LOCATE/OK             D7D7E3C5 , 22DA5B30                                                           =000265=
00772 L8001 LD 0001 LDLD        ENTRY ACQUIRE_PROGRAM       22C871A0                                                                      =000266=
00772 L8001 LD 0002 LDLD        EXIT  ACQUIRE_PROGRAM/OK    A43002D8,243002B0,D8,0,REUSABLE,ESDSA,OLD_COPY                                =000267=
00772 L8001 AP 1940 APLI        ENTRY START_PROGRAM         DB2PLAN,CEDF,FULLAPI,URM,NO,22F89A94,22C1E678 , 0000001C,3                    =000268=
00772 L8001 SM 0C01 SMMG        ENTRY GETMAIN               190,YES,00,TASK                                                               =000269=
00772 L8001 SM 0C02 SMMG        EXIT  GETMAIN/OK            226E1788                                                                      =000270=
00772 L8001 AP 00E1 EIP         ENTRY RETURN                                       0004,226E1798 .>.q,08000E08 ....                       =000271=
00772 L8001 AP E160 EXEC        ENTRY RETURN                ASM                                                                           =000272=
00772 L8001 SM 0301 SMGF        ENTRY FREEMAIN              226E1788,TASK                                                                 =000273=
00772 L8001 SM 0302 SMGF        EXIT  FREEMAIN/OK                                                                                         =000274=
00772 L8001 AP 1941 APLI        EXIT  START_PROGRAM/OK      ....,NO,DB2PLAN                                                               =000275=
00772 L8001 LD 0001 LDLD        ENTRY RELEASE_PROGRAM       22C871A0,A43002D8                                                             =000276=
00772 L8001 LD 0002 LDLD        EXIT  RELEASE_PROGRAM/OK    243002B0,D8,ESDSA                                                             =000277=
00772 L8001 PG 0A02 PGLU        EXIT  LINK_URM/OK                                                                                         =000278=
00772 L8001 AP 3250 D2D2        ENTRY DB2_API_CALL          230D7030                                                                      =000279=
00772 L8001 AP 3251 D2D2        EXIT  DB2_API_CALL/OK                                                                                     =000285=
00772 L8001 AP 3181 D2EX1       EXIT  APPLICATION-REQUEST   SQLCODE 0 RETURNED ON EXEC SQL SELECT                                         =000286=
00772 L8001 MN 0201 MNMN        ENTRY ACCUMULATE_RMI_TIME   DSNCSQL                                                                       =000287=
00772 L8001 MN 0202 MNMN        EXIT  ACCUMULATE_RMI_TIME/OK                                                                              =000288=
00772 L8001 AP D500 UEH         EVENT LINK-TO-USER-EXIT-PROGRAM XXXRMI AT EXIT POINT XRMIOUT                                              =000289=
00772 L8001 SM 0C01 SMMG        ENTRY GETMAIN               198,YES,00,TASK                                                               =000290=
00772 L8001 SM 0C02 SMMG        EXIT  GETMAIN/OK            226E1788                                                                      =000291=
00772 L8001 SM 0D01 SMMF        ENTRY FREEMAIN              226E1788                                                                      =000292=
00772 L8001 SM 0D02 SMMF        EXIT  FREEMAIN/OK           USER storage at 226E1788                                                      =000293=
00772 L8001 AP D501 UEH         EVENT RETURN-FROM-USER-EXIT-PROGRAM XXXRMI WITH RETURN CODE 0                                             =000294=
00772 L8001 RM 0301 RMLN        ENTRY SET_LINK              0154000C,24C57CEC , 0000000C , 00000008,YES,NECESSARY                         =000295=
00772 L8001 RM 0302 RMLN        EXIT  SET_LINK/OK           24C57CEC , 0000000C , 00000008,                                               =000296=
00772 L8001 AP 2521 ERM         EXIT  ASSEMBLER-APPLICATION-CALL-TO-TRUE(DSNCSQL )                                                        =000297=
00772 L8001 AP 2520 ERM         ENTRY ASSEMBLER-APPLICATION-CALL-TO-TRUE(DSNCSQL )                                                        =000298=
00772 L8001 AP D500 UEH         EVENT LINK-TO-USER-EXIT-PROGRAM XXXRMI AT EXIT POINT XRMIIN                                               =000299=
00772 L8001 SM 0C01 SMMG        ENTRY GETMAIN               198,YES,00,TASK                                                               =000300=
00772 L8001 SM 0C02 SMMG        EXIT  GETMAIN/OK            226E1788                                                                      =000301=
00772 L8001 SM 0D01 SMMF        ENTRY FREEMAIN              226E1788                                                                      =000302=
00772 L8001 SM 0D02 SMMF        EXIT  FREEMAIN/OK           USER storage at 226E1788                                                      =000303=
00772 L8001 AP D501 UEH         EVENT RETURN-FROM-USER-EXIT-PROGRAM XXXRMI WITH RETURN CODE 0                                             =000304=
00772 L8001 AP 3180 D2EX1       ENTRY APPLICATION           REQUEST EXEC SQL SELECT                                                       =000305=
00772 L8001 AP 3250 D2D2        ENTRY DB2_API_CALL          230D7030                                                                      =000306=
00772 L8001 AP 3251 D2D2        EXIT  DB2_API_CALL/OK                                                                                     =000307=
00772 L8001 AP 3181 D2EX1       EXIT  APPLICATION-REQUEST   SQLCODE 0 RETURNED ON EXEC SQL SELECT                                         =000308=
00772 L8001 MN 0201 MNMN        ENTRY ACCUMULATE_RMI_TIME   DSNCSQL                                                                       =000309=
00772 L8001 MN 0202 MNMN        EXIT  ACCUMULATE_RMI_TIME/OK                                                                              =000310=
00772 L8001 AP D500 UEH         EVENT LINK-TO-USER-EXIT-PROGRAM XXXRMI AT EXIT POINT XRMIOUT                                              =000311=
00772 L8001 SM 0C01 SMMG        ENTRY GETMAIN               198,YES,00,TASK                                                               =000312=
00772 L8001 SM 0C02 SMMG        EXIT  GETMAIN/OK            226E1788                                                                      =000313=
00772 L8001 SM 0D01 SMMF        ENTRY FREEMAIN              226E1788                                                                      =000314=
00772 L8001 SM 0D02 SMMF        EXIT  FREEMAIN/OK           USER storage at 226E1788                                                      =000315=
00772 L8001 AP D501 UEH         EVENT RETURN-FROM-USER-EXIT-PROGRAM XXXRMI WITH RETURN CODE 0                                             =000316=
00772 L8001 AP 2521 ERM         EXIT  ASSEMBLER-APPLICATION-CALL-TO-TRUE(DSNCSQL )                                                        =000317=
00772 L8001 AP 00E1 EIP         ENTRY RETURN                                       0004,226E1458 .>..,08000E08 ....                       =000318=
```

8.2 Migrating WebSphere MQSeries regions

The WMQ adapter supplied with CICS Transaction Server Version 3.2 is now enabled as OPENAPI by CICS. Therefore the CICS-WMQ TRUE now uses L8 TCBs and not the eight private TCBs used by previous versions of the TRUE.

The potential for unnecessary TCB switches for WMQ applications is very similar to that for DB2 applications. As for DB2 calls, WMQ calls will invoke the RMI exits XRMIIN and XRMIOUT. In addition for WMQ there is also the API crossing exit which is executed before and after each WMQ call.

> **Note:** The definition for the API crossing exit (CSQCAPX) is supplied by CICS in CSD group DFHMQ. By default it is defined as THREADSAFE and should *not* be changed.

Figure 8-5 on page 184 shows the flow of a single WMQ call from CICS where the XRMIIN and XRMIOUT exits are defined as QUASIRENT and also the application program is defined as QUASIRENT.

We have not changed the definition of the API crossing exit from its default of THREADSAFE. If it were changed then both calls to the crossing exit would also be executed over on the QR TCB, thus adding four more TCB switches to the call.

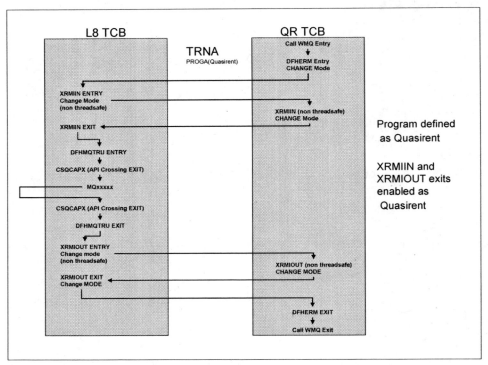

Figure 8-5 Call flow for a WMQ call with non threadsafe XRMIIN & XRMIOUT exits

If we enable the XRMI exits to be threadsafe there will be no switches back to the QR TCB when they are executed. This can be seen in Figure 8-6 on page 185.

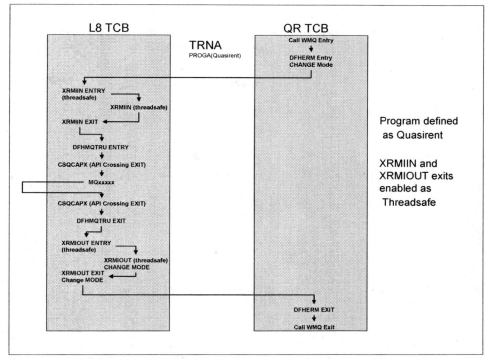

Figure 8-6   Call flow for a WMQ transaction with the XRMI exits enabled as threadsafe

Example 8-4   Example trace of an MQPUT operation.

```
***
        ***   MQPUT
        ***
00052 L8001 AP 2520 ERM    ENTRY COBOL-APPLICATION-CALL-TO-TRUE(MQM   )                                                  =001236=
00052 L8001 AP D500 UEH    EVENT LINK-TO-USER-EXIT-PROGRAM GENGEXIT AT EXIT POINT XRMIIN                                  =001237=
00052 L8001 AP D501 UEH    EVENT RETURN-FROM-USER-EXIT-PROGRAM GENGEXIT WITH RETURN CODE 790568                           =001238=
00052 L8001 AP 2522 ERM    EVENT PASSING-CONTROL-TO-OPENAPI-TRUE(MQM   )                                                  =001239=
00052 L8001 AP A090 MQTRU  ENTRY APPLICATION-REQUEST     MQPUT                                                            =001240=
00052 L8001 AP A099 MQTRU  EVENT CSQCPMGH                       & CSQCPMGD ABOUT TO ISSUE MQPUT                           =001241=


        ***
        ***   CSQCAPX
        ***
00052 L8001 AP 00E1 EIP    ENTRY LINK                                          0004,266ADE6C ...%,08000E02 ....           =001242=
00052 L8001 AP E110 EISR   ENTRY TRACE_ENTRY             266AD734                                                         =001243=
00052 L8001 AP E160 EXEC   ENTRY LINK                    'CSQCAPX ' AT X'279F2A96','..Q........&...Y................-y...' AT X =001244=
00052 L8001 AP E111 EISR   EXIT  TRACE_ENTRY/OK                                                                           =001245=
00052 L8001 PG 1101 PGLE   ENTRY LINK_EXEC               CSQCAPX,266AEB98 , 00000024,NO,NO                                =001246=
00052 L8001 DD 0301 DDLO   ENTRY LOCATE                  2592AE60,26CD46AC,PPT,CSQCAPX                                    =001247=
00052 L8001 DD 0302 DDLO   EXIT  LOCATE/OK               D7D7E3C5 , 26DF0108                                              =001248=
00052 L8001 LD 0001 LDLD   ENTRY ACQUIRE_PROGRAM         26DEF750                                                         =001249=
00052 L8001 LD 0002 LDLD   EXIT  ACQUIRE_PROGRAM/OK      A6D84828,26D84800,550,REUSABLE,ECDSA,OLD_COPY,                   =001250=
00052 L8001 AP 1940 APLI   ENTRY START_PROGRAM           CSQCAPX,NOCEDF,FULLAPI,EXEC,NO,2594C880,266AEB98 , 00000024,3,NO =001251=
00052 L8001 SM 0C01 SMMG   ENTRY GETMAIN                 20C,YES,00,TASK                                                  =001252=
00052 L8001 SM 0C02 SMMG   EXIT  GETMAIN/OK              266AEBD8                                                         =001253=
00052 L8001 AP 00E1 EIP    ENTRY RETURN                                        0004,266AEBE8 ...Y,08000E08 ....           =001254=
00052 L8001 AP E110 EISR   ENTRY TRACE_ENTRY             266AEC50                                                         =001255=
```

```
00052 L8001 AP E160 EXEC  ENTRY RETURN                ASM                                                                           =001256=
00052 L8001 AP E111 EISR  EXIT  TRACE_ENTRY/OK                                                                                      =001257=
00052 L8001 SM 0301 SMGF  ENTRY FREEMAIN              266AEBD8,TASK                                                                 =001258=
00052 L8001 SM 0302 SMGF  EXIT  FREEMAIN/OK                                                                                         =001259=
00052 L8001 AP 1941 APLI  EXIT  START_PROGRAM/OK      ,NO,CSQCAPX                                                                   =001260=
00052 L8001 LD 0001 LDLD  ENTRY RELEASE_PROGRAM       26DEF750,A6D84828                                                             =001261=
00052 L8001 LD 0002 LDLD  EXIT  RELEASE_PROGRAM/OK    26D84800,550,ECDSA                                                            =001262=
00052 L8001 PG 1700 PGCH  ENTRY DELETE_OWNED_CHANNELS                                                                               =001263=
00052 L8001 PG 1701 PGCH  EXIT  DELETE_OWNED_CHANNELS/OK                                                                            =001264=
00052 L8001 PG 1102 PGLE  EXIT  LINK_EXEC/OK          ,,,                                                                           =001265=
00052 L8001 AP E110 EISR  ENTRY TRACE_EXIT            266AD734                                                                      =001266=
00052 L8001 AP E161 EXEC  EXIT  LINK                  'CSQCAPX ' AT X'279F2A96','..Q........&...Y...............-y...' AT X         =001267=
00052 L8001 AP E111 EISR  EXIT  TRACE_EXIT/OK                                                                                       =001268=
00052 L8001 AP 00E1 EIP   EXIT  LINK                  OK                          00F4,00000000 ....,00000E02 ....                  =001269=


         ***
         *** CSQCAPX
         ***
00052 L8001 AP 00E1 EIP   ENTRY LINK                                              0004,266ADE6C ...%,08000E02 ....                  =001270=
00052 L8001 AP E110 EISR  ENTRY TRACE_ENTRY           266AD734                                                                      =001271=
00052 L8001 AP E160 EXEC  ENTRY LINK                  'CSQCAPX ' AT X'279F2A96','..Q........&...Y...............-y...' AT X         =001272=
00052 L8001 AP E111 EISR  EXIT  TRACE_ENTRY/OK                                                                                      =001273=
00052 L8001 PG 1101 PGLE  ENTRY LINK_EXEC             CSQCAPX,266AEB98 , 00000024,NO,NO                                             =001274=
00052 L8001 DD 0301 DDLO  ENTRY LOCATE                2592AE60,26CD46AC,PPT,CSQCAPX                                                 =001275=
00052 L8001 DD 0302 DDLO  EXIT  LOCATE/OK             D7D7E3C5 , 26DF0108                                                           =001276=
00052 L8001 LD 0001 LDLD  ENTRY ACQUIRE_PROGRAM       26DEF750                                                                      =001277=
00052 L8001 LD 0002 LDLD  EXIT  ACQUIRE_PROGRAM/OK    A6D84828,26D84800,550,REUSABLE,ECDSA,OLD_COPY,                                =001278=
00052 L8001 AP 1940 APLI  ENTRY START_PROGRAM         CSQCAPX,NOCEDF,FULLAPI,EXEC,NO,2594C880,266AEB98 , 00000024,3,NO              =001279=
00052 L8001 SM 0C01 SMMG  ENTRY GETMAIN               20C,YES,00,TASK                                                               =001280=
00052 L8001 SM 0C02 SMMG  EXIT  GETMAIN/OK            266AEBD8                                                                      =001281=
00052 L8001 AP 00E1 EIP   ENTRY RETURN                                            0004,266AEBE8 ...Y,08000E08 ....                  =001282=
00052 L8001 AP E110 EISR  ENTRY TRACE_ENTRY           266AEC50                                                                      =001283=
00052 L8001 AP E160 EXEC  ENTRY RETURN                ASM                                                                           =001284=
00052 L8001 AP E111 EISR  EXIT  TRACE_ENTRY/OK                                                                                      =001285=
00052 L8001 SM 0301 SMGF  ENTRY FREEMAIN              266AEBD8,TASK                                                                 =001286=
00052 L8001 SM 0302 SMGF  EXIT  FREEMAIN/OK                                                                                         =001287=
00052 L8001 AP 1941 APLI  EXIT  START_PROGRAM/OK      ,NO,CSQCAPX                                                                   =001288=
00052 L8001 LD 0001 LDLD  ENTRY RELEASE_PROGRAM       26DEF750,A6D84828                                                             =001289=
00052 L8001 LD 0002 LDLD  EXIT  RELEASE_PROGRAM/OK    26D84800,550,ECDSA                                                            =001290=
00052 L8001 PG 1700 PGCH  ENTRY DELETE_OWNED_CHANNELS                                                                               =001291=
00052 L8001 PG 1701 PGCH  EXIT  DELETE_OWNED_CHANNELS/OK                                                                            =001292=
00052 L8001 PG 1102 PGLE  EXIT  LINK_EXEC/OK          ,,,                                                                           =001293=
00052 L8001 AP E110 EISR  ENTRY TRACE_EXIT            266AD734                                                                      =001294=
00052 L8001 AP E161 EXEC  EXIT  LINK                  'CSQCAPX ' AT X'279F2A96','..Q........&...Y...............-y...' AT X         =001295=
00052 L8001 AP E111 EISR  EXIT  TRACE_EXIT/OK                                                                                       =001296=
00052 L8001 AP 00E1 EIP   EXIT  LINK                  OK                          00F4,00000000 ....,00000E02 ....                  =001297=


00052 L8001 AP A09A MQTRU EVENT CSQCPMGI              MESSAGE ID                                                                    =001298=
00052 L8001 AP A091 MQTRU EXIT  APPLICATION-REQUEST   MQPUT 00000000,00000000                                                       =001299=
00052 L8001 AP 2523 ERM   EVENT REGAINING-CONTROL-FROM-OPENAPI-TRUE(MQM    )                                                        =001300=
00052 L8001 AP D500 UEH   EVENT LINK-TO-USER-EXIT-PROGRAM GENGEXIT AT EXIT POINT XRMIOUT                                             =001301=
00052 L8001 AP D501 UEH   EVENT RETURN-FROM-USER-EXIT-PROGRAM GENGEXIT WITH RETURN CODE 790568                                       =001302=
00052 L8001 RM 0301 RMLN  ENTRY SET_LINK              01000009,26FEC31C , 0000000C , 00000008,YES,NECESSARY                         =001303=
00052 L8001 RM 0302 RMLN  EXIT  SET_LINK/OK           26FEC31C , 0000000C , 00000008,                                               =001304=
00052 L8001 AP 2521 ERM   EXIT  COBOL-APPLICATION-CALL-TO-TRUE(MQM       )                                                          =001305=
```

8.2.1 The API crossing exit (CSQCAPX)

Care should be taken when changing the WMQ API crossing exit (CSQCAPX). It is possible to execute CICS API commands. If you amend this exit to make calls to non threadsafe CICS API commands, be aware that this will cause a switch to the QR TCB in order to execute this command and then a switch back to the open TCB in order to continue with the WMQ call.

8.3 OPENAPI programs and additional TCB switching

CICS Transaction Server Version 3 allows programs to be defined with API(OPENAPI) and so run almost independently of the QR TCB. Such programs run on an L8 or L9 open TCB, depending upon their EXECKEY value. The OPENAPI definition is introduced in 2.2.5, "CICS Transaction Server 3.1" on page 21.

OPENAPI programs must be threadsafe and defined to CICS as such.

Because OPENAPI programs can potentially use non-CICS APIs, the key of the TCB is important and must match the execution key. This is unlike CICSAPI threadsafe programs that can execute in the CICS key or the user key irrespective of the TCB key. CICS services are implemented irrespective of the key of the TCB they are running under, unlike MVS services, which care about the TCB key.

> **Important note:** Use of non-CICS APIs within CICS is entirely at the risk of the user. No testing of non-CICS APIs within CICS has been undertaken by IBM, and use of such APIs is not supported by IBM service.

The use of OPENAPI programs can increase TCB switching within CICS. If an OPENAPI program is defined to run with an execution key of user, it is given control under an L9 TCB rather than an L8 TCB. Should the program issue a call to an OPENAPI TRUE, the task is switched to an L8 TCB for the duration of the call. This is because OPENAPI TRUEs have to run in CICS key under an L8 TCB. Those IBM-supplied TRUES are:

DFHD2EX1	CICS DB2 Adapter
DFHMQTRU	CICS MQ Adapter
EZACIC01	IP CICS Sockets Adapter

On completion of the call, CICS returns control to the application program on its L9 TCB.

Likewise, an OPENAPI program that invokes non threadsafe EXEC CICS commands will be switched from its L8 or L9 TCB to the QR TCB for the duration of the CICS request, then switched back to the open TCB when returning control to the application program. This is because when a program is defined as being OPENAPI it means it *must* run its application logic under an open L8 or L9 TCB. This is different from a CICSAPI threadsafe program, which does not have affinity to any one TCB and executes under whatever TCB CICS deems appropriate to use.

To avoid such additional TCB switching, user key applications that make calls to OPENAPI enabled TRUEs are best left defined as CICSAPI threadsafe programs. Other good candidates for threadsafe programs defined with API(CICSAPI) are those that invoke non threadsafe CICS API requests.

Programs that are good candidates to be defined as API(OPENAPI) are:

- Those with an execution key of CICS that make calls to OPENAPI-enabled TRUEs
- Those that only invoke threadsafe CICS API requests
- CPU-intensive applications

A summary of good and bad candidates can be seen in "OPENAPI good and bad candidates" on page 53.

> **Note:** The EXECKEY program attribute will determine the mode of open TCB that is assigned for an OPENAPI program to run under. User key programs will run under an L9 TCB, CICS key programs under an L8 TCB. There is an exception to this behavior, however. If a CICS system does not have storage protection active (that is, STGPROT=NO is specified), all OPENAPI programs will run under L8 TCBs, regardless of their EXECKEY value. This is because STGPROT=NO makes CICS operate without any storage protection, and so run in a single storage key (key 8).

8.4 Function shipped commands

The temporary storage API commands (equally valid for function shipped transient data, interval control, file control, and DLI calls) are threadsafe. This is true when the commands are performed against locally defined resources or against shared temporary storage queues residing within a coupling facility. However, if these commands are performed against remote resources, they must be function shipped to the remote region to execute. This involves extra TCB switching due to Multi-Region Operation (MRO) and Intersystem Communication (ISC) CICS components not being threadsafe. The same is true for an EXEC CICS LINK command to a remote program (that is, a DPL call).

The following examples show these commands being performed in both local and remote scenarios.

Example 8-5 is a CICS trace of a threadsafe CICSAPI application program making a DB2 call on an open L8 TCB. It then does an EXEC CICS LINK to program DUMMY, which is defined as a local program. The LINK command is threadsafe, so there is no mode switch to the QR TCB and the request is processed on the L8 TCB.

Example 8-5   CICS trace of link command on local region

```
54728 L800I AP 3180 D2EX1 ENTRY APPLICATION          REQUEST EXEC SQL SELECT                                        =000268=
54728 L800I AP 3250 D2D2  ENTRY DB2_API_CALL         22F76330                                                        =000269=
54728 L800I AP 3251 D2D2  EXIT  DB2_API_CALL/OK                                                                      =000270=
54728 L800I AP 3181 D2EX1 EXIT  APPLICATION-REQUEST  SQLCODE -805 RETURNED ON EXEC SQL SELECT                        =000271=
54728 L800I MN 0201 MNMN  ENTRY ACCUMULATE_RMI_TIME  DSNCSQL                                                         =000272=
54728 L800I MN 0202 MNMN  EXIT  ACCUMULATE_RMI_TIME/OK                                                               =000273=
54728 L800I RM 0301 RMLN  ENTRY SET_LINK             01CF034D,22DE21EC , 0000000C , 00000008,YES,NECESSARY           =000274=
54728 L800I RM 0302 RMLN  EXIT  SET_LINK/OK          22DE21EC , 0000000C , 00000008,                                 =000275=
54728 L800I AP 2521 ERM   EXIT  ASSEMBLER-APPLICATION-CALL-TO-TRUE(DSNCSQL )                                         =000276=
54728 L800I AP 00E1 EIP   ENTRY LINK                                           0004,226D1458 ._...,08000E02 ....     =000277=
54728 L800I AP E160 EXEC  ENTRY LINK                 'DUMMY    ' AT X'A43037D8',ASM                                  =000278=
54728 L800I PG 1101 PGLE  ENTRY LINK_EXEC            DUMMY,NO,NO                                                     =000279=
54728 L800I DD 0301 DDLO  ENTRY LOCATE               21C27B70,22B956DC,PPT,DUMMY                                     =000280=
54728 L800I DD 0302 DDLO  EXIT  LOCATE/OK            D7D7E3C5 , 2410F6B8                                             =000281=
54728 L800I LD 0001 LDLD  ENTRY ACQUIRE_PROGRAM      24199988                                                        =000282=
54728 L800I AP 00E1 EIP   ENTRY LINK                                           0004,226D1458 ._...,08000E02 ....     =000277=
54728 L800I AP E160 EXEC  ENTRY LINK                 'DUMMY    ' AT X'A43037D8',ASM                                  =000278=
54728 L800I PG 1101 PGLE  ENTRY LINK_EXEC            DUMMY,NO,NO                                                     =000279=
54728 L800I DD 0301 DDLO  ENTRY LOCATE               21C27B70,22B956DC,PPT,DUMMY                                     =000280=
54728 L800I DD 0302 DDLO  EXIT  LOCATE/OK            D7D7E3C5 , 2410F6B8                                             =000281=
54728 L800I LD 0001 LDLD  ENTRY ACQUIRE_PROGRAM      24199988                                                        =000282=
54728 L800I LD 0002 LDLD  EXIT  ACQUIRE_PROGRAM/OK   A4303C30,24303C30,138,0,REUSABLE,ESDSA,OLD_COPY                 =000283=
54728 L800I AP 1940 APLI  ENTRY START_PROGRAM        DUMMY,CEDF,FULLAPI,EXEC,NO,2410D6B8,00000000 , 00000000,2,NO    =000284=
54728 L800I SM 0C01 SMMG  ENTRY GETMAIN              190,YES,00,TASK                                                 =000285=
54728 L800I SM 0C02 SMMG  EXIT  GETMAIN/OK           226D1788                                                        =000286=
54728 L800I AP 00E1 EIP   ENTRY RETURN                                         0004,226D1798 ._.q,08000E08 ....      =000287=
54728 L800I AP E160 EXEC  ENTRY RETURN               ASM                                                             =000288=
54728 L800I SM 0301 SMGF  ENTRY FREEMAIN             226D1788,TASK                                                   =000289=
54728 L800I SM 0302 SMGF  EXIT  FREEMAIN/OK                                                                          =000290=
54728 L800I AP 1941 APLI  EXIT  START_PROGRAM/OK     ....,NO,DUMMY                                                   =000291=
54728 L800I LD 0001 LDLD  ENTRY RELEASE_PROGRAM      24199988,A4303C30                                               =000292=
54728 L800I LD 0002 LDLD  EXIT  RELEASE_PROGRAM/OK   24303C30,138,ESDSA                                              =000293=
54728 L800I PG 1102 PGLE  EXIT  LINK_EXEC/OK         ,,,                                                             =000294=
54728 L800I AP E161 EXEC  EXIT  LINK                 'DUMMY    ' AT X'A43037D8',0,0,ASM                              =000295=
54728 L800I AP 00E1 EIP   EXIT  LINK                 OK                        00F4,00000000 ....,00000E02 ....      =000296=
```

Example 8-6 on page 190 is a CICS trace of a threadsafe CICSAPI application program making a DB2 call on an open L8 TCB. It then does a distributed program link (DPL) request to program DUMMY. Although the link command itself is threadsafe, there is a mode switch to the QR TCB in order to ship the request to the remote region. When the link to program DUMMY returns, notice that the application continues to run on the QR TCB and does not switch back to the L8 TCB. The application will not be switched to the L8 TCB until another DB2 request is made.

Example 8-6   CICS trace of distributed program link (DPL)

```
54734 L800I AP 3180 D2EX1 ENTRY APPLICATION            REQUEST EXEC SQL SELECT                                        =000262=
54734 L800I AP 3250 D2D2  ENTRY DB2_API_CALL           22F76330                                                       =000263=
54734 L800I AP 3251 D2D2  EXIT  DB2_API_CALL/OK                                                                       =000264=
54734 L800I AP 3181 D2EX1 EXIT  APPLICATION-REQUEST    SQLCODE -805 RETURNED ON EXEC SQL SELECT                       =000265=
54734 L800I MN 0201 MNMN  ENTRY ACCUMULATE_RMI_TIME    DSNCSQL                                                        =000266=
54734 L800I MN 0202 MNMN  EXIT  ACCUMULATE_RMI_TIME/OK                                                                =000267=
54734 L800I RM 0301 RMLN  ENTRY SET_LINK               01020035,22DE21EC , 0000000C , 00000008,YES,NECESSARY          =000268=
54734 L800I RM 0302 RMLN  EXIT  SET_LINK/OK            22DE21EC , 0000000C , 00000008,                                =000269=
54734 L800I AP 2521 ERM   EXIT  ASSEMBLER-APPLICATION-CALL-TO-TRUE(DSNCSQL )                                          =000270=
54734 L800I AP 00E1 EIP   ENTRY LINK                                                          0004,226D1458 ._...,08000E02 ....  =000271=
54734 L800I AP E160 EXEC  ENTRY LINK                   'DUMMY    ' AT X'A43037D8',ASM                                 =000272=
54734 L800I PG 1101 PGLE  ENTRY LINK_EXEC              DUMMY,NO,NO                                                    =000273=
54734 L800I DD 0301 DDLO  ENTRY LOCATE                 21C27B70,22B956DC,PPT,DUMMY                                    =000274=
54734 L800I DD 0302 DDLO  EXIT  LOCATE/OK              D7D7E3C5 , 2410F6B8                                            =000275=
54734 L800I PG 1102 PGLE  EXIT  LINK_EXEC/EXCEPTION    REMOTE_PROGRAM,PJA7,DUMMY,,                                    =000276=
54734 L800I DS 0002 DSAT  ENTRY CHANGE_MODE            QR                                                             =000277=
54734 QR    DS 0003 DSAT  EXIT  CHANGE_MODE/OK                                                                        =000278=
54734 QR    AP 00DF ISP   ENTRY CONVERSE                                                      0003,04000000 ....,D7D1C1F7 PJA7  =000279=
54734 QR    AP D900 XFP   ENTRY TRANSFORMER_1          226D14C0,0E0200000000000000000003C090000                       =000280=
54734 QR    PG 0500 PGIS  ENTRY INQUIRE_CURRENT_PROGRAM                                                               =000281=
54734 QR    PG 0501 PGIS  EXIT  INQUIRE_CURRENT_PROGRAM/OK FUNCSHIP                                                   =000282=
54734 QR    AP D901 XFP   EXIT  TRANSFORMER_1          226D14C0,0E024C6E00580010FD016054734C00D5                      =000283=
54734 QR    AP FD01 ZARQ  ENTRY APPL_REQ               22F077F0,WRITE,READ,WAIT,FMH                                   =000284=
54734 QR    AP FD0D ZIS2  ENTRY IRC                    22F077F0,IOR,WRITE,WAIT,READ                                   =000285=
54734 QR    AP DD21 ZIS2  EVENT IRC                    SWITCH SUBSEQUENT TO SYSTEM (SCSCPJA7) RETURN CODE WAS 00000000 =000286=
54734 QR    AP DD22 ZIS2  EVENT IRC                    OUTBOUND REQUEST HEADER: FMH RQE CD , 12                       =000287=
54734 QR    DS 0004 DSSR  ENTRY WAIT_MVS               IRLINK,7F656CC0,YES,INHIBIT,YES,CONV,PJA7>ALA                  =000288=
54734 QR    DS 0005 DSSR  EXIT  WAIT_MVS/OK                                                                           =000289=
54734 QR    AP DD24 ZIS2  EVENT IRC                    INBOUND REQUEST HEADER: FMH RQE CD , 12                        =000290=
54734 QR    AP FD8D ZIS2  EXIT  IRC                    22F077F0,NORMAL                                                =000291=
54734 QR    AP FC01 ZARQ  EVENT MRO/LU6.1              STATE SETTING TO SEND                                          =000292=
54734 QR    AP FD81 ZARQ  EXIT  APPL_REQ                                                                              =000293=
54734 QR    AP D900 XFP   ENTRY TRANSFORMER_4          226D14C0,0E024C6E00330010D9016054734C00D5                      =000294=
54734 QR    AP D901 XFP   EXIT  TRANSFORMER_4          226D14C0,0E024C6E003C001000DF6054734C00D5                      =000295=
54734 QR    AP 00DF ISP   EXIT  CONVERSE                                                      0005,04000000 ....,D7D1C1F7 PJA7  =000296=
54734 QR    AP E161 EXEC  EXIT  LINK                   'DUMMY    ' AT X'A43037D8',0,0,ASM                             =000297=
54734 QR    AP 00E1 EIP   EXIT  LINK                   OK                                     00F4,00000000 ....,00000E02 ....  =000298=
54734 QR    AP 00E1 EIP   ENTRY SEND-TEXT                                                     0004,226D1458 ._...,08001806 .... =000299=
54734 QR    AP E160 EXEC  ENTRY SEND                   TEXT 'TRANSACTION COMPLETE            ' AT X'24303714',30 AT X'A4303802 =000300=
54734 QR    SM 0C01 SMMG  ENTRY GETMAIN                22,YES,00,CICS24_SAA                                           =000301=
54734 QR    SM 0C02 SMMG  EXIT  GETMAIN/OK             00041008                                                       =000302=
54734 QR    SM 0D01 SMMF  ENTRY FREEMAIN               22FA8020,22CBD6F0                                              =000303=
54734 QR    SM 0D02 SMMF  EXIT  FREEMAIN/OK            TERMINAL storage at 22FA8020                                   =000304=
54734 QR    AP 00FA BMS   ENTRY SEND-OUT               CTRL                                   0003,00000800 ....,04000020 ....  =000305=
54734 QR    SM 0301 SMGF  ENTRY GETMAIN                464,YES,00,MCPOSPWA,CICS                                       =000306=
54734 QR    SM 0302 SMGF  EXIT  GETMAIN/OK             22FA9008                                                       =000307=
54734 QR    PG 0500 PGIS  ENTRY INQUIRE_CURRENT_PROGRAM                                                               =000308=
```

Example 8-7 on page 191 is a CICS trace of a threadsafe CICSAPI application program making a DB2 call on an open L8 TCB. It then issues a WRITEQ-TS request to temporary storage queue TCBTEST, which is defined as a local queue. The WRITEQ-TS command is threadsafe, so there is no mode switch to the QR TCB and the request is processed on the L8 TCB.

Example 8-7   CICS trace of WRITEQ-TS command on local region

```
54910 L800I AP 3250 D2D2  ENTRY DB2_API_CALL         22F76330                                              =000257=
54910 L800I AP 3251 D2D2  EXIT  DB2_API_CALL/OK                                                            =000258=
54910 L800I AP 3181 D2EX1 EXIT  APPLICATION-REQUEST  SQLCODE -805 RETURNED ON EXEC SQL SELECT              =000259=
54910 L800I MN 0201 MNMN  ENTRY ACCUMULATE_RMI_TIME  DSNCSQL                                               =000260=
54910 L800I MN 0202 MNMN  EXIT  ACCUMULATE_RMI_TIME/OK                                                     =000261=
54910 L800I RM 0301 RMLN  ENTRY SET_LINK             01020037,22DE21EC , 0000000C , 00000008,YES,NECESSARY =000262=
54910 L800I RM 0302 RMLN  EXIT  SET_LINK/OK          22DE21EC , 0000000C , 00000008,                       =000263=
54910 L800I AP 2521 ERM   EXIT  ASSEMBLER-APPLICATION-CALL-TO-TRUE(DSNCSQL )                               =000264=
54910 L800I AP 00E1 EIP   ENTRY WRITEQ-TS                                  0004,23C41458 .D..,08000A02 ... =000265=
54910 L800I AP E160 EXEC  ENTRY WRITEQ               TS 'TCBTEST ' AT X'24303850','THIS IS THE POST-SQL WRITEQ =000266=
54910 L800I TS 0C01 TSMB  ENTRY MATCH                TCBTEST                                               =000267=
54910 L800I TS 0C02 TSMB  EXIT  MATCH/OK             ,,,TCBTEST,,00000000,,ANY,NO,NO                       =000268=
54910 L800I TS 0201 TSQR  ENTRY WRITE                TCBTEST,23C41660 , 00000050,YES,AUXILIARY,EXEC        =000269=
54910 L800I TS 0901 TSAM  ENTRY WRITE_AUX_DATA       23C41660 , 00000050,TCBTEST,BB1A867EE0360C42,8,1,NO,NO,YES =000270=
54910 L800I TS 0902 TSAM  EXIT  WRITE_AUX_DATA/OK    1,00000001                                            =000271=
54910 L800I TS 0202 TSQR  EXIT  WRITE/OK             8                                                     =000272=
54910 L800I AP E161 EXEC  EXIT  WRITEQ               TS 'TCBTEST ' AT X'24303850','THIS IS THE POST-SQL WRITEQ =000273=
54910 L800I AP 00E1 EIP   EXIT  WRITEQ-TS            OK                    00F4,00000000 ....,00000A02 ... =000274=
```

Example 8-8 on page 192 is a CICS trace of a threadsafe CICSAPI application program making a DB2 call on an open L8 TCB. It then issues a WRITEQ-TS request to temporary storage queue TCBTEST, which is defined as remote. Although the WRITEQ-TS command itself is threadsafe, there is a mode switch to the QR TCB in order to function ship the request to the remote region. When the WRITEQ-TS returns, notice that the application continues to run on the QR TCB and does not switch back to the L8 TCB. The application will not be switched to the L8 TCB until another DB2 request is made.

Example 8-8 CICS trace of WRITEQ-TS command being function shipped

```
54915 L800I AP 3180 D2EX1 ENTRY APPLICATION             REQUEST EXEC SQL SELECT                                                =000381=
54915 L800I AP 3250 D2D2  ENTRY DB2_API_CALL            22F76330                                                                =000382=
54915 L800I AP 3251 D2D2  EXIT  DB2_API_CALL/OK                                                                                 =000383=
54915 L800I AP 3181 D2EX1 EXIT  APPLICATION-REQUEST     SQLCODE -805 RETURNED ON EXEC SQL SELECT                                =000384=
54915 L800I MN 0201 MNMN  ENTRY ACCUMULATE_RMI_TIME     DSNCSQL                                                                 =000385=
54915 L800I MN 0202 MNMN  EXIT  ACCUMULATE_RMI_TIME/OK                                                                          =000386=
54915 L800I RM 0301 RMLN  ENTRY SET_LINK                01CF034F,22DE21EC , 0000000C , 00000008,YES,NECESSARY                   =000387=
54915 L800I RM 0302 RMLN  EXIT  SET_LINK/OK             22DE21EC , 0000000C , 00000008,                                         =000388=
54915 L800I AP 2521 ERM   EXIT  ASSEMBLER-APPLICATION-CALL-TO-TRUE(DSNCSQL )                                                    =000389=
54915 L800I AP 00E1 EIP   ENTRY WRITEQ-TS                                            0004,23C41458 .D..,08000A02 ....           =000390=
54915 L800I AP E160 EXEC  ENTRY WRITEQ                  TS 'TCBTEST ' AT X'24303850','THIS IS THE POST-SQL WRITEQ                =000391=
54915 L800I TS 0C01 TSMB  ENTRY MATCH                   TCBTEST                                                                 =000392=
54915 L800I TS 0C02 TSMB  EXIT  MATCH/OK                TCBTEST,TCBTEST,,TCBTEST,,00000000,PJA7,NO,NO,NO                        =000393=
54915 L800I DS 0002 DSAT  ENTRY CHANGE_MODE             QR                                                                      =000394=
54915 QR    DS 0003 DSAT  EXIT  CHANGE_MODE/OK                                                                                  =000395=
54915 QR    AP 00DF ISP   ENTRY CONVERSE                                             0003,04000000 ....,D7D1C1F7 PJA7           =000396=
54915 QR    AP D902 XFX   ENTRY TRANSFORMER_1           23C414C0,0A024C6E00330010D9036054915C00CD                               =000397=
54915 QR    AP D903 XFX   EXIT  TRANSFORMER_1           23C414C0,0A024C6E00580010DF016054915C00CD                               =000398=
54915 QR    AP FD01 ZARQ  ENTRY APPL_REQ                22F077F0,WRITE,READ,WAIT,FMH                                            =000399=
54915 QR    AP FD00 ZIS2  ENTRY IRC                     22F077F0,IOR,WRITE,WAIT,READ                                            =000400=
54915 QR    AP DD21 ZIS2  EVENT IRC                     SWITCH SUBSEQUENT TO SYSTEM (SCSCPJA7) RETURN CODE WAS 00000000          =000401=
54915 QR    AP DD22 ZIS2  EVENT IRC                     OUTBOUND REQUEST HEADER: FMH RQE CD , 15                                =000402=
54915 QR    DS 0004 DSSR  ENTRY WAIT_MVS                IRLINK,7F656CC0,YES,INHIBIT,YES,CONV,PJA7>ALA                            =000403=
54915 QR    DS 0005 DSSR  EXIT  WAIT_MVS/OK                                                                                     =000404=
54915 QR    AP DD24 ZIS2  EVENT IRC                     INBOUND REQUEST HEADER: FMH RQE CD , 15                                 =000405=
54915 QR    AP FD8D ZIS2  EXIT  IRC                     22F077F0,NORMAL                                                         =000406=
54915 QR    AP FC01 ZARQ  EVENT MRO/LU6.1               STATE SETTING TO SEND                                                   =000407=
54915 QR    AP FD81 ZARQ  EXIT  APPL_REQ                                                                                        =000408=
54915 QR    AP D902 XFX   ENTRY TRANSFORMER_4           23C414C0,0A024C6E00330010D9036054915C00CD                               =000409=
54915 QR    AP D903 XFX   EXIT  TRANSFORMER_4           23C414C0,0A024C6E003C001000DF6054915C00CD                               =000410=
54915 QR    AP 00DF ISP   EXIT  CONVERSE                                             0005,04000000 ....,D7D1C1F7 PJA7           =000411=
54915 QR    AP E161 EXEC  EXIT  WRITEQ                  TS 'TCBTEST ' AT X'24303850','THIS IS THE POST-SQL WRITEQ                =000412=
54915 QR    AP 00E1 EIP   EXIT  WRITEQ-TS               OK                           00F4,00000000 ....,00000A02 ....           =000413=
54915 QR    AP 00E1 EIP   ENTRY SEND-TEXT                                            0004,23C41458 .D..,08001806 ....           =000414=
54915 QR    AP E160 EXEC  ENTRY SEND                    TEXT 'TRANSACTION COMPLETE                ' AT X'24303738',30 AT X'A43038CC =000415=
54915 QR    SM 0C01 SMMG  ENTRY GETMAIN                 22,YES,00,CICS24_SAA                                                    =000416=
54915 QR    SM 0C02 SMMG  EXIT  GETMAIN/OK              0004C008                                                                =000417=
54915 QR    SM 0D01 SMMF  ENTRY FREEMAIN                22FA88C0,22CBD6F0                                                       =000418=
54915 QR    SM 0D02 SMMF  EXIT  FREEMAIN/OK             TERMINAL storage at 22FA88C0                                            =000419=
54915 QR    AP 00FA BMS   ENTRY SEND-OUT                CTRL                         0003,00000800 ....,04000020 ....           =000420=
54915 QR    SM 0301 SMGF  ENTRY GETMAIN                 464,YES,00,MCPOSPWA,CICS                                                =000421=
54915 QR    SM 0302 SMGF  EXIT  GETMAIN/OK              22FF3008                                                                =000422=
```

Example 8-9 on page 193 is a CICS trace of a threadsafe CICSAPI application program making a DB2 call on an open L8 TCB. It then issues a WRITEQ-TS request to a shared temporary storage queue TCBTEST, which resides within a coupling facility. In this scenario there is no need to function ship the WRITEQ-TS request. The application continues to run on the L8 TCB with no additional TCB switches to the QR TCB. Conversion of remote temporary storage queues to shared temporary storage queues within a coupling facility is a recommended solution within a threadsafe environment.

Note that the initial call to the shared temporary storage server is always issued from the QR TCB, regardless of which TCB the program is currently on.

Example 8-9 CICS trace of WRITEQ-TS request to shared temporary storage queue

```
00300 QR    AP 2520 ERM   ENTRY ASSEMBLER-APPLICATION-CALL-TO-TRUE(DSNCSQL )                                                              =000219=
00300 QR    US 0401 USXM  ENTRY INQUIRE_TRANSACTION_USER                                                                                  =000220=
00300 QR    US 0402 USXM  EXIT  INQUIRE_TRANSACTION_USER/OK 00000000                                                                      =000221=
00300 QR    RM 0301 RMLN  ENTRY ADD_LINK              RMI,22F914A4 , 22C1D640 , 00000008,000949D0 , 21B06F30 , 00000008,22F               =000222=
00300 QR    RM 0302 RMLN  EXIT  ADD_LINK/OK           01C8000F,22F914A4 , 22C1D640 , 00000008,000949D0 , 21B06F30 , 0000000               =000223=
00300 QR    DS 0002 DSAT  ENTRY CHANGE_MODE           0000000C                                                                            =000224=
00300 L8000 DS 0003 DSAT  EXIT  CHANGE_MODE/OK                                                                                            =000225=
00300 L8000 AP D500 UEH   EVENT LINK-TO-USER-EXIT-PROGRAM XXXRMI AT EXIT POINT XRMIIN                                                     =000226=
00300 L8000 SM 0C01 SMMG  ENTRY GETMAIN               198,YES,00,TASK                                                                     =000227=
00300 L8000 SM 0C02 SMMG  EXIT  GETMAIN/OK            22661788                                                                            =000228=
CICS - AUXILIARY TRACE FROM 04/26/04 - APPLID SCSCPJA6 - TIME OF FIRST ENTRY ON THIS PAGE 09:58:10.4188565405                      PAGE 00003

00300 L8000 SM 0D01 SMMF  ENTRY FREEMAIN              22661788                                                                            =000229=
00300 L8000 SM 0D02 SMMF  EXIT  FREEMAIN/OK           USER storage at 22661788                                                             =000230=
00300 L8000 AP D501 UEH   EVENT RETURN-FROM-USER-EXIT-PROGRAM XXXRMI WITH RETURN CODE 0                                                   =000231=
00300 L8000 AP 3180 D2EX1 ENTRY APPLICATION           REQUEST EXEC SQL SELECT                                                             =000232=
00300 L8000 AP 3250 D2D2  ENTRY DB2_API_CALL          230D7330                                                                            =000233=
00300 L8000 AP 3251 D2D2  EXIT  DB2_API_CALL/OK                                                                                           =000234=
00300 L8000 AP 3181 D2EX1 EXIT  APPLICATION-REQUEST   SQLCODE 0 RETURNED ON EXEC SQL SELECT                                               =000235=
00300 L8000 MN 0201 MNMN  ENTRY ACCUMULATE_RMI_TIME   DSNCSQL                                                                             =000236=
00300 L8000 MN 0202 MNMN  EXIT  ACCUMULATE_RMI_TIME/OK                                                                                    =000237=
00300 L8000 AP D500 UEH   EVENT LINK-TO-USER-EXIT-PROGRAM XXXRMI AT EXIT POINT XRMIOUT                                                    =000238=
00300 L8000 SM 0C01 SMMG  ENTRY GETMAIN               198,YES,00,TASK                                                                     =000239=
00300 L8000 SM 0C02 SMMG  EXIT  GETMAIN/OK            22661788                                                                            =000240=
00300 L8000 SM 0D01 SMMF  ENTRY FREEMAIN              22661788                                                                            =000241=
00300 L8000 SM 0D02 SMMF  EXIT  FREEMAIN/OK           USER storage at 22661788                                                             =000242=
00300 L8000 AP D501 UEH   EVENT RETURN-FROM-USER-EXIT-PROGRAM XXXRMI WITH RETURN CODE 0                                                   =000243=
00300 L8000 RM 0301 RMLN  ENTRY SET_LINK              01C8000F,22F914AC , 0000000C , 00000008,YES,NECESSARY                               =000244=
00300 L8000 RM 0302 RMLN  EXIT  SET_LINK/OK           22F914AC , 0000000C , 00000008,                                                     =000245=
00300 L8000 AP 2521 ERM   EXIT  ASSEMBLER-APPLICATION-CALL-TO-TRUE(DSNCSQL )                                                              =000246=
00300 L8000 AP 00E1 EIP   ENTRY WRITEQ-TS                                         0004,22661458 ....,08000A02 ....                        =000247=
00300 L8000 AP E160 EXEC  ENTRY WRITEQ                TS 'TCBTEST ' AT X'24300730','THIS IS THE POST-SQL WRITEQ                           =000248=
00300 L8000 TS 0C01 TSMB  ENTRY MATCH                 TCBTEST                                                                             =000249=
00300 L8000 TS 0C02 TSMB  EXIT  MATCH/OK              TCBTEST,TCBTEST,,TCBTEST,TSQSPQA1,22571FE0,,NO,NO,NO                                =000250=
00300 L8000 TS 0A01 TSSH  ENTRY WRITE                 TCBTEST,22661660 , 00000050,22571FE0,YES,NO                                         =000251=
00300 L8000 TS 0A0B TSSH  EVENT Before_server_request WRITE,TCBTEST,22661660 , 00000050,22571FE0,FUNC,YES,NO,0000300C                     =000252=
00300 L8000 TS 0A0C TSSH  EVENT After_server_request  WRITE,OK,4                                                                          =000253=
00300 L8000 TS 0A02 TSSH  EXIT  WRITE/OK              4                                                                                   =000254=
00300 L8000 AP E161 EXEC  EXIT  WRITEQ                TS 'TCBTEST ' AT X'24300730','THIS IS THE POST-SQL WRITEQ                           =000255=
00300 L8000 AP 00E1 EIP   EXIT  WRITEQ-TS             OK                          00F4,00000000 ....,00000A02 ....                        =000256=
```

8.5 COBOL calls

If your application makes use of COBOL calls to invoke sub programs, you need to be aware that the concurrency value used will be the value set for the program at the calling level. So, if PROGA is defined as CONCURRENCY(QUASIRENT) and PROGB is defined as CONCURRENCY(THREADSAFE), the concurrency attribute that will be honored will be QUASIRENT when we call PROGB from PROGA. This can be demonstrated by looking at the following two trace examples.

This behavior can be seen when using dynamic COBOL calls or static COBOL calls or both.

8.5.1 PROGA (Quasirent) calls PROGB (threadsafe)

In Example 8-10 PROGA is defined as QUASIRENT and PROGB is defined as THREADSAFE. The trace shows that once all the DB2 calls have completed (including the call in PROGB, which is defined as THREADSAFE), the program returns to the QR TCB.

Example 8-10   PROGA - Quasirent and PROGB - threadsafe

```
11281 QR         AP 1940 APLI    ENTRY START_PROGRAM          PROGA ,CEDF,FULLAPI,EXE
11281 QR         AP 1948 APLI    EVENT CALL-TO-LE/370         Thread_Initialization CAL
11281 QR         AP 1949 APLI    EVENT RETURN-FROM-LE/370     Thread_Initialization OK
11281 QR         AP 1948 APLI    EVENT CALL-TO-LE/370         Rununit_Init_&_Begin_Invo
11281 QR         AP 00E1 EIP     ENTRY DELETEQ-TS
11281 QR         AP E160 EXEC    ENTRY DELETEQ                TS 'TONYQ    ' AT X'A266AB
11281 QR         AP E161 EXEC    EXIT  DELETEQ                TS 'TONYQ    ' AT X'A266AB
11281 QR         AP 00E1 EIP     EXIT  DELETEQ-TS             OK
11281 QR         AP 2520 ERM     ENTRY COBOL-APPLICATION-CALL-TO-TRUE(DSNCSQL )
                                 ****
                                 **** First SQL Call in PROGA           *****
                                 ****
11281 L802I AP D500 UEH          EVENT LINK-TO-USER-EXIT-PROGRAM XXXRMI AT EXIT POINT
11281 L802I AP D501 UEH          EVENT RETURN-FROM-USER-EXIT-PROGRAM XXXRMI WITH RETUR
11281 L802I AP 3180 D2EX1        ENTRY APPLICATION            REQUEST EXEC SQL SELECT
11281 L802I AP 3250 D2D2         ENTRY DB2_API_CALL           230D7330
11281 L802I AP 3251 D2D2         EXIT  DB2_API_CALL/OK
11281 L802I AP 3181 D2EX1        EXIT  APPLICATION-REQUEST    SQLCODE 0 RETURNED ON EXE
11281 L802I AP D500 UEH          EVENT LINK-TO-USER-EXIT-PROGRAM XXXRMI AT EXIT POINT
11281 L802I AP D501 UEH          EVENT RETURN-FROM-USER-EXIT-PROGRAM XXXRMI WITH RETUR
                                 ****
                                 **** First SQL Complete - back to QR    *****
                                 ****
11281 QR         AP 2521 ERM     EXIT  COBOL-APPLICATION-CALL-TO-TRUE(DSNCSQL )
11281 QR         AP 00E1 EIP     ENTRY WRITEQ-TS
11281 QR         AP E160 EXEC    ENTRY WRITEQ                 TS 'TONYQ    ' AT X'2266AB
11281 QR         AP E161 EXEC    EXIT  WRITEQ                 TS 'TONYQ    ' AT X'2266AB
11281 QR         AP 00E1 EIP     EXIT  WRITEQ-TS              OK
11281 QR         AP 00E1 EIP     ENTRY GETMAIN
11281 QR         AP E160 EXEC    ENTRY GETMAIN                AT X'226600F8',4080 AT X'
11281 QR         AP E161 EXEC    EXIT  GETMAIN                X'2266C948' AT X'226600F8
11281 QR         AP 00E1 EIP     EXIT  GETMAIN                OK
11281 QR         AP 00E1 EIP     ENTRY ADDRESS
11281 QR         AP E160 EXEC    ENTRY ADDRESS                AT X'A266D23C',SYSEIB,ASM
11281 QR         AP E161 EXEC    EXIT  ADDRESS                X'0005D494' AT X'A266D23C
11281 QR         AP 00E1 EIP     EXIT  ADDRESS                OK
                                 ****
                                 **** About to start PROGB             *****
                                 ****
11281 QR         AP 00E1 EIP     ENTRY LOAD
11281 QR         AP E160 EXEC    ENTRY LOAD                   'PROGB' AT X'2266D380'
11281 QR         AP E161 EXEC    EXIT  LOAD                   'PROGB' AT X'2266D380'
11281 QR         AP 00E1 EIP     EXIT  LOAD                   OK
11281 QR         AP 00E1 EIP     ENTRY PUSH
11281 QR         AP E160 EXEC    ENTRY PUSH                   HANDLE SYSEIB NOHANDLE AS
11281 QR         AP E161 EXEC    EXIT  PUSH                   HANDLE 0,0,SYSEIB,NOHANDL
11281 QR         AP 00E1 EIP     EXIT  PUSH                   OK
11281 QR         AP 2520 ERM     ENTRY COBOL-APPLICATION-CALL-TO-TRUE(DSNCSQL )
                                 ****
                                 **** SQL Call in PROGB - switch to L8   *****
                                 ****
11281 L802I AP D500 UEH          EVENT LINK-TO-USER-EXIT-PROGRAM XXXRMI AT EXIT POINT
11281 L802I AP D501 UEH          EVENT RETURN-FROM-USER-EXIT-PROGRAM XXXRMI WITH RETUR
11281 L802I AP 3180 D2EX1        ENTRY APPLICATION            REQUEST EXEC SQL SELECT
11281 L802I AP 3250 D2D2         ENTRY DB2_API_CALL           230D7330
```

```
11281 L802I AP 3251 D2D2   EXIT  DB2_API_CALL/OK
11281 L802I AP 3181 D2EX1  EXIT  APPLICATION-REQUEST     SQLCODE 0 RETURNED ON EXE
11281 L802I AP D500 UEH    EVENT LINK-TO-USER-EXIT-PROGRAM XXXRMI AT EXIT POINT
11281 L802I AP D501 UEH    EVENT RETURN-FROM-USER-EXIT-PROGRAM XXXRMI WITH RETUR
                ****
                **** First SQL Complete - back to QR    *****
                ****
11281 QR    AP 2521 ERM    EXIT  COBOL-APPLICATION-CALL-TO-TRUE(DSNCSQL )
11281 QR    AP 00E1 EIP    ENTRY WRITEQ-TS
11281 QR    AP E160 EXEC   ENTRY WRITEQ                  TS 'TONYQ    ' AT X'2266AE
11281 QR    AP E161 EXEC   EXIT  WRITEQ                  TS 'TONYQ    ' AT X'2266AE
11281 QR    AP 00E1 EIP    EXIT  WRITEQ-TS               OK
11281 QR    AP 00E1 EIP    ENTRY POP
11281 QR    AP E160 EXEC   ENTRY POP                     HANDLE SYSEIB NOHANDLE AS
11281 QR    AP E161 EXEC   EXIT  POP                     HANDLE 0,0,SYSEIB,NOHANDL
11281 QR    AP 00E1 EIP    EXIT  POP                     OK
11281 QR    AP 00E1 EIP    ENTRY WRITEQ-TS
11281 QR    AP E160 EXEC   ENTRY WRITEQ                  TS 'TONYQ    ' AT X'2266AB
11281 QR    AP E161 EXEC   EXIT  WRITEQ                  TS 'TONYQ    ' AT X'2266AB
11281 QR    AP 00E1 EIP    EXIT  WRITEQ-TS               OK
11281 QR    AP 00E1 EIP    ENTRY RETURN
11281 QR    AP E160 EXEC   ENTRY RETURN                  COBOLII 00008
11281 QR    AP 1948 APLI   EVENT CALL-TO-LE/370          Rununit_End_Invocation CA
11281 QR    AP 1949 APLI   EVENT RETURN-FROM-LE/370      Rununit_End_Invocation OK
11281 QR    AP 1948 APLI   EVENT CALL-TO-LE/370          Rununit_Termination CALLP
11281 QR    AP 00E1 EIP    ENTRY ADDRESS
11281 QR    AP E160 EXEC   ENTRY ADDRESS                 AT X'A2669800',SYSEIB,ASM
11281 QR    AP E161 EXEC   EXIT  ADDRESS                 X'0005D494' AT X'A2669800
11281 QR    AP 00E1 EIP    EXIT  ADDRESS                 OK
11281 QR    AP 00E1 EIP    ENTRY RELEASE
11281 QR    AP E160 EXEC   ENTRY RELEASE                 'PROGB' AT X'A2669948'
11281 QR    AP E161 EXEC   EXIT  RELEASE                 'PROGB' AT X'A2669948'
11281 QR    AP 00E1 EIP    EXIT  RELEASE                 OK
11281 QR    AP 00E1 EIP    ENTRY FREEMAIN
11281 QR    AP E160 EXEC   ENTRY FREEMAIN                AT X'A266C948',SYSEIB,NOH
11281 QR    AP E161 EXEC   EXIT  FREEMAIN                AT X'A266C948',0,0,SYSEIB
11281 QR    AP 00E1 EIP    EXIT  FREEMAIN                OK
11281 QR    AP 1949 APLI   EVENT RETURN-FROM-LE/370      Rununit_Termination OK CA
11281 QR    AP 1948 APLI   EVENT CALL-TO-LE/370          Thread_Termination
11281 QR    AP 1949 APLI   EVENT RETURN-FROM-LE/370      Thread_Termination OK
11281 QR    AP 1941 APLI   EXIT  START_PROGRAM/OK        ....,NO,PROGA
11281 QR    AP 2500 ERMSP  ENTRY PERFORM_PREPARE         NO,0005D264
11281 QR    AP 2501 ERMSP  EXIT  PERFORM_PREPARE/OK      READ_ONLY
11281 QR    AP 1760 LTRC   ENTRY PERFORM_PREPARE         NO,22CD04B0
11281 QR    AP 1761 LTRC   EXIT  PERFORM_PREPARE/OK      READ_ONLY
11281 QR    AP 05A8 APRC   ENTRY PERFORM_PREPARE         NO,00000001
11281 QR    AP 05A9 APRC   EXIT  PERFORM_PREPARE/OK      READ_ONLY
11281 QR    AP 2500 ERMSP  ENTRY SEND_DO_COMMIT          241FC030,NO,YES,01380036,
11281 QR    AP 2520 ERM    ENTRY SYNCPOINT-MANAGER-CALL-TO-TRUE(DSNCSQL )
                ****
                **** Return briefly to the L8 for commit processing  *****
                ****
11281 L802I AP 3180 D2EX1  ENTRY SYNCPOINT-MANAGER       REQUEST
11281 L802I AP 3250 D2D2   ENTRY SINGLE_PHASE_COMMIT     230D7330
11281 L802I AP 3251 D2D2   EXIT  SINGLE_PHASE_COMMIT/OK
11281 L802I AP 3181 D2EX1  EXIT  SYNCPOINT-MANAGER       REQUEST
11281 QR    AP 2521 ERM    EXIT  SYNCPOINT-MANAGER-CALL-TO-TRUE(DSNCSQL )
11281 QR    AP 2501 ERMSP  EXIT  SEND_DO_COMMIT/OK       YES,YES,DSNCSQL
11281 QR    AP 2500 ERMSP  ENTRY PERFORM_COMMIT          241FC030,NO,YES,YES,NO,NO
11281 QR    AP 2501 ERMSP  EXIT  PERFORM_COMMIT/OK       YES,YES,YES,NO,UNNECESSAR
11281 QR    AP 2500 ERMSP  ENTRY PERFORM_COMMIT          NO,FORWARD,0005D264
11281 QR    AP 2520 ERM    ENTRY CALL-TRUES-FOR-TASK-END
11281 QR    AP 2521 ERM    EXIT  CALL-TRUES-FOR-TASK-END
11281 QR    AP 2501 ERMSP  EXIT  PERFORM_COMMIT/OK       YES
11281 QR    AP 1760 LTRC   ENTRY PERFORM_COMMIT          NO,FORWARD,22CD04B0
11281 QR    AP 1710 TFRF   ENTRY RELEASE_FACILITY        NO,NORMAL,22CD04B0,TC51
11281 QR    AP FD0B ZISP   ENTRY FACILITY_REQ            22CD04B0,FREE_DETACH,IMPL
```

```
11281 QR      AP FD03 ZDET    ENTRY DETACH                  22CD04B0,TC51
11281 QR      AP FD18 ZSDS    ENTRY SEND_DFSYN              22CD04B0,TC51
11281 QR      AP FD1D ZSDR    ENTRY SEND_DFSYN_RESP         22CD04B0,TC51
11281 QR      AP FC90 VIO     EVENT TCTTE(22CD04B0)         SC38TC51,01CA,SEND,DATA,0
11281 QR      AP FD8B ZISP    EXIT  FACILITY_REQ
11281 QR      AP 1711 TFRF    EXIT  RELEASE_FACILITY/OK     TC51
11281 QR      AP 1761 LTRC    EXIT  PERFORM_COMMIT/OK       NO
11281 QR      AP 05A8 APRC    ENTRY PERFORM_COMMIT          NO,FORWARD,00000001
11281 QR      AP 05A9 APRC    EXIT  PERFORM_COMMIT/OK       NO
11281 QR      AP 0590 APXM    ENTRY RELEASE_XM_CLIENT       NORMAL
```

8.5.2 PROGA (threadsafe) calls PROGB (Quasirent)

If we swap over the definitions of PROGA and PROGB so that PROGA is now THREADSAFE and PROGB is QUASIRENT, we should see the opposite effect. That is, PROGB will remain on the L8 TCB after any DB2 calls due to the definition of PROGA are set to THREADSAFE. PROGB will start on the L8 TCB and continue there until completion. This can be seen in Example 8-11.

Example 8-11   PROGA - threadsafe and PROGB Quasirent

```
00108 QR       AP 1940 APLI    ENTRY START_PROGRAM           PROGA,CEDF,FULLAPI,EXE
00108 QR       AP 1948 APLI    EVENT CALL-TO-LE/370          Thread_Initialization CAL
00108 QR       AP 1949 APLI    EVENT RETURN-FROM-LE/370      Thread_Initialization OK
00108 QR       AP 1948 APLI    EVENT CALL-TO-LE/370          Rununit_Init_&_Begin_Invo
00108 QR       AP 00E1 EIP     ENTRY DELETEQ-TS
00108 QR       AP 00E1 EIP     EXIT  DELETEQ-TS              OK
00108 QR       AP 2520 ERM     ENTRY COBOL-APPLICATION-CALL-TO-TRUE(DSNCSQL )
              ****
              **** First SQL Call in PROGA            *****
              ****
00108 L8000 AP 3180 D2EX1  ENTRY APPLICATION             REQUEST EXEC SQL SELECT
00108 L8000 AP 3250 D2D2   ENTRY DB2_API_CALL            22DDF030
00108 L8000 AP 3251 D2D2   EXIT  DB2_API_CALL/OK
00108 L8000 AP 3181 D2EX1  EXIT  APPLICATION-REQUEST     SQLCODE -805 RETURNED ON
00108 L8000 AP 2521 ERM    EXIT  COBOL-APPLICATION-CALL-TO-TRUE(DSNCSQL )
              ****
              **** PROGA continues on L8 TCB          *****
              ****
00108 L8000 AP 00E1 EIP    ENTRY WRITEQ-TS
00108 L8000 AP 00E1 EIP    EXIT  WRITEQ-TS               OK
00108 L8000 AP 00E1 EIP    ENTRY GETMAIN
00108 L8000 AP 00E1 EIP    EXIT  GETMAIN                 OK
00108 L8000 AP 00E1 EIP    ENTRY ADDRESS
00108 L8000 AP 00E1 EIP    EXIT  ADDRESS                 OK
              ****
              **** Here we are about to call PROGB    *****
              ****     remaining on the L8 TCB        *****
              ****
00108 L8000 AP 00E1 EIP    ENTRY LOAD
00108 L8000 AP 00E1 EIP    EXIT  LOAD                    OK
00108 L8000 AP 00E1 EIP    ENTRY PUSH
00108 L8000 AP 00E1 EIP    EXIT  PUSH                    OK
00108 L8000 AP 2520 ERM    ENTRY COBOL-APPLICATION-CALL-TO-TRUE(DSNCSQL )
00108 L8000 AP 3180 D2EX1  ENTRY APPLICATION             REQUEST EXEC SQL SELECT
00108 L8000 AP 3250 D2D2   ENTRY DB2_API_CALL            22DDF030
00108 L8000 AP 3251 D2D2   EXIT  DB2_API_CALL/OK
00108 L8000 AP 3181 D2EX1  EXIT  APPLICATION-REQUEST     SQLCODE -805 RETURNED ON
00108 L8000 AP 2521 ERM    EXIT  COBOL-APPLICATION-CALL-TO-TRUE(DSNCSQL )
00108 L8000 AP 00E1 EIP    ENTRY WRITEQ-TS
00108 L8000 AP 00E1 EIP    EXIT  WRITEQ-TS               OK
00108 L8000 AP 00E1 EIP    ENTRY POP
```

```
00108 L8000 AP 00E1 EIP   EXIT  POP                    OK
00108 L8000 AP 00E1 EIP   ENTRY WRITEQ-TS
00108 L8000 AP 00E1 EIP   EXIT  WRITEQ-TS              OK
00108 L8000 AP 00E1 EIP   ENTRY RETURN
00108 L8000 AP 1948 APLI  EVENT CALL-TO-LE/370         Rununit_End_Invocation CA
00108 L8000 AP 1949 APLI  EVENT RETURN-FROM-LE/370     Rununit_End_Invocation OK
00108 L8000 AP 1948 APLI  EVENT CALL-TO-LE/370         Rununit_Termination CALLP
00108 L8000 AP 00E1 EIP   ENTRY ADDRESS
00108 L8000 AP 00E1 EIP   EXIT  ADDRESS                OK
00108 L8000 AP 00E1 EIP   ENTRY RELEASE
00108 L8000 AP 00E1 EIP   EXIT  RELEASE                OK
00108 L8000 AP 00E1 EIP   ENTRY FREEMAIN
00108 L8000 AP 00E1 EIP   EXIT  FREEMAIN               OK
00108 L8000 AP 1949 APLI  EVENT RETURN-FROM-LE/370     Rununit_Termination OK CA
00108 L8000 AP 1948 APLI  EVENT CALL-TO-LE/370         Thread_Termination
00108 L8000 AP 1949 APLI  EVENT RETURN-FROM-LE/370     Thread_Termination OK
00108 L8000 AP 1941 APLI  EXIT  START_PROGRAM/OK       ....,NO,PROGA
                    ****
                    **** Program End Return to QR TCB   *****
                    ****
00108 QR    AP 2500 ERMSP ENTRY PERFORM_PREPARE        NO,0005B264
00108 QR    AP 2501 ERMSP EXIT  PERFORM_PREPARE/OK     READ_ONLY
00108 QR    AP 1760 LTRC  ENTRY PERFORM_PREPARE        NO,22CD04B0
00108 QR    AP 1761 LTRC  EXIT  PERFORM_PREPARE/OK     READ_ONLY
00108 QR    AP 05A8 APRC  ENTRY PERFORM_PREPARE        NO,00000001
00108 QR    AP 05A9 APRC  EXIT  PERFORM_PREPARE/OK     READ_ONLY
00108 QR    AP 2500 ERMSP ENTRY SEND_DO_COMMIT         22F91450,NO,YES,01030001,
00108 QR    AP 2520 ERM   ENTRY SYNCPOINT-MANAGER-CALL-TO-TRUE(DSNCSQL )
                    ****
                    **** Return briefly to the L8 for commit processing  *****
                    ****
00108 L8000 AP 3180 D2EX1 ENTRY SYNCPOINT-MANAGER      REQUEST
00108 L8000 AP 3250 D2D2  ENTRY SINGLE_PHASE_COMMIT    22DDF030
00108 L8000 AP 3251 D2D2  EXIT  SINGLE_PHASE_COMMIT/OK
00108 L8000 AP 3181 D2EX1 EXIT  SYNCPOINT-MANAGER      REQUEST
00108 QR    AP 2521 ERM   EXIT  SYNCPOINT-MANAGER-CALL-TO-TRUE(DSNCSQL )
00108 QR    AP 2501 ERMSP EXIT  SEND_DO_COMMIT/OK      YES,YES,DSNCSQL
00108 QR    AP 2500 ERMSP ENTRY PERFORM_COMMIT         22F91450,NO,YES,YES,NO,NO
00108 QR    AP 2501 ERMSP EXIT  PERFORM_COMMIT/OK      YES,YES,YES,NO,UNNECESSAR
00108 QR    AP 2500 ERMSP ENTRY PERFORM_COMMIT         NO,FORWARD,0005B264
00108 QR    AP 2520 ERM   ENTRY CALL-TRUES-FOR-TASK-END
00108 QR    AP 2521 ERM   EXIT  CALL-TRUES-FOR-TASK-END
00108 QR    AP 2501 ERMSP EXIT  PERFORM_COMMIT/OK      YES
00108 QR    AP 1760 LTRC  ENTRY PERFORM_COMMIT         NO,FORWARD,22CD04B0
00108 QR    AP 1710 TFRF  ENTRY RELEASE_FACILITY       NO,NORMAL,22CD04B0,TC3F
00108 QR    AP 1711 TFRF  EXIT  RELEASE_FACILITY/OK    TC3F
00108 QR    AP 1761 LTRC  EXIT  PERFORM_COMMIT/OK      NO
00108 QR    AP 05A8 APRC  ENTRY PERFORM_COMMIT         NO,FORWARD,00000001
00108 QR    AP 05A9 APRC  EXIT  PERFORM_COMMIT/OK      NO
00108 QR    AP 0590 APXM  ENTRY RELEASE_XM_CLIENT      NORMAL
```

With CICS Transaction Server Version 3, the API attribute of the calling program is also inherited by the called program. If, for example, PROGA had been defined with API(OPENAPI) and EXECKEY(USER), it would have been invoked under an L9 TCB, and would have called PROGB under the L9 TCB also.

The programs used to create these examples can be found in Appendix B, "COBOL call program listings" on page 321.

8.6 The CSACDTA field

Historically, the CSACDTA field provided the address of the task control area (TCA) for the currently dispatched task running within CICS. Before OTE was introduced, all tasks ran under the control of the QR TCB, and this provided a guarantee that a running task would retrieve the address of its own TCA if it accessed the CSACDTA field.

With the introduction of OTE, it is *no longer safe* to assume that the TCA address held within CSACDTA is the TCA of the task that is accessing the CSA. CSACDTA contains the address of the task currently dispatched on the QR TCB. The program that is referencing CSACDTA may be running under an open TCB. In this case the wrong TCA address will be used by the program, leading to unpredictable results.

Since CICS/ESA® Version 4.1, direct access to CICS control blocks is not supported. The CICS system programming interface (SPI) should be used for programs wishing to access state information about a task.

Prior to CICS TS 3.1

In the releases of CICS prior to CICS Transaction Server 3.1 the CSACDTA field will return the address of the currently dispatched task executing under the QR TCB.

CICS TS 3.1

In CICS Transaction Server Version 3.1, CSACDTA is renamed CSAQRTCA to further discourage its use.

CICS TS 3.2

In CICS Transaction Server Version 3.2 IBM has *withdrawn* the ability to reference a TCA using this field. This has been done by loading CSAQRTCA with the address of an area of fetch-protected storage. This will result in an abend ASRD with message DFHSR0618 if it is referenced.

9

Migration scenario

This chapter describes a threadsafe migration from beginning to end using a sample application. Using a migration plan based on the concepts that are developed and detailed in Chapter 4, "Threadsafe tasks" on page 57, the authors of this book took a CICS-DB2 application running as quasi-reentrant under CICS Transaction Server Version 1.3 and converted it to threadsafe running under CICS Transaction Server Version 2.3. Each step of the migration process is illustrated with displays of the required system and application changes.

DB2 is one example of a user of the CICS Resource Manager Interface (RMI) which has been enhanced to exploit OTE. In addition, the z/OS Communications Server IP CICS Sockets Version 1 Release 7 and later can be configured to use OTE and also, from CICS Transaction Server 3.2, the WebSphere MQseries CICS adapter will now also exploit OTE.

While in this exercise CICS Transaction Server Version 2.3 is the target release, the migration process described is the same if we take any quasi-reentrant program and convert it to be a threadsafe program. However, note that additional considerations apply when migrating the program to be an OPENAPI program in CICS Transaction Server Version V3. We discuss at the end of the chapter why this is not recommended for RMI users that exploit OTE (CICS-DB2 applications, IP CICS Sockets applications, or WebSphere MQSeries applications).

The chapter is organized into the following sections:

- 9.1, "Application overview" on page 201

This section describes the sample application that we used in the migration.

- 9.2, "Migration plan" on page 201

    This section provides an overview of our migration plan.

- 9.3, "Migration part 1" on page 202

    This section details each of the steps taken to ensure that the application does not incur the overhead of extra TCB switches under CICS Transaction Server Version 2.3 compared to Version 1.3, without fully converting it from quasi-reentrant to threadsafe.

- 9.4, "Migration part 2" on page 218

    This section details each of the steps taken to fully convert the application from quasi-reentrant to threadsafe, in order to achieve a performance improvement.

- 9.5, "Performance measurement" on page 236

    This section details the actions taken to measure the application performance post-migration, and compares the threadsafe results with the quasi-reentrant results.

- 9.6, "Additional considerations for OPENAPI programs" on page 242

    This section details additional considerations involved should an application be migrated to run as OPENAPI under CICS Transaction Server Version 3.1 rather than threadsafe.

9.1 Application overview

This section describes the sample application that we used in the migration.

It should be noted that although the application is not realistic (it is designed to generate a large volume of CICS DB2 tasks rather than to serve any useful business purpose), the profile of the individual tasks are not dissimilar to some of the typical CICS transactions in large DB2 applications.

9.1.1 Description of the application

The application is designed to generate a large volume of CICS DB2 transactions. It consists of a driver transaction, which asynchronously starts 10 daughter transactions. Each of the daughter transactions, on completion, restarts itself a finite number of times.

There are 11 application programs, corresponding to the 11 transactions described previously. Each program issues a large number of EXEC SQL requests. The 10 daughter programs are similar, but not identical. In addition to the EXEC SQL requests, a variety of EXEC CICS commands are issued, and there are some updates to shared resources.

In addition to the 11 application programs, there are 3 global user exit programs, a PLTPI program, and a dynamic plan exit program.

Full source code listings of the application programs are provided in Appendix C, "Assembler routines" on page 327.

9.2 Migration plan

This section provides an overview of the plan we used to migrate the application from running as quasi-reentrant under CICS Transaction Server Version 1.3, to running as threadsafe under CICS Transaction Server Version 2.3.

A key decision we made at the outset was that we did not want to implement simultaneously what for most organizations would be two major changes. They are:

- Migrating the application from a CICS Transaction Server Version 1.3 region to a CICS Transaction Server Version 2.3 region
- Migrating the application to be fully threadsafe

At first glance, the first of the two changes above may not appear to have any relevance to a threadsafe migration. However, we have already discussed in this book that this is not the case. Chapter 8, "Migration pitfalls" on page 173, explains in detail why user exit programs must be considered when migrating a DB2 application to CICS Transaction Server Version 2 or later.

We therefore split our migration plan into two major parts to reflect the fact that most organizations will migrate to threadsafe in two stages. Table 9-1 outlines our migration plan.

Table 9-1 Migration plan

Threadsafe migration plan	
Part 1 - Migrate application from CICS TS V1.3 to V2.3	
Step 1	Identify exits in scope for part 1.
Step 2	Convert in-scope exits to be threadsafe.
Step 3	Address non threadsafe commands within in-scope exits.
Step 4	Confirm performance after migration to CICS TS 2.3.
Part 2 - Migrate application to be fully threadsafe	
Step 1	Identify programs in scope for part 2.
Step 2	Convert user exits to be threadsafe.
Step 3	Convert application programs to be threadsafe.
Step 4	Address non threadsafe commands.
Step 5	CICS system changes.

9.3 Migration part 1

As outlined in 9.2, "Migration plan" on page 201, the migration plan is split into two major parts:

- Upgrading to CICS Transaction Server Version 2.3 without incurring extra TCB switches
- Convert application to be fully threadsafe

This section covers part 1 of the migration, converting a quasi-reentrant DB2 application running under CICS Transaction Server Version 1.3, to run as largely quasi-reentrant under CICS Transaction Server Version 2.3, with the minimum of threadsafe-related changes.

> **Note:** Upgrading a CICS region from one release to another is not what this book is about, and therefore this particular aspect of the migration is not covered. The focus of this section is on ensuring that the sample application can run as quasi-reentrant under CICS Transaction Server Version 2.3 and incur the same number of TCB switches as it did running under CICS Transaction Server Version 1.3. (The circumstances under which a quasi-reentrant application will incur additional TCB switches under CICS Transaction Server Version or later is discussed in detail in Chapter 8, "Migration pitfalls" on page 173.)

9.3.1 Step 1: Identify exits in scope for part 1

For the purposes of part 1 of the migration, we are only interested in programs, user exits, and commands that can be invoked on the call path of an EXEC SQL statement. These are the entities that can cause an increase in TCB switches under CICS Transaction Server Version 2 or later.

We know there are only two exit points invoked directly as a result of an EXEC SQL statement, XRMIIN and XRMIOUT, and that there is one user-replaceable module (URM) that can be invoked directly on the first SQL call of each unit of work—the dynamic plan exit program. The following sections cover each of these in turn.

XRMIIN and XRMIOUT

To determine whether this CICS region has programs running at the XRMIIN and XRMIOUT exit points, we ran the CICS-supplied sample statistics program, DFH0STAT, requesting a global user exit report.

```
Global User Exits

    Exit       Program     Entry       <------- Global Area ------->    Number      Program
    Name       Name        Name        Entry Name  Length  Use Count    of Exits    Status

    XTSQRIN    XXXTS       XXXTS       XXXTS         64         1          1        Started
    XEIIN      XXXEI       XXXEI                      0         0          2        Started
    XEIOUT     XXXEI       XXXEI                      0         0          2        Started
    XRMIIN     XXXRMI      XXXRMI                     0         0          2        Started
    XRMIOUT    XXXRMI      XXXRMI                     0         0          2        Started
```

Figure 9-1   GLUE section of DFH0STAT report

As can be seen from Figure 9-1, program XXXRMI is enabled at both exit points. Therefore we now know that we have at least one program in scope for part 1. Next we need to determine whether it is possible for any of the other enabled exit points (XEIIN, XEIOUT, or XTSQRIN) to be invoked via XXXRMI, and the only accurate method of doing this is by examining the source code.

An examination of the XXXRMI source code in Appendix C, "Assembler routines" on page 327, shows that it does *not* contain any code that will cause the other exit points to be invoked, so the scope of this step is limited to XXXRMI itself.

Dynamic plan exit program

To determine whether any dynamic plan exit (DPE) programs exist, we again ran the CICS-supplied sample statistics program, DFH0STAT, this time requesting reports for DB2 connection and DB2 entries.

As can be seen in Figure 9-2, there is a single DPE program in use named PLANEXIT, so this can be added to the list of in-scope programs. We also need to determine whether PLANEXIT calls any other programs or invokes any user exits. The best method of achieving this is by examining the source code.

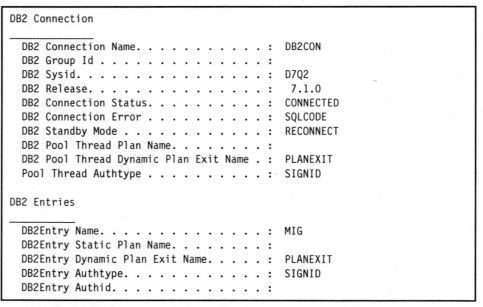

Figure 9-2   DB2 section of DFH0STAT report

We can see from the PLANEXIT source code in Appendix C, "Assembler routines" on page 327, that it does *not* call any other programs, but that it does issue an EXEC CICS ASSIGN command. We have already established the list of active exit points (see Figure 9-1 on page 203), so we can therefore conclude that PLANEXIT will cause program XXXEI to be invoked at the XEIIN and XEIOUT exit points.

We now know the full scope of the programs that need to be addressed in part 1 of the migration:

- User exit program XXXRMI, which is invoked twice (at XRMIIN and XRMIOUT) on every SQL call
- URM PLANEXIT, which is invoked on the first SQL call each unit of work,
- User exit program XXXEI, which is invoked twice (at XEIIN and XEIOUT) every time PLANEXIT executes

9.3.2 Step 2: Convert in-scope exits to threadsafe

Having established the list of in-scope exit programs for part 1, we now need to determine whether they can be redefined as threadsafe. This means identifying any instances of updates to shared resources, and removing or serializing access if they exist. Once completed, it is then safe to redefine the programs as threadsafe.

The actions taken to achieve this are listed here and described in the subsequent sections:

1. Run DFH0STAT to find shared program storage.
2. Run DFH0STAT to find GWAs.
3. Run DFHEISUP to find other potential shared resources.
4. Examine source code.
5. Redefine programs as threadsafe.

Run DFH0STAT to find shared program storage

The supplied sample statistics program, DFH0STAT, can provide useful information about the use of shared storage. First of all, the System Status section shows us whether reentrant programs reside in read-only storage (Figure 9-3).

```
System Status

  MVS Product Name. . . . . . . :  MVS/SP7.0.4
  CICS Startup. . . . . . . . . :  INITIAL
  CICS Status . . . . . . . . . :  ACTIVE
Storage Protection. . . . . . . :  INACTIVE
Transaction Isolation . . . . . :  INACTIVE
Reentrant Programs. . . . . . . :  PROTECT
```

Figure 9-3   System Status section of DFH0STAT report

Moreover, the Programs section shows us where each program resides.

```
Programs

    Program    Data    Exec                      Program    Program
    Name       Loc     Key     Times Used  ...   Size       Location

    DB2MANY    Any     USER         1            1,536      ERDSA
    DB2PROGA   Any     USER        12            1,312      ERDSA
    DB2PROG1   Any     USER        12            1,256      ERDSA
    DB2PROG2   Any     USER        12            1,256      ERDSA
    DB2PROG3   Any     USER        12            1,256      ERDSA
    DB2PROG4   Any     USER        12            1,216      ERDSA
    DB2PROG5   Any     USER        12            1,216      ERDSA
    DB2PROG6   Any     USER        12            1,216      ERDSA
    DB2PROG7   Any     USER        12            1,216      ERDSA
    DB2PROG8   Any     USER        12            1,304      ERDSA
    DB2PROG9   Any     USER        12            1,304      ERDSA
    EXITENBL   Any     USER         1              432      ERDSA
    PLANEXIT   Any     USER       121              208      ERDSA
    XXXEI      Any     USER         1              184      ERDSA
    XXXRMI     Any     USER         1              184      ERDSA
    XXXTS      Any     USER         1              104      ERDSA
```

Figure 9-4   Programs section of DFH0STAT report

Figure 9-3 on page 205 and Figure 9-4 together allow us to conclude that all application programs and exits are reentrant, reside in protected ERDSA storage, and therefore cannot use the program itself as a form of shared storage.

Run DFH0STAT to find GWAs

We have already run the supplied sample statistics program DFH0STAT to determine which user exit programs are enabled for the application. In addition to listing the exit programs, DFH0STAT also displays whether each one has a global work area (GWA).

```
Exit Programs

                         <---- Global Area ---->    No.
   Program    Entry       Entry           Use        of     Program
    Name      Name         Name   Length  Count    Exits    Status

   DFHEDP     DLI                   0       0        0     Started
   DFHD2EX1   DSNCSQL     DSNCSQL  16       1        0     Started
   XXXEI      XXXEI                 0       0        2     Started
   XXXRMI     XXXRMI                0       0        2     Started
   XXXTS      XXXTS       XXXTS    64       1        1     Started
```

Figure 9-5   Exit Programs section of DFH0STAT report

By referring to Figure 9-5, we can see that both of the user exit programs in scope for part 1 of the migration, XXXRMI and XXXEI, have a GWA length of zero. We can also rule out the possibility that they share a GWA that is owned by another exit program, because the Entry Name column is blank for these programs, and the programs that do own a GWA have a use count of 1.

Run DFHEISUP to find potential shared resources

As a next step, we ran the CICS-supplied load module scanner DFHEISUP against *all* of the programs and exits, using our own modified version of the supplied threadsafe inhibitors table, DFHEIDTH.

> **Attention:** It is important to note that scanning the in-scope programs alone might not be sufficient, as the commands to create or address a shared resource may not necessarily be confined to the programs that access or update it.

The changes we made to DFHEIDTH are shown in Figure 9-6, and the output from DFHEISUP is shown in Figure 9-7 on page 208.

```
EXTRACT EXIT GASET *
GETMAIN SHARED *
ADDRESS CWA *
LOAD SET *            LOAD SET * command added to the supplied list
```

Figure 9-6   Modified DFHEIDTH threadsafe inhibitors table

```
Module Name        'CICSRS4.MIG.LOAD(DB2PROG4)'
Module Language    Assembler
Offset/EDF         Command
-----------------  ------------------------------------------
00001387/no-edf    ADDRESS CWA

Module Name        'CICSRS4.MIG.LOAD(DB2PROG5)'
Module Language    Assembler
Offset/EDF         Command
-----------------  ------------------------------------------
00001387/no-edf    ADDRESS CWA

Module Name        'CICSRS4.MIG.LOAD(DB2PROG6)'
Module Language    Assembler
Offset/EDF         Command
-----------------  ------------------------------------------
00001387/no-edf    ADDRESS CWA

Module Name        'CICSRS4.MIG.LOAD(DB2PROG7)'
Module Language    Assembler
Offset/EDF         Command
-----------------  ------------------------------------------
00001387/no-edf    ADDRESS CWA

Total possible commands located = 4
```

Figure 9-7   DFHEISUP detailed report using DFHEIDTH filter table

Figure 9-7 shows that XXXRMI, XXXEI, and PLANEXIT are not mentioned in the DFHEISUP report, which means that none of them issue any of the threadsafe inhibitor commands. Also significant is that there is no instance anywhere in the application of the LOAD, GETMAIN SHARED, and EXTRACT EXIT commands. However, it is important to note that the application does make use of the common work area (CWA). It is possible for the CWA address to be passed to other programs as a parameter.

Examine source code

Although running utilities such as DFH0STAT and DFHEISUP can help determine whether a program is likely to be threadsafe, ultimately this is no substitute for a full understanding of the application.

However, we are off to a good start. The previous steps have already allowed us to conclude that:

► All programs are reentrant and reside in read-only storage.
► XXXRMI and XXXEI do not use GWAs.

- There is no use of EXEC CICS SHARED GETMAIN within the application.
- There is no use of EXEC CICS EXTRACT EXIT within the application.
- There is no use of EXEC CICS LOAD within the application.
- The application uses the CWA, but not necessarily in the in-scope programs.

All that remains is to examine the source code of the in-scope programs for evidence of CWA access, and any nonstandard programming techniques that could result in access to a shared resource. The source code for XXXRMI, PLANEXIT, and XXXEI is listed in Appendix C, "Assembler routines" on page 327, and it is clear from this that there is nothing to cause us any concern in this regard.

Redefine programs as threadsafe

Now that we have established that XXXRMI, PLANEXIT, and XXXEI are all truly threadsafe, we can redefine them as such.

Figure 9-8 shows the program definition for PLANEXIT after it has been redefined as threadsafe. The same change was made to the XXXRMI and XXXEI definitions. Figure 9-9 on page 210 shows how CEMT can be used to confirm this.

```
 CEDA   View PROGram( PLANEXIT )
  PROGram           : PLANEXIT
  Group             : THDSAFE
  DEscription       :
  Language          :
  RELoad            : No
  RESident          : No
  USAge             : Normal
  USElpacopy        : No
  Status            : Enabled
  RSl               : 00
  CEdf              : Yes
  DAtalocation      : Any
  EXECKey           : User
  COncurrency       : Threadsafe
  REMOTE ATTRIBUTES
```

Figure 9-8 CEDA VIEW PROGRAM display

```
I PROG(XXX*)
STATUS:   RESULTS - OVERTYPE TO MODIFY
 Prog(XXXEI   ) Leng(0000000184) Ass Pro Ena Pri       Ced
      Res(001) Use(0000000001) Any Uex Ful Thr             Nat
 Prog(XXXRMI  ) Leng(0000000184) Ass Pro Ena Pri       Ced
      Res(001) Use(0000000001) Any Uex Ful Thr             Nat
 Prog(XXXTS   ) Leng(0000000104) Ass Pro Ena Pri       Ced
      Res(001) Use(0000000001) Any Uex Ful Qua             Nat
```

Figure 9-9   CEMT INQUIRE PROGRAM display

9.3.3 Step 3: Address non threadsafe commands

Having successfully converted each of the programs in scope for part 1 to be threadsafe, the final step is to determine whether any of these programs issues non threadsafe commands. These programs are invoked on the SQL call path, and are therefore critical to performance. Any non threadsafe commands issued within an SQL flow will cause a TCB switch from L8 to QR and back again. Refer to chapter Chapter 2, "OTE and threadsafe overview" on page 11, for a full discussion on this topic.

To determine which commands are issued by XXXRMI, PLANEXIT, and XXXEI, we ran the load module scanner utility, DFHEISUP, with the supplied non threadsafe command table, DFHEIDNT.

```
CICS LOAD MODULE SCANNER UTILITY
SCAN PERFORMED ON Fri May  7 11:21:25 2004 USING TABLE RSTABLE2.3

SUMMARY LISTING OF CICSRS4.MIG.LOAD.PART1
=======================================
Module Name    Commands Found    Language

LOAD LIBRARY STATISTICS
=======================
Total modules in library                             =      3
Total modules Scanned                                =      3
Total CICS modules/tables not scanned                =      0
Total modules possibly containing requested commands =      0
```

Figure 9-10   DFHEISUP summary report using DFHEIDNT filter table

Figure 9-10 on page 210 shows the DFHEISUP summary report when run against XXXRMI, PLANEXIT, and XXXEI, and shows that the number of non threadsafe commands in these three programs is zero.

We can conclude therefore that we have no further work to do to address non threadsafe commands in part 1 of the migration.

9.3.4 Step 4: Confirm performance after migration to CICS TS 2.3

> **Important:** The results shown in this section are specific to the sample application and the system it was running on at the time. The purpose is to illustrate the importance of converting user exits on the SQL call path to be threadsafe when upgrading to CICS Transaction Server Version 2 or later. However, these specific results should not be used as a benchmark for other applications or any other system.

We have now completed part 1 of the migration, that is, migrated the application from CICS Transaction Server Version 1.3 to CICS Transaction Server Version 2.3, and converted the user exit programs on the SQL call path to be threadsafe.

To confirm that the application is not incurring extra TCB switches under CICS Transaction Server Version 2.3, and therefore has comparable performance with CICS Transaction Server Version 1.3, we used CICS Performance Analyzer Version 1 Release 3 to interrogate the SMF type 110 records. Figure 9-11 on page 212 shows the selection criteria we used to generate the reports. We used 5-minute intervals (that is, the difference between SMFSTART and SMFSTOP) in each of the reports

For more information about CICS Performance Analyzer (CICS PA) see the IBM Redbooks publication *CICS Performance Analyzer*, SG24-6063.

```
CICSPA IN(SMFIN001),
       SMFSTART(yyyy/mm/dd,hh:mm:ss.00),
       SMFSTOP(yyyy/mm/dd,hh:mm:ss.00),
       APPLID(cicsapplid),
       LINECNT(60),
       FORMAT(':','/'),
    SUMMARY(OUTPUT(TESTSUM),
       BY(TRAN),
       SELECT(PERFORMANCE(
       INC(TRAN(DB21,DB22,DB23,DB24,DB25,
       DB26,DB27,DB28,DB29,DB2A)))),
       FIELDS(TRAN,
              TASKCNT,
              DB2REQCT(TOTAL),
              CHMODECT(TOTAL)))
```

Figure 9-11   Selection criteria for CICS PA report

First, we measured our baseline. Figure 9-12 shows the result of running CICS PA prior to part 1 of the migration, when the application was running under CICS Transaction Server Version 1.3.

```
V1R3M0         CICS Performance Analyzer
                   Performance Summary

Data from 02:44:58  5/13/2004 to 02:49:59  5/13/200


                        Total     Total
Tran        #Tasks   DB2 Reqs  ChngMode

DB2A           482     482000         0
DB21           470     470000         0
DB22           479     479000         0
DB23           483     483000         0
DB24           484     484000         0
DB25           461     461000         0
DB26           481     481000         0
DB27           494     494000         0
DB28           482     482000         0
DB29           490     490000         0
```

Figure 9-12   CICS PA report showing SQL calls in CICS TS 1.3

> **Note:** The number of switches between the QR TCB and DB2 subtask thread TCBs is not captured in SMF type 110 records for CICS Transaction Server Version 1.3. However, it is possible to calculate this value from the number of SQL calls. The formula is:
>
> ```
> TCB switches = (SQL calls * 2) + (syncpoints * 4) - (read-only syncpoints * 2)
> ```
>
> (Units of work with no DB2 updates will perform single-phase commit rather than two-phase commit, and therefore two switches will occur during sync point instead of four.)

As expected, the ChngMode field is zero for our CICS Transaction Server Version 1.3 transactions (see Figure 9-12 on page 212). However, the number of TCB switches can be calculated using the formula defined above. From our knowledge of the sample application, we know we have a read-only workload with only one syncpoint per task, so the total TCB switches for each transaction shown in Figure 9-12 on page 212 can be calculated using the following modified formula:

```
TCB switches = (2 * DB2 Reqs) + (2 * #tasks)
```

Now that we know our baseline, we measured application performance under CICS Transaction Server Version 2.3. Figure 9-13 on page 214 shows the result of running the same CICS PA report after part 1 of the migration was completed.

```
V1R3M0       CICS Performance Analyzer
             Performance Summary

Data from 15:09:58  5/13/2004 to 15:14:59  5/13/2004


                     Total    Total
Tran       #Tasks   DB2 Reqs  ChngMode

DB2A         498    498000    996996
DB21         499    499000    998998
DB22         500    500000    1001E3
DB23         498    498000    996996
DB24         498    498000    996996
DB25         498    498000    996996
DB26         499    499000    998998
DB27         499    499000    998998
DB28         498    498000    996996
DB29         498    498000    996996
```

Figure 9-13 CICS PA report showing TCB switches in CICS TS 2.3

To compare the figures from CICS Transaction Server Version 1.3 and CICS Transaction Server Version 2.3, we calculated the averages across all transactions and tabulated the results (Table 9-2).

Table 9-2 CICSTS 1.3 versus CICS TS 2.3

	CICS TS 1.3	CICS TS 2.3
Avg. SQL calls per task	1000	1000
Avg. TCB switches per task	2002	2002
Transaction throughput	15.97 tps	16.56 tps

The figures in Table 9-2 confirm that we have achieved the goal of part 1 of the migration plan. The application is now running as quasi-reentrant under CICS Transaction Server Version 2.3, without extra TCB switches, and with a transaction throughput that is similar to CICS Transaction Server Version 1.3. In fact, we measured a slight improvement in throughput.

What will happen if

Throughout this book we have continually highlighted the benefit of converting all user exit programs on the SQL call path to threadsafe when upgrading to CICS

Transaction Server Version 2 or later, even if the initial intention is to leave application code as quasi-reentrant. This is why we split the migration plan into two parts in this chapter.

To further illustrate this point, we decided to measure what the sample application performance *would have been* had we simply upgraded to CICS Transaction Server Version 2.3 without converting the user exit programs on the SQL call path to threadsafe.

We therefore redefined XXXRMI, PLANEXIT, and XXXEI as quasi-reentrant under CICS Transaction Server Version 2.3, and generated the same CICS PA report that we produced with the programs defined as threadsafe. To differentiate this from what we actually did in part 1 of the migration, we have called this approach the *simplistic conversion* to CICS Transaction Server Version 2.3. The results are shown in Figure 9-14.

```
V1R3M0        CICS Performance Analyzer
                 Performance Summary

Data from 16:39:58  5/13/2004 to 16:44:59  5/13/2004


                        Total     Total
Tran      #Tasks     DB2 Reqs  ChngMode

DB2A         368      368000    2209E3
DB21         368      368000    2209E3
DB22         368      368000    2209E3
DB23         367      367000    2203E3
DB24         368      368000    2209E3
DB25         368      368000    2209E3
DB26         367      367000    2203E3
DB27         367      367000    2203E3
DB28         368      368000    2209E3
DB29         369      369000    2215E3
```

Figure 9-14 CICS PA report showing TCB switches after simplistic conversion

To compare the simplistic conversion figures with both CICS Transaction Server Version 1.3 and our actual CICS Transaction Server Version 2.3 migration, we again calculated the averages across all transactions and added the results to our table. See Table 9-3.

Table 9-3   CICS TS 1.3 vs. CICS TS 2.3 actual conversion vs. simplistic conversion

	CICS TS 1.3	CICS TS 2.3 (actual conversion)	CICS TS 2.3 (simplistic conversion)
Avg. SQL calls per task	1000	1000	1000
Avg. TCB switches per task	2002	2002	**6003**
Transaction throughput	15.97 tps	16.56 tps	**12.26tps**

As can be seen in Table 9-3, failure to define all the user exit programs on the SQL call path within the sample application as threadsafe would have resulted in a significant increase in TCB switches after the upgrade from CICS Transaction

Server Version 1.3 to CICS Transaction Server Version 2.3 and a corresponding decline in transaction throughput. This point is reinforced by the two charts shown in Figure 9-15 and Figure 9-16 on page 218.

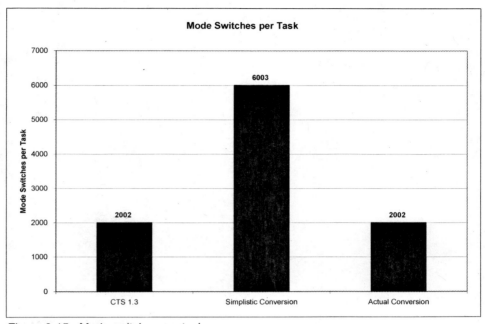

Figure 9-15   Mode switches per task

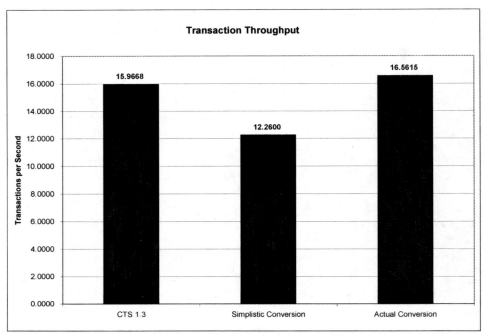

Figure 9-16   Transaction throughput

9.4 Migration part 2

As outlined in 9.2, "Migration plan" on page 201, the migration plan is split into two major parts:

- Upgrading to CICS Transaction Server Version 2.3 without incurring extra TCB switches
- Converting application to be fully threadsafe

This section covers part 2 of the migration, which converts the application to be threadsafe.

9.4.1 Step 1: Identify programs in scope for part 2

The first step is to identify the application programs (including PLT programs), user exits, and user-replaceable modules that are defined as quasi-reentrant. If program autoinstall is in operation, it is not sufficient to use a list of programs defined to CICS—we need to start with the application load libraries concatenated within DFHRPL.

The list of modules in the sample application load library is shown in Figure 9-17, while Figure 9-18 on page 220 shows the corresponding entries from the Programs by DSA section of a DFH0STAT print.

Name	Size	TTR	AC	AM	RM	Attributes
DB2MANY	00000558	001D46	00	31	ANY	RN RU
DB2PROGA	00000480	001E06	00	31	ANY	RN RU
DB2PROG1	00000448	001E0F	00	31	ANY	RN RU
DB2PROG2	00000448	001E18	00	31	ANY	RN RU
DB2PROG3	00000448	001E21	00	31	ANY	RN RU
DB2PROG4	00000420	001E2A	00	31	ANY	RN RU
DB2PROG5	00000420	001E33	00	31	ANY	RN RU
DB2PROG6	00000420	001E3C	00	31	ANY	RN RU
DB2PROG7	00000420	001F02	00	31	ANY	RN RU
DB2PROG8	00000478	001F0B	00	31	ANY	RN RU
DB2PROG9	00000478	001F14	00	31	ANY	RN RU
EXITENBL	000001B0	001D1A	00	31	ANY	RN RU
PLANEXIT	000000D0	001D23	00	31	ANY	RN RU
XXXEI	000000B8	001D2C	00	31	ANY	RN RU
XXXRMI	000000B8	001D35	00	31	ANY	RN RU
XXXTS	00000068	001D3E	00	31	ANY	RN RU

Figure 9-17 Application load library member list

```
Programs by DSA and LPA

Program    Concurrency               Program    Program
Name       Status       Times Used   Size       Location

DB2MANY    Quasi Rent        3       1,368      ERDSA
DB2PROGA   Quasi Rent       36       1,152      ERDSA
DB2PROG1   Quasi Rent       36       1,096      ERDSA
DB2PROG2   Quasi Rent       36       1,096      ERDSA
DB2PROG3   Quasi Rent       36       1,096      ERDSA
DB2PROG4   Quasi Rent       36       1,056      ERDSA
DB2PROG5   Quasi Rent       36       1,056      ERDSA
DB2PROG6   Quasi Rent       36       1,056      ERDSA
DB2PROG7   Quasi Rent       36       1,056      ERDSA
DB2PROG8   Quasi Rent       36       1,144      ERDSA
DB2PROG9   Quasi Rent       36       1,144      ERDSA
EXITENBL   Quasi Rent        1         432      ERDSA
PLANEXIT   Thread Safe     363         208      ERDSA
XXXEI      Thread Safe       1         184      ERDSA
XXXRMI     Thread Safe       1         184      ERDSA
XXXTS      Quasi Rent        1         104      ERDSA
```

Figure 9-18   Programs by DSA section of DFH0STAT report

Taking the information displayed in Figure 9-17 on page 219 and Figure 9-18 together, we now have a definitive list of the application programs and exits that are defined as quasi-reentrant:

- DB2MANY
- DB2PROG1
- DB2PROG2
- DB2PROG3
- DB2PROG4
- DB2PROG5
- DB2PROG6
- DB2PROG7
- DB2PROG8
- DB2PROG9
- DB2PROGA
- EXITENBL
- XXXTS

These programs constitute the full scope of part 2 of the migration.

9.4.2 Step 2: Convert user exits to be threadsafe

This step has a variety of tasks, such as gathering information and examining code, as well as other tasks.

Gather information using DFH0STAT

To determine whether any user exits are in scope for part 2, we again look at the Exit Programs section of the DFH0STAT print.

Figure 9-19 shows that we have one global user exit in scope for migration. Program XXXTS is enabled at the XTSQRIN exit point. (The CICS Customization Guide tells us that XTSQRIN is invoked prior to each user temporary storage request.)

```
User Exit Programs

                        <---- Global Area ---->   No.
    Program     Entry   Entry                     Use       of      Program     Program
    Name        Name    Name         Length      Count    Exits    Status      Concurrency

    XXXEI      XXXEI                    0          0        2      Started     Thread Safe
    XXXRMI     XXXRMI                   0          0        2      Started     Thread Safe
    XXXTS      XXXTS   XXXTS           64          1        1      Started     Quasi Rent

Global User Exits

    Exit       Program  Entry       <------- Global Area ------->   Number      Program
    Name       Name     Name        Entry Name   Length  Use Count  of Exits    Status

    XTSQRIN    XXXTS    XXXTS       XXXTS          64       1          1        Started
    XEIIN      XXXEI    XXXEI                       0       0          2        Started
    XEIOUT     XXXEI    XXXEI                       0       0          2        Started
    XRMIIN     XXXRMI   XXXRMI                      0       0          2        Started
    XRMIOUT    XXXRMI   XXXRMI                      0       0          2        Started
```

Figure 9-19   User Exits section of DFH0STAT report

Highly significant is the fact that DFH0STAT also shows that XXXTS owns a global work area (see Figure 9-19). A GWA is, by definition, a shared resource, and we now must determine which programs access it. As owner of the GWA, it is probable that the XXXTS code is not threadsafe, but we will need to look at the source code to confirm this.

Examine source code

The source code for XXXTS is listed in Appendix C, "Assembler routines" on page 327. An examination of this code confirms that this program is not threadsafe, because it updates a counter field in the GWA without serialization.

Gather information using DFHEISUP

Having discovered a shared resource (that is, the XXXTS GWA) we now need to determine which other programs access this resource. DFH0STAT has already told us that no other user exits programs share this GWA (see Figure 9-19 on page 221). However, we also need to look for programs that address it via an EXEC CICS EXTRACT EXIT command.

DFHEISUP is designed for this purpose, and we ran it against the entire application using a single filter table entry: EXEC CICS EXTRACT EXIT GASET *. Figure 9-20 shows the output from DFHEISUP.

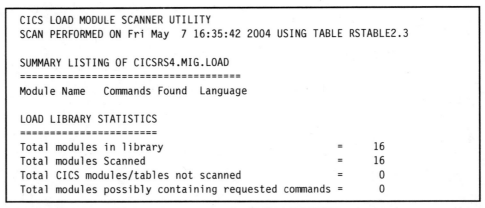

```
CICS LOAD MODULE SCANNER UTILITY
SCAN PERFORMED ON Fri May  7 16:35:42 2004 USING TABLE RSTABLE2.3

SUMMARY LISTING OF CICSRS4.MIG.LOAD
=======================================
Module Name    Commands Found   Language

LOAD LIBRARY STATISTICS
=========================
Total modules in library                                =     16
Total modules Scanned                                   =     16
Total CICS modules/tables not scanned                   =      0
Total modules possibly containing requested commands    =      0
```

*Figure 9-20   DFHEISUP summary report for EXTRACT EXIT * command*

DFHEISUP tells us that no program issues the EXEC CICS EXTRACT EXIT command, so it is safe for us to conclude that access to this GWA is limited to program XXXTS.

Important: We were able to reach this conclusion because we know the sample application always uses standard CICS interfaces to address GWAs. Applications using other methods to address GWAs would need further investigation before this conclusion could be reached.

Serialize access to GWAs

Having established that XXXTS is the only program to update the GWA, we now need to ensure that this update is serialized. Figure 9-21 shows the appropriate extract from the source code.

```
GWAUPDT  EQU  *
         L    R6,GWACOUNT      GET THE COUNTER
         LA   R6,1(R6)         INCREMENT
         ST   R6,GWACOUNT        AND STORE
         B    RETURN           EXIT
```

Figure 9-21   XXXTS source code (quasi-reentrant)

We can see in Figure 9-21 that the update is performed with a store (ST) instruction. Using XPI enqueue and dequeue commands to serialize this update would be perfectly valid, but since a single field is being updated, we decided to replace the store with a Compare and Swap (CS) routine. Figure 9-22 shows the changed code.

```
GWAUPDT  EQU  *
         L    R6,GWACOUNT      PUT ORIGINAL COUNTER IN R6
LOOP     LR   R7,R6            CREATE A COPY IN R7 TO MODIFY
         LA   R7,1(R7)         INCREMENT THE COPY IN R7
         CS   R6,R7,GWACOUNT   USE COMPARE & SWAP TO UPDATE
         BC   4,LOOP             AND REPEAT IF UNSUCCESFUL
         B    RETURN           EXIT
```

Figure 9-22   XXXTS source code (threadsafe)

Having serialized access to the GWA, XXXTS now contains threadsafe code.

Redefine exits as threadsafe

Having completed an analysis of all user exits, identified and serialized access to their shared resources (from all application programs, not just user exit programs), it is now safe to redefine all exits as threadsafe.

Figure 9-23 shows XXXTS redefined as threadsafe.

```
 OBJECT CHARACTERISTICS
  CEDA   View PROGram( XXXTS     )
   PROGram           : XXXTS
   Group             : MIGAPPL3
   DEscription       :
   Language          :
   RELoad            : No
   RESident          : No
   USAge             : Normal
   USElpacopy        : No
   Status            : Enabled
   RSl               : 00
   CEdf              : Yes
   DAtalocation      : Any
   EXECKey           : User
   COncurrency       : Threadsafe
   REMOTE ATTRIBUTES
   DYnamic           : No
 + REMOTESystem      :
```

Figure 9-23   CEDA view program display

9.4.3 Step 3: Convert application programs to be threadsafe

For most applications, this is likely to be the single biggest step in a threadsafe migration, and the step most dependent on user application knowledge. The migration process described in this section is valid for the sample application because we know that this application uses standard CICS interfaces to create and address shared resources.

Run DFH0STAT to find shared program storage

This is a step we have already performed in part 1 of the migration, but it must be repeated now if the application has changed in the meantime. (In a real-life scenario, months may have elapsed between the implementation of parts 1 and 2 of the migration plan.) This is not the case for the sample, and therefore the conclusion reached in part 1 is still valid—program storage is not used as a shared resource within the application.

Refer to "Run DFH0STAT to find shared program storage" on page 205 for a full discussion of the results of this step.

Run DFHEISUP to find potential shared resources

This is also a step that has already been performed in part 1 of the migration, and would only need to be repeated if the application had changed in the meantime. The details are discussed in "Run DFHEISUP to find potential shared resources" on page 207, but since the results are more relevant to this part of the migration, they are repeated here in Figure 9-24.

```
Module Name         'CICSRS4.MIG.LOAD(DB2PROG4)'
Module Language     Assembler
Offset/EDF          Command
----------------    ------------------------------------
00001387/no-edf     ADDRESS CWA

Module Name         'CICSRS4.MIG.LOAD(DB2PROG5)'
Module Language     Assembler
Offset/EDF          Command
----------------    ------------------------------------
00001387/no-edf     ADDRESS CWA

Module Name         'CICSRS4.MIG.LOAD(DB2PROG6)'
Module Language     Assembler
Offset/EDF          Command
----------------    ------------------------------------
00001387/no-edf     ADDRESS CWA

Module Name         'CICSRS4.MIG.LOAD(DB2PROG7)'
Module Language     Assembler
Offset/EDF          Command
----------------    ------------------------------------
00001387/no-edf     ADDRESS CWA

Total possible commands located = 4
```

Figure 9-24   DFHEISUP detailed report using DFHEIDTH filter table

Running DFHEISUP with the threadsafe inhibitors table DFHEIDTH reveals that the programs listed here all address the CWA (Figure 9-24):

- DB2PROG4
- DB2PROG5
- DB2PROG6
- DB2PROG7

The absence within the application of the GETMAIN SHARED, EXTRACT EXIT, and LOAD SET commands is confirmed by DFHEISUP, and therefore since we know that *the sample always uses standard CICS interfaces*, we can conclude that the CWA is the only remaining shared resource we need to address.

Examine source code

We have reached the point in the migration where we know we have one remaining shared resource—the CWA—to investigate, and we have also identified the programs that access it: DB2PROG4, DB2PROG5, DB2PROG6, and DB2PROG7.

An examination of the source code (listed in Appendix C, "Assembler routines" on page 327) shows us that each of the four programs access and update the data in the CWA using the same sequence of instructions. An appropriate extract is shown in Figure 9-25.

```
****************************************************************
*                                     INCREMENT COUNTER IN CWA
        EXEC CICS ADDRESS CWA(R10)
        USING CWASTG,R10
        L     R9,CWACOUNT
        LA    R9,1(R9)
        ST    R9,CWACOUNT
****************************************************************
```

Figure 9-25   DB2PROG4-7 source code (quasi-reentrant)

Figure 9-25 shows that all four programs take a counter from the CWA, increment it by 1, and then store it back. This code is not threadsafe, and unless changed, all four programs must remain defined as quasi-reentrant.

> **Note:** For the purposes of our test we decided to use enqueue/dequeue to serialize access. It should be noted though that Compare and Swap is less costly than using enqueue/dequeue.

Serialize access to shared resources

We have identified that we have non threadsafe code in the application. Programs DB2PROG4, DB2PROG5, DB2PROG6, and DB2PROG7 all update a counter field in the CWA. To convert this code to be threadsafe, we decided to serialize access to the CWA.

To achieve this, all four programs must be changed to use an identical serialization technique. The option we chose was an enqueue/dequeue on the address of the CWA. Figure 9-26 shows the appropriate extract of code after the EXEC CICS ENQ and DEQ commands have been added. (The code prior to the change was shown previously in Figure 9-25 on page 226.)

```
****************************************************************
*                                    INCREMENT COUNTER IN CWA
       EXEC CICS ADDRESS CWA(R10)
       USING CWASTG,R10
       EXEC  CICS ENQ RESOURCE(CWASTG)
       L     R9,CWACOUNT              UPDATE CWA WHILE
       LA    R9,1(R9)                  OWNING ENQ ON
       ST    R9,CWACOUNT               CWA ADDRESS
       EXEC  CICS DEQ RESOURCE(CWASTG)
****************************************************************
```

Figure 9-26   DB2PROG4-7 source code (threadsafe)

The code illustrated in Figure 9-26 is threadsafe and enables programs DB2PROG4, DB2PROG5, DB2PROG6, and DB2PROG7 to be redefined as such.

Redefine application programs as threadsafe

Having completed an analysis of all application programs, identified and serialized access to their shared resources, it is now safe to redefine all programs as threadsafe.

Figure 9-27 shows a CEMT display of the application programs after they have been redefined as threadsafe.

```
I PROG(DB2*)
STATUS:   RESULTS - OVERTYPE TO MODIFY
 Prog(DB2MANY ) Leng(0000000000)        Pro Ena Pri       Ced
    Res(000) Use(0000000000) Any Uex Ful Thr
 Prog(DB2PROGA) Leng(0000000000)        Pro Ena Pri       Ced
    Res(000) Use(0000000000) Any Uex Ful Thr
 Prog(DB2PROG1) Leng(0000000000)        Pro Ena Pri       Ced
    Res(000) Use(0000000000) Any Uex Ful Thr
 Prog(DB2PROG2) Leng(0000000000)        Pro Ena Pri       Ced
    Res(000) Use(0000000000) Any Uex Ful Thr
 Prog(DB2PROG3) Leng(0000000000)        Pro Ena Pri       Ced
    Res(000) Use(0000000000) Any Uex Ful Thr
 Prog(DB2PROG4) Leng(0000000000)        Pro Ena Pri       Ced
    Res(000) Use(0000000000) Any Uex Ful Thr
 Prog(DB2PROG5) Leng(0000000000)        Pro Ena Pri       Ced
    Res(000) Use(0000000000) Any Uex Ful Thr
 Prog(DB2PROG6) Leng(0000000000)        Pro Ena Pri       Ced
    Res(000) Use(0000000000) Any Uex Ful Thr
 Prog(DB2PROG7) Leng(0000000000)        Pro Ena Pri       Ced
    Res(000) Use(0000000000) Any Uex Ful Thr
 Prog(DB2PROG8) Leng(0000000000)        Pro Ena Pri       Ced
    Res(000) Use(0000000000) Any Uex Ful Thr
 Prog(DB2PROG9) Leng(0000000000)        Pro Ena Pri       Ced
    Res(000) Use(0000000000) Any Uex Ful Thr
```

Figure 9-27   CEMT INQUIRE PROGRAM display

9.4.4 Step 4: Address non threadsafe commands

Having successfully converted and redefined all application programs and exits as threadsafe, our one remaining migration task is to investigate the extent to which non threadsafe commands are used within the application. In particular, we are looking for commands that can be issued between the first and last SQL call within a CICS task. Non threadsafe commands that are issued either prior to the first SQL call or after the last SQL call will not have a detrimental impact on performance.

> **Note:** In CICS Transaction Server Version 3.1 if the application is an OPENAPI application then all non threadsafe commands, wherever they are in the program, are an issue. They would cause two TCB switches per command.

To determine which commands are issued within the application, we ran the load module scanner utility, DFHEISUP, with the supplied non threadsafe command table, DFHEIDNT, against the whole application.

```
SUMMARY LISTING OF CICSRS4.MIG.LOAD
=======================================
Module Name                     Commands Found  Language
'CICSRS4.MIG.LOAD(DB2MANY)'                  2  Assembler
'CICSRS4.MIG.LOAD(DB2PROGA)'                 3  Assembler
'CICSRS4.MIG.LOAD(DB2PROG1)'                 4  Assembler
'CICSRS4.MIG.LOAD(DB2PROG2)'                 4  Assembler
'CICSRS4.MIG.LOAD(DB2PROG3)'                 4  Assembler
'CICSRS4.MIG.LOAD(DB2PROG4)'                 2  Assembler
'CICSRS4.MIG.LOAD(DB2PROG5)'                 2  Assembler
'CICSRS4.MIG.LOAD(DB2PROG6)'                 2  Assembler
'CICSRS4.MIG.LOAD(DB2PROG7)'                 2  Assembler
'CICSRS4.MIG.LOAD(DB2PROG8)'                 3  Assembler
'CICSRS4.MIG.LOAD(DB2PROG9)'                 3  Assembler
'CICSRS4.MIG.LOAD(EXITENBL)'                 2  Assembler

LOAD LIBRARY STATISTICS
========================
Total modules in library                              =     16
Total modules Scanned                                 =     16
Total CICS modules/tables not scanned                 =      0
Total modules possibly containing requested commands  =     12
```

Figure 9-28   DFHEISUP summary report using DFHEIDNT filter table

Figure 9-28 shows the summary output from DFHEISUP and highlights the programs that will need further investigation. From our knowledge of the sample application, we know that each application program listed in the report is a self-contained CICS transaction, so we can examine the use of commands on a program-by-program basis.

The source code for the programs discussed in the following sections is listed in Appendix C, "Assembler routines" on page 327.

Program DB2MANY

Figure 9-29 details the two non threadsafe commands discovered by DFHEISUP in program DB2MANY: EXEC CICS START and EXEC CICS SEND.

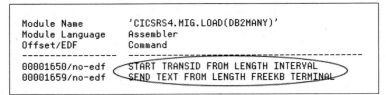

```
Module Name        'CICSRS4.MIG.LOAD(DB2MANY)'
Module Language    Assembler
Offset/EDF         Command
-----------------  --------------------------------------------
00001650/no-edf    START TRANSID FROM LENGTH INTERVAL
00001659/no-edf    SEND TEXT FROM LENGTH FREEKB TERMINAL
```

Figure 9-29 DFHEISUP detailed report for program DB2MANY

We can see from the source code in Appendix C, "Assembler routines" on page 327, that DB2MANY contains EXEC SQL calls, but both the START and SEND commands will always be executed after the last call, and so will not impact performance. No action is therefore required.

(The ASKTIME command, which will be executed between SQL calls, was made threadsafe in CICS Transaction Server Version 2.3).

Programs DB2PROG1, DB2PROG2, and DB2PROG3

Figure 9-30 details the four non threadsafe commands discovered by DFHEISUP in programs DB2PROG1, 2, and 3:

- EXEC CICS RETRIEVE
- EXEC CICS POST
- EXEC CICS WAITCICS
- EXEC CICS START

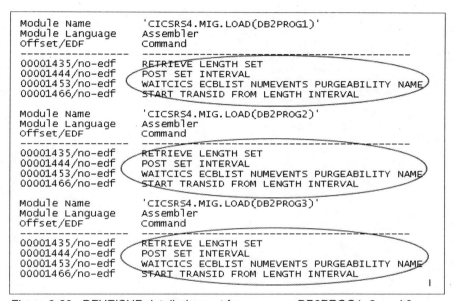

Figure 9-30   DFHEISUP detailed report for programs DB2PROG1, 2, and 3

We can see from the source code in Appendix C, "Assembler routines" on page 327, that these three programs contain EXEC SQL calls, but both the RETRIEVE and POST will always be executed before the first call, and the START will always be executed after the last call, and so these commands will not impact performance.

However, the WAITCICS command presents a problem, because it is non threadsafe and it will always be executed between SQL calls. Our options are:

- Leave the code unchanged and not gain the performance benefit from defining the programs as threadsafe.
- Redesign the code so that the WAITCICS does not execute between SQL calls.
- Change the code so that the WAITCICS is no longer required.

In actual fact, there is a simple solution in this particular case that makes the last option viable. The EXEC CICS WAIT EXTERNAL command *is* threadsafe, and can be substituted in our application for the WAITCICS command. Figure 9-31 and Figure 9-32 show the code change that we implemented.

```
        LA      R9,ECB1                 WAIT UNTIL ECB POSTED
        EXEC    CICS WAITCICS                                           X
                ECBLIST(R9)                                             X
                NUMEVENTS(=F'1')                                        X
                NAME(=C'APPLWAIT')                                      X
                PURGEABLE
```

Figure 9-31   Unchanged code contains a non threadsafe command

```
        LA      R9,ECB1                 WAIT UNTIL ECB POSTED
        EXEC    CICS WAIT EXTERNAL                                      X
                ECBLIST(R9)                                             X
                NUMEVENTS(=F'1')                                        X
                NAME(=C'APPLWAIT')                                      X
                PURGEABLE
```

Figure 9-32   Code changed to use a threadsafe command

Programs DB2PROG4, DB2PROG5, DB2PROG6, and DB2PROG7

Figure 9-33 details the two non threadsafe commands discovered by DFHEISUP in programs DB2PROG4, 5, 6, and 7:

- EXEC CICS RETRIEVE
- EXEC CICS START

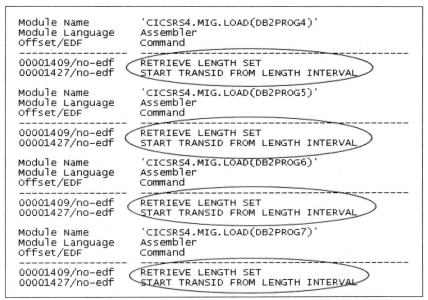

Figure 9-33   DFHEISUP detailed report for programs DB2PROG4, 5, 6, and 7

We can see from the source code in Appendix C, "Assembler routines" on page 327, that these four programs contain EXEC SQL calls, but the RETRIEVE will always be executed before the first call, and the START will always be executed after the last call, and so neither will impact performance. No action is therefore required.

The ASKTIME command, which will be executed between SQL calls, was made threadsafe in CICS Transaction Server Version 2.3.

Programs DB2PROG8, DB2PROG9, and DB2PROGA

Figure 9-34 details the three non threadsafe commands discovered by DFHEISUP in programs DB2PROG8, 9, and A:

- EXEC CICS RETRIEVE
- EXEC CICS WRITEQ TD
- EXEC CICS START

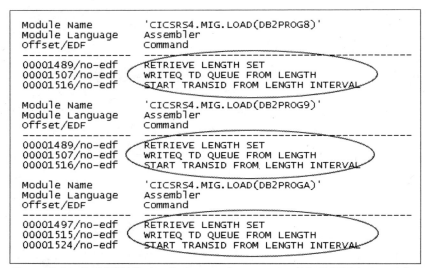

Figure 9-34 DFHEISUP detailed report for programs DB2PROG8, 9 and A

We can see from the source code in Appendix C, "Assembler routines" on page 327, that these three programs contain EXEC SQL calls, but the RETRIEVE will always be executed before the first call, and both the WRITEQ TD and START will always be executed after the last call, and so will not impact performance. No action is therefore required.

(The READQ TS command, which will be executed between SQL calls, was made threadsafe in CICS Transaction Server Version 2.2.)

Program EXITENBL

Figure 9-35 details the two non threadsafe commands discovered by DFHEISUP in program EXITENBL—both were EXEC CICS ENABLE.

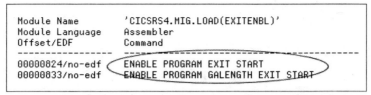

Figure 9-35   DFHEISUP detailed report for program EXITENBL

We can see from the source code (listed in Example C-6 on page 342) that this program does not contain EXEC SQL calls and, from our knowledge of the application, we know is executed via the PLTPI. No action is therefore required.

This completes our investigation of EXEC CICS commands within the application. We were able to confirm, with one exception, that all non threadsafe commands are executed either prior to the first SQL call or after the last SQL call in every CICS program. Moreover, we were able to address the one instance of a non threadsafe command executing between SQL calls by substituting it with a similar command that is threadsafe.

9.4.5 Step 5: CICS system changes

We are now in a good position. We have an application we know is fully threadsafe, and does not issue non threadsafe commands between SQL calls. The final step in the migration is to make appropriate changes to the CICS region in order to let the application exploit the open transaction environment.

Table 9-4 shows the parameter values we implemented in the CICS Transaction Server Version 2.3 region. The CICS Transaction Server Version 1.3 region values are shown for comparison.

Table 9-4   CICS system parameters pre- and post-migration

Parameter	Pre-migration (CICS TS 1.3)	Post-migration (CICS TS 2.3)
SIT		
MXT	110	110
DSA	4M	4M
MAXOPENTCBS	N/A to application	130

Parameter	Pre-migration (CICS TS 1.3)	Post-migration (CICS TS 2.3)
FORCEQR	N/A to application	NO
DB2CONN		
TCBLIMIT	130	130
DB2ENTRY		
THREADLIMIT	120	120
PRIORITY	LOW	LOW

As illustrated by Table 9-4 on page 235, the only changes required in our CICS Transaction Server Version 2.3 region was to set FORCEQR to NO (this is the default in any case) and MAXOPENTCBS to be the same value as TCBLIMIT. The key thing to note is that MAXOPENTCBS, TCBLIMIT, and THREADLIMIT are all higher than MXT; that is, MXT is the parameter we chose to throttle the CICS workload in the event that throttling is ever required.

The CICS system changes complete our migration of the application to threadsafe. The final step in the plan is to confirm that we have achieved what we set out to achieve: improved application performance.

9.5 Performance measurement

This section describes what we did to measure the performance of the sample application after it was fully converted to threadsafe. The results are shown and compared with the corresponding figures measured when the application was quasi-reentrant.

> **Important:** The results shown in this chapter are specific to the sample application and the system it was running on at the time. The purpose is to show that threadsafe migrations will improve application performance, but these specific results should not be used as a benchmark for any other application or system.

9.5.1 Reports

We used SMF type 110 records to gather the following key measurements for each transaction:

- The number of SQL calls
- The number of TCB switches
- The response time
- The CPU time
- The throughput (tasks per second)

We used CICS Performance Analyzer Version 1 Release 3 (CICS PA) to report against the SMF data. Figure 9-36 shows the selection criteria we used to generate the reports. We used 5-minute intervals (that is, the difference between SMFSTART and SMFSTOP) in all our reports.

```
CICSPA IN(SMFIN001),
       SMFSTART(yyyy/mm/dd,hh:mm:ss.nn),
       SMFSTOP(yyyy/mm/dd,hh:mm:ss.nn),
       APPLID(cicsapplid),
       LINECNT(60),
       FORMAT(':','/'),
    SUMMARY(OUTPUT(TESTSUM),
       BY(TRAN),
       SELECT(PERFORMANCE(
       INC(TRAN(DB21,DB22,DB23,DB24,DB25,
       DB26,DB27,DB28,DB29,DB2A)))),
       FIELDS(TRAN,
              TASKCNT,
              RESPONSE(TOTAL),
              DB2REQCT(TOTAL),
              CHMODECT(TOTAL),
              CPU(TIME(TOT)),
              QRCPU(TIME(TOT)),
              L8CPU(TIME(TOT))))
```

Figure 9-36   CICS PA report - selection criteria

Figure 9-37 shows the report generated for the application after part 1 of the migration was completed (that is, quasi-reentrant application, with threadsafe exits on the SQL call path), and Figure 9-38 on page 239 shows the corresponding report after part 2 was completed (that is, the is application fully threadsafe).

> **Note:** In the next few CICS PA performance reports we decided to use totals, not averages. If averages are required you must divide the number of tasks by the whichever total you are interested in.

```
V1R3M0                    CICS Performance Analyzer
                             Performance Summary

                Data from 15:09:58  5/13/2004 to 15:14:59  5/13/2004


                        Total    Total    Total    Total    Total    Total
Tran        #Tasks    Response  DB2 Reqs ChngMode User CPU  QR CPU   L8 CPU
                        Time                        Time     Time     Time
DB2A           498    300.471   498000   996996   37.8468  8.2547   29.5920
DB21           499    301.155   499000   998998   37.0994  7.4055   29.6939
DB22           500    301.048   500000   1001E3   36.6220  7.3962   29.2258
DB23           498    300.426   498000   996996   36.7766  7.3603   29.4164
DB24           498    300.475   498000   996996   37.4116  7.8154   29.5961
DB25           498    300.414   498000   996996   37.1906  7.8236   29.3670
DB26           499    300.977   499000   998998   37.6047  7.9280   29.6767
DB27           499    301.023   499000   998998   37.4565  7.8656   29.5908
DB28           498    300.599   498000   996996   37.8501  8.2476   29.6025
DB29           498    300.456   498000   996996   37.7188  8.2497   29.4691
```

Figure 9-37   Performance report before full migration to threadsafe

```
V1R3M0                   CICS Performance Analyzer
                            Performance Summary

             Data from 17:19:59  5/13/2004 to 17:24:59  5/13/2004


                 Total     Total    Total     Total    Total    Total
   Tran  #Tasks Response    DB2 Reqs ChngMode User CPU  QR CPU   L8 CPU
                  Time                          Time    Time     Time
   DB2A    813  303.524    813000    3252    49.1480   .2283   48.9198
   DB21    959  304.113    959000    3836    54.2789   .2374   54.0415
   DB22    967  303.960    967000    3868    53.7371   .2400   53.4971
   DB23    959  304.398    959000    3836    54.1888   .2366   53.9522
   DB24    951  303.937    951000    3804    53.9875   .2169   53.7706
   DB25    955  303.988    955000    3820    53.9665   .2187   53.7478
   DB26    951  303.723    951000    3804    54.0771   .2176   53.8595
   DB27    956  303.770    956000    3824    54.1474   .2174   53.9300
   DB28    813  303.917    813000    3252    49.1606   .2285   48.9321
   DB29    817  303.342    817000    3268    49.0784   .2247   48.8537
```

Figure 9-38   Performance report after full migration to threadsafe

Looking at the data in Figure 9-37 on page 238 and Figure 9-38 together, we can see that our threadsafe migration has delivered the reduction in TCB switches we set out to achieve, and this in turn has resulted in substantial improvements in all of our key performance indicators (KPIs):

- Transaction CPU time
- Transaction response time
- Transaction throughput (tasks per second)

We used the figures in the CICS PA reports to calculate our KPIs and tabulated the results (Table 9-5).

Table 9-5   KPIs: quasi-reentrant versus threadsafe

	Quasi-reentrant	Threadsafe	Improvement
Avg. SQL calls per task	1000	1000	
Avg. TCB switches per task	2002	4	
Avg. cpu time per task	0.0749 sec	0.0575 sec	**23%**
Avg. response time	0.6032 sec	0.3324 sec	**45%**
Transaction throughput	16.62 tps	30.47 tps	**83%**

To illustrate this more clearly, we created charts for each of the KPIs, and these are shown in 9.5.2, "Charts" on page 240.

9.5.2 Charts

In this section we provide charts for each of the KPIs.

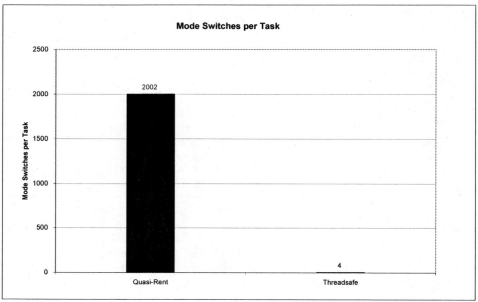

Figure 9-39   Mode switches per task CICS TS 2.3

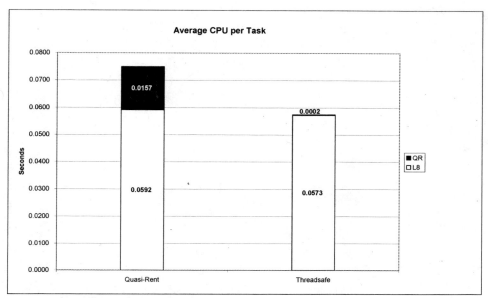

Figure 9-40   Average CPU per task

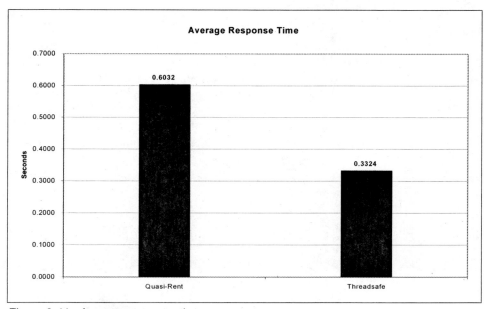

Figure 9-41   Average response time

Chapter 9. Migration scenario

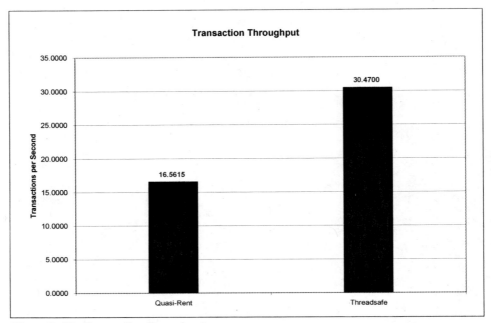

Figure 9-42   Transaction throughput

9.5.3 Conclusions

The performance measurements complete the migration of the sample application from quasi-reentrant to threadsafe. The reports and charts shown in 9.5.1, "Reports" on page 237, and 9.5.2, "Charts" on page 240, illustrate that we have achieved our goal. By migrating the entire application to threadsafe, we delivered substantial improvements in each of our key performance indicators:

- 23% improvement in transaction CPU time
- 45% improvement in transaction response times
- 83% improvement in transaction throughput

9.6 Additional considerations for OPENAPI programs

CICS Transaction Server Version 3.1 extends OTE and allows applications to be defined not only as THREADSAFE, but also with an API attribute that takes values of CICSAPI or OPENAPI (CICSAPI being the default). Hence, a threadsafe application in CICS Transaction Server Version 2 is a threadsafe, CICSAPI program in CICS Transaction Server Version 3.1.

The OPENAPI attribute mandates that the application also be defined as THREADSAFE because it must be coded to threadsafe standards, as it will execute on an open TCB. Hence, an OPENAPI application is one that is defined as THREADSAFE and OPENAPI.

THREADSAFE, OPENAPI applications differ from THREADSAFE, CICSAPI applications programs in that they *always* execute on an open TCB, whereas THREADSAFE, CICSAPI applications execute on *either* QR TCB or an open TCB, whichever is being used at the time. This allows THREADSAFE, OPENAPI programs to safely use non-CICS APIs because they are guaranteed not to be running on the QR TCB. Any non-CICS API command that halts the TCB will halt just that open TCB and not the whole of CICS.

For non-CICS APIs to function correctly the key of the TCB is important, and it must match the execution key. For example, an MVS getmain determines the key of storage required by examining the key of the TCB rather than the PSW execution key. (For CICSAPI programs, the TCB key is irrelevant, as the CICS API works independently of the TCB key.) This means that THREADSAFE, OPENAPI, EXECKEY(USER) programs *always* run on an L9 TCB, and THREADSAFE, OPENAPI, EXECKEY(CICS) applications *always* run on an L8 TCB (assuming storage protection is active).

Task-related user exits (TRUEs) always run in EXECKEY(CICS). OPENAPI TRUEs such as the CICS-DB2 TRUE, or the IP CICS Sockets TRUE in z/OS Communications Server Version 1 Release 7 (if configured), therefore always run on an L8 TCB. Hence a conflict exists between a EXECKEY(USER) application that is defined as OPENAPI that must run on an L9 TCB, and an OPENAPI TRUE that must run on an L8 TCB. Two TCB switches will occur for *every* call to an OPENAPI TRUE, L9 to L8 and L8 to L9 afterwards.

> **Note**: We strongly recommend that EXECKEY(USER) CICS-DB2 applications that have previously been made threadsafe, and defined to CICS as such, remain as THREADSAFE, CICSAPI PROGRAMS, unless storage protection is not being used. The applications should not be defined as OPENAPI.
>
> The same recommendation applies to EXECKEY(USER) IP CICS Sockets applications.

Performance case studies

This chapter documents the results obtained by some benchmark comparisons performed by IBM for applications running on CICS Transaction Server Version 3.2, and utilizing DB2, WMQ, and EXEC CICS file control calls. It is intended to provide a comparison of the benefits obtained when redefining such applications from quasi-reentrant to threadsafe. In these benchmarked examples, it is taken as a given that the applications are already analyzed and written to threadsafe standards, so there are no issues such as shared storage areas or serialization techniques to consider.

10.1 CICS DB2 and file control application

The test involved driving a transaction that carried out the following work. An initial (quasi-reentrant) COBOL program EXEC CICS LINKed to another COBOL application program. This second application then performed a variety of DB2 and CICS commands. The sequence followed was:

EXEC CICS READ

EXEC SQL OPEN

EXEC SQL FETCH

EXEC CICS ASKTIME

EXEC SQL UPDATE

EXEC SQL CLOSE

> **Note:** The application logic involves EXEC CICS commands that are threadsafe in CICS Transaction Server Version 3.2, and so can execute under an open TCB or QR TCB. In the same way, EXEC SQL calls to DB2 also execute under open (L8) TCBs.

This application looped internally 100 times when linked to, so this series of commands was issued 100 times per task.

Testing involved defining the second program as CONCURRENCY(QUASIRENT), API(CICSAPI) and then redefining it as CONCURRENCY(THREADSAFE), API(OPENAPI). In both cases, performance and diagnostic data was gathered to provide metrics for the comparative results. This included CICS Performance Analyzer reports, CICS statistics, RMF™ data and CICS auxiliary trace.

The CICS system was not using storage protection for these tests: STGPROT=NO was specified.

> **Note:** This is not an example intended to demonstrate issues with serialization of shared data; nor is it intended to demonstrate performance problems with TCB switching due to interleaved threadsafe and non threadsafe EXEC CICS commands. It is provided to quantify benefits when taking such a program that is or has been made a good threadsafe candidate application, and redefining if as threadsafe to CICS. In a similar vein, it is not intended to reveal performance issues when having to switch between L9 and L8 TCBs for OPENAPI programs that are defined with EXECKEY(USER) and that issue calls to DB2.

The application can be considered a good candidate for being redefined threadsafe in CICS Transaction Server Version 3.2 since it:

- Includes EXEC SQL calls to DB2, which require an L8 TCB
- Has EXEC CICS commands that are threadsafe and so have no affinity to a given TCB environment
- Does not interleave threadsafe and non-threadsafe commands

In fact, this sort of application would be a good model for one that had been prepared for threadsafe use prior to migrating to CICS Transaction Server Version 3.2, because prior to that release EXEC CICS READ commands were non threadsafe, while EXEC CICS ASKTIME commands were threadsafe. Hence the application has already been well structured to separate its non threadsafe and threadsafe work, and so avoid TCB switching where possible. It has good construction with regard to threadsafety.

10.1.1 Environment

Performance testing was carried out on a dedicated IBM test system to provide comparable results. The hardware and software environment was as follows:

- Z990 2084-303 with 3 dedicated CPs
- z/OS Version 1.7
- CICS Transaction Server Version 3.2
- CICS Performance Analyzer 2.1
- DB2 Version 7.1

10.1.2 Results

Two sets of results were obtained, first when the application was defined as CONCURRENCY(QUASIRENT), API(CICSAPI) and then after it was redefined as CONCURRENCY(THREADSAFE), API(OPENAPI).

CICS Performance Analyzer was used to investigate the CPU usage and response times for the application, and compare the number of invocations of the transaction (that is, CICS tasks) that executed for the tests.

RMF workload activity was used to review the total CPU usage, transaction rates and internal response time for the comparison tests.

In addition, a review of the CICS auxiliary trace taken during the tests could be used (if so desired) to verify the TCB switching activity taking place during the execution of the transactions.

```
CICS Performance Analyzer
Performance Summary

                             Avg        Avg                Avg       Avg       Avg        Avg
                    Tran     User CPU   Dispatch   #Tasks  L8 CPU    L9 CPU    Response   DSCHMDLY
                             Time       Time               Time      Time      Time       Count
Results when
quasirent:          FCDB     .010710    .020827    2313    .007678   .000000   .031925    9050757

Results when
threadsafe:         FCDB     .008057    .013630    3452    .007944   .000000   .014356    1806209
```

Figure 10-1   Comparison of transaction performance between quasirent and threadsafe

Figure 10-1 shows the results from CICS Performance Analyzer when comparing the transaction's characteristics for both a quasirent and a threadsafe definition of the main application. As can be seen, the average user CPU time and average dispatch time were reduced after the program was redefined. This can be explained by the reduction in TCB switches that took place when the program was redefined as threadsafe. Prior to that, each EXEC SQL command required a switch from QR to L8 for the duration of the call to DB2, followed by a switch from L8 back to QR upon return to CICS. With 100 iterations of the loop within the application, this resulted in 800 switches for the EXEC SQL calls and 2 switches for the end-of-task syncpoint flows to DB2. When the program was redefined as CONCURRENCY(THREADSAFE), API(OPENAPI), there were 2 switches for the EXEC CICS LINK to the second program, and 2 switches for the syncpoint flows to DB2. The switch from QR to L8 on the link to the second program was because it was defined as API(OPENAPI) and so had to execute under an open TCB. Likewise, the switch back from L8 to QR on the return from the link was because the top level linking program was still defined as quasirent.

The results also show that the comparison is even more favorable when the program was redefined as threadsafe, since more than 1000 additional tasks were able to be executed within the test time frame.

Note that the average L8 CPU time did increase when the application was redefined as threadsafe; however, this was more than countered by the reduction in QR TCB CPU usage, as reflected in the total value shown by the average user CPU time.

L9 TCB CPU usage was 0 since storage protection was not active, and the application's execution key was therefore not pertinent. An L8 TCB could be used instead.

Also note that the average response time for using the threadsafe application was less than half that of the quasirent version.

Finally, the DSCHMDLY value (redispatch wait time caused by a change mode to switch TCBs) was reduced by eighty percent, a direct reflection of the fact that far fewer TCB switches were having to take place.

```
CICS Performance Analyzer
DB2 - Long Summary

                                      Avg        Max        Avg        Max        Avg        Max
         Tran/   Program/  #Tasks/   DB2Rqst    DB2Rqst    UserCPU    UserCPU    Response   Response
         SSID    Planname  #Threads   Count      Count      Time       Time       Time       Time

Results when quasirent:
         FCDB    FCDB2001    2313      400.0       400      .010710    .012918    .0319     .1539

         DF2A    DB9A        2313             Thread Utilization    Entry=    0     Pool=   2313
                                       Class1: Thread Time Avg: Elapsed=  .0312    CPU=  .008933
                                                            Max: Elapsed=  .1533    CPU=  .011068

Results when threadsafe:
         FCDB    FCDB2001    3452      400.0       400      .008056    .018088    .0144     .0546

         DF2A    DB9A        3452             Thread Utilization    Entry=    0     Pool=   3452
                                       Class1: Thread Time Avg: Elapsed=  .0126    CPU=  .007693
                                                            Max: Elapsed=  .0462    CPU=  .017703
```

Figure 10-2   Comparison of DB2 performance activity between quasirent and threadsafe

Figure 10-2 shows the results from CICS Performance Analyzer when comparing the transaction's DB2 performance characteristics for both a quasirent and a threadsafe definition of the main application. As before, the response time can be seen to have reduced when redefining the application as threadsafe. The same is true for the average user CPU time.

```
W O R K L O A D   A C T I V I T Y

z/OS V1R7        SYSPLEX PLEX3      DATE 07/10/2007      INTERVAL 00.45.546      MODE = GOAL
RPT VERSION V1R7 RMF                TIME 11.51.14

Results when quasirent:

REPORT BY: POLICY=POLICY

    TRANSACTIONS       TRANS-TIME HHH.MM.SS.TTT      ---SERVICE----    SERVICE TIMES    ---APPL %---
    AVG       1.00     ACTUAL              36.024    IOC      160      CPU     30.9     CP     68.19
    MPL       1.00     EXECUTION           36.024    CPU    6209K      SRB      0.1     AAPCP   0.00
    ENDED        2     QUEUED                   0    MSO    2663M      RCT      0.0     IIPCP   0.00
    END/S     0.04     R/S AFFIN                0    SRB    26214      IIT      0.0

    TRANSACTIONS       TRANS-TIME HHH.MM.SS.TTT
    AVG       0.00     ACTUAL                  49
    ENDED     2250
    END/S    49.40




Results when threadsafe:

REPORT BY: POLICY=POLICY

    TRANSACTIONS       TRANS-TIME HHH.MM.SS.TTT      ---SERVICE----    SERVICE TIMES    ---APPL %---
    AVG       1.00     ACTUAL              38.026    IOC        0      CPU     28.4     CP     62.73
    MPL       1.00     EXECUTION           38.026    CPU    5696K      SRB      0.2     AAPCP   0.00
    ENDED        2     QUEUED                   0    MSO    2444M      RCT      0.0     IIPCP   0.00
    END/S     0.04     R/S AFFIN                0    SRB    38026      IIT      0.0


    TRANSACTIONS       TRANS-TIME HHH.MM.SS.TTT
    AVG       0.00     ACTUAL                  13
    ENDED     3506
    END/S    76.99
```

Figure 10-3 Comparison of RMF workload activity between quasirent and threadsafe

Figure 10-3 shows the results from RMF workload activity when comparing the transaction's CPU and throughput characteristics for both a quasirent and a threadsafe definition of the main application. The transaction rate can be seen to have increased from 49.40 per second up to 76.99 per second. This is because the use of L8 TCBs has allowed for parallel processing to exploit multiple CPs in the hardware, and increased the transaction throughput as a result. Likewise, the transaction time has reduced from 49 to 13 seconds. The CPU time has reduced, reflecting the reduction in TCB switches when redefining the program as threadsafe.

```
CICS TCB Mode Statistics


TCB    < TCBs Attached >    TCB       Attach     MVS        Accumulated           Accumulated          Accumulated
Mode   Current      Peak    Attaches  Failures   Waits      Time in MVS wait      Time Dispatched      Time / TCB

Results when quasirent:

QR     1            1       0         0          538040     00:00:35.590807       00:00:10.394348      00:00:10.552730
L8     81           81      71        0          916768     00:14:08.888409       00:01:19.872928      00:00:20.877639

Results when threadsafe:

QR     1            1       0         0          7474       00:00:44.388717       00:00:01.596551      00:00:00.637270
L8     10           10      0         0          7333       00:06:58.286155       00:00:45.715037      00:00:28.074048


TRANSACTION MANAGER STATISTICS


Results when quasirent:

Peak number of active user transactions       :        82
Total number of active user transactions      :        2287

Results when threadsafe:

Peak number of active user transactions       :        12
Total number of active user transactions      :        3547
```

Figure 10-4   Comparison of CICS statistics data between quasirent and threadsafe

Figure 10-4 shows the output from the DFHSTUP CICS statistics utility program for the comparison between TCB activity when the application was defined first as quasi-reentrant and then as threadsafe.

In the quasi-reentrant case, both the QR and L8 TCBs entered many more MVS waits than in the threadsafe case. For the L8 TCBs, the accumulated time spent in MVS waits was over twice as long as for the threadsafe case. Note too that the quasirent workload required a peak of 81 L8 TCBs to accommodate the transactions, whereas the threadsafe workload peaked at 10 L8 TCBs. This is because (in the quasi-reentrant case), work built up in the CICS system as tasks were attached and competing for subdispatch processing under the QR TCB. This led to a higher peak of user transactions in the system (82 as opposed to 12). Since L8 TCBs can only be reused once their owning task has completed, there was the resultant need to attach more L8 TCBs in this case to accommodate these additional concurrently attached tasks as they issued their interleaving EXEC SQL calls to DB2. The higher number of L8 TCBs, coupled with the greater number of TCB switches between them and the QR TCB in the quasi-reentrant case, led to the L8 TCBs experiencing more MVS waits than in the threadsafe case because there were more occasions when they had no further work to perform and so relinquished control back to the operating system.

The total accumulated time for the TCBs was lower in the threadsafe case, which reflects the fewer TCB switches that were required.

Since fewer peak L8 TCBs were required in the threadsafe case, the need for below the line storage was reduced as a result, thereby assisting with virtual storage constraint relief for this given workload.

10.2 CICS WMQ and file control application

The test involved driving a transaction that carried out the following work. An initial (quasi-reentrant) COBOL program EXEC CICS LINKed to another COBOL application program. This second application then performed a variety of WMQ and CICS commands. The sequence followed was:

   EXEC CICS READ

   WMQ PUT

   WMQ GET

This application looped internally 100 times when linked to, so this series of commands was issued 100 times per task. In addition, an MQOPEN was issued before the loop, and an MQCLOSE was issued after the loop had completed.

Testing involved defining this second program first as CONCURRENCY(QUASIRENT), API(CICSAPI) and then redefining it as CONCURRENCY(THREADSAFE), API(OPENAPI). In both cases, performance and diagnostic data was gathered to provide metrics for the comparative results. This included CICS Performance Analyzer reports, CICS statistics, RMF data and CICS auxiliary trace.

As before, the CICS system was not using storage protection for these tests: STGPROT=NO was specified.

Once again, this was not a test designed to demonstrate serialization issues.

10.2.1 Environment

Performance testing was carried out on a dedicated IBM test system to provide comparable results. The hardware and software environment was as follows:

- Z990 2084-303 with 3 dedicated CPs

- z/OS Version 1.7
- CICS Transaction Server Version 3.2
- CICS Performance Analyzer 2.1
- WMQ Version 6.1

10.2.2 Results

Two sets of results were obtained, first when the application was defined as CONCURRENCY(QUASIRENT), API(CICSAPI) and then after it was redefined as CONCURRENCY(THREADSAFE), API(OPENAPI).

CICS Performance Analyzer was used to investigate the CPU usage and response times for the application, and to compare the number of invocations of the transaction (that is, CICS tasks) that executed for the tests.

RMF workload activity was used to review the total CPU usage, transaction rates, and internal response time for the comparison tests.

In addition, a review of the CICS auxiliary trace taken during the tests could be used (if so desired) to verify the TCB switching activity taking place during the execution of the transactions.

The following results are a summary from these various sources.

```
CICS Performance Analyzer
Performance Summary

                         Avg       Avg               Avg       Avg       Avg       Avg       Avg
              Tran       User CPU  Dispatch  #Tasks  L8 CPU    L9 CPU    Response  DSCHMDLY  DSCHMDLY
                         Time      Time              Time      Time      Time      Time      Count
Results when
quasirent:    FCMQ       .011992   .014209   1500    .009574   .000000   .019020   .004250   7141728

Results when
threadsafe:   FCMQ       .011003   .013148   1500    .010866   .000000   .015339   .000076   312592
```

Figure 10-5   Comparison of transaction performance between quasirent and threadsafe

Figure 10-5 shows the results from CICS Performance Analyzer when comparing the transaction's characteristics for both a quasirent and a threadsafe definition of the main application. As can be seen, the average user CPU time and average dispatch time were reduced after the program was redefined. This can be explained by the reduction in TCB switches that took place when the program was redefined as threadsafe. Prior to that, each WMQ call required a switch from QR to L8 for the duration of the call to WMQ, followed by a switch from L8 back to QR upon return to CICS. With 100 iterations of the loop within the application, this resulted in 400 switches for the WMQ calls and 2 switches for the end-of-task syncpoint flows to WMQ. When the program was redefined as CONCURRENCY(THREADSAFE), API(OPENAPI), there were 2 switches for the EXEC CICS LINK to the second program, and 2 switches for the syncpoint flows to WMQ. The switch from QR to L8 on the link to the second program was because it was defined as API(OPENAPI) and so had to execute under an open TCB. Likewise, the switch back from L8 to QR on the return from the link was because the top level linking program was still defined as quasirent.

The reduction in the average user CPU time and average dispatch time was less marked than in the case of the file control/DB2 application. This can be explained by the fact that the WMQ application only issued two WMQ calls (the WMQ PUT and WMQ GET) within the scope of its loop. There were four EXEC SQL calls in the file control/DB2 example program. So, the CPU benefits of remaining on an L8 TCB, and the reduction in TCB switching, is less marked in the WMQ example than in the DB2 example. This is another indication of the scaleability of benefits that threadsafe exploitation brings: the more an application has the need to drive an OTE-enabled TRUE such as for DB2 or WMQ calls, the more the savings can be if that application is suitable for redefining as a threadsafe program.

Note that the average L8 CPU time did increase when the application was redefined as threadsafe. As with the DB2 tests earlier, L9 TCB CPU usage was 0 since storage protection was not active, and the application's execution key was therefore not pertinent. An L8 TCB could be used instead.

Also note that the average response time for using the threadsafe application was reduced compared with that of the quasi-reentrant version.

Finally, the DSCHMDLY value (redispatch wait time caused by a change mode to switch TCBs) and DSCHMDLY count (number of TCB switches) was reduced by orders of magnitude, a direct reflection of the fact that far fewer TCB switches were having to take place once the application was redefined as CONCURRENCY(THREADSAFE), API(OPENAPI).

```
CICS Performance Analyzer
WebSphere MQ Class 1 Summary
                                                       ----- Average -----
                          SSID    APPLID    TRAN    Count    CPU        Calls

Results when
quasirent:                VICC    IYCUZC19  FCMQ    15282    0.007768   200.0

Results when
threadsafe:               VICC    IYCUZC19  FCMQ    6088     0.007634   200.0
```

Figure 10-6   Comparison of WMQ performance activity between quasirent and threadsafe

Figure 10-6 shows the results from CICS Performance Analyzer when comparing the transaction's WMQ performance characteristics for both a quasirent and a threadsafe definition of the main application. As before, the CPU usage can be seen to have reduced when redefining the application as threadsafe.

```
CICS TCB Mode Statistics

TCB    < TCBs Attached >    TCB       Attach     MVS       Accumulated         Accumulated         Accumulated
Mode   Current      Peak    Attaches  Failures   Waits     Time in MVS wait    Time Dispatched     Time / TCB

Results when quasirent:

QR       1           1        0         0        264838    00:00:40.827822     00:00:05.157484     00:00:05.228039
L8      81          81       71         0        312696    00:01:13.668300     00:00:18.511194     00:00:15.920050

Results when threadsafe:

QR       1           1        0         0        5305      00:00:45.505023     00:00:00.480204     00:00:00.340059
L8      10          10        0         0        4651      00:01:12.057051     00:00:19.912177     00:00:16.667971

TRANSACTION MANAGER STATISTICS

Results when quasirent:

Peak number of active user transactions     :        6
Total number of active user transactions    :     1535

Results when threadsafe:

Peak number of active user transactions     :        8
Total number of active user transactions    :     1535
```

Figure 10-7   Comparison of CICS statistics data between quasirent and threadsafe

Figure 10-7 shows the output from the DFHSTUP CICS statistics utility program for the comparison between TCB activity when the application was defined first as quasi-reentrant and then as threadsafe.

In the quasi-reentrant case, both the QR and L8 TCBs entered many more MVS waits than in the threadsafe case. The total accumulated time for the TCBs was lower in the threadsafe case, which reflects the fewer TCB switches that were required.

Note too that the quasi-reentrant workload required a peak of 81 L8 TCBs to accommodate the transactions, whereas the threadsafe workload peaked at 10 L8 TCBs. As in the DB2 tests, this is because (in the quasi-reentrant case) work built up in the CICS system as tasks were attached and competing for subdispatch processing under the QR TCB. Since L8 TCBs can only be reused once their owning task has completed, there was the resultant need to attach more L8 TCBs, in this case to accommodate these additional concurrently attached tasks as they issued their interleaving WMQ calls. The higher number of L8 TCBs, coupled with the greater number of TCB switches between them and the QR TCB in the quasi-reentrant case, led to the L8 TCBs experiencing more MVS waits than in the threadsafe case because there were more occasions when they had no further work to perform and so relinquished control back to the operating system.

The total accumulated time for the TCBs was lower in the threadsafe case, which reflects the fewer TCB switches that were required.

As with the DB2 example, since fewer peak L8 TCBs were required in the threadsafe case, the resultant need for below the line storage was reduced when the application was redefined as threadsafe.

Part 3

Customer examples and general questions

This part explains performance indicators, describes an actual threadsafe conversion project, presents the results from a real customer's benchmark tests for a threadsafe conversion, and answers a few frequently asked questions of a general nature about threadsafe.

Danske Bank threadsafe conversion

This chapter shows the results obtained during a customer threadsafe conversion of intensive CICS/DB2 applications.

This chapter covers the following topics:

- Hardware and software configuration
- Online application infrastructure
- Threadsafe project definition
- Threadsafe analysis and resolution
- The autoinstall process
- Threadsafe conversion results
- Summary and conclusions

11.1 Hardware and software configuration

Danske Bank is the second largest bank in Scandinavia and is an integrated banking solution, providing continuous real-time processing in a CICS/DB2 environment.

The Danske Bank online systems are characterized by:

- High transaction volume. This is approximately 66 million transactions on an average day for all production CICS systems and 77 million transactions including all CICS systems, production, test, and development.
- High transaction rate in a peak hour. This is approximately 6.5 million transactions on an average day for all production CICS systems and 7.5 million transactions including all CICS systems, production, test, and development.
- Continuous use. CICS systems run 24/7.

The Danske Bank threadsafe conversion project involved all applications, with a few exceptions that are described later. The implication of this was that thousands of programs were made threadsafe overnight.

Hardware configuration

During the time of conversion the hardware configuration was:

- 6 CECs on two physical sites consisting of 2 Z9 and 4 Z900 machines. A CEC is a physical CPU including memory, engines, OSA adapters, and Coupling Facility (CF) links.
- Usage of CF for each environment: production, test, and so forth.
- M800 as the storage system.

Software configuration

The software details and levels are:

- z/OS 1.8
- CICS Transaction Server for z/OS V3.1
- DB2 UDB for z/OS V8
- IBM Websphere MQ for z/OS V6

11.2 Online application infrastructure

Figure 11-1 and Figure 11-2 show the overall online application-related topology for Danske Bank.

The application infrastructure consists of a CISCO router where data arrives from the network. The transactions are then routed as follows:

- The CISCO router selects a CEC with an LPAR with a z/OS system. In the z/OS selection process, the CISCO router uses a round robin algorithm. In a round robin algorithm, the different z/OS systems are selected one at a time in a sequence. When the last system is selected, the iteration starts all over again
- On the z/OS system, the front-end CICS initiates the transactions.

CICSPlex SM is not used for routing purposes, but only for monitoring purposes.

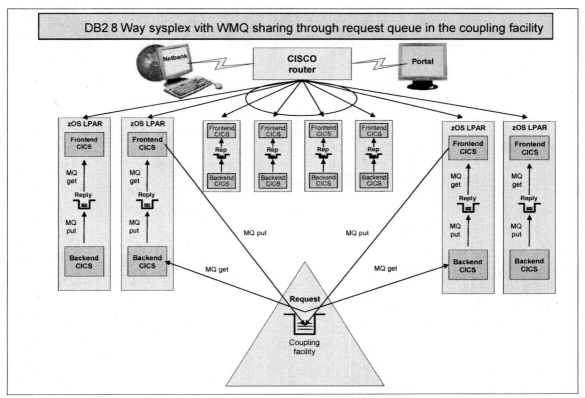

Figure 11-1 Danske Bank 8-way sysplex with WMQ shared queues

Figure 11-1 shows that transactions are routed dynamically from the front-end CICS to a back-end CICS using WMQ shared queues.

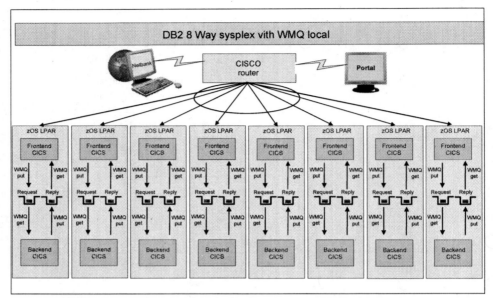

Figure 11-2   Danske Bank with 8 way sysplex showing static routing

The result of the Danske Bank threadsafe conversion was a MIPS saving of a little below 300 MIPS during the peak processing one hour period.

Figure 11-2 shows that transactions are statically routed from the front-end CICS system to a back-end CICS system.

The routing mechanism (static or dynamic) is managed by the CISCO router and is decided on a individual transaction basis.

11.3 Threadsafe project definition

Danske Bank had eight primary objectives for the threadsafe project:

- Maximizing throughput and increasing concurrency by exploiting the CICS Open Transaction Environment.
- Decreasing capacity needs by reducing the MIPS usage during peak hours.
- Exploiting the use of non-CICS API in the future.
- Minimizing resources required during the change of applications to threadsafe standard.

- Minimizing resources required for the threadsafe conversion process.
- Not allowing the size of the CSD to grow.
- Automating the decision of threadsafe or non-threadsafe at program execution, thus reducing the likelihood of human error. For this reason the CICS auto-install program was used.
- Delaying the threadsafe execution until the next weekly run to give the Danske Bank development team a week to analyze the program for threadsafe execution problems.

To help validate the outcome of the conversion project, the following measurement milestones were defined:

- Establish a *before* and *after* threadsafe conversion measurement of the number of TCB switches in the transactions. The number of changes in TCB switches should then be used to calculate the changes in the MIPS capacity requirements during peak hours.
- To validate the threadsafe conversion before and after measurements, MIPS changes in peak hour were compared to actual MIPS used in the production systems before and after threadsafe conversion.

11.4 Threadsafe analysis and results

Danske Bank separated their programs into the following categories:

- **Completely threadsafe programs**
  Whether making SQL calls or not, these programs could all in general be defined as threadsafe.
- **Completely non-threadsafe programs that would not endanger data integrity by updating shared resources (like CWA and so forth)**
  An analysis of the different programs would show whether or not they should be made threadsafe.
- **Non-threadsafe programs that would endanger data integrity by updating shared resources (like CWA and others)**
  An analysis of the different programs would show whether these programs are important enough to be changed. Importance here is defined as the relative execution frequency related to the amount of effort to change the program. We also made the decision here on whether or not they should be made threadsafe.
- **Programs not being linked reentrant**
  An analysis must be done to see if this is just a matter of changing the linkage option or not.

- **Threadsafe or non-threadsafe programs linked together with a non-threadsafe run-time module**
  For Danske Bank this meant that all VAGen (Visual Age Generator) programs were defined as non-threadsafe because the Language Environment run-time module was non-threadsafe.

11.4.1 Programs used in threadsafe analysis

Danske Bank used the CICS Transaction Affinities Utility load module scanner to identify threadsafe/non-threadsafe programs.

11.4.2 Resolution

The result of the threadsafe analysis was:

- Libraries that contain only threadsafe programs.
- Libraries that contain non-threadsafe programs only.
- Libraries that contain a mixture of threadsafe and non-threadsafe programs.
- Programs that should be defined as non-threadsafe for different reasons, for example not reetrant.
- Programs that should be defined as threadsafe but that come from a mixed library.

All of the this information was used in the autoinstall threadsafe conversion process described in next.

11.5 The autoinstall process

The Danske Bank changed the existing autoinstall program exit to correctly install programs as threadsafe or not. This was done for the following reasons:

- Ease of maintenance to an ongoing automated process.
- The decision whether a program should be defined threadsafe or not must be determined at autoinstall time. The CICS autoinstall program only knows program type and name; some additional information needs to be supplied.

Because Danske Bank has more than 100,000 programs, the reasons for defining the programs threadsafe or non-threadsafe at autoinstall time was:

- Cold start: Time to add 100,000 programs
- Warm start: Time to reinstall 100,000 programs
- Maintenance: CEDA definitions of 100,000 programs

- CICS storage: Avoid having unused program definitions filling up CICS storage

11.5.1 Data extract process for the CICS CFDT information

The question was how to supply the additional information apart from program name and type.

It must be remembered that the CICS autoinstall program executes on the QR TCB. No MVS API can be used without blocking the QR TCB, which in turn would block the complete CICS address space if this function resulted in an MVS wait. For these reasons Danske Bank decided to supply the additional information from a batch job and store the information in a CFDT that could be accessed from all CICS systems' autoinstall programs. A CFDT is a CICS-defined data table that resides in the CF.

To supply the necessary data the following processes were implemented as a series of batch programs. To control this, the information from 11.4.2, "Resolution" on page 264 was used:

- All relevant PDS/PDSE directories were read and controlled by a parameter list.
    - The information supplied here was linkage conventions (reentrant, addressing-mode).
    - Special checks were added for duplicates, large programs, and so forth.
    - Another parameter was used to determine whether certain programs required special treatment. This could, for example, be linkage relations to other programs like the inheritance of threadsafe from main programs to sub programs. If the main program is threadsafe, all subsequent programs must be threadsafe because of the inheritance rules.
- The output generated several lists showing all the information just identified, and a dataset with all the necessary threadsafe information covering all the relevant programs.
- The threadsafe information dataset was used as input to another program. This program copied the information to a CICS CFDT.

It was decided to execute this process once a week for the three different environments:

- Production systems
- Test systems
- Development systems

11.5.2 Data information structure in CICS CFDT

The key to the CFDT was the program name, which could be defined generically to avoid having too many entries.

The data information structure for the CICS CFDT is described in Table 11-1. Only the most important information related to the threadsafe determination is showed. Danske Bank also kept other kinds of information but these are irrelevant in understanding the general concept.

Table 11-1 CICS CFDT data structure

Name	Type	Description
CMDT_NRN	B'00000001'	Non-reentrant
CMDT_FOR	B'00000100'	DSN non-threadsafe
CMDT_EXT	B'00100000'	Exception = threadsafe
CMDT_EXN	B'01000000'	Exception = non-threadsafe

11.5.3 Danske Bank CICS autoinstall program

The following functionality was added to the standard CICS autoinstall program to use the information in Table 11-1:

- A prerequisite is that the definition to be installed is of type program.
- If autoinstall mask is '*' for a given program, a default autoinstall model is used that defines programs as threadsafe, unless the program is:
  - Not found
  - Non rentrant
  - Non threadsafe library
  - Special non threadsafe action

Programs used during CICS startup, like PLT programs, are always CEDA defined.

11.6 Threadsafe results

The results were generated based on CICS SMF 110 record analysis.

The following CICS SMF 110 records were collected.

1. A point in time *before* converting to threadsafe for the Danske Bank applications. This was further subdivided into those applications that were issuing SQL calls and all other applications.

2. A point in time *after* conversion to threadsafe for the Danske Bank applications. This was further subdivided into those applications that were issuing SQL calls and to all other applications.

The basis for the measurement was the peak hour between 10-11 AM, during which Danske Bank expects a high transaction rate. The transaction rate per peak hour is shown in Table 11-2.

Table 11-2   Transaction measurements

Date	Description	# Transactions	# TCB switches
10-02-2006 Before	Before converting, including those transactions issuing SQL calls.	3,179,639	250,820,638
11-27-2006 After	After converting, including those transactions issuing SQL calls.	2,678,469	104,224,554
10-02-2006 Before	Before converting, including all transactions.	7,859,741	280,879,869
11-27-2006 After	After converting, including all transactions.	6,462,891	128,826,384

Figure 11-3 on page 268 shows the average number of TCB switches before and after threadsafe conversion for all eight z/OS systems, and a total. This figure includes all transactions.

As seen from Figure 11-3, the average number of TCB switches for the total transactions doing SQL calls was reduced from 79 (before threadsafe conversion) to 39 (after threadsafe conversion). This is a reduction to approximately half of the TCB switches after threadsafe conversion.

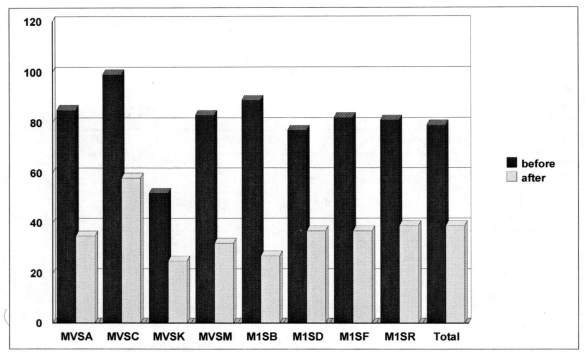

Figure 11-3   TCB switches average per transaction, DB2

Figure 11-4 on page 269 shows the average number of TCB switches before and after threadsafe conversion for all eight z/OS systems (MVSA, MVSC, and so forth) and a total. This figure only includes transactions performing SQL calls.

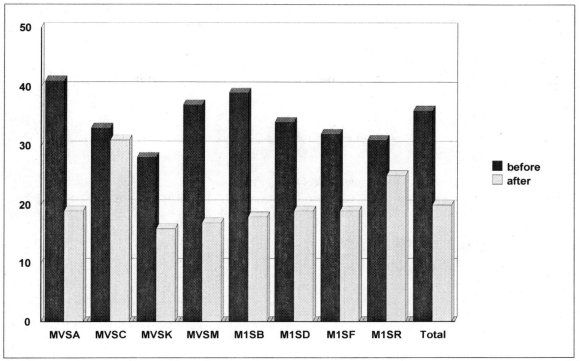

Figure 11-4   TCB switches average per transaction

As seen from Figure 11-4, the average number of TCB switches for all transactions was reduced from 36 (before threadsafe conversion) to 20 (after threadsafe conversion). This is a reduction of 44% in TCB switches after threadsafe conversion.

11.7 Threadsafe summary and conclusion

The decision to make the threadsafe or non-threadsafe definitions for CICS programs an automated process at CICS autoinstall time had several major advantages:

- Elimination of human errors
- Fast converting process overnight
- Optimizing CICS start up time
- Limiting the reliance on program definition changes via the CEDA transaction
- Minimizing CICS storage usage by only installing active program definitions

> **Note:** The automated process was specific to the autoinstall phase. Human expertise and analysis were very much required prior to this.

The result of the Danske Bank threadsafe conversion was a MIPS saving of a little below 300 MIPS during the peak processing period. This can be directly attributed to reduced TCB switching.

Danske Bank is looking forward to CICS Transaction Server Version 3.2 since WMQ, local File Control, and VSAM RLS are threadsafe. They have many WMQ applications and want to use VSAM RLS for application tracing.

In general, if you design and write application code to threadsafe standards, you can define the CICS program as threadsafe. It then has the benefit of being able to run on its own dedicated L8 open TCB, and avoids two TCB switches per DB2 request.

CoreBank benchmark: Quasirent versus threadsafe

This chapter provides the results obtained from a real customer benchmark test with a threadsafe conversion for a very high-end CICS/DB2 application.

This chapter covers the following topics:

- Scope of the benchmark
- Benchmark hardware and software resources and configuration
- Is the application code threadsafe? Analysis and resolution
- Results
- Conclusion

12.1 Scope of the benchmark

CoreBank is an integrated banking solution, providing continuous real-time processing in a relational database environment. The CoreBank V4 application developed by Fidelity Information Services in partnership with IBM was used to execute a performance benchmark at Montpellier, looking at different contexts to measure and evaluate the capabilities of the application and the CICS-DB2 environment. It compared running as a Quasirent application to running as a threadsafe application. The benchmark involved:

- Running at a very high transaction rate
- Collecting the various requested performance data (measurements, logs, traces, and so on)
- Tuning the system, subsystems, and application along the way where possible so as to increase the throughput

12.2 Benchmark hardware and software resources

Here we review the hardware and software resources and the configuration we used for the benchmark environment.

Hardware resources

We used an IBM @server zSeries environment based on Z900 Processors hosting the CICS application servers and the DB2 databases. One S/390 processor was linked to this cluster through the usage of an ISC type 2 link. It hosted the many CICS injectors. The DASD subsystem was a 2105-800 ESS with 3.3 TB.

Software resources

The software details and levels are:

- z/OS 1.3
- CICS Transaction Server for z/OS V2.2
- CICS Performance Analyzer V1.2
- DB2 UDB for z/OS V7
- CoreBank V4 application (Fidelity Information Services)

Configuration

The following configuration was used for the threadsafe versus Quasirent comparison:

- z/OS, LPAR
  - Based on z/OS 1.3 with 1 LPAR
- CICSPlex
  - The CICSPlex configuration used for this workload activity was composed of three layers:
    i. The first layer is an injector part, which is composed of six cloned CICS TS V2.2 regions in one separate S/390.
    ii. The second layer is composed of six cloned CICS TS V2.2 Terminal Owning Regions (TORs).
    iii. The third layer is composed of ten cloned CICS TS V2.2 Application Owning Regions (AORs).
  - The dynamic distributed program link (DPL) was used for routing the programs to the AORs driven by a CICSPlex/SM Workload Specification.
  - Each injector is connected with only one TOR using an LU6.2 connection.
- CoreBank V4
  - List of transaction IDs used and DB2 calls.

	Av. No. SQL calls (CICS)	Select SQL	Fetch SQL	Open SQL	Close SQL	Insert SQL	SQL Sorts	Total SQL
BI	21	3	6	6	6	0	1	21
BP	96	6	28	28	28	3	7	93
CAL	29	2	11	8	8	0	0	29
CD	98	4	30	30	30	2	7	96
CDO	133	8	29	29	29	4	11	98
CDT	86	8	24	24	24	3	5	83
CW	106	6	32	32	32	2	7	104
PIA	19	1	8	5	5	0	1	19
PIC	85	8	29	24	24	0	4	85
TOF	96	9	27	27	27	3	7	93
TWF	126	6	38	39	39	2	11	124

Figure 12-1 CoreBank transaction and DB2 call details

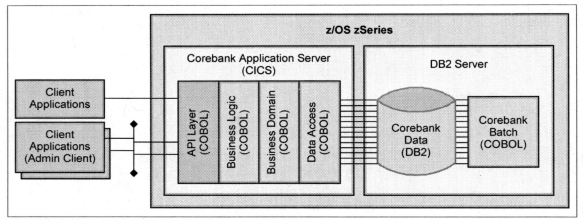

Figure 12-2   CoreBank architecture

12.3 Determining whether the application code is threadsafe

The key to determining whether the application is threadsafe is to properly understand the application. For the benchmark this involved discussions with the application architect to understand where there were resource serialization issues and to understand use of non threadsafe commands, which would not prevent the application from being defined as threadsafe, but would add a performance overhead in terms of TCB switching.

12.3.1 Analysis

From an online point of view there are a couple of architectural paths through to the CoreBank business function, depending on whether you use the provided MQ entry path or another path based on the COMMAREA.

The CoreBank application is based on several components. Only the first component (the API Layer) issues the non threadsafe commands path based on the COMMAREA. All other components are dynamically called by COBOL and issue only DB2 calls.

During the benchmark an LU6.2 path was used which directly invoked the application through the use of the COMMAREA.

The CoreBank application issued GETMAIN SHARED commands in one module in order to cache arrays of commonly retrieved static data when the first transaction is requested during the CICS session or at the start of a day. ENQ and DEQ were used to establish exclusive access at these setup times. An ADDRESS CWA is also used for storing the caches's pointer, and an ASKTIME was also done by this module.

CoreBank issued a few non threadsafe commands in the API layer. The rest of the time Corebank issue threadsafe commands.

12.3.2 Resolution

The caches were implemented purely to speed up I/O data retrieval and were set up in each AOR. It was decided to develop a new program to run as a PLT program during CICS initialization to set up the caches. This removed the need for ENQ and DEQ for synchronization in the API layer.

The use of ASKTIME was left in the application and other administration programs. No modifications were made for ASKTIME because it has been made threadsafe in CICS Transaction Server V2.3.

12.4 Results

The results shown used the data in the CICS SMF 110 and were analyzed by using CICS Performance Analyzer V1.2. The transaction rates for both comparison runs was the same, 100 transactions per second specified via the injection script. The same injection script and same properties (for example ramp-up, think time, number of users simulated) was used for both runs.

12.4.1 CICS performance records

Here are the benchmark records in the form of performance reports, statistics, and transactions.

CICS performance totals report

The performance totals report provides a comprehensive analysis of the resource usage of your CICS system and can be used to gain a system-wide perspective of CICS system performance.

Resource utilization statistics

The following CICS PA performance total report (Figure 12-3) shows the average and maximum numbers of TCB switches (change-TCB mode requests) running the application with Concurrency(Quasirent) and running the application with Concurrency(Threadsafe). The report interval was three minutes.

Example 12-1   CICS performance analyzer command

```
CICSPA IN(SMFIN001),
                    APPLID(A6PTRA*),
                        TOTAL(OUTPUT(PTOT0001))
```

```
........................................................ C O U N T S ......
From Selected Performance Records                Total      Avg/Task    Max/Task

PCSTGHWM Program Storage HWM above and below 16MB 13538E6    500708.4    901376
PC24BHWM Program Storage HWM below 16MB                0          .0         0
PC31AHWM Program Storage HWM above 16MB          13538E6    500708.4    901376
PC24CHWM Program Storage (CDSA) HWM below 16MB         0          .0         0
PC31CHWM Program Storage (ECDSA) HWM above 16MB        0          .0         0
PC24SHWM Program Storage (SDSA) HWM below 16MB         0          .0         0
PC31SHWM Program Storage (ESDSA) HWM above 16MB        0          .0         0
PC24RHWM Program Storage (RDSA) HWM below 16MB         0          .0         0
PC31RHWM Program Storage (ERDSA) HWM above 16MB  13538E6    500708.4    901376
DB2REQCT DB2 requests                            1886033        69.8       156
IMSREQCT IMS (DBCTL) requests                          0          .0         0
CHMODECT CHANGE-TCB MODES REQUESTS               3826198       141.5       314
```

Figure 12-3   Performance total report extract in quasi-reentrant

Figure 12-3 shows the average at 141.5 and the maximum at 314 change-TCB mode requests per task when running Quasi-reentrant.

```
.................................................... C O U N T S ......
From Selected Performance Records                   Total   Avg/Task  Max/Task

PCSTGHWM Program Storage HWM above and below 16MB   13524E6  500913.0   901376
PC24BHWM Program Storage HWM below 16MB                   0       .0        0
PC31AHWM Program Storage HWM above 16MB             13524E6  500913.0   901376
PC24CHWM Program Storage (CDSA) HWM below 16MB            0       .0        0
PC31CHWM Program Storage (ECDSA) HWM above 16MB           0       .0        0
PC24SHWM Program Storage (SDSA) HWM below 16MB            0       .0        0
PC31SHWM Program Storage (ESDSA) HWM above 16MB           0       .0        0
PC24RHWM Program Storage (RDSA) HWM below 16MB            0       .0        0
PC31RHWM Program Storage (ERDSA) HWM above 16MB     13524E6  500913.0   901376
DB2REQCT DB2 requests                               1887552     69.9      798
IMSREQCT IMS (DBCTL) requests                             0       .0        0
CHMODECT Change-TCB modes requests                   108050      4.0        8
```

Figure 12-4   Performance total report extract in threadsafe

Figure 12-4 shows the previous average of 141.5 in Quasi-reentrant change-TCB modes reduced to 4, when the application was defined and run as threadsafe. This is an improvement of 98%. The previous maximum at 314 change-TCB mode request Threadsafe mode reduced to 8, which is also an improvement of 98%.

The report shows that the average DB2 requests had not changed, but the DB2 request maximum was now 798. This was due to the new PLTPI program for initializing the cache arrays.

CICS performance totals report

Now we discuss the CICS performance totals report.

CPU and dispatch statistics

We show in this CICS PA performance total report the overall CICS system usage in terms of CPU and dispatch time broken down by TCB modes (Figure 12-5).

```
                                Dispatched Time           CPU Time
                                DD HH:MM:SS      Secs    DD HH:MM:SS      Secs

Total Elapsed Run Time             00:03:00       180


From Selected Performance Records

QR Dispatch/CPU Time               00:02:01       121      00:01:48       108
MS Dispatch/CPU Time               00:00:00         0      00:00:00         0
                                   --------     -----     --------      ------
  TOTAL (QR + MS)                  00:02:01       121      00:01:48       108

L8 CPU Time                                                 00:03:17       197
J8 CPU Time                                                 00:00:00         0
S8 CPU Time                                                 00:00:00         0
                                   --------     -----     --------      ------
  TOTAL (L8 + J8 + S8)             00:10:05       605      00:03:17       197

                                   --------     -----     --------      ------
Total CICS TCB Time                00:02:01       121      00:05:05       305
```

Figure 12-5 Performance total report extract for quasi-reentrant application

Figure 12-5 shows the global usage of dispatch time and CPU time in seconds when running as a quasi-reentrant application.

The total dispatch time is the time the transaction was dispatched by the CICS dispatcher.

The total CPU time is the portion of the dispatch time during which the task is using the processor.

The total CPU time consumed for the Quasi-reentrant TCB (QR) is 108 seconds and the total CPU time consumed for the open TCB (L8) is 197 seconds. This report shows that the breakdown of CPU time between the QR and L8 is approximately Figure 12-6 35% for the QR and 65% for the L8.

```
                              Dispatched Time        CPU Time
                              DD HH:MM:SS    Secs    DD HH:MM:SS    Secs

Total Elapsed Run Time           00:02:59    179


From Selected Performance Records

QR Dispatch/CPU Time             00:01:05     65       00:01:00      60
MS Dispatch/CPU Time             00:00:00      0       00:00:00       0
                                 --------    ---       --------     ---
  TOTAL (QR + MS)                00:01:05     65       00:01:00      60

L8 CPU Time                                            00:03:41     221
J8 CPU Time                                            00:00:00       0
S8 CPU Time                                            00:00:00       0
                                 --------    ---       --------     ---
  TOTAL (L8 + J8 + S8)           00:11:29    689       00:03:41     221

                                 --------    ---       --------     ---
Total CICS TCB Time              00:01:05     65       00:04:40     280
```

Figure 12-6 Performance total report extract for threadsafe application

Figure 12-6 shows the global usage of dispatch time and CPU time in seconds when running as a threadsafe application.

The previous total CPU time consumed by the QR and L8 TCB was 305 seconds and is now 280 seconds, an improvement of 8%.

The report shows the breakdown of CPU between the QR and L8 TCBs changed. It is now 21% for the QR and 79% for the L8.

The number of transactions processed for these two runs was:

- 27037 for Quasi-reentrant run
- 26999 for threadsafe run

CICS PA obtains the data shown in these performance total reports from the CICS SMF 110 performance monitoring (task termination) records.

CICS performance summary report
Now we discuss the CICS performance summary report.

Summary by transaction
The following CICS PA performance summary report shows an average of per-transaction principal wait times and the number of change-TCB modes requests for the Quasi-reentrant and threadsafe versions of the application (Example 12-2).

Example 12-2   CICS performance analyzer commands

```
CICSPA IN(SMFIN001),
                              APPLID(A6PTRA*),
                              SUMMARY(OUTPUT(SUMM0001),
                                BY(TRAN),
                                FIELDS(TRAN,
                                       CHMODECT(AVE),
                                       RESPONSE(AVE),
                                       DISPATCH(TIME(AVE)),
                                       KY8DISPT(TIME(AVE)),
                                       QRDISPT(TIME(AVE)),
                                       QRMODDLY(TIME(AVE)),
                                       MAXOTDLY(TIME(AVE)),
                                       SUSPEND(TIME(AVE)),
                                       DSPDELAY(TIME(AVE)),
                                       DISPWAIT(TIME(AVE)),
                                       RMITIME(TIME(AVE)),
                                       RMISUSP(TIME(AVE)))),
```

Tran	Avg ChngMode	Avg Response Time	Avg Dispatch Time	Avg KY8 Disp Time	Avg QR Disp Time	Avg QRModDly Time	Avg MaxOTDly Time	Avg Suspend Time	Avg DispDly Time	Avg DispWait Time	Avg RMI Elap Time	Avg RMI Susp Time
BI	43	.2550	.0121	.0096	.0024	.0769	.0000	.2429	.1639	.0778	.0095	.0000
BP	194	.4510	.0393	.0333	.0060	.2454	.0000	.4118	.1602	.2494	.0326	.0000
CAL	58	.3867	.0306	.0277	.0029	.1917	.0000	.3560	.1618	.1929	.0275	.0000
CD	215	.4596	.0354	.0294	.0060	.2524	.0000	.4242	.1651	.2568	.0286	.0000
CDO	289	.4828	.0404	.0333	.0071	.2742	.0000	.4424	.1596	.2800	.0322	.0000
CDT	191	.4490	.0379	.0317	.0062	.2441	.0000	.4111	.1610	.2480	.0310	.0000
CW	224	.4103	.0314	.0253	.0060	.2111	.0000	.3789	.1609	.2156	.0245	.0000
PIA	34	.2735	.0137	.0110	.0028	.0908	.0000	.2597	.1670	.0916	.0108	.0000
PIC	158	.5013	.0494	.0444	.0051	.2806	.0000	.4518	.1661	.2838	.0437	.0000
TOF	200	.4187	.0318	.0255	.0064	.2115	.0000	.3868	.1691	.2156	.0247	.0000
TWF	283	.4395	.0343	.0277	.0066	.2295	.0000	.4053	.1672	.2352	.0266	.0000

Figure 12-7   Summary report by transaction for Quasi-reentrant application

This report shows the average change-TCB modes and the principal wait times when running as a quasi-reentrant application, summarized by transaction.

Tran	Avg ChngMode	Avg Response Time	Avg Dispatch Time	Avg KY8 Disp Time	Avg QR Disp Time	Avg QRModDly Time	Avg MaxOTDly Time	Avg Suspend Time	Avg DispDly Time	Avg DispWait Time	Avg RMI Elap Time	Avg RMI Susp Time
BI	4	.0967	.0137	.0116	.0021	.0173	.0000	.0830	.0642	.0174	.0111	.0000
BP	4	.1295	.0418	.0391	.0027	.0249	.0000	.0877	.0612	.0250	.0355	.0000
CAL	4	.1181	.0300	.0281	.0019	.0234	.0000	.0881	.0631	.0235	.0269	.0000
CD	4	.1284	.0381	.0354	.0027	.0237	.0000	.0902	.0649	.0239	.0319	.0000
CDO	4	.1321	.0412	.0384	.0028	.0280	.0000	.0910	.0613	.0282	.0339	.0000
CDT	4	.1295	.0405	.0378	.0027	.0247	.0000	.0890	.0627	.0248	.0341	.0000
CW	4	.1151	.0319	.0292	.0027	.0180	.0000	.0831	.0635	.0182	.0256	.0000
PIA	4	.0958	.0134	.0113	.0021	.0153	.0000	.0825	.0657	.0154	.0104	.0000
PIC	4	.1427	.0497	.0472	.0025	.0268	.0000	.0930	.0646	.0270	.0444	.0000
TOF	4	.1171	.0329	.0301	.0028	.0191	.0000	.0842	.0635	.0193	.0262	.0000
TWF	4	.1235	.0339	.0313	.0026	.0214	.0000	.0895	.0665	.0215	.0273	.0000

Figure 12-8   Summary report by transaction for threadsafe application

This report (Figure 12-8) shows the average change-TCB modes and principal wait times when running as a threadsafe application, summarized by transaction.

- DispDly: Wait for QR Mode TCB is elapsed time a task waited for re-dispatch on the CICS QR TCB. This is a subset of dispatch wait time.

- DispWait: Wait for re-dispatch time is a measure of the length of time following the posting of the ECB until CICS re-dispatches the task on the QR TCB.

The reduction of the response time for each transaction is between 60% to 80%.

The reduction in re-dispatch wait time is the principal reason for the reduction in response time, and this is due to the reduction in the number of TCB switches. The application spent less time on the QR TCB and more time on its own dedicated L8 TCB.

Figure 12-9 shows the reduction of between 60% and 80% in response time for each separate transaction.

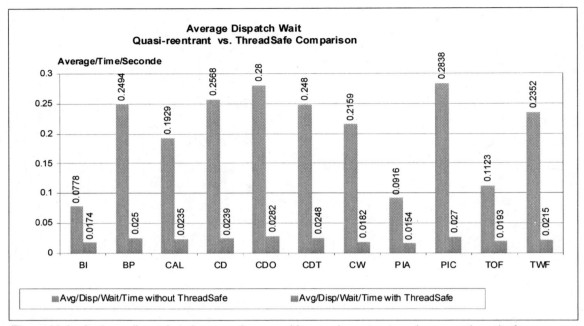

Figure 12-9   Average dispatch wait comparison graphic, quasi-reentrant mode versus threadsafe

Figure 12-10 shows the final transaction response times achieved for quasi-reentrant and threadsafe.

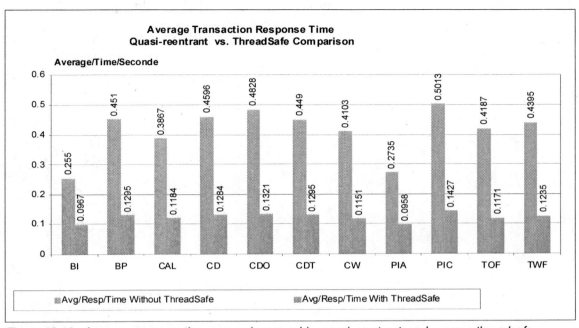

Figure 12-10   Average response time comparison graphic, quasi-reentrant mode versus threadsafe

Figure 12-11 shows, for each individual transaction, the average change-TCB modes for Quasi-reentrant versus Threadsafe.

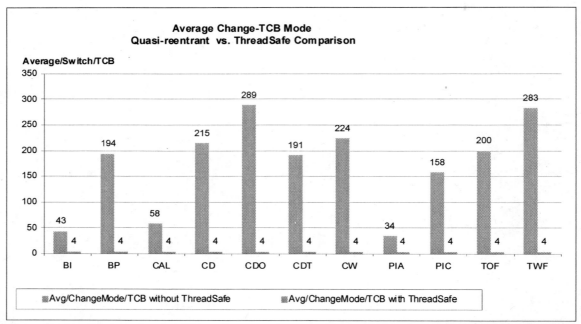

Figure 12-11 Average change-TCB mode comparison graphic in quasi-reentrant mode versus threadsafe

Figure 12-12 shows the CPU time consumed for each individual transaction. The reduction of the CPU time used for each transaction is the result of the elimination of TCB switches. The instruction saved per TCB switch is approximately 5000.

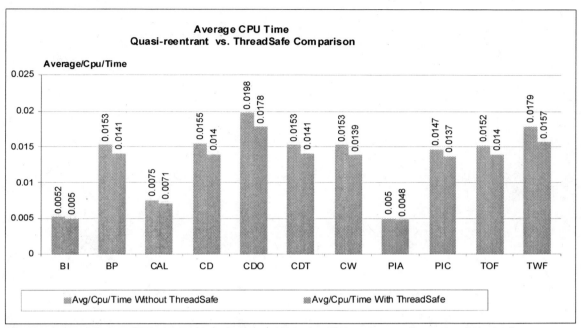

Figure 12-12   Average CPU time comparison graphic in quasi-reentrant mode versus threadsafe

12.5 Conclusions

If you design and write application code to threadsafe standards, you can define the CICS program as threadsafe. It then has the benefit of being able to run on its own dedicated L8 open TCB, and avoids two TCB switches per DB2 request. Avoiding use of non threadsafe CICS commands will reduce TCB switching further. In our experience, the conversion of this application to a threadsafe application was helped by good communication and real teamwork between the Fidelity Information Services application architect and developer.

13

Diagnosing performance problems

This chapter provides an overview of diagnosing performance problems using the following data sources:

- Message IEF374I
- SMF Type 30
- RMF workload activity reports
- CICS statistics
- CICS monitoring

13.1 Introduction

Here we look at two types of performance problem, which are:

- Increased response time
- CPU increase

We also need to review the following areas:

- What is the scope?
- When did it start?
- What changed?
  - Applications
  - Other software
  - Maintenance applied
  - Hardware

13.2 Define the problem

Usually, performance problems fall into two major categories: poor response time or increased CPU consumption. Each of these problems requires slightly different approaches, and often different data to diagnose the cause and resolve the problem:

- Poor response time

    Users have begun to complain that their response time has increased. This is usually an indication of resource constraint somewhere in the system: waits of various types (enqueues, locks, slow I/O, string, or buffer waits), file, journal or logger bottlenecks, slowdowns in DB2, DBCTL or another subsystem, and of course, not enough CPU cycles to support the workload.

    - The bottleneck could be within the CICS region. For example, applications are doing many more GETMAINs/FREEMAINs after implementing new functionality in the Language Environment.
    - Applications might be spending much more time in DB2, IMS, or another database product after implementing a new release.
    - The bottleneck could be outside the region. For example, DASD contention is slowing writes and causing applications to wait.

- Increased CPU time

    Either the end user paying the bill is complaining that his CPU costs have gone up, or someone has noticed that she is using more CPU than before. First, determine how the CPU increase is being measured: is it from SMF records or perhaps a report from a vendor product?

    - If the reported increase is from a vendor product, how is the CPU usage determined? Is it calculated from a formula based on the hardware type, or is it calculated from data reported by SMF or RMF?

    - If the increase is reported following a change in hardware, was the formula used in the vendor product updated to reflect the new hardware? In other words, is there a real increase, or are we being misled by erroneous reports?

A few more questions are:

- What is the scope?

    Identify the scope of the problem. Is it an overall slowdown—that is, are all transactions affected, or are only a few transactions affected, perhaps a single application? The scope of the symptoms will help determine where to look next. Since you are trying to identify the resources that are adversely affecting response time, you will need to look at information that tells you about resource usage in the system: either system-wide resource usage (CICS statistics) or usage by individual transactions (CICS monitoring data), or even MVS-wide data in RMF reports.

- When did the problem start?

    Can you associate the onset of the problem with a change of any kind, or with a specific time?

- What changed?

    - Was maintenance applied (*any* maintenance, not just CICS but also MVS, VTAM, LE, OEM products, and so on)?

    - Were there application changes? Hardware changes? (Processor, DASD, LPAR configuration, new NCP or I/O configuration, and so on?) Were there any new releases of software?

13.3 Performance hierarchy

Performance problems represent a class of problems that are often difficult and time consuming to resolve. Like learning to diagnose an 0C1 program check, we must learn to use and understand the tools and methodologies that can assist in problem resolution.

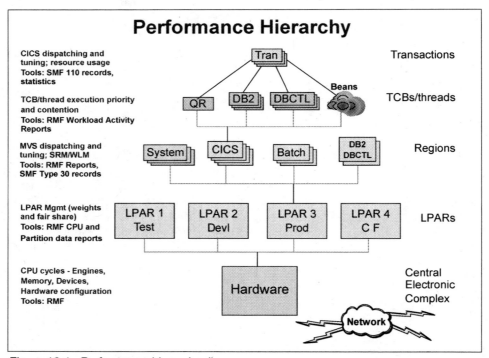

Figure 13-1   Performance hierarchy diagram

The Central Electronic Complex (CEC) is a physical collection of hardware that consists of central storage, one or more central processors (CP), timers, and channels.

The hardware resources of a CEC (central processors, central storage, expanded storage, and channel paths) can be divided into logical partitions (LPARs). Each LPAR executes a separate copy of an operating system (z/OS, MVS, VM, VSE, Linux®, and so on).

Each layer shown in Figure 13-1 builds on the resources of the lower levels. For example, in order for CICS to dispatch a task, an engine (CP, central processor) must have been made available (allocated) to the z/OS image. This in turn dispatches the CICS region (that is, assigns a CP to the CICS region). The CICS region can then dispatch CICS tasks using the CP allocated by z/OS.

Difficulty in solving a performance problem is reduced by a better understanding of the layers that provide the execution environment. The underlying resources allocated to CICS are provided by the hardware. If there are insufficient or poorly configured hardware resources, CICS performance will be affected. Tuning and application changes can reduce resource demand.

The MVS (z/OS) dispatcher, with assistance from Workload Manager (WLM), allocates the available LPAR resources between regions (address spaces). MVS tuning can be performed to increase a region's share of these resources, within the scope of the resources available to the LPAR. If it is felt that an LPAR has insufficient resources, consider investigating the reports produced that detail the LPAR management data.

> **Important:** A basic premise to remember is that a lack of underlying hardware resources is nearly impossible to tune away with software.

Problem Sources

- **Transactions**
  - ►Application design
    - ENQ, locks
    - Resource usage
  - ►Routing
  - ►Priority
  - ►Classing
- **TCBs/Threads**
  - ►TCB usage
    - Open TCBs
    - Subtasking
    - JAVA
  - ►DB2
    - DPMODE
- **Region/Operating System**
  - ►Region priority
  - ►Resource allocation
    - SRM
    - WLM Goals, definitions, SLA
    - Strings, buffers, etc.
- **LPAR**
  - ►Configuration
    - Weights, fair share, CPs
- **Hardware**
  - ►DASD
  - ►CPU
  - ►Timers

Figure 13-2   Problem sources

13.4 Key performance indicators

In this section we discuss key performance indicators.

13.4.1 Indicators from System Management Facilities (SMF)

Here are performance indicators for CICS performance records (SMF 110 subtype 1):

- Wait for redispatch time (DISPWAIT) is a measure of the length of time following the posting of the ECB until CICS redispatches the task.
- Wait for QR Mode TCB time (QRMODDLY) is the elapsed time a task waited for redispatch on the CICS QR TCB.
    - QRMODDLY is a subset of DISPWAIT time.
- Average CPU per task.
- Average response time.
- Wait times associated with resources, for example:
    - File wait
    - MRO link wait time
    - RMI time
    - RMI suspend time
    - TCLASS delay
    - First dispatch delay
- QR TCB CPU to dispatch ratio.
- Transaction rate.
- Logwrites per second.

13.4.2 Indicators from Resource Management Facility (RMF)

Here are the key performance indicators that can be obtained from RMF:

- Workload activity reports
    - TCB CPU seconds in the interval
    - APPL% (the percent an engine (CP) used in the interval)
    - Average CPU per task
    - Divide APPL% by RMF transaction rate
    - MVS busy
- RMF transaction level report classes
    - Average response time
    - Transaction rate

- Partition data report
    - LPAR logical and physical busy
    - CEC busy

13.5 Performance data sources

The following performance data sources are discussed in more detail in the following sections.

- Message IEF374I
    - Written at step termination
    - Contains TCB and SRB accumulated time for the address space
    - Some of the information contained in SMF 30 records
    - Job/address space
- SMF type 30 records
    - Subtype 2 and 3 (interval records):
        - Written every SMF interval - similar to CICS interval statistics
        - Information such as *CPU seconds used* is available at the end of the SMF interval
- RMF workload activity reports, SMF interval information
    - SMF 70–78 records
    - TCB and SRB times
    - DASD I/O counts and response times
    - Indication of CP usage (APPL%)
    - Region level statistics
- CICS monitoring records
    - SMF 110 subtype 1 records
    - CICS task level data - performance and exception
- CICS statistics
    - SMF 110 subtype 2 records
    - Information collected on an interval basis and/or end of day
    - Information is similar to RMF data but CICS-based
    - CICS resource based

13.5.1 Message IEF374I

This is written to the JESYSMSG log for the job during step termination. It shows you the virtual storage above and below the 16-MB line.

- The sample in Figure 13-3 shows a one-step CICS job.

    Job and step numbers are the same.

- Includes all TCB and SRB time in the region.

```
IEF373I STEP/CICS/START 2002349.1112
IEF374I STEP/CICS/STOP  2002349.1310 CPU 62MIN 37.76SEC SRB 10MIN 28SEC VIRT 5420K SYS 344K EXT 116612K SYS 16896K
IEF375I JOB/IYOT122/START 2002349.1112
IEF376I JOB/IYOT122/STOP  2002349.1310 CPU    62MIN 37.76SEC SRB    10MIN 28.05SEC
```

Figure 13-3   IEF374I message

13.5.2 SMF records

Performance data is captured in many places within a z/OS system. During step termination, information is collected as SMF type 30 records. The processor time used by the collective TCBs and SRBs in the address space is written to the JES log (JESYSMSG) during step termination, as message IEF374I.

This data can be used to define the overall CPU time associated with an address space. From a CICS perspective, these numbers include all time that is not associated with the actual transactions processed. Simply dividing the total CPU time by the number of transactions processed does not give a true representation of resources used.

For example, suppose 50% of the transactions simply read a record from a VSAM file and display a message on the terminal and 50% of the transactions issue 100 EXEC SQL calls. Dividing the processor time by the total transactions does not provide a true picture of resource usage. In the case where the CPU per transaction suddenly increases, it is quite difficult to understand the root cause.

z/OS collects statistical information about an System Management Facilities interval. The interval is defined using the INTVAL(tt) option in the SMFPRMxx member of SYS1.PARMLIB. To display the status of the SMF datasets, use the command D SMF. The SMF options in use can be displayed using a D SMF,O command (Figure 13-4).

```
COMMAND INPUT ===> /d smf,o
IEE967I 13.10.10 SMF PARAMETERS 330
    MEMBER = SMFPRMZI     <----------------------------------- SYS1.PARMLIB member
        MULCFUNC -- DEFAULT
        . . . . .
        SUBSYS(OMVS,TYPE(0,30,70:79,90,88,89,99,101,110,245)) -- PARMLIB
        SUBSYS(OMVS,INTERVAL(SMF,SYNC)) -- PARMLIB
        SUBSYS(OMVS,NOEXITS) -- PARMLIB
        SUBSYS(STC,NODETAIL) -- SYS
        SUBSYS(STC,TYPE(0,30,70:79,88,89,90,99,101,110,245)) -- PARMLIB <- Record types collected
        SUBSYS(STC,INTERVAL(SMF,SYNC)) -- PARMLIB
        SUBSYS(STC,EXITS(IEFACTRT)) -- PARMLIB
    INTVAL(05) -- PARMLIB         <--------------------------- SMF Interval
    NOPROMPT -- PARMLIB
    LISTDSN -- PARMLIB
    DSNAME(SYSD.MAN4) -- PARMLIB
    DSNAME(SYSD.MAN3) -- PARMLIB                              SMF dataset names
    DSNAME(SYSD.MAN2) -- PARMLIB
    DSNAME(SYSD.MAN1) -- PARMLIB
```

Figure 13-4   d smf, o command

The Resource Measurement Facility (RMF) function of z/OS gathers a large amount of information regarding resource usage, which is written to SMF as record types 70 to 78. The information includes TCB and SRB times, DASD I/O counts, along with a breakdown of the response times, Central Processor (CP) usage, and more.

It is also possible to obtain the number and rate of CICS transactions completed during the SMF interval. However, as in the case of the contents of IEF374I, this information is presented at a region level. For example, in order to calculate the CPU time per transaction, the total CPU consumed in the interval is divided amongst the number of transactions completing in the interval.

RMF reports are generated using the RMF post processor (ERBRMFPP). For maximum granularity, each CICS region should be assigned to a separate reporting class. In addition, we strongly recommend that report classes be defined to display the CICS transactions that complete during the interval. For example, a report class might be generated for all transactions that begin with JOR (JOR1, JOR2, JOR3, and so on) with a second report class defined for transactions beginning with DB2 (DB21, DB22, and so on). This would allow transaction rates and response times to be reported for individual sets of transactions rather than the region as a whole. There can be up to 999 report classes in a sysplex. Report classes are defined using the Work Load Manager facilities (=WLM in ISPF).

SMF Type 110 subtype 1 records

CICS collects performance data at the task level (activated via the MNPER SIT parm, CEMT SET MONITOR, or EXEC CICS SET MONITOR). Three classes of performance monitoring may be selected: performance class data (MNPER), exception class data (MNEXE), and a new transaction resource class data (MNRES), with the addition of CICS Transaction Server 2.2 APAR PQ63143. This class data is present at the base code level in later releases of CICS.

Performance class data is detailed at the transaction level. It provides information such as response time, time spent waiting for a resource or I/O, and CPU time. At least one performance record is written for each transaction at task termination time. For long-running tasks, the MNFREQ option can be used to cause periodic records to be written.

Exception class monitoring data provides information about CICS resource shortages at the transaction level. This data can be used to identify system constraints that affect transaction performance. An exception record is written to SMF when the shortage has been resolved. Refer to the *CICS Performance Guide* for a detailed description of exception records.

With the addition of PQ63143, transaction resource class data provides additional transaction level information about file resources. To activate transaction resource collection for files, an Monitor Control Table (MCT) must be assembled with FILE=parm.

SMF Type 110 subtype 2 records

CICS interval statistics are collected for CICS resource usage at the expiration of each statistics recording interval and written to SMF as type 110 subtype 2 records. The interval can be specified using the STATINT SIT (System Initialization Table) parameter, and STATRCD=ON must also be specified. Otherwise, as is the case with older releases of CICS, the interval is set using the CICS master terminal function CEMT SET STATISTICS, or EXEC CICS SET STATISTICS command.

The the interval statistics can be considered as CICS region level data, but at a more granular level than RMF data (for example, dataset level statistics versus the actual DASD activity in RMF).

SMF Type 30 records

The SMF 30 records contain *region level* statistics. There are a number of methods that can be used to view the records. The record shown in Figure 13-5 was selected by using a SORT with the control cards shown in Example 13-1 on page 298.

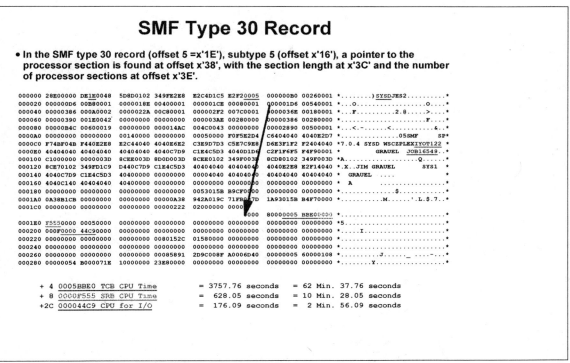

Figure 13-5 An example of an SMF type 30 record

```
                        SMF Type 30 Record: Notes

Processor Section:

Offsets           Name        Length   Format    Description
0       0         SMF30PTY    2        binary    Address space dispatching priority
                                                   (note this field is not valid in goal mode)
4       4         SMF30CPT    4        binary    Step CPU time under the task control block (TCB), in
                                                   hundredths of a second (including enclave time,
                                                   preemptable class SRB time, and client SRB time).

8       8         SMF30CPS    4        binary    Step CPU time under the service request block (SRB),
                                                   in hundredths of a second.

44      2C        SMF30IIP    4        binary    Amount of CPU time used to process I/O interrupts, in
                                                   hundredths of a second.

52      34        SMF30HPT    4        binary    CPU time consumed for the step, in hundredths of a
                                                   second, to support requests for data to be transferred
                                                   between a hiperspace and an address space, when the
                                                   hiperspace is backed by expanded storage. The CPU
                                                   time may vary depending on the availability of
                                                   expanded storage.

68      44        SMF30ASR    4        binary    Additional CPU time accumulated by the preemptable
                                                   SRBs and client SRBs for this job, in hundredths of a
                                                   second. This value is also included in the value in
                                                   SMF30CPT.

Refer to OS/390 V2R4.0 MVS System Management Facilities (SMF) - SMF30COF
```

Figure 13-6   SMF Type 30 record layout

Example 13-1   Sort example

```
//SYSIN    DD *
     SORT FIELDS=(47,8,CH,A,11,4,PD,A,7,4,BI,A)
       INCLUDE COND=(6,1,FI,EQ,30)
```

DFHJUP was then used to print the records in hex.

SMF 30 records consist of a header plus a number of sections, that is, processor, performance, I/O, and so on.

The processor section contains information such as the TCB (+4) and SRB (+8) times, which are reported in the IEF374I message.

▶ An SMF 30 subtype 2 record is written at the completion of each SMF interval.

▶ A subtype 5 record is written at job termination.

Refer to z/OS V1R7.0 MVS System Management Facilities (SMF) -Record Type 30 (1E)

13.5.3 RMF Workload Activity reports

RMF provides a wealth of information that is invaluable in the resolution of performance problems. This information can be used to understand how changes affect CPU, storage, and DASD usage.

Figure 13-8 on page 300 contains a WLM Workload Activity Report that presents data collected for report classes RIYOT122 and RJORIY1. Report class RIYOT122 provides RMF information about a CICS region called IYOT122. Report class RJORIY1 was defined to show the number of transactions beginning with JOR, which ended in the given SMF interval.

Report classes are defined using the WLM ISPF panels (=WLM option 2.6, then enter a 3 beside CICS). shows report classes for TRANIDs starting with JOR (report class RJORIY1), and a second report class (RCICSIY1) for all transactions starting with C.

```
 Subsystem-Type  Xref  Notes  Options  Help
 ------------------------------------------------------------------
              Modify Rules for the Subsystem Type     Row 1 to 8 of 10
 Command ===> _____  SCROLL ===> PAGE

 Subsystem Type . : CICS        Fold qualifier names?  Y  (Y or N)
 Description  . . . CICS transaction level rules

 Action codes:    A=After      C=Copy       M=Move      I=Insert rule
                  B=Before     D=Delete row R=Repeat    IS=Insert Sub-rule
                                                                More ===>
                  --------Qualifier--------        -------Class--------
 Action  Type       Name          Start           Service     Report
                                         DEFAULTS: _____   _____
 ____    1  SI     IYOT1         ___               _____   _____
 ____    2  TN     JOR*          ___               _____   RJORIY1
 ____    2  TN     C*            ___               _____   RCICSIY1
```

Figure 13-7 RMF report classes

The report interval is listed in the start and end times at the top of the page. A word of caution: T Figure 13-8 on page 300 he minimum interval is defined by the INTVAL() parm in the SMFPRMxx member of SYS1.PARMLIB. In the samples collected, the interval was set to 5 minutes:

```
INTVAL(05)                    /* SMF GLOBAL RECORDING INTERVAL */
```

It is also important to ensure that the SMF 70 to 79 records are being collected, along with the CICS 110 records. The records to be collected are also defined in the SMFPRMxx member:

```
SUBSYS(STC,EXITS(IEFACTRT),INTERVAL(SMF,SYNC),
                    TYPE(0,30,70:79,88,89,90,99,110,245))
       SUBSYS(OMVS,NOEXITS,INTERVAL(SMF,SYNC),
                    TYPE(0,30,70:79,90,88,89,99,110,245))
```

When the reports are formatted, it is possible to report a larger interval than was specified in the SMFPRMxx member, via the DINTV parm. However, do not forget that the length of the minimum interval is the value specified for INTVAL. One word of caution: SMF88 data that is formatted using IXGRPT1 does not have the ability to summarize at a larger interval than the interval used for data collection (the INTVAL value specified in the current SMFPRMxx).

Workload Activity Reports by Class

• Report Class by Transactions

```
REPORT BY: POLICY=WLMPOL                REPORT CLASS=RJORIY1
                                        DESCRIPTION =Report class -JOR trans IYOT1

TRANSACTIONS      TRANS.-TIME   HHH.MM.SS.TTT
AVG      0.00     ACTUAL                 161
MPL      0.00     EXECUTION                0
ENDED   27713     QUEUED                   0
END/S   92.39     R/S AFFINITY             0
#SWAPS      0     INELIGIBLE               0
EXCTD       0     CONVERSION               0
AVG ENC  0.00     STD DEV                 56
REM ENC  0.00
MS ENC   0.00
```

- **27713 JOR* tasks completed in the interval**
- **92.39 transactions ended per second**
- **Average transaction response time is .161 seconds**

• Report Class by Region

```
REPORT BY: POLICY=WLMPOL                REPORT CLASS=RIYOT122
                                        DESCRIPTION =

TRANSACTIONS   TRANS.-TIME   HHH.MM.SS.TTT   --DASD I/O--   ---SERVICE----   --SERVICE RATES--   PAGE-IN RATES   ----STORAGE----
AVG    1.00    ACTUAL                    0   SSCHRT  3881   IOC    116525   ABSRPTN  123986    SINGLE    0.0   AVG      7756.33
MPL    1.00    EXECUTION                 0   RESP     1.2   CPU     2048K   TRX SERV 123986    BLOCK     0.0   TOTAL    7755.58
ENDED     0    QUEUED                        CONN     0.9   MSO    34897K   TCB        156.5   SHARED    0.0   CENTRAL  7755.58
END/S  0.00    R/S AFFINITY              0   DISC     0.1   SRB    127300   SRB          9.7   HSP       0.0   EXPAND      0.00
#SWAPS    0    INELIGIBLE                0   Q+PEND   0.3   TOT    37189K   RCT          0.0   HSP MISS  0.0
EXCTD     0    CONVERSION                0   IOSQ     0.0   /SEC   123974   IIT          7.4   EXP SNGL  0.0   SHARED      1.00
AVG ENC 0.00   STD DEV                   0                                  HST          0.0   EXP BLK   0.0
REM ENC 0.00                                                                APPL %      57.9   EXP SHR   0.0
MS ENC  0.00
```

Figure 13-8 Workload Activity Reports by class

Referring to Figure 13-8:

▶ The following fields should be noted in the reports:

- MPL: Multiprogramming level. Number of address spaces active in this service/report class during the interval

- TCB: provides the CPU seconds accumulated in TCB mode during the collection interval
- SRB: provides the CPU seconds accumulated in SRB mode during the collection interval
- APPL%: percentage of an engine (CP) used during the collection interval

▶ The following field should be noted under STORAGE:
- AVG: average number of central and expanded storage frames allocated to ASIDs in the report class

▶ The following field should be noted under PAGE-IN RATES:
- SINGLE: average rate at which pages are read into central storage from aux (DASD)

▶ The following fields should be noted under DASD I/O:
- SSCHRT: number of start subchannels (SSCHs) per second in the reported interval
- RESP: average DASD response time (in milliseconds).

▶ The following fields should be noted in the transaction report:
- ENDED: reports the number of CICS transactions that ended during the SMF interval
- END/S: provides the transaction rate for those transactions reported, as defined in the report class
- TRANS. TIME: transaction response time

13.5.4 CICS PA reports

CICS PA can provide a report on transaction response time as reported by WLM. It provides a slightly different perspective. Notice in Figure 13-9 on page 302 that it reports by both service class (which is not being used) and report class. In addition to the information provided in the RMF report, CICS PA provides data showing the standard deviation and 90% peak.

```
                        CICS PA Workload Report

    V1R2M0                          CICS Performance Analyzer
                          Workload Manager Activity Summary by Service Class
    WKLD0001 Printed at 12:21:12 10/06/2003 Data from 16:44:59 10/02/2003 to 16:49:59 10/02/2003

    Service                          -------------- Response Time --------------
    Class    APPLID    Phase        #Tasks    Average    Std Dev    90% Peak    Maximum

    *Other*  IYOT1     BTE          29051     .1566      .0671      .2426       .6043

    V1R2M0                          CICS Performance Analyzer
                          Workload Manager Activity Summary by Report Class
    WKLD0001 Printed at 12:21:12 10/06/2003 Data from 16:44:59 10/02/2003 to 16:49:59 10/02/2003

    Report                           -------------- Response Time --------------
    Class    APPLID    Phase        #Tasks    Average    Std Dev    90% Peak    Maximum

    RCICSIY1 IYOT1     BTE           1330     .0320      .0177      .0547       .1138
    RJORIY1  IYOT1     BTE          27721     .1625      .0627      .2429       .6043
```

Figure 13-9   CICS PA workload report

CICS PA provides extensive reports and analysis of the CICS performance monitoring record. CICS writes a performance monitoring record to SMF as 110 record subtype 1 when each task completes. The records contain an extensive amount of information about the task showing everything from response time, CPU used, to suspend/wait times. Each segment of response time is reported. For example, if the task issues 100 file control calls, the calls will be detailed as to the type (read, read/update, rewrite, and so on). The total file I/O wait time is recorded. An example CICS PA report is shown in Figure 13-10.

```
V1R2M0                          CICS Performance Analyzer
                                   Performance Summary

SUMM0001 Printed at  7:53:10 10/05/2003    Data from 01:00:00 10/03/2003 to 01:04:59 10/03/2003
Summary of DB2* and JOR* task records in the SMF dataset

        Avg      Avg      Avg   Avg   Avg   Avg      Avg      Avg      Avg   Avg    Avg     Avg
Tran #Tasks Response Dispatch User  QR    L8   Suspend DispWait ChngMode QRModDly FCAMRq FC Wait DB2 Reqs
        Time     Time     CPU   CPU   CPU    Time     Time              Time             Time
                                Time  Time  Time
DB2A  2506  .1204    .0110    .0065 .0004 .0061 .1094   .0464    404    .0288    0      .0000   200
JORB  1806  .1660    .0079    .0056 .0056 .0000 .1581   .0483    0      .0483    168    .0983   0
```

Figure 13-10   CICS PA performance summary

13.5.5 DFH0STAT

DFH0STAT is supplied as a compiled sample program. The source continues to be available as a sample COBOL program in SDFHSAMP. You need to install CSD group DFH$STAT. It is run as the STAT transaction to collect CICS statistics and write them to the JES spool. The output can then be viewed under TSO. The SIT parm SPOOL=YES is required.

The information provided via DFH0STAT is also available in the CICS shutdown statistics.

> **Note:** DFH0STAT must not be used in place of the shutdown statistics. It will only report information provided in the current statistics interval. In addition, the unsolicited records will be lost.

```
Applid IYOT1    Sysid IY01   Jobname IYOT122   Date 12/15/2002  Time 11:57:13           CICS 6.2.0

System Status

  MVS Product Name. . . . . . . :  MVS/SP7.0.4         CICS Transaction Server Level . . :  02.02.00
  CICS Startup. . . . . . . . . :  INITIAL
  CICS Status . . . . . . . . . :  ACTIVE              RLS Status. . . . . . . . . . . . :  RLS=NO
  Storage Protection. . . . . . :  ACTIVE              RRMS/MVS Status . . . . . . . . . :  OPEN
  Transaction Isolation . . . . :  ACTIVE
  Reentrant Programs. . . . . . :  NOPROTECT           VTAM Open Status. . . . . . . . . :  OPEN
                                                       IRC Status. . . . . . . . . . . . :  OPEN
  Force Quasi-Reentrant . . . . :  No                  TCP/IP Status . . . . . . . . . . :  OPEN

  Program Autoinstall . . . . . :  ACTIVE              Max IP Sockets. . . . . . . . . . :      255
  Terminal Autoinstall. . . . . :  ENABLED             Active IP Sockets.. . . . . . . . :        0

  Activity Keypoint Frequency. . . . . . . :  1,000    WEB Garbage Collection Interval . :       60
  Logstream Deferred Force Interval. . . . :      0    Terminal Input Timeout Interval . :        5

  DB2 Connection Name . . . . . :  SYSD
```

Figure 13-11 DFH0STAT sample output

The dispatcher summary is used to track information such as the TCB and SRB time accumulated in the address space since the start of the CICS region or the beginning of the last statistics interval. For the QR TCB, the CPU-to-dispatch ratio is calculated. CPU and dispatch time information is provided for all TCB modes, but the ratio is only calculated for the QR TCB. For open TCB modes like J8 and L8, the TCBs are not necessarily permanent, that is, they can be attached and detached during the CICS run or within a statistics interval.

```
Dispatcher
   Current ICV time . . . . . . . . . . . . . . :        3,000ms
   Current ICVR time. . . . . . . . . . . . . . :       20,000ms
   Current ICVTSD time. . . . . . . . . . . . . :          100ms
   Current PRTYAGING time . . . . . . . . . . . :          500ms
   MRO (QR) Batching (MROBTCH) value. . . . . . :            1
   Concurrent Subtasking (SUBTSKS) value. . . . :            1
   Current number of CICS Dispatcher tasks. . . :           27
   Peak number of CICS Dispatcher tasks . . . . :           29
   Current number of TCBs attached. . . . . . . :            7
   Current number of TCBs in use. . . . . . . . :            7
   Number of Excess TCB Scans . . . . . . . . . :            0
   Excess TCB Scans - No TCB Detached . . . . . :            0
   Number of Excess TCBs Detached . . . . . . . :            0
   Average Excess TCBs Detached per Scan. . . . :            0
   Number of CICS TCB MODEs . . . . . . . . . . :           18
   Number of CICS TCB POOLs . . . . . . . . . . :            4
Dispatcher TCB Modes
   Dispatcher Start Time and Date . . . . . . . :    13:10:00.00569   05/05/2006
   Address Space Accumulated CPU Time . . . . . :    00:17:53.38121   (Not Reset)
   Address Space Accumulated SRB Time . . . . . :    00:02:31.70997   (Not Reset)
   Address Space CPU Time (Since Reset) . . . . :    00:00:55.93860
   Address Space SRB Time (Since Reset) . . . . :    00:00:07.58986

  TCB    TCBs Attached    Op. System    Op. System       Total TCB        Total TCB        DS TCB          TCB CPU/Disp
  Mode   Current  Peak      Waits        Wait Time      Dispatch Time     CPU Time         CPU Time           Ratio
  QR        1      1       90,525      00:00:41.30698   00:01:31.49197   00:00:55.93948   00:00:01.49983      61.1%
  R0        1      1            0      00:00:00.00000   00:00:00.00000   00:00:00.00000   00:00:00.00000
  C0        1      1            0      00:00:00.00000   00:00:00.00000   00:00:00.00000   00:00:00.00000
  SZ        0      0            0      00:00:00.00000   00:00:00.00000   00:00:00.00000   00:00:00.00000
  RP        0      0            0      00:00:00.00000   00:00:00.00000   00:00:00.00000   00:00:00.00000
  F0        1      1            0      00:00:00.00000   00:00:00.00000   00:00:00.00000   00:00:00.00000
  SL        1      1            0      00:00:00.00000   00:00:00.00000   00:00:00.00000   00:00:00.00000
  S0        1      1            0      00:00:00.00000   00:00:00.00000   00:00:00.00000   00:00:00.00000
  SP        1      1            1      00:00:00.00000   00:00:00.00996   00:00:00.00000   00:00:00.00000
  D2        1      1            4      00:02:00.00270   00:00:00.00010   00:00:00.00008   00:00:00.00003
  JM        0      0            0      00:00:00.00000   00:00:00.00000   00:00:00.00000   00:00:00.00000
  S8        0      0            0      00:00:00.00000   00:00:00.00000   00:00:00.00000   00:00:00.00000
  L8        0      0            0      00:00:00.00000   00:00:00.00000   00:00:00.00000   00:00:00.00000
  L9        0      0            0      00:00:00.00000   00:00:00.00000   00:00:00.00000   00:00:00.00000
  J8        0      0            0      00:00:00.00000   00:00:00.00000   00:00:00.00000   00:00:00.00000
  J9        0      0            0      00:00:00.00000   00:00:00.00000   00:00:00.00000   00:00:00.00000
  X8        0      0            0      00:00:00.00000   00:00:00.00000   00:00:00.00000   00:00:00.00000
  X9        0      0            0      00:00:00.00000   00:00:00.00000   00:00:00.00000   00:00:00.00000

  Totals    8                                                            00:00:55.93957   00:00:01.49987
```

Figure 13-12   DFH0STAT dispatcher report

CICS Transaction Server Version 2.2 APAR PQ76702 introduced the ability to collect additional TCB information for the CICS address space. This function is present at the base code level in later releases of CICS. DFH0STAT has been changed to display the TCB structure along with CPU and storage information for each TCB.

It is very important to remember that this display, like all DFH0STAT displays, is a snapshot captured at a particular point in time. It shows the TCBs and their status as they were when the STAT transaction was run. The number of TCBs can and will change over the course of a CICS run. It is very important to understand that open TCBs (S8, L8, L9, J8, J9, X8, and X9) can be detached and a new TCB attached at a later time, which might be located at the exact same address. Therefore the CPU values may seem incorrect over an extended period of time, because there is actually more than a single TCB being reported. Multiple displays provide a trend but they should not be used as a substitute for the dispatcher shutdown statistics and RMF data produced for the region.

The address space accumulated TCB and SRB CPU time is displayed. Storage allocated information is provided at both address space and TCB levels.

```
Dispatcher - MVS TCBs
  Dispatcher Start Time and Date . . . . . . :  10:22:47.81766  01/16/2004
  Address Space Accumulated CPU Time . . . . :  00:20:14.25838  (Not Reset)
  Address Space Accumulated SRB Time . . . . :  00:00:00.44907  (Not Reset)
  Address Space CPU Time (Since Reset) . . . :  00:20:15.00231
  Address Space SRB Time (Since Reset) . . . :  00:00:00.44711

  Current number of CICS TCBs . . . . . . . . . . . . :           36
  Current CICS TCB CPU time . . . . . . . . . . . . . :  00:20:15.04754
  Current CICS TCB Private Storage below 16MB . . . . :        5,368K
  Current CICS TCB Private Storage above 16MB . . . . :      121,860K
  Current number of non-CICS TCBs . . . . . . . . . . :            1
  Current non-CICS TCB CPU time . . . . . . . . . . . :  00:00:00.75399
  Current non-CICS TCB Private Storage below 16MB . . :          104K
  Current non-CICS TCB Private Storage above 16MB . . :        1,248K

  TCB               CICS       Current TCB        Current TCB  Private Stg  Task    Tran  Task    Mother    Sister    Daughter
  Address  TCB Name TCB    <--- TCB CPU Time--->  Below 16MB   Above 16MB   Number  ID    Status  TCB       TCB       TCB
  009F0860 IEFIIC   No     00:00:00.75399 100.0%       104K       1,248K    None                  009FFD90            009F0A40
  009F0A40 DFHSIP   Yes    00:00:00.03861   0.0%     5,312K     121,340K    None                  009F0860            009DD9C0
  009DD9C0 F0       Yes    00:00:00.02274   0.0%        12K          32K    None                  009F0A40  009F0058  009DD610
  009DD610 R0       Yes    00:00:00.29527   0.0%        16K          32K    None                  009DD9C0            009DD260
  009F0058 DFHTRTCB Yes    00:00:00.00002   0.0%         0K           0K    None                  009F0A40
  009DD260 QR       Yes    00:05:21.69479  26.4%        16K         260K      35   STAT   Run     009DD610            009A65F0
  009A65F0 L800Q    Yes    00:00:38.52774   3.1%         0K           0K    None                  009DD260  009A6AE8
  009A6AE8 L800P    Yes    00:01:21.47988   6.7%         0K           4K    None                  009DD260  009A6D90

  009B2868 L800A    Yes    00:01:12.86450   5.9%         0K           4K    None                  009DD260  009B2B10
  009B2B10 L8009    Yes    00:01:10.83851   5.8%         0K           4K    None                  009DD260  009B5308

  009B4348 L8001    Yes    00:00:00.34601   0.0%         0K           4K    None                  009DD260  009B4C00
  009B4C00 L8000    Yes    00:00:00.00545   0.0%         0K           4K    None                  009DD260  009B4E88
  009B4E88 DFHSKTSK Yes    00:00:00.01054   0.0%         8K           4K    None                  009DD260  009B9418
  009B9418 D2000    Yes    00:00:00.00001   0.0%         0K           0K    None                  009DD260  009B9A68
  009B9A68 S0       Yes    00:00:00.00187   0.0%         4K         116K    None                  009DD260  009B9D90
  009B9D90 SL       Yes    00:00:00.00025   0.0%         0K           8K    None                  009DD260
```

Figure 13-13   DFH0STAT Dispatcher MVS TCBs report

Each TCB entry in the display shows the TCB address, the TCB name, and the current TCB accumulated CPU time, and storage allocation is given. The TCB name is taken from the PRB CDE (Contents Directory Entry) for non-CICS TCBs or the CICS name found in the KTCB (in the Kernel Domain). Additional information displayed includes the active task (if the TCB is executing when the inquiry is issued), the mother (attaching) TCB, sister (attached by the same mother) TCB, and daughter (attached by this TCB) TCBs.

If we look at the QR TCB in Figure 13-13 we can see the TCB located at 009DD260. It was attached by the TCB located at 009DD610 (the RO), and it has attached a number of daughter TCBs. The daughter TCBs are listed in reverse order starting with L800Q at location 009A65F0. Following the sister TCB chain, it is observed that the L8, a DFHSKTSK, the D2000, SO, and SL TCBs are all daughters of the QR TCB. (Note that due to space limitations, not all TCBs have been displayed.)

Also notice that the QR TCB has accumulated 26.4% of the address space CPU time: 5 minutes and 21.69479 seconds of the 20 minutes—15.04754 seconds of the TCB time in the address space.

The QR TCB has allocated 16-K bytes of storage below the 16 MB line and 260 K above the line. The current task is task number 35 (a STAT transaction).

13.6 Conclusions

You must consider many different areas when reviewing performance. There are many tools out there to help. However, no one tool can be used alone to get a picture of your overall performance. The steps and guidelines listed here provide you with a clearer picture of the performance of your systems.

You must:

- Define the problem.
- Understand the workload.
- Understand the physical configuration.
- If CPU has increased:
    - Establish a baseline before a new function is implemented
        - CICS Performance data (SMF 110 records)
        - SMF 70-78, SMF 30
        - CICS trace
        - CPU to Dispatch ratio
        - Measure with the following three data collectors:
            - DFH0STAT
            - Shutdown statistics
            - CICS PA
- If response time has increased:
    - Establish a baseline using
        - CICS Performance data (SMF 110 records)
        - SMF 70-78, SMF 30
- Remember that capacity problems usually manifest themselves as response time problems.

Common threadsafe questions

In this chapter we answer some of the most frequently asked questions about threadsafe.

14.1 General threadsafe questions

Can I go ahead and define all my applications as threadsafe?

Answer: No. A full analysis of each of your applications must be performed before making the definition change. Otherwise you could compromise your application's shared data and also see a performance degradation due to excessive TCB switches caused by non threadsafe CICS commands and non threadsafe user exits. Just changing a program's definition is not enough.

If my application is reentrant can I define it as threadsafe?

Answer: No. Reentrancy is just one aspect of being threadsafe. You need to check whether the application accesses any shared resources, and if so does it have the necessary serialization logic in place. An application can be reentrant, link-edited with RENT, and reside in a CICS read-only DSA, but if it incorrectly accesses shared data without serialization logic, then it is non threadsafe.

Are there automatic tools I can run to tell me if my application code is threadsafe or to convert my application automatically?

Answer: No, there is no automatic way of making your programs threadsafe. CICS provides the load module scanner to help you identify those commands that could cause your application code to be non threadsafe and to identify those CICS commands that are non threadsafe and will cause a switchback to the QR TCB. However, the load module scanner is an aid to be used as a starting point in analyzing your application.

What happens if I define an application program as threadsafe to CICS when it is not threadsafe?

Answer: CICS cannot protect you from the consequences, and the results are unpredictable. You risk the integrity of the shared data as multiple instances of the program each running on its own TCB can access the data at the same time. There is no protection provided via quasi-reentrancy because the application is not running on the QR TCB. The loss of data integrity may not be instantly detected and may become apparent later. This is similar to the victim of a storage overwrite finding out long after the storage overwrite occurred.

What is a non threadsafe CICS command, and do such commands have a data integrity exposure?

Answer: A non threadsafe CICS command is a CICS command that insists on running on QR TCB. The CICS code that implements the command relies on quasi-reentrancy, that is, serialization provided by running on the QR TCB. No, there is no data integrity exposure, as serialization of shared resources is provided by QR TCB. On the other hand, a threadsafe CICS command is one in which the CICS code does not rely on running on QR TCB and can execute safely on open TCBs concurrently.

Can I define a program as threadsafe if it contains non threadsafe CICS commands?

Answer: Yes. By defining a program as threadsafe you are telling CICS the application code (for example, the COBOL source code) is threadsafe, you are not telling CICS about what API commands the program uses. (CICS manages the threadsafety issues of its own code.) Non threadsafe EXEC CICS commands will cause a switch back to the QR TCB. This affects the performance of the application, but it does not affect the integrity of your data.

For a program defined as CONCURRENCY(THREADSAFE) API(CICSAPI), following execution of a non threadsafe CICS command, the program remains on the QR TCB until the next request to an OPENAPI TRUE (for example, a DB2 or WMQ request). For a program defined as CONCURRENCY(THREADSAFE) API(OPENAPI), following execution of a non threadsafe EXEC CICS command, the program receives control back on the open TCB (either L8 or L9).

Will a program defined with CONCURRENCY(QUASIRENT) calling DB2 V6 or later use L8 TCBs?

Answer: Yes, CICS always uses L8 TCBs with DB2 V6 and later irrespective of whether the application is threadsafe or not. For every DB2 call the DB2 work will be done on the L8 TCB and, once complete, CICS will switch back to the QR TCB before returning to the non threadsafe application. This will happen for every DB2 call.

Will an application running on CICS Transaction Server Version 3.2 that calls WMQ use L8 TCBs?

Answer: Yes, CICS Transaction Server Version 3.2 uses an OTE-enabled TRUE for handling CICS-WMQ calls. L8 TCBs are used for the requests to WMQ. If the application is defined as threadsafe, control will remain on the open TCB upon return from WMQ. If the application is defined as quasi-reentrant, control will switch back to the QR TCB upon return from WMQ.

Can I stop using L8 TCBs by specifying FORCEQR=YES in the SIT?

Answer: No, DB2 calls for DB2 V6 and later will always switch to an L8 TCB. FORCEQR=YES will override the CONCURRENCY(THREADSAFE) API(CICSAPI) setting for any program defined as such, forcing a switchback to the QR TCB following the DB2 call. FORCEQR=YES has no affect on a program defined as CONCURRENCY(THREADSAFE) API(OPENAPI) that must run on an open TCB.

Prior to CICS Transaction Server Version 2.2, did TCB switching occur for DB2 requests?

Answer: Yes, for each DB2 request two TCB switches occurred. One switch from QR TCB to a DB2 thread TCB before calling DB2, and then one switchback to QR TCB after the DB2 call has completed. Activity on the DB2 thread TCB was not visible in a CICS trace.

Prior to CICS Transaction Server Version 3.2, did TCB switching occur for WMQ requests?

Answer: Yes, for each WMQ request two TCB switches occurred: one switch to a WMQ thread TCB before calling WMQ, and then one switch back to the original TCB after the WMQ call has completed. Activity on the WMQ thread TCB was not visible in a CICS trace.

Can I stop using L8 TCBs by specifying FCQRONLY=YES in the SIT?

Answer: It depends what you mean. CICS Transaction Server Version 3.2 will allow EXEC CICS file control requests to be processed under an open TCB. If your application were running under an L8 or L9 TCB when it issued a file control command, CICS would execute this threadsafe API request under the open TCB. This is the same as for other threadsafe EXEC CICS commands. However, the file control threadsafety implementation also provides the option of disabling threadsafe support for EXEC CICS file control API commands by means of the FCQRONLY SIT parameter. If this is set to YES, file control commands are processed under the QR TCB within CICS, as per earlier releases. However, this will not remove support for and use of L8 TCBs for, for instance, WMQ or DB2 calls, nor for programs defined with CONCURRENCY(THREADSAFE) API(OPENAPI), which have to execute their application logic under an L8 or L9 open TCB. FCQRONLY is specific to the execution path within CICS for EXEC CICS file control commands only.

Can I still address a task's TCA by using the CSACDTA field?

Answer: No. With the introduction of OTE it is no longer safe to assume the TCA address held within CSACDTA is the TCA of the task that is accessing the CSA. CSACDTA contains the address of the task currently dispatched *under the QR TCB*. The task that is looking at the value in CSACDTA may be running under an open TCB. This can lead to the wrong TCA address being used by the program, with unpredictable results. The CICS system programming interface (SPI) should be used whenever possible for programs wishing to access state information about a task.

Note also that CSACDTA was renamed CSAQRTCA in CICS Transaction Server Version 3.1, to further discourage using the CSA to address the running task's TCA. In CICS Transaction Server Version 3.2, IBM has now withdrawn the ability to reference a TCA using this field, by loading CSAQRTCA with the address of an area of fetch-protected storage. This will result in an abend ASRD with message DFHSR0618 if it is referenced.

What is the difference between a THREADSAFE program and an OPENAPI program in CICS Transaction Server Version 3?

Answer: A threadsafe program is a program defined as CONCURRENCY(THREADSAFE) and API(CICSAPI). It can run on QR TCB or an open TCB. Part of it may run on QR TCB, and then after a DB2 or WMQ request, part of it can run on an open TCB. A threadsafe program has no TCB affinity, and no affinity to the key of the TCB. Use of non-CICS APIs is not allowed, as they may execute on QR TCB and so damage the CICS environment.

An OPENAPI program is a program defined as CONCURRENCY(THREADSAFE) and API(OPENAPI). It always runs on an open TCB. It starts on an open TCB, and all application code runs on an open TCB. If CICS has to switch to QR TCB to execute a non threadsafe CICS command, then CICS will switch back to the open TCB when it returns control to the program. An OPENAPI program runs on an open TCB whose key matches the program's execution key, that is, an L8 TCB for EXECKEY(CICS) or an L9 TCB for EXECKEY(USER). Use of non-CICS APIs is allowed at the user's own risk, as they will not run on QR TCB and will not block main CICS processing.

If STGPROT=NO is specified, does CICS still need to use L9 TCBs for EXECKEY(USER) programs?

Answer: No. If CICS is not utilizing storage protection, there is no need for open TCBs that match user key storage and execution. L9 TCBs do not have to be used for CONCURRENCY(THREADSAFE) API(OPENAPI) EXECKEY(USER) programs. L8 TCBs can be used instead.

If SUBTSKS is specified, to allow CICS to utilize the CO TCB for concurrent VSAM calls on busy systems, is this still honored for those file control requests that are issued under an open TCB?

Answer: No. If a CICS Transaction Server Version 3.2 application were running under an open TCB, and issued an EXEC CICS file control command, it would not be sensible to then switch to another TCB in order to process the request. The SUBTSKS SIT parameter is only honored by CICS if the application were running on the QR TCB when the file control command was issued.

What differences will be seen when tasks are running in CICS Transaction Server Version 3.2 and issue file control commands?

Answer: CICS Transaction Server Version 3.2 supports threadsafe file control. Applications that are running on an open TCB can therefore call VSAM under the open TCB as part of a file control request.

Prior to CICS Transaction Server Version 3.2, file control was a non-threadsafe EXEC CICS API, and so all file control commands were processed under the QR TCB. If VSAM had to suspend a task during its execution of a request to an LSR file, it drove the supplied UPAD exit in CICS and the task was suspended by the CICS dispatcher. If the request was NSR, CICS issued the request to VSAM asynchronously and could then suspend the task if needed. For example, tasks would be suspended on FCIOWAITs or FCXCWAITs. The reason a task was suspended could be analyzed, for example by using CEMT online, or by investigating a CICS system dump offline. The IPCS system dump formatter could be run against a system dump and return, for example, the task environment (using the KE VERBEXIT) or the dispatcher environment (using the DS VERBEXIT). Since non-threadsafe commands have to run under the serialized QR TCB, only one task would be seen to be running on this TCB at any one time, and the KE VERBEXIT data would clearly identify the running task at the time of the dump.

With CICS Transaction Server Version 3.2, VSAM requests can be executed under an open TCB. If they are, any suspends due to VSAM do not require calling the UPAD exit since there is no danger that blocking the TCB will affect other tasks within CICS (unlike the effect that a blocking operation on the QR TCB would have). This means that such requests will not result in the CICS dispatcher being invoked to suspend the task. Tasks will still appear to be running when investigated using techniques such as CEMT or IPCS. This may affect the analysis of task activity when using performance monitors or equivalent pieces of software.

14.2 Questions about CICS exits

How do I find out what exits I use, and whether they are defined as threadsafe?

Answer: Use the CICS-supplied sample DFH0STAT to look at user exits. It will report what exit programs are active and what the concurrency setting of the exit program is. The report will include any exits supplied by third-party vendors in support of their products.

If my exits are for a vendor product, can I just define them as threadsafe and improve my performance?

Answer: No, you must contact the vendor and have them tell you whether it is safe to change the concurrency attribute of the exit's program definition.

14.3 Performance questions

I am planning on migrating to CICS Transaction Server Version 3 and am worried about the potential performance impacts. Can I do the migration and then set FORCEQR to FORCE to allow the system to run like my current CICS system?

Answer: No, you must review and set your exits to threadsafe before you perform the migration to be safe. You cannot turn off the use of L8 open TCBs.

What is the cost of a TCB switch?

Answer: The pathlength of a single TCB switch (say from QR to L8) is approximately 2000 instructions. So, a non-threadsafe application issuing an EXEC SQL call to DB2 would incur 4000 additional instructions (half when switching from the QR TCB onto an L8 TCB in order to call DB2, and half when switching back to the QR TCB upon return to CICS).

The benefits of being threadsafe can be seen when such additional pathlength is scaled up by the number of calls to OPENAPI TRUEs such as DB2 and WMQ from within busy quasi-reentrant applications. In addition to the execution time required to execute the TCB switches, there is also the corresponding CPU cost, together with the increased contention of having to use the QR TCB for non-threadsafe application work.

14.4 Load module scanner questions

Are the commands listed in table DFHEIDTH non threadsafe?

Answer: Some of the commands in DFHEIDTH are non threadsafe, but that is not its purpose. The commands listed in DFHEIDTH give the application programmer access to shared storage. There is potential for the application program code being non threadsafe unless it has implemented serialization logic around updates to the shared storage. Therefore the purpose of DFHEIDTH is to report programs that may contain non threadsafe code.

I ran the load module scanner DFHEISUP with table DFHEIDTH against my programs and found they were using EXEC CICS ADDRESS CWA, but when searching the code I could not find any reference to the CWA. Are these programs therefore threadsafe?

Answer: If the report from DFHEISUP flags use of a command that gives you access to shared storage, if you never reference the storage in question, then there is no threadsafety issue. Perhaps someone changed the code years ago but never removed the reference to the shared storage. If that is the only potential shared storage issue reported, then your program is threadsafe.

Is there a table that lists all non threadsafe CICS commands?

Answer: Yes, table DFHEIDNT lists all non threadsafe CICS commands. Note that use of this table tells you whether you may experience excessive TCB switching due to having to return to QR TCB to execute the non threadsafe CICS command. It does not tell you anything about the application code and whether it is threadsafe. How much TCB switching will occur depends upon how many CICS commands there are and their relative position in the code to DB2 or WMQ calls, or both.

Part 4

Appendixes

CICS, DB2, and WMQ maintenance

This appendix provides a list of the recommended maintenance to be applied to CICS, DB2, and WMQ.

CICS TS 2.3 APARs

- PQ78987

    CPU increase in regions connecting to DB2 when migrating to CICS Transaction Server V2

- PQ93953 and PK04677

    Purge and forcepurge of task using OPENAPI True fails

- PK05932

    Sqlcode -922 after COBOL program precompiled in DB2 V8 new function mode

- PK12632

    Task stuck in resumed early state

- PK18498

RMI 0C4 abend
- PK26061

  Abend AD3K and AEXZ on a task purge of a DB2 threadsafe transaction

CICS TS 3.1 APARs

- PQ05771

  Purge and forcepurge of task using OPENAPI True fails

- PK05933

  Sqlcode -922 after COBOL program precompiled in DB2 V8 new function mode

- PK14003

  Task stuck in resumed early state

- PK20040

  RMI 0C4 abend

- PK21134

  Abend AD3K due to recovery backout failure after a task is purged

- PK31859

  Abend AD3K and AEXZ on a task purge of a DB2 threadsafe transaction

CICS TS 3.2 APARs

- PK45354

  File control threadsafety modifications

  Change default for FCQRONLY parameter to YES

DB2 7.1 APARs

- PQ44614

  Subsystem init changes for group attach

- PQ45691

  Group attach fixes

- PQ45692

  Group attach fixes
- PQ46501

  ERLY code changes for OTE
- PQ50703

  Incorrect accounting class 1 TCB time reported when threads switch TCB
- PQ65357

  CICS-DB2 thread is not released properly at sync point if the package is bound with OPTHHINT

> **Note:** Some of the above DB2 maintenance affects DB2 ERLY code that resides in the LPA, and so having applied the maintenance, an MVS IPL is required for it to become active. For this reason, for DB2 V7.1 we also list those apars that hit ERLY code pertaining to group attach as well as that required to support OTE.

DB2 8.1 APARs

- PK21892

  Excessive stack storage for identified signed on connections

WMQ 5.3.1 APARs

- PK39200

  Checks CICS release and alias changes

WMQ 6.1 APARs

- PK42616

  Checks CICS release
- PK38772

  Bridge code does not provide a reason code for signon failures after migrating to Version 6.0

DFHEISUP APARs

- PQ73890

    DFHEISUP does not list the EXEC CICS SEND MAP command when the command contains the option MAPONLY.

- PQ76545

    Abend 0C4 in module DFHEISUP scanning application load libraries.

- PQ77185

    CEE3204S THE SYSTEM DETECTED A PROTECTION EXCEPTION (SYSTEM COMPLETION CODE=0C4).

- PQ78531

    DFHEISUP Library problem. Runs short on storage.

- PQ82603

    Running the DFHEISUP utility returns an undocumented error message when certain commands are encountered.

- PQ87863 (CICS TS 2.3 only)

    ASKTIME ABSTIME is listed as non threadsafe in DFHEIDNT.

COBOL call program listings

This appendix contains the COBOL programs used to demonstrate the effect of using COBOL calls as described in 8.5, "COBOL calls" on page 193.

Program listings for COBOL call examples

Program PROGA

Example: B-1 PROGA

```
IDENTIFICATION DIVISION.
      PROGRAM-ID. PROGA .
      ENVIRONMENT DIVISION.
      DATA DIVISION.
      WORKING-STORAGE SECTION.

      01 ws-PROGB                      pic x(08)
             VALUE 'PROGB'.
      01 ws-queue                      pic x(08)
             VALUE 'TONYQ'.
      01 WS-MSG.
         03 ws-before-after            pic x(12).
         03 filler                     pic x(10)
            value 'PROGA : '.
         03 filler                     pic x(17)
            value 'Counter value :- '.
         03 ws-counter                 pic 9(8).

      01 ws-counter-s9                 pic s9(8) comp.

          EXEC SQL INCLUDE SQLCA END-EXEC.

          EXEC SQL
              DECLARE DSN8710.EMP TABLE (
              EMPNO                    CHAR(6),
              FIRSTNME                 CHAR(12),
              MIDINIT                  CHAR(1),
              LASTNAME                 CHAR(15),
              WORKDEPT                 CHAR(3),
              PHONENO                  CHAR(4),
              HIREDATE                 DATE,
              JOB                      CHAR(8),
              EDLEVEL                  SMALLINT,
              SEX                      CHAR(1),
              BIRTHDATE                DATE,
              SALARY                   DECIMAL,
              BONUS                    DECIMAL,
              COMM                     DECIMAL )
          END-EXEC.

      PROCEDURE DIVISION.
```

```
        EXEC CICS DELETEQ TS QUEUE(WS-QUEUE) NOHANDLE END-EXEC.

        EXEC SQL
            SELECT count(*)
            INTO :WS-COUNTER-S9
            FROM DSN8710.EMP
            WHERE EMPNO = "000990"
        END-EXEC.

        MOVE ZEROES TO WS-COUNTER.

        MOVE 'Before CALL' to ws-before-after.

        EXEC CICS
          WRITEQ TS MAIN
          QUEUE(WS-QUEUE) FROM(WS-msg)
        END-EXEC.

        Call ws-PROGB using dfheiblk
                            ws-counter.

        MOVE 'After CALL ' to ws-before-after.

        EXEC CICS
          WRITEQ TS MAIN
          QUEUE(WS-QUEUE) FROM(WS-msg)
        END-EXEC.

        EXEC CICS RETURN END-EXEC.
```

Program PROGB

Example: B-2 PROGB

```cobol
IDENTIFICATION DIVISION.
      PROGRAM-ID. PROGB.
      ENVIRONMENT DIVISION.
      DATA DIVISION.
      WORKING-STORAGE SECTION.

      01 WS-COUNTER-S9              PIC S9(8) COMP.
      01 WS-QUEUE                   PIC X(08)
          VALUE 'TONYQ'.
      01 WS-MSG.
         03 filler                  pic x(10)
             value 'PROGB: '.
         03 filler                  pic x(17)
             value "Counter value :- ".
         03 filler                  pic x(12)
             value spaces.
         03 ws-counter              pic 9(8).

         EXEC SQL INCLUDE SQLCA END-EXEC.

         EXEC SQL
             DECLARE DSN8710.EMP TABLE (
             EMPNO                  CHAR(6),
             FIRSTNME               CHAR(12),
             MIDINIT                CHAR(1),
             LASTNAME               CHAR(15),
             WORKDEPT               CHAR(3),
             PHONENO                CHAR(4),
             HIREDATE               DATE,
             JOB                    CHAR(8),
             EDLEVEL                SMALLINT,
             SEX                    CHAR(1),
             BIRTHDATE              DATE,
             SALARY                 DECIMAL,
             BONUS                  DECIMAL,
             COMM                   DECIMAL )
         END-EXEC.

      Linkage section.
      01 dfhcommarea.
         03 ls-count                pic 9(8).

      PROCEDURE DIVISION.
          move 99999 to ls-count
                        ws-counter.
```

```
    EXEC SQL
        SELECT count(*)
        INTO :WS-COUNTER-S9
        FROM DSN8710.EMP
        WHERE EMPNO = "000990"
    END-EXEC.

    EXEC CICS WRITEQ TS MAIN
      QUEUE(WS-QUEUE) FROM(WS-MSG) END-EXEC.

AA-EXIT.
    EXIT.
    GOBACK.
```

Assembler routines

This appendix lists the assembler routines we used in our migration.

DB2MANY

Example C-1 is a list of code for the DB2MANY program.

Example: C-1   iDB2MANY example

```
***********************************************************************
DFHEISTG DSECT
         EXEC SQL INCLUDE SQLCA
*
**************************************************
DFHEISTG DSECT
**************************************************
 VVEMP      DS    CL80
 EMPNO      DS    CL6
 FIRSTNME   DS    CL12
 MIDINIT    DS    CL1
 LASTNAME   DS    CL15
 WORKDEPT   DS    CL3
 PHONENO    DS    CL4
 HIREDATE   DS    CL10
 JOB        DS    CL8
 EDLEVEL    DS    HL2
 SEX        DS    CL1
 BIRTHDATE  DS    CL10
 SALARY     DS    PL3
 BONUS      DS    PL3
 COMM       DS    PL3
**************************************************
 TERMNL        DC     F'0'
 DATALEN       DS     F'0'
               DS     0D
               DC     C'EISTG   '
 MESSAGES DS   CL80                  TEMP STORE
 KEYNUM   DS   CL9                   TEMP STORE
 COMLEN   DS   1H                    LENGTH OF C
          DS   0F
 SQDWSTOR DS   (SQLDLEN)C    RESERVE STORAGE TO BE USED FOR SQLDSECT
 SDARGDATA     DC     50F'0'
               DC     C'EISTG END'
 SDARG         DSECT
 SDREPEAT      DC     X'00000000'  NUMBER OF TIMES TO REPEAT DB2 CALL
 SDTERMID      DS     CL4          TERMINAL ID
 SDREPCNT      DC     F'0'         CURRENT NUMBER TO BE ATTACHED
 SDPASSCT      DC     F'0'         NUMBER OF START TASK PASSES
 SDTRAN        DS     F'0'
 SDASKTIM      DS     CL4
 SDEMPNO       DS     CL6          EMPLOYEE NUMBER TO USE
 INPUT         DC     20F'0'       INPUT DATA
```

```
         INMSGLEN         DS     0H         MESSAGE LENGTH
*
         ***********************************************************
         SQDWSREG  EQU    7
         RETREG    EQU    2                 SET UP REGISTER USAGE
         COUNTER   EQU    5
         R06       EQU    6
         R08       EQU    8
         R9        EQU    9
         COMPTR    EQU    4                 POINTER TO COMMAREA
         SDPASSR   EQU    11                PASS COUNT REG
         ***********************************************************
         DB2MANY   CSECT
         DB2MANY   AMODE 31
         DB2MANY   RMODE ANY
         ****************************************************************
         * OBTAIN INPUT DATA
                 LA    R08,SDARGDATA
                 USING SDARG,R08
                 MVC   SDREPEAT,REPEAT   SET TO THE NUMBER OF DB2 CALLS
         ****************************************************************
         *
         * SQL WORKING STORAGE
                 LA    SQDWSREG,SQDWSTOR   GET ADDRESS OF SQLDSECT
                 USING SQLDSECT,SQDWSREG   AND TELL ASSEMBLER ABOUT IT
         *
                 EXEC SQL
                     DECLARE DSN8710.EMP TABLE (
                     EMPNO                 CHAR(6),
                     FIRSTNME              CHAR(12),
                     MIDINIT               CHAR(1),
LASTNAME                       CHAR(15),                             *
                     WORKDEPT              CHAR(3),                  *
                     PHONENO               CHAR(4),                  *
                     HIREDATE              DATE,                     *
                     JOB                   CHAR(8),                  *
                     EDLEVEL               SMALLINT,                 *
                     SEX                   CHAR(1),                  *
                     BIRTHDATE             DATE,                     *
                     SALARY                DECIMAL,                  *
                     BONUS                 DECIMAL,                  *
                     COMM                  DECIMAL )
         *
         *
         RESET     L     COUNTER,COUNT
         *
         READLOOP  DS    0H
                 EXEC CICS ASKTIME
         *
```

```
         EXEC SQL SELECT * INTO :VVEMP FROM DSN8710.EMP WHERE EMPNO='000140'
         LA    COUNTER,1(COUNTER)
         C     COUNTER,MAXREAD
         BNH   READLOOP
*
**********************************************************************
**   NOW START THE NEXT TASK                                      ****
**                                                                ****
         L     SDPASSR,SDPASSCT       LOAD THE WORK REG
         C     SDPASSR,NUMPASS
         BE    NOSTART
STARTLP  DS    0H
         LA    R08,SDARGDATA
         USING SDARG,R08
         MVC   SDTERMID,EIBTRMID
         MVC   SDREPEAT,REPEAT SET THE NUMBER OF DB2 CALLS PER TRAN
         MVC   SDREPCNT,NUMTRAN  PASS THE NUMBER OF TIMES TO RESTART
         MVC   SDTRAN,=CL4'DB21'
         MVC   TERMNL,EIBTRMID
         EXEC CICS START TRANSID(SDTRAN) INTERVAL(0)
               FROM(SDARG) LENGTH(SDLENG)
**********************************************************************
         MVC   SDTRAN,=CL4'DB22'
         MVC   TERMNL,EIBTRMID
         EXEC CICS START TRANSID(SDTRAN) INTERVAL(0)
               FROM(SDARG) LENGTH(SDLENG)
**********************************************************************
         MVC   SDTRAN,=CL4'DB23'
         MVC   TERMNL,EIBTRMID
         EXEC CICS START TRANSID(SDTRAN) INTERVAL(0)
               FROM(SDARG) LENGTH(SDLENG)
**********************************************************************
         MVC   SDTRAN,=CL4'DB24'
    MVC  TERMNL,EIBTRMID
         EXEC CICS START TRANSID(SDTRAN) INTERVAL(0)
               FROM(SDARG) LENGTH(SDLENG)
**********************************************************************
         MVC   SDTRAN,=CL4'DB25'
         MVC   TERMNL,EIBTRMID
         EXEC CICS START TRANSID(SDTRAN) INTERVAL(0)
               FROM(SDARG) LENGTH(SDLENG)
**********************************************************************
         MVC   SDTRAN,=CL4'DB26'
         MVC   TERMNL,EIBTRMID
         EXEC CICS START TRANSID(SDTRAN) INTERVAL(0)
               FROM(SDARG) LENGTH(SDLENG)
**********************************************************************
         MVC   SDTRAN,=CL4'DB27'
         MVC   TERMNL,EIBTRMID
```

```
              EXEC CICS START TRANSID(SDTRAN) INTERVAL(0)
                    FROM(SDARG) LENGTH(SDLENG)
***************************************************************
         MVC    SDTRAN,=CL4'DB28'
         MVC    TERMNL,EIBTRMID
         EXEC CICS START TRANSID(SDTRAN) INTERVAL(0)
                    FROM(SDARG) LENGTH(SDLENG)
***************************************************************
         MVC    SDTRAN,=CL4'DB29'
         MVC    TERMNL,EIBTRMID
EXEC CICS START TRANSID(SDTRAN) INTERVAL(0)                    *
              FROM(SDARG) LENGTH(SDLENG)
***************************************************************
         MVC    SDTRAN,=CL4'DB2A'
         MVC    TERMNL,EIBTRMID
         EXEC CICS START TRANSID(SDTRAN) INTERVAL(0)           *
                    FROM(SDARG) LENGTH(SDLENG)
***************************************************************
         LA     SDPASSR,1(SDPASSR)   INCREMENT THE COUNTER
         C      SDPASSR,NUMPASS
         BNL    NOSTART
         B      STARTLP
NOSTART  DS 0H
         EXEC CICS SEND TEXT FROM(AREA) FREEKB
         EXEC CICS RETURN
         DS     0F
AREA     DC     CL40'TRANSACTION COMPLETE'
***************************************************************
         DC F'0'
REPEAT   DC     X'000000C8'     TEST NUMBER OF TIMES TO REPEAT
COUNT    DC     X'00000000'
MAXREAD  DC     X'000000C8'     NUMBER OF DB2 CALLS FOR DB2M XACTION
SDEND    DC     X'00000001'     LAST ONE
NUMTRAN  DC     F'01000000'     NUMBER OF TIMES A TASK IS TO RESTART
NUMPASS  DC     F'00000001'     THE NUMBER OF PASSES AT STARTING TASKS
***************************************************************
SDLENG   DC     X'0030'     LENGTH OF TS RECORD
***************************************************************
         END
```

DB2PROG1

Programs DB2PROG1, 2, and 3 (EXEC CICS RETRIEVE, EXEC CICS POST, EXEC CICS WAITCICS and EXEC CICS START).

We show a list of the DB2PROG1 code in Example C-2.

Example: C-2   DB2PROG1 example (same as DB2PROG2 and DB2PROG3)

```
DFHEISTG DSECT
         EXEC SQL INCLUDE SQLCA
*
**************************************************
DFHEISTG DSECT
**************************************************
         VVEMP       DS     CL80
         EMPNO       DS     CL6
         FIRSTNME    DS     CL12
         MIDINIT     DS     CL1
         LASTNAME    DS     CL15
         WORKDEPT    DS     CL3
         PHONENO     DS     CL4
         HIREDATE    DS     CL10
         JOB         DS     CL8
         EDLEVEL     DS     HL2
         SEX         DS     CL1
         BIRTHDATE   DS     CL10
         SALARY      DS     PL3
         BONUS       DS     PL3
         COMM        DS     PL3
**************************************************
         TERMNL      DC     F'0'
         DATALEN     DS     F'0'
                     DS     0D
ECB1                 DS     1F
**************************************************
* THE FORMAT OF THE TS QUEUE RECORD PASSED TO
**************************************************
                     DC     C'EISTG    '
MESSAGES  DS    CL80                  TEMP STORE
KEYNUM    DS    CL9                   TEMP STORE
COMLEN    DS    1H                    LENGTH OF C
          DS    0F
SQDWSTOR  DS    (SQLDLEN)C    RESERVE STORAGE TO BE USED FOR SQLDSECT
SDARGDATA       DC     20F'0'
                DC     C'EISTG END'
SDARG           DSECT
SDREPEAT        DC     X'00000000'  NUMBER OF TIMES TO MAKE THE DB2 CALL
SDTERMID        DS     CL4          TERMINAL ID
```

```
SDREPCNT        DC      F'0'        CURRENT NUMBER TO BE ATTACHED
SDTRAN          DS      F'0'
SDASKTIM        DS      CL4         YES ISSUE ASKTIME,NO SKIP ASKTIMES
SDEMPNO         DC      2F'0'       EMPLOYEE NUMBER TO USE
*
***************************************************************
R1              EQU     1
SQDWSREG        EQU     7
RETREG          EQU     2                       SET UP REGISTER USAGE
R06             EQU     6
R08             EQU     8
R9              EQU     9
SDREPCTR        EQU     5
COMPTR          EQU     4                       POINTER TO COMMAREA
***************************************************************
DB2PROG1 CSECT
DB2PROG1 AMODE 31
DB2PROG1 RMODE ANY
***************************************************************
         MVC     TERMNL,EIBTRMID
* OBTAIN START DATA
         EXEC CICS RETRIEVE SET(R08) LENGTH(DATALEN)
         USING SDARG,R08
***************************************************************
*
* SQL WORKING STORAGE
         LA      SQDWSREG,SQDWSTOR   GET ADDRESS OF SQLDSECT
         USING SQLDSECT,SQDWSREG     AND TELL ASSEMBLER ABOUT IT
*
         EXEC SQL                                                   *
             DECLARE DSN8710.EMP TABLE (                             *
             EMPNO                           CHAR(6),                *
             FIRSTNME                        CHAR(12),               *
             MIDINIT                         CHAR(1),                *
             LASTNAME                        CHAR(15),               *
WORKDEPT                     CHAR(3),
             PHONENO                         CHAR(4),
             HIREDATE                        DATE,
             JOB                             CHAR(8),
             EDLEVEL                         SMALLINT,
             SEX                             CHAR(1),
             BIRTHDATE                       DATE,
             SALARY                          DECIMAL,
             BONUS                           DECIMAL,
             COMM                            DECIMAL )
*
***************************************************************
         L       6,SDREPEAT
         EXEC CICS POST SET(R9)
```

```
              ST    R9,ECB1                POST EVENT & STORE ADDRESS
*
AGAIN         DS    0H
              LA    R9,ECB1                WAIT UNTIL ECB POSTED
              EXEC  CICS WAITCICS
                    ECBLIST(R9)
                    NUMEVENTS(=F'1')
                    NAME(=C'APPLWAIT')
                    PURGEABLE
*
        EXEC SQL SELECT EMPNO INTO :EMPNO FROM DSN8710.EMP
                    WHERE EMPNO='000070'
BCT  6,AGAIN
*
*********************************************************************
**   NOW START THE NEXT TASK                                      ****
**                                                                ****
              L     SDREPCTR,SDREPCNT      LOAD THE WORK REG
              LTR   SDREPCTR,SDREPCTR
              BZ    NOSTART
              S     SDREPCTR,SDEND         DECREMENT THE COUNTER
              ST    SDREPCTR,SDREPCNT      SAVE IT BACK FOR NEXT START
              EXEC CICS START TRANSID('DB21') INTERVAL(0)
                    FROM(SDARG) LENGTH(DATALEN)
*********************************************************************
*         EXEC CICS PERFORM STATISTICS RECORD DISPATCHER
NOSTART   DS 0H
*         EXEC CICS SEND TEXT FROM(AREA) FREEKB
          EXEC CICS RETURN
          DS    0F
BIG_NUMBER DC   X'00000500'       XXX,XXX   1280 TIMES
AREA       DC   CL30'TRANSACTION COMPLETE'
*********************************************************************
          DC  F'0'
REPEAT    DC   X'00007500'         NUMBER OF TIMES TO REPEAT
MAXREAD   DC   X'00000600'         MAX READ COUNT
MAXREAD2  DC   X'00000005'         MAX READ COUNT
SDEND     DC   X'00000001'    LAST ONE
*********************************************************************
SDLENG    DC   X'0030'    LENGTH OF TS RECORD
*********************************************************************
          END
```

DB2PROG4

Programs DB2PROG4, 5, 6, and 7 (EXEC CICS RETRIEVE and EXEC CICS START).

Example C-3 is a list of the source code for the DB2PROG4.

Example: C-3 DB2PROG4 example (same as DB2PROG5, 6, and 7)

```
DFHEISTG DSECT
         EXEC SQL INCLUDE SQLCA
*
**********************************************
DFHEISTG DSECT
**********************************************
         VVEMP     DS    CL80
         EMPNO     DS    CL6
         FIRSTNME  DS    CL12
         MIDINIT   DS    CL1
         LASTNAME  DS    CL15
         WORKDEPT  DS    CL3
         PHONENO   DS    CL4
         HIREDATE  DS    CL10
         JOB       DS    CL8
         EDLEVEL   DS    HL2
         SEX       DS    CL1
         BIRTHDATE DS    CL10
         SALARY    DS    PL3
         BONUS     DS    PL3
         COMM      DS    PL3
**********************************************
         TERMNL    DC    F'0'
         DATALEN   DS    F'0'
**********************************************
* THE FORMAT OF THE TS QUEUE RECORD PASSED TO
**********************************************
                   DC    C'EISTG    '
         MESSAGES DS     CL80              TEMP STORE
         KEYNUM   DS     CL9               TEMP STORE
         COMLEN   DS     1H                LENGTH OF C
                  DS     0F
         SQDWSTOR DS    (SQLDLEN)C   RESERVE STORAGE TO BE USED FOR SQLDSECT
         SDARGDATA       DC    20F'0'
                         DC    C'EISTG END'
         SDARG           DSECT
         SDREPEAT        DC    X'00000000' NUMBER OF TIMES TO MAKE THE DB2 CALL
         SDTERMID        DS    CL4         TERMINAL ID
         SDREPCNT        DC    F'0'        CURRENT NUMBER TO BE ATTACHED
         SDTRAN          DS    F'0'
```

```
         SDASKTIM        DS      CL4       YES ISSUE ASKTIME,NO SKIP ASKTIMES
         SDEMPNO         DC      2F'0'     EMPLOYEE NUMBER TO USE
*************************************************************
         CWASTG          DSECT
         CWACOUNT        DS      F         COUNTER TO UPDATE
*************************************************************
         SQDWSREG  EQU   7
         RETREG    EQU   2                 SET UP REGISTER USAGE
         R08       EQU   8
         R9        EQU   9
         R10       EQU   10
         COUNT2    EQU   9
         SDREPCTR  EQU   5
         COMPTR    EQU   4                 POINTER TO COMMAREA
*************************************************************
         DB2PROG4 CSECT
         DB2PROG4 AMODE 31
         DB2PROG4 RMODE ANY
******************************************************************
                 MVC    TERMNL,EIBTRMID
* OBTAIN START DATA
                 EXEC CICS RETRIEVE SET(R08) LENGTH(DATALEN)
                 USING SDARG,R08
******************************************************************
*        EXEC CICS PERFORM STATISTICS RECORD DISPATCHER
*
* SQL WORKING STORAGE
                 LA     SQDWSREG,SQDWSTOR  GET ADDRESS OF SQLDSECT
                 USING SQLDSECT,SQDWSREG   AND TELL ASSEMBLER ABOUT IT
*
                 EXEC SQL                                              *
                     DECLARE DSN8710.EMP TABLE (                       *
                     EMPNO                    CHAR(6),                 *
                     FIRSTNME                 CHAR(12),                *
                     MIDINIT                  CHAR(1),                 *
                     LASTNAME                 CHAR(15),                *
                     WORKDEPT                 CHAR(3),                 *
                     PHONENO                  CHAR(4),                 *
                     HIREDATE                 DATE,
                     JOB                      CHAR(8),
                     EDLEVEL                  SMALLINT,
                     SEX                      CHAR(1),
                     BIRTHDATE                DATE,
                     SALARY                   DECIMAL,
                     BONUS                    DECIMAL,
                     COMM                     DECIMAL )
*
******************************************************************
             L     6,SDREPEAT
```

```
AGAIN     DS    0H
          EXEC CICS ASKTIME
NOASKT    DS    0H
*****************************************************************
      EXEC SQL SELECT EMPNO INTO :EMPNO FROM DSN8710.EMP
                     WHERE EMPNO='000100'
          BCT   6,AGAIN
*****************************************************************
*                                        INCREMENT COUNTER IN CWA
          EXEC CICS ADDRESS CWA(R10)
          USING CWASTG,R10
          L     R9,CWACOUNT
          LA    R9,1(R9)
          ST    R9,CWACOUNT
*****************************************************************
**   NOW START THE NEXT TASK                                 ****
**                                                           ****
          L     SDREPCTR,SDREPCNT   LOAD THE WORK REG
          LTR   SDREPCTR,SDREPCTR
          BZ    NOSTART
          S     SDREPCTR,SDEND      DECREMENT THE COUNTER
          ST    SDREPCTR,SDREPCNT   SAVE IT BACK FOR NEXT START
          EXEC CICS START TRANSID('DB24') INTERVAL(0)
                    FROM(SDARG) LENGTH(DATALEN)
*****************************************************************
*         EXEC CICS PERFORM STATISTICS RECORD DISPATCHER
NOSTART   DS 0H
*         EXEC CICS SEND TEXT FROM(AREA) FREEKB
          EXEC CICS RETURN
          DS    0F
BIG_NUMBER DC   X'00000500'     XXX,XXX   1280 TIMES
AREA      DC    CL30'TRANSACTION COMPLETE'
*****************************************************************
          DC    F'0'
REPEAT    DC    X'00007500'         NUMBER OF TIMES TO REPEAT
MAXREAD   DC    X'00000600'         MAX READ COUNT
MAXREAD2  DC    X'00000005'         MAX READ COUNT
SDEND     DC    X'00000001'    LAST ONE
*****************************************************************
SDLENG    DC    X'0030'    LENGTH OF TS RECORD
*****************************************************************
END
```

DB2PROG8

Programs DB2PROG8, 9, and A (EXEC CICS RETRIEVE, EXEC CICS WRITEQ TD and EXEC CICS START).

Example C-4 is a list of the source code for program DB2PROG8.

Example: C-4 (DB2PROG8 example (same as DB2PROG9 and DB2PROGA)

```
***********************************************************************
DFHEISTG DSECT
         EXEC SQL INCLUDE SQLCA
*
************************************************
DFHEISTG DSECT
************************************************
         VVEMP     DS    CL80
         EMPNO     DS    CL6
         FIRSTNME  DS    CL12
         MIDINIT   DS    CL1
         LASTNAME  DS    CL15
         WORKDEPT  DS    CL3
         PHONENO   DS    CL4
         HIREDATE  DS    CL10
         JOB       DS    CL8
         EDLEVEL   DS    HL2
         SEX       DS    CL1
         BIRTHDATE DS    CL10
         SALARY    DS    PL3
         BONUS     DS    PL3
         COMM      DS    PL3
************************************************
         TERMNL        DC    F'0'
         DATALEN       DS    F'0'
************************************************
* THE FORMAT OF THE TS QUEUE RECORD PASSED TO
************************************************
                       DC    C'EISTG   '
         MSG      DS    CL80
         KEYNUM   DS    CL9            TEMP STORE
         COMLEN   DS    1H             LENGTH OF C
         QTEST    DS    CL8
                  DS    0F
         SQDWSTOR DS    (SQLDLEN)C    RESERVE STORAGE TO BE USED FOR SQLDSECT
         SDARGDATA      DC    20F'0'
                        DC    C'EISTG END'
         SDARG         DSECT
         SDREPEAT      DC    X'00000000'  NUMBER OF TIMES TO MAKE THE DB2 CALL
         SDTERMID      DS    CL4       TERMINAL ID
```

```
         SDREPCNT       DC      F'0'       CURRENT NUMBER TO BE ATTACHED
         SDTRAN         DS      F'0'
         SDASKTIM       DS      CL4        YES ISSUE ASKTIME,NO SKIP ASKTIMES
         SDEMPNO        DC      2F'0'      EMPLOYEE NUMBER TO USE
*
***************************************************************
SQDWSREG EQU    7
RETREG   EQU    2                          SET UP REGISTER USAGE
R06      EQU    6
R08      EQU    8
RA       EQU    10
COUNT2   EQU    9
SDREPCTR EQU    5
COMPTR   EQU    4                          POINTER TO COMMAREA
***************************************************************
DB2PROG8 CSECT
DB2PROG8 AMODE 31
DB2PROG8 RMODE ANY
***************************************************************
         MVC    TERMNL,EIBTRMID
* OBTAIN START DATA
         EXEC CICS RETRIEVE SET(R08) LENGTH(DATALEN)
         USING SDARG,R08
***************************************************************
*        EXEC CICS PERFORM STATISTICS RECORD DISPATCHER
*
* SQL WORKING STORAGE
         LA     SQDWSREG,SQDWSTOR     GET ADDRESS OF SQLDSECT
         USING SQLDSECT,SQDWSREG      AND TELL ASSEMBLER ABOUT IT
*
         EXEC SQL                                                   *
              DECLARE DSN8710.EMP TABLE (                           *
              EMPNO                      CHAR(6),                   *
              FIRSTNME                   CHAR(12),                  *
              MIDINIT                    CHAR(1),                   *
              LASTNAME                   CHAR(15),                  *
              WORKDEPT                   CHAR(3),
              PHONENO                    CHAR(4),
              HIREDATE                   DATE,
              JOB                        CHAR(8),
              EDLEVEL                    SMALLINT,
              SEX                        CHAR(1),
              BIRTHDATE                  DATE,
              SALARY                     DECIMAL,
              BONUS                      DECIMAL,
              COMM                       DECIMAL )
*
***************************************************************
         L      6,SDREPEAT
```

```
AGAIN    DS    0H
****************************************************************
         EXEC CICS READQ TS QUEUE(QTEST) SET(RA) LENGTH(COMLEN)
                 NOHANDLE
****************************************************************
NOASKT   DS    0H
 EXEC SQL SELECT EMPNO INTO :EMPNO FROM DSN8710.EMP
                 WHERE EMPNO='000140'
*
         BCT   6,AGAIN
*
****************************************************************
         MVC   MSG,=CL80'DB2PROG8 ENDED'
EXEC  CICS WRITEQ TD QUEUE(=C'THDS') FROM(MSG) NOHANDLE
****************************************************************
**   NOW START THE NEXT TASK                                 ****
**                                                           ****
         L     SDREPCTR,SDREPCNT     LOAD THE WORK REG
         LTR   SDREPCTR,SDREPCTR
         BZ    NOSTART
         S     SDREPCTR,SDEND        DECREMENT THE COUNTER
         ST    SDREPCTR,SDREPCNT     SAVE IT BACK FOR NEXT START
         EXEC CICS START TRANSID('DB28') INTERVAL(0)                  *
                 FROM(SDARG) LENGTH(DATALEN)
****************************************************************
NOSTART DS 0H
****************************************************************
         EXEC  CICS RETURN
         DS    0F
BIG_NUMBER DC  X'00000500'     XXX,XXX   1280 TIMES
AREA     DC    CL30'TRANSACTION COMPLETE'
****************************************************************
         DC F'0'
REPEAT    DC    X'00007500'         NUMBER OF TIMES TO REPEAT
MAXREAD   DC    X'00000600'         MAX READ COUNT
MAXREAD2  DC    X'00000005'         MAX READ COUNT
SDEND     DC    X'00000001'    LAST ONE
****************************************************************
SDLENG    DC    X'0030'    LENGTH OF TS RECORD
****************************************************************
         END
```

Planexit

Example C-5 shows the example code used for our Planexit.

Example: C-5   Planexit

```
TITLE 'PLANEXIT - DB2 CICS ATTACH, DYNAMIC PLAN ALLOCATION EXIT'
*
PLANEXIT AMODE 31                         CAN ADDR STORAGE ABOVE THE LINE
PLANEXIT RMODE ANY                        CAN RUN ABOVE THE LINE
PLANEXIT DFHEIENT CODEREG=(3),EIBREG=(11),DATAREG=(13)
*
A100     EQU   *                          ADDRESS COMMAREA
         USING CPRMPARM,R2
         L     R2,DFHEICAP
         EXEC  CICS ASSIGN USERID(USERID) NOHANDLE
*
RETURN   EQU   *                          RETURN TO CALLER
         EXEC  CICS RETURN
*
*
         LTORG
*
*                                         WORKING STORAGE
         DFHEISTG
USERID   DS    1CL8
         DFHEIEND
*
*
                DSNCPRMA                  COMMAREA
*
*
R0       EQU   0
R1       EQU   1
R2       EQU   2
R3       EQU   3
R4       EQU   4
R5       EQU   5
R6       EQU   6
R7       EQU   7
R8       EQU   8
R9       EQU   9
R10      EQU   10
R11      EQU   11
R12      EQU   12
```

```
            R13       EQU     13
            R14       EQU     14
            R15       EQU     15
*
                      END     PLANEXIT
```

EXITENBL

Example C-6 shows the example code used to enable all exits.

Example: C-6   Program to enable all exits

```
TITLE 'ENABLE - ENABLE EXITS FOR SAMPLE APPLICATION'
*
EXITENBL  AMODE 31                        CAN ADDR STORAGE ABOVE THE LINE
EXITENBL  RMODE ANY                       CAN RUN ABOVE THE LINE
EXITENBL  DFHEIENT CODEREG=(3),EIBREG=(11),DATAREG=(13)
*
A100      EQU   *
          EXEC  CICS ENABLE PROGRAM(=CL8'XXXEI')                          X
                            EXIT(=CL8'XEIIN')                             X
                            START
*
          EXEC  CICS ENABLE PROGRAM(=CL8'XXXEI')                          X
                            EXIT(=CL8'XEIOUT')                            X
                            START
*
          EXEC  CICS ENABLE PROGRAM(=CL8'XXXRMI')                         X
                            EXIT(=CL8'XRMIIN')                            X
                            START
*
          EXEC  CICS ENABLE PROGRAM(=CL8'XXXRMI')                         X
                            EXIT(=CL8'XRMIOUT')                           X
                            START
*
          EXEC  CICS ENABLE PROGRAM(=CL8'XXXTS')                          X
                            EXIT(=CL8'XTSQRIN')                           X
                            GALENGTH(=H'64')                              X
                            START
*
RETURN    EQU   *                         RETURN TO CALLER
          EXEC  CICS RETURN
*
          LTORG
*                                         WORKING STORAGE
```

```
              DFHEISTG
              DFHEIEND
*
              END   EXITENBL
```

XXXEI exit

Example C-7 shows the example source code for our XXXEI exit.

Example: C-7   Example XXXEI

```
DFHUEXIT TYPE=EP,ID=(XEIIN,XEIOUT)
         COPY  DFHTSUED           COMMAND LEVEL PLIST DEFINITIONS
*
DFHEISTG DSECT                    WORKING STORAGE
RETCODE       DS XL4
RESPONSE      DS F
*
XXXEI    DFHEIENT
XXXEI    AMODE 31
XXXEI    RMODE ANY
         LR    R2,R1              DFHUEPAR PLIST PROVIDED BY CALLER
         USING DFHUEPAR,R2        ADDRESS UEPAR PLIST
*
         LA    R15,UERCNORM       SET OK RESPONSE
         ST    R15,RETCODE          IN WORKING STORAGE
*
RETURN   EQU   *
         L     R15,RETCODE        FETCH RETURN CODE
         DFHEIRET RCREG=15        RETURN TO CICS
*
R0       EQU   0
R1       EQU   1
R2       EQU   2
R3       EQU   3
R4       EQU   4
R5       EQU   5
R6       EQU   6
R7       EQU   7
R8       EQU   8
R9       EQU   9
R10      EQU   10
R11      EQU   11
R12      EQU   12
R13      EQU   13
```

```
            R14      EQU      14
            R15      EQU      15
                     END      XXXEI
```

XXXRMI exit

Example C-8 shows the source code for our example XXXRMi exit.

Example: C-8   Example XXXRMI

```
DFHUEXIT TYPE=EP,ID=(XRMIIN,XRMIOUT)
         COPY    DFHTSUED           COMMAND LEVEL PLIST DEFINITIONS
*
DFHEISTG DSECT                      WORKING STORAGE
RETCODE        DS XL4
RESPONSE       DS F
*
XXXRMI   DFHEIENT
XXXRMI   AMODE 31
XXXRMI   RMODE ANY
         LR      R2,R1              DFHUEPAR PLIST PROVIDED BY CALLER
         USING DFHUEPAR,R2          ADDRESS UEPAR PLIST
*
         LA      R15,UERCNORM       SET OK RESPONSE
         ST      R15,RETCODE          IN WORKING STORAGE
*
RETURN   EQU     *
         L       R15,RETCODE        FETCH RETURN CODE
         DFHEIRET RCREG=15          RETURN TO CICS
*
R0       EQU     0
R1       EQU     1
R2       EQU     2
R3       EQU     3
R4       EQU     4
R5       EQU     5
R6       EQU     6
R7       EQU     7
R8       EQU     8
R9       EQU     9
R10      EQU     10
R11      EQU     11
R12      EQU     12
```

```
R13          EQU    13
R14          EQU    14
R15          EQU    15
             END    XXXRMI
```

XXXTS exit

Example C-9 shows the source code used for XXXTS exit.

Example: C-9   Example XXXTS

```
DFHUEXIT TYPE=EP,ID=(XTSQRIN)
*
GWA          DSECT                          GLOBAL WORK AREA
GWACOUNT     DS     F
GWAL         EQU    *-GWA
*
XXXTS        CSECT
XXXTS        AMODE  31
XXXTS        RMODE  ANY
             SAVE   (14,12)                 SAVE REGS
             LR     R12,R15                 SET-UP BASE REGISTER
             USING  XXXTS,R12               ADDRESSABILITY
             LR     R2,R1                   DFHUEPAR PLIST PROVIDED BY CAL
             USING  DFHUEPAR,R2             ADDRESS UEPAR PLIST
             L      R8,UEPGAA               GET GWA ADDRESS
             USING  GWA,R8                  ADDRESSABILITY
*
GWA_CHECK_LENGTH EQU *
             L      R10,UEPGAL              LOAD ADDRESS OF LENGTH OF GWA
             LH     R9,0(,R10)              LOAD LENGTH OF GWA
             LA     R10,GWAL                LOAD EXPECTED LENGTH OF GWA
             CLR    R9,R10                  IS IT BIG ENOUGH?
             BNL    GWAUPDT                 YES, CAN UPDATE DATA IN GWA
GWAERROR     EQU    *
             B      RETURN                  GWA NOT BIG ENOUGH, EXIT
*
GWAUPDT      EQU    *
             L      R6,GWACOUNT             GET THE COUNTER
             LA     R6,1(R6)                INCREMENT
             ST     R6,GWACOUNT              AND STORE
             B      RETURN                  EXIT
*
RETURN       EQU    *
             L      R13,UEPEPSA             ADDRESS OF EXIT SAVE AREA
             RETURN (14,12),RC=UERCNORM  RESTORE REGS AND RETURN
*
```

```
         LTORG
R0       EQU   0
R1       EQU   1
R2       EQU   2
R3       EQU   3
R4       EQU   4
R5       EQU   5
R6       EQU   6
R7       EQU   7
R8       EQU   8
R9       EQU   9
R10      EQU   10
R11      EQU   11
R12      EQU   12
R13      EQU   13
R14      EQU   14
R15      EQU   15
         END   XXXTS
```

Related publications

The publications listed in this section are considered particularly suitable for a more detailed discussion of the topics covered in this redbook.

IBM Redbooks

For information on ordering these publications, see "How to get IBM Redbooks" on page 348. Note some of the documents referenced here may be available in softcopy only.

- *CICS Interdependency Analyzer, SG24-6458*
- *CICS Performance Analyzer*, SG24-6063

Other publications

These publications are also relevant as further information sources:

- *CICS Customization Guide,* SC34-6227, for CICS TS V2
- *CICS Application Programming Reference*, SC34-6232, for CICS TS V2
- *CICS Transaction Server for z/OS V3.1 CICS Application Programming Reference,* SC34-6434, for CICS TS V3
- *CICS System Programming Reference*, SC34-6233, for CICS TS V2
- *CICS Transaction Server for z/OS CICS System Programming Reference*, SC34-6435, for CICS TS V3
- *CICS Application Programming Guide*, SC34-6231, for CICS TS V2
- *CICS Transaction Server for z/OS CICS Application Programming Guide*, SC34-6433, for CICS TS V3
- *CICS Performance Guide*, SC34-6247, for CICS TS V2
- *CICS Transaction Server for z/OS Performance Guide*, SC34-6452, for CICS TS V3
- *CICS Operations and Utilities Guide, V3.1 CICS Operations and Utilities Guide*, SC34-6431, for CICS TS V3
- *CICS DB2 Guide*, SC34-6252, for CICS TS V2

- *CICS Transaction Server for z/OS V3.1 CICS DB2 Guide*, SC34-6457, for CICS TS V3
- *ESA/390 Principles of Operation*, SA22-7201
- *z/Architecture Principles of Operations*, SA22-7832
- *CICS Performance Analyzer for z/OS User's Guide*, SC34-6307
- *CICS Performance Analyzer for z/OS Report Reference*, SC34-6308

Online resources

These Web sites and URLs are also relevant as further information sources:

- CICS home page

    http://www.ibm.com/cics

How to get IBM Redbooks

You can search for, view, or download Redbooks, Redpapers, Hints and Tips, draft publications and Additional materials, as well as order hardcopy Redbooks or CD-ROMs, at this Web site:

ibm.com/redbooks

Help from IBM

IBM Support and downloads

ibm.com/support

IBM Global Services

ibm.com/services

Index

A
ADDRESS CWA 61, 121, 275
APARS
    CICS TS 2.3
        PQ78987 317
    DB2 6.1
        PQ43242 317–318
    DB2 7.1
        PQ44614 318
        PQ45691 318
        PQ45692 319
        PQ46501 319
        PQ50703 319
        PQ65357 319
    DFHEISUP
        PQ73890 320
        PQ76545 320
        PQ77185 320
        PQ78531 320
        PQ82603 320
        PQ87863 320
API TRUE 19
application programming interface (API) 72
application-owning region (AOR) 71–72
ASKTIME 20, 275
ASRA abend 113

B
BASEAPI 28

C
CEDA Transaction 27
CEMT commands 141
Central Electronic Complex (CEC) 290
central processors (CP) 290
CHANGE_MODE 153
channels 290
CHMODECT 171
CICS 106
    CEDA transaction 27
    Exits 144
    QR TCB 7
    supplied filter tables 62
    System Parameters 141
    temporary storage queue 121
    TRANCLASS 25
CICS API 17, 112
CICS API commands 38
CICS API Enqueue / Dequeue 46
CICS API Enqueue/Dequeue 43
CICS application
    programming interface 72
    resource 70
CICS Auxiliary Trace 139
CICS BMS 74
CICS command level interface 38
CICS Commands
    CEMT SET DB2CONN 142
    CEMT SET DB2ENTRY 143
    CEMT SET STATISTICS 296
CICS DB2 attachment facility 17
CICS DB2 task-related user exit 17
CICS dispatcher 5, 33
    wait 4
CICS EXITS
    dynamic plan exit 34
    XEIIN 34
    XEIOUT 34
    XPCFTCH 34
    XRMIIN 34
    XRMIOUT 34
CICS IA
    Collector 84
CICS IA client 74
CICS IA Collector
    CINB 84
    CINT 84
    global user exit program 84
CICS Indiana 70, 72–75
    Collector component 72
    interactive interface 72
    Scanner component 73
CICS Interdependency Analyzer
    Architecture 75
    Collector Component 73
    components of CICS IA? 73

Enhancements in CICS IA Version 1 Release 3   72
   Query Component   74
   Reporter Component   74
   Scanner Component   73
CICS Monitoring   287
CICS PA   168, 212
CICS Pa   104
CICS Performance Analyzer (CICS PA)   105
CICS Performance Analyzer for z/OS   104
CICS RDO
   COncurrency attribute   13
CICS region   70–72
   collected information   72
CICS shutdown   303
CICS SPI commands   40
CICS Statistics   287
CICS TCB   4
CICS Temporary Storage   44
CICS Transaction
   Server   70
CICS Transaction Server for OS/390, Version 1 Release 3   17
CICS Transaction Server for z/OS, Version 2 Release 2   18
CICS TS 1.3   17, 174
CICS TS 2.2   132, 174–175
   APARs   317
CICS TS 2.3   20
   APARs   317
CICS XPI Enqueue / Dequeue   46
CICS XPI Enqueue/Dequeue   43
CICS-DB2 attach code   140
CICS-DB2 Interface   17
CICSPlex/SM   273
CICSs injectors   272
CICS-WMQ API crossing exit CSQCAPX   134
CIU4_SCAN _DETAIL table   94
CIUJCLCS - IA CSECT Scanner JCL   83
CIUJCLTD.   81
CIUJCLTS - IA detailed scanner   81
CIUJCLTS - IA summary scanner JCL   79
CIUTLOAD.   83
CIUUPDB1 - DB2 update JCL   91
CIUUPDB1.   90
COBOL   193, 302
   Call Examples   322
Cobol   37
COBOL/BMS   74

COMMAREA   274
Compare and Swap   43
   instructions   157
   techniques   157
Compare and Swap (CS)   223
COMPARE DOUBLE AND SWAP   47
count   171
count of TCB switches   171
CP SHARE   7
CSA   112
CSACDTA   198, 310
CSAQRTCA   198, 311
CSECT scanner   83
CTHREAD parameter   141
Customer Information Control System (CICS)   xiii
CWA   6, 13, 44, 208
CWAPROG   114

D

DASD   272
Data Tables   122
DB2
   applications   201
   call   38
   Call Path   153
   Path   152
   path   59
   resources   17
   System Parameters   141
   Version 6   58
   ZPARM   141
DB2 6.1
   APARs   318
DB2 7.1
   APARs   318
DB2 8.1
   APARs   319
DB2 table   71
DB2 V5   19
DB2CONN definition   32
DB2PLAN   155
DBCTL   288
DETAILMODS parameter   64
DFH0STAT   59–60, 208
   GWAs find   206
   print   221
   print.   219
   report   149

DFHAUXT 81, 83
DFHD2EX1 174
DFHD2PXT 34
DFHDUMP 81, 83
DFHEIDNT 63, 123
DFHEIDTH 14, 62, 113, 313
DFHEILMS 61
DFHEISUP 14, 61, 113, 208
   APARs 320
   Detail Mode 65
   Filter Tables 62
   Summary 67
   Summary Mode 63
DFHJUP 298
DFHNQEDX 46
DFHRPL 122, 218
DFHSKTSK 305
DPLs 45
DSCHMDLY 171
DSNCUEXT 34
Dynamic Plan Exit 34, 174, 178
dynamic storage area (DSA) 12

E
ERDSA 113
EXEC CICS 71, 73
   ADDRESS CWA 14, 61
   ASKTIME 20
   commands 8
   ENABLE 235
   ENABLE PROGRAM 45
   ENQ 25
   EXTRACT EXIT 14, 61, 222
   FORMATTIME 20
   GETMAIN SHARED 14, 61
   LINK command 37
   RETRIEVE 233–234, 335, 338
   START 233, 335
   WAIT EXTERNAL 232
   WRITEQ TD 234, 338
EXEC SQL 8
Exit
   review 147
EXTRACT EXIT 61
EXTRACT EXIT command 45

F
FCQRONLY 144

File Owning Region (FOR) 74
FORCEQR Parameter 143
FORMATTIME 20
FREEMAIN 288
function shipping 45

G
GALENGTH 45
GETMAIN 288
GETMAIN SHARED 61
global user exit programs 26
global work areas (GWAs) 45
GWA 45

I
IMS 288
Inter System Communication (ISC) 41
Interdependency Analyzer (IA) 70, 72–75
Intersystem Communication (ISC) 188
ISC 41

J
Java Hotpooling applications 17
Java Virtual Machines 17

K
key performance indicators (KPIs) 239
KTCB (in the Kernel Domain) 305

L
L8
   mode 28
   TCB 8, 134, 174–175
   TCBs 19
Language Environment (LE) 112
LINK, WRITEQ-TS 188
Linux 290
Logical Partitions (LPARs) 290
Logwrites per second 292
LPAR 164
   configuration 289
   management data 291
LU6.2 connection 273

M
MAXACTIVE 25

MAXOPENTCBS 32, 142
   limit 33
MCT (Monitor Control Table) 296
Message IEF374I 287, 294
MNFREQ option 296
MRO 41
MRO Link wait time 292
Multi-Region Operation (MRO) 41, 188
MVS 5
MVS (z/OS) dispatcher 291
MVS data space 74
MVS WAIT state 44
MXT 236

N
non-CICS APIs 19

O
Open TCBs 11
Open Transaction Environment (OTE) 4, 11
OPENAPI 19, 28, 174
OPENPOOL wait 33
OS/390 17
OTE
   function 17

P
Performance Analyzer (PA) 104
PLT programs 26, 44
PLTPI program 201
PRB CDE (Contents Directory Entry) 305
programming language 73

Q
QR
   TCB 4, 17, 134, 174–175, 181
QRMODDLY 292
Quasi-reentrant (QR) xiii, 11, 119
   programs 5
   TCB 4
QUASIRENT
   Results 165
Quasirent 25

R
RDSA 113
READQ-TS 188

Redbooks Web site 348
   Contact us xvi
RENT option 112–113
RENTPGM=PROTECT 122
RENTTPGM=NOPROTECT 113
RLS 74
RMF (Resource Measurement Facility) 295
RMF post processor (ERBRMFPP) 295
RMF Workload Activity reports 287
RMI suspend time 292
RMI Time 292
RMIXIT 160
RMODE(24) 113
RMODE(ANY) 113

S
SDFHINST 61
SDFHSAMP 302
serialization techniques 5
Serialize
   access to GWAs 223
Serializing
   shared resources 156
SIT Parameter
   FORCEQR=YES 309–310
   MNPER 296
   RENTPGM=PROTECT 44
   STATRCD=ON 296
   WRKAREA=0 44
SMF 110 subtype 1 records 293
SMF 110 subtype 2 records 293
SMF 30 subtype 2 298
SMF 70-78 records 293
SMF type 110 records 237
SMF Type 30 287
SMF type 30 records 294
SMFSTART 237
SMFSTOP 237
SPI commands 41
SQL call 35
static call 37
Store (ST) instruction 223
subtask TCBs 19
System Programming Interface (SPI) 72

T
task control block (TCB) xiii
task related user exit (TRUE) 11, 18, 174

TCB   176
TCB limits   11
TCB stealing   32
TCB steals   33
TCB switches   17, 19, 61
TCBLIMIT   32
TCBLIMIT parameter   142
TCLASS delay   292
TCP/IP   17
Terminal Owning Regions (TOR)   273
THREADLIMIT   236
THREADSAFE
    Results   163
Threadsafe   7, 11, 194
    Code Example   164
    Convert exits to Threadsafe   205
    converting exits to Threadsafe   155
    Data Integrity Issues   136
    Define programs as threadsafe   209
    implementation   58
    inhibitors   62, 76
    Migration Path   59
    Migration Plan   201
    Migration Planning   58
    Operation   132
    Performance Issues   132
    processing   25
    Redefine exits as threadsafe   223
TRANISO   32
transaction isolation (TRANISO)   32
Transaction rate   292
Transaction Server (TS)   70
transient data queues   13
TRUE   9, 174

U
UNIX System Services   17
URMs   45

V
VSAM file   71, 74
VSAM files   71
VSE   290
VTAM   289

W
WAITCICS   231

WLM
    ISPF panels   299
    Workload Activity Report   299
WLM (Workload Manager)   291
WMQ   153

X
XEIIN   147
XEIN   34
XEIOUT   34, 147
XGRPT1   300
XPCFTCH   34
XPI Commands   41
XPI ENQUEUE   25, 45
XRMIIN   34, 174, 178, 180–181
XRMIOU   174
XRMIOUT   34, 178, 180–181

Z
z/OS   16, 18, 290
    image   290
Z900 Processors   272